Thank You!

T hank you for buying this *Fix-It and Forget-It PINK Cookbook*. By doing so, you have guaranteed that we at Good Books will contribute $1.00 to The Avon Breast Cancer Crusade. (Good Books has pledged a minimum donation of $100,000.)

When you give the *Pink Cookbook* to others—or encourage them to buy copies— you're supporting the work of this life-saving crusade against breast cancer.

Phyllis
Pellman Good

. . . .

O n behalf of the Avon Foundation for Women, thank you for your contribution to our Breast Cancer Crusade. We are truly grateful. And the multitude of women and men who are served by the 300-plus cancer centers and community organizations, partners that we fund across the country annually, also thank you. Together we are **IN IT TO END IT**!

Carol Kurzig,
President,
Avon Foundation
for Women

Fix-It and Forget-It®
PINK Cookbook

More Than 700 Great Slow-Cooker Recipes!

With a 64-page
Bonus Section
featuring Survivor
Stories, Breast Health
Information,
and Tips

by **Phyllis Pellman Good**

For each copy of this cookbook sold,
a minimum of $1.00 will be donated to —

AVON
Foundation
for Women
Breast Cancer Crusade

Good Books®

Intercourse, PA 17534 • 800/762-7171 • www.GoodBooks.com

I owe a special thank you to JoAnne Fairchild, Eloise Caggiano, and Carolyn Ricci, from the Avon Foundation team. And to Merle Good, Kate Good, and Cliff Snyder, from Good Books, thank you for the many ways you helped this book to happen. I am grateful.

— *Phyllis Pellman Good*

Fix-It and Forget-It Pink Cookbook is based on
Fix-It and Forget-It Cookbook: Revised and Updated,
published by Good Books, 2010.

Food photography by Jeremy Hess
Illustrations throughout the book by Cheryl Benner
Design by Cliff Snyder

FIX-IT AND FORGET-IT® PINK COOKBOOK
Copyright © 2012 by Good Books, Intercourse, PA 17534

International Standard Book Number: 978-1-56148-773-8
Library of Congress Catalog Control Number: 2012944353

Publisher's Cataloging-in-Publication Data
Good, Phyllis Pellman
   Fix-it and forget-it pink cookbook : more than 700 great slow-cooker recipes / Phyllis Pellman Good.
     p. cm.
     ISBN 978-1-56148-773-8
1. Electric cooking, Slow. 2. Cooking. 3. Breast --Cancer. I. Fix-it and forget-it pink cookbook : more than seven hundred great slow-cooker recipes. II. Title.

TX827 .G65 2012
641.5/884 –dc23   2012944353

Table of Contents

(continued)

Welcome to *Fix-It and Forget-It PINK* Cookbook

Food is usually more than food

When I cook, I'm not thinking fuel. I'm usually hungry, so I'm imagining flavor and often the prospect of eating with someone else.

Food can settle us down, bring us together, strengthen our friendships, distract us from our fears, underline hope, remind us that we are not alone.

Funny how often food came up when I was talking to the fiercely courageous people whom we feature in the front section of this *Cookbook*. In fact, for many of them, fixing food was a burden—until—some good souls stepped in and brought them meals. This food took care of an immediate need, but it quietly whispered another message from those who brought it—"We're with you."

Why this partnership?

Nearly all of us know someone who's had breast cancer. We are incensed and fearful. And then we want to act. The Avon Foundation has moved right into the neediest of places, providing funds so that women who've been diagnosed have support while they go through treatment. They fund education about breast health, access to care programs, and efforts to accelerate research. Avon Foundation programs raise money for these critical projects—but they also create a powerful community.

Fix-It and Forget-It PINK Cookbook brings two communities together—those who want to feed their families good food at home, and those who want passionately to support those with breast cancer and to eradicate the disease.

You join these two sister causes when you buy and use this book.

We at Good Books are giving $1.00 to the Avon Foundation for every copy of this book that sells.

We've put together 700 great slow cooker recipes—for ordinary times, and for those special occasions when you want to especially celebrate life. Let's multiply the good!

Phyllis Pellman Good

3

Eloise Caggiano

PROGRAM DIRECTOR FOR THE AVON WALK FOR BREAST CANCER, AND SURVIVOR

Pot Roast with Gingersnap Gravy

❧❧

Makes 8 servings • Ideal Slow-Cooker Size: 6-qt.
Prep. Time: 10 minutes • Cooking Time: 6 hours

3- to 4-lb. beef rump roast

salt to taste

pepper to taste

1 large yellow onion, cut in 8 wedges

1 cup beef stock

1 tsp. Kitchen Bouquet Seasoning

20 gingersnaps, finely crushed

1. Season roast with salt and pepper. Place in slow cooker.

2. Scatter onion wedges over top of beef.

3. Spoon beef stock into cooker, being careful not to wash the seasoning or onion pieces off the beef.

4. Cover and cook on High for 6 hours.

5. Remove roast from cooker and keep warm on a platter covered with a tent of foil.

6. Add Kitchen Bouquet to liquid in cooker. Stir in gingersnap crumbs, until thickened.

7. Slice meat and top with sauce for serving.

"This isn't fancy, but I remember it well from my childhood. Dinner-time was important in our family—a time to spend together with no TV or other distractions, and my mom worked hard to make a lovely home-cooked dinner for us each and every night. I, of course, tortured her with my ridiculously picky eating habits, but bless her, she always made sure there was something good for me to eat."

Eloise Caggiano

PROGRAM DIRECTOR FOR THE AVON WALK FOR BREAST CANCER, AND SURVIVOR

I was healthy and active and 33 years old when I was diagnosed with breast cancer. I went alone to the surgeon for my biopsy results, assuming I'd get good news.

She told me that I had breast cancer, and when I left her office that day, I literally did not know what to do in that minute. My parents were on a flight, and I couldn't reach them. So I went to work, which seemed like a weird thing to do, but I didn't want to go home and sit there alone.

I was so surprised by how many decisions were left up to me. It was tough, because I felt fine, but I knew that whatever surgery and treatment options I chose would make me feel bad. I didn't feel equipped to make such life-changing and life-saving decisions.

On the day I was diagnosed, my surgeon gave me a "Cancer 101" organizer. It was a binder that included the many steps I would need to go through, plus a calendar, a guide for tracking insurance, a glossary, and much more. It kept me organized and gave me a real sense of empowerment.

Eloise speaks to a crowd of walkers as financial expert and Avon supporter, Suze Orman, looks on.

I tried to keep as much normalcy in my life as I could, since so much felt out of my control. I had five surgeries, so I was out of work briefly for each of them. Otherwise, going to work helped keep me going. And I still went to the gym, even though I needed to alter my workouts to suit my surgeries and chemo side-effects. Mentally, it helped to stay active. Physically, I think I healed faster.

A friend lined up other friends to accompany me to each chemo treatment. She took care of all the details and always prepared whoever was meeting me, telling them what to bring, and warning them that I'd likely fall asleep on them at some point! It was so comforting to have someone with me each time.

I would have preferred not to have breast cancer, but I've certainly learned a lot. The experience brought me closer to a lot of people. I've learned to open up more. I'm by nature a private person, but I made a choice to let people in. I'm so glad I did because I don't think I could have gotten through this on my own.

I even found a new job! After my breast cancer battle, I wanted to find a more rewarding career. As Program Director for the Avon Walk for Breast Cancer, my job now gives me the chance to put my breast cancer experience to good use.

"I wished for a little cancer angel on my shoulder to help me. I was so afraid of making a wrong decision."

Noelle Krejci

SURVIVOR, AND AVON WALKER

• • • • • • • • • • • • • •

Noelle Krejci is a 2-year survivor, and Avon Walker. She's done 8 Walks and has spoken at both opening and closing ceremonies. Noelle is a nurse.

Cheesy Slow-Cooker Chicken

Makes 6 servings • Prep Time: 10 minutes
Cooking Time: 6-7 hours • Ideal slow-cooker size: 4½- to 5-qt.

6 boneless, skinless chicken breast halves

salt to taste

pepper to taste

garlic powder to taste

2 10½-oz. cans cream of chicken soup

1 10½-oz. can cheese soup

1. Spray slow cooker with low-fat cooking spray.

2. Season each piece of chicken to your liking, and then place in slow cooker.

3. Whisk soups together in bowl until smooth.

4. Pour over chicken pieces, covering them as well as possible with the sauce.

5. Cover. Cook on Low for 6-7 hours, or until chicken is tender but not dry.

"Here's a quick and easy recipe that our entire family loves!"

Noelle Krejci

SURVIVOR, AND AVON WALKER

I did the entire Avon Santa Barbara Walk 11 days after my mastectomy. I hadn't trained; it was a tough year. But I am very determined!

Oddly enough, about six years before I was diagnosed, a girlfriend and I decided that we wanted to see if we could do an Avon Walk physically. I ended up doing it alone because she had to have knee surgery, but it was such a good experience that I said, "I'm going to do this forever."

I had started out walking alone because I knew no one, but I came upon a woman who was about 65 years old. I learned she was going through chemo—and still walking—and she became my inspiration.

During those first years I walked alone, hooked by the moving stories I heard and the spirit of the event. Now I have a team that I've put together. They're amazing people whom I've met along the way.

A girlfriend who I grew up with in Texas is part of my team. My best friend is on the team. When I went in for my double mastectomy, my nurse that day said, "I'm doing the Avon Walk." She told me she was going alone. I said, "No, you're not." So now she's on my team.

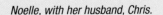

Noelle, with her husband, Chris.

When I was first diagnosed, the first thing I did was to go home, go onto the Avon Walk message board, and put my message out there. The women reached out to me and gave me advice and support.

The cancer and mastectomy are the most challenging experiences I've ever been through. Chris and I have four children; our oldest was 19 at the time.

Losing my breasts changed me hugely. I was 41. I was in a very happy and intimate relationship with my husband. But he told me that no matter how my body changed, he would still love me. And he never failed in that.

When I lost my hair, I was clearly a cancer patient. I couldn't hide that loss under a shirt. People looked at me with such pity.

I had been an active person. I'd done half-marathons. While going through chemo, I gained 35 pounds. I felt like a freak. I was always very go-go-go, keeping myself very busy. But when I was in chemo, I couldn't be busy.

On the days when my mom was helping me, my dad would often stop in. He passed away the week before my last chemo. I was so glad for the special times I got to spend with him, which wouldn't have happened if I hadn't been sick. It's been a big lesson for me—slow down and enjoy your family and friends. They aren't going to be here forever.

"My husband told me that no matter how my body changed, he would still love me. He never made me feel like a freak when I had no hair and no breasts."

Early Breast Cancer Detection

In the fall of 2009, the U.S Preventive Services Task Force recommended changing mammography screening guidelines, which was met with mixed reviews from medical experts, advocates, and the public.

The Avon Foundation continues to support guidelines recommended by expert groups—American Cancer Society, American College of Radiology and others – including:

- Breast self exam (BSE)—Experts now recommend BSE as optional but encourage all women to become familiar with their own bodies and watch for changes. BSE is an option for women starting in their 20s. You should report any changes in your breast health to your medical provider right away.

- Women in their 20s and 30s should have a clinical breast exam (CBE) as a part of their periodic health exam by a health professional, preferably every 3 years. (Community based groups that can help link you to CBE can be found at www.avonbreastcare.org)

- Women of average risk should begin annual screening mammography at age 40 and continue annual screening mammography for as long as the woman is in good health. (Programs to link you to mammography providers can be found by visiting www.avonbreastcare.org)

- And don't forget, men can get breast cancer, too!

- Talk to your doctor about your risk and when you should start screening.

What Everyone Should Know About Breast Cancer

BREAST CANCER FACTS

- More than 240,000 women and 1,000 men are diagnosed with breast cancer in the U.S. each year.

- One person is diagnosed approximately every 3 minutes, and one person dies of breast cancer approximately every 14 minutes.

- People over the age of 50 account for 76% of breast cancer cases, while only 5% of breast cancer diagnoses are in people under the age of 40 and 18% are in their 40s.

- More than 40,000 women and 400 men die each year from the disease.

- There are more than 2 million breast cancer survivors in the United States.

- The majority of breast cancers found today are "hormone receptor positive," and excellent treatments exist. Nearly 1 out of 5 breast cancers diagnosed will be HER2-positive breast cancer, a form that tends to grow and spread more aggressively than other breast cancer.

MORE FACTS

- 43% of breast cancer patients skip treatments because they can't afford them.

- 5 African American women die needlessly from breast cancer every day because they do not have access to care.

- Government-backed breast cancer screening supports only 20%, or 1 in 5, eligible low-income women.

- Only 26% of uninsured women over the age of 40 had a mammogram within the past year, compared to 56% of insured women. This means that more uninsured women risk a late-stage diagnosis and worse outcomes.

13

Barbara Jo Kirshbaum

9-CITY AVON WALKER

. . . .

Barbara Jo Kirshbaum has done more than 120 long-distance walks in the crusade against breast cancer and has raised more than $1.45 million. She has done all 9 of the Avon Walks year after year.

Pineapple Carrot Cake ala Kirshbaum

Makes 12-15 servings • Prep Time: 20-30 minutes • Baking Time: 40-45 minutes

2 cups sugar

1 cup chopped nuts

½ cup grated coconut

1 cup crushed pineapple, drained

4 beaten eggs

¾ cup buttermilk

2 cups grated carrots

2 cups flour

2½ tsp. cinnamon

½ tsp. allspice

2 tsp. baking soda

1. In a large mixing bowl, combine sugar, nuts, coconut, pineapple, eggs, buttermilk, and carrots.

2. In a separate bowl, mix together flour, cinnamon, allspice, and baking soda.

3. Stir dry ingredients into wet ingredients until well mixed.

4. Pour into well greased and floured 9" x 13" baking pan, or 2 8" round baking pans.

5. Bake at 350° for 40-45 minutes, or until tester stuck in middle of cake comes out clean.

CREAM CHEESE FROSTING

8-oz. pkg. cream cheese, softened to room temperature

½ stick (¼ cup) butter, softened

1 tsp. vanilla or lemon flavoring

1 cup powdered sugar

1. Beat cream cheese, butter, and vanilla together until creamy and well blended.

2. Blend in powdered sugar until creamy.

3. Frost slightly warm cake.

"You'll see this has our name in the title. It's a favorite family recipe!"

14

Barbara Jo Kirshbaum

9-CITY AVON WALKER

When I turned 60 in 1998, I wanted a physical challenge. I had just done the Los Angeles marathon when I heard about the breast cancer walks. I am a marriage and family counselor, and my husband was a physician. It wasn't about the breast cancer cause or about fund-raising. It was about exercise for me.

When I heard you were expected to fundraise, I decided not to do the Walk. But I kept thinking about it, wondering if I could raise any money even though I'm not a breast cancer survivor. So that became my second challenge. I put together a letter in which I listed things I had done through the years to challenge myself. I used that as my hook. I raised $17,000 that first year.

In 2002, I signed up to do all nine of Avon's City Walks. I was growing emo-tionally attached to these events! In 2008 I did 15 walks, and I reached the million-dollar total that year. My husband, Bob, was a major part of the effort. He came to every event I participated in, putting up 60 signs each time.

In 2009, he was diagnosed with esophageal cancer; he survived 10 months. He said on the day he was diagnosed, "I want you to keep doing this. And when

I die, I want people to make donations to the Avon Foundation, instead of giving flowers."

One woman told me recently that when she saw an article in the paper about my fundraising and walking, she was reminded that she hadn't had a mammogram in a while. So she went – and she had breast cancer. She said I saved her life. That's why I do this.

Every year something amazing happens. One year a man, who was a senior himself, was participating. His elderly mother had given him a $100 bill and told him to give it to someone who especially inspired him on the Walk. He gave it to me, and then he bought Bob's and my flights to the next Walk. I've been so fortunate.

I walk because I can't walk away.

"I walk because
I can't walk away."

About the Avon Walks

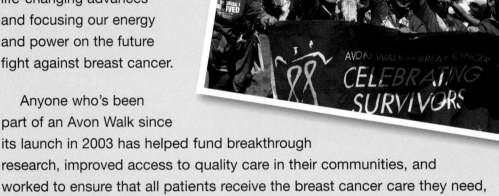

Each Avon Walk is 2 days and 39 miles and celebrates a decade of life-changing advances and focusing our energy and power on the future fight against breast cancer.

Anyone who's been part of an Avon Walk since its launch in 2003 has helped fund breakthrough research, improved access to quality care in their communities, and worked to ensure that all patients receive the breast cancer care they need, regardless of their ability to pay.

Since the Avon Walks began, Avon Walkers have collectively traveled the equivalent of more than 210 trips around the globe.

SEE PASSION AT WORK

There's a spirit you feel throughout an Avon Walk, a current of hope and joy that connects the participants. They cheer each other on as they achieve personal goals. They walk together with their hearts full and heads held high, knowing they're making a real difference to people living with this devastating disease, as well as those who may be diagnosed in the future.

When you join an Avon Walk, you share stories and laughs and make incredible memories. You form new friendships and deepen old ones. You hear how

Avon Foundation-funded organizations in your own community are helping breast cancer patients navigate the daunting journey from diagnosis through treatment. You realize you're changing the world by participating.

At an Avon Walk, complete strangers become friends, because everyone is connected by the same belief—that putting one foot in front of the other truly can help put an end to breast cancer.

Avon Walks take place in 8 cities: Houston, Washington D.C., Boston, Chicago, San Francisco, Santa Barbara, New York, and Charlotte. Every Walk route is designed to bring out the best that city has to offer.

WHERE THE MONEY GOES

All money raised by the Avon Walk is managed by the Avon Foundation for Women, a 501(c)(3) public charity that funds a comprehensive network of programs and services dedicated to serving breast cancer patients and their families through five areas of the breast cancer cause: awareness and education, screening and diagnosis, access to treatment, support services, and scientific research.

Show the world you're **IN IT TO END IT**. Bring your friends and family and come together for an unforgettable celebration of life and hope. Please visit **avonwalk.org** for more information.

The Avon Foundation places a special emphasis on reaching the medically under-served, including low-income, elderly and minority individuals, and those who are under-insured.

The destination?
A world without
breast cancer.

Dr. Mita Sanghavi Goel

PROVIDER OF ACCESS TO CARE, AND SURVIVOR

• • • • • • • • • • • • • •

Dr. Mita Sanghavi Goel is part of the Avon Center for Excellence and Assistant Professor of Medicine at the Feinberg School of Medicine at Northwestern University.

Zucchini-Lemon Open-Faced Sandwiches

4-6 servings • Prep Time: 20 minutes • Cooking Time: 15-18 minutes

2 Tbsp. olive oil

1 onion, chopped

2-3 zucchini, sliced in half lengthwise, and then sliced in half-moon shapes

3 Tbsp. fresh lemon, squeezed from half a lemon

salt to taste

pepper to taste

4-6 tsp. balsamic vinegar, or more (preferably a tangy, sweet variety such as aged balsamic or fig balsamic)

4-6 slices toasted French or Italian bread

1-1½ cups shredded cheddar cheese (2-year-old Grafton or Cabot Hunter's Sharp are especially good)

1. Heat olive oil in a skillet. Saute onions until translucent, approximately 5 minutes.

2. Add sliced zucchini. Cook for another 5 minutes.

3. Stir in lemon juice. Continue cooking until zucchini slices are soft, approximately 5 minutes.

4. Salt and pepper to taste.

5. Assemble the sandwich as follows: Drizzle balsamic vinegar over slices of bread. Place cooked mixture in generous quantities on top of vinegar. Divide cheese among open-faced sandwiches. It will melt on its own from the heat. Serve.

"This is my made-up recipe that satisfies my entire family's taste buds (even our 2-year-old!), as well as my desire to eat healthily as a family. It is a wonderful weeknight dinner for a working couple."

Dr. Mita Sanghavi Goel

PROVIDER OF ACCESS TO CARE, AND SURVIVOR

In my work as a physician, I've helped to develop a video for patients to watch as they wait for their doctor appointments.

The video is in both English and Spanish and is a straight narrative—practical and efficient—about five minutes long. In it we describe how mammography detects cancer. We show a woman having a mammogram to demystify the process. The message is intended to encourage and motivate women to think of their doctors as partners. We want them to talk to their doctors about whether a mammogram is right for them.

I've had a long interest in the disparities in cancer care, especially for Latina women. I wanted to partner with an agency who worked actively with persons who were especially vulnerable because of their culture and economic standing.

The women we've met are quite interested in their health and want to learn more. We were afraid that the video might be too graphic, but they're very receptive to it. In fact, when we tracked who was having mammograms, twice as many who watched the video got mammograms compared to those who didn't.

Dr. Goel with her daughter.

I was diagnosed with breast cancer just about a year and a half ago, not long after I began working with the video. I underwent the full range of treatment. That has underscored for me the importance of this work—and how hard it can be to balance family life and a job alongside treatment.

I am very fortunate to have an outpouring of support. I have two young kids—5 and 2½. My mother came and lived with us for a few months during my surgery and treatments. We had friends bringing food and offering all kinds of help.

I kept working during my treatment, and I had wonderful support from my colleagues and my patients, too. In fact, I had to make a big effort to get them to talk about their situations and not mine!

One other thing I found helpful was keeping an online journal at CaringBridge.org. It was a wonderful way to keep my community and friends up to date. It allowed them to write back to me in a way that was comfortable and supportive. I found it therapeutic to write and then to read the wonderful messages I received. I am learning now that surviving is a very active process.

I had always been so healthy, so it's a new experience for me to focus on my health beyond making sure that I eat right and exercise regularly.

"I am learning now that surviving breast cancer is a very active process. Complications from treatment come up. I wasn't planning on any setbacks, but I developed some swelling in my arm that took me completely by surprise."

Deb Wills

**SURVIVOR OF
26 YEARS, AND
AVON WALKER**

. . . .

Deb Wills is a 26-year survivor, an avid Walker (she's done 13 Walks), and has so far raised $400,000 for the Avon Foundation, including more than $101,000 in 2012. She spoke at the Closing Ceremony of the Washington D.C. Walk in 2010.

Slow-Cooker Chicken Fricassee

*Makes 4 servings • Prep Time: 15 minutes
Cooking Time: 4-6 hours • Ideal Slow-Cooker Size: 4-qt.*

4 boneless, skinless chicken breast halves

1 can reduced-fat cream of chicken soup

½ soup can of water

2 medium carrots, peeled and cut into chunks

½ cup chopped onions

1 tsp. paprika

¾ tsp. dried thyme

1 tsp. dried rosemary

1 tsp. lemon juice

1 tsp. salt

¼ tsp. pepper

1. Spray slow cooker with nonstick cooking spray.

2. Place chicken in slow cooker.

3. Mix remaining ingredients together in a bowl. Pour over chicken.

4. Cover. Cook on Low 4-6 hours, or until chicken is tender but not dry and the vegetables are as tender as you like them.

5. Serve over cooked noodles or rice.

"I especially like this recipe served to me by my very dear friend."

Deb Wills

SURVIVOR OF 26 YEARS, AND AVON WALKER

I n 1986, I felt a lump in my breast when showering one day. Something told me it was cancer. I had lost my mom at 42 from ovarian cancer. Mine turned out to be Stage 2 breast cancer, having moved into my lymph nodes. The world was different in the '80s. Then, cancer meant the death sentence. I was embarrassed; I didn't even tell the people I worked with. I'd do my radiation first thing in the morning and then go straight to work.

I shared a house with three other women. They were quite supportive. One of the best things they did for me was to help me find a therapist.

I was 32 years old and I was so angry. The therapist helped me with my anger by asking me to get a kid's punching bag. I also made a pile of bricks behind my house. Each brick represented a week of chemo. At the end of each week, I'd go out with a sledgehammer and beat the daylights out of a brick.

When I was diagnosed, lumpectomies were relatively new in the U.S. You had to go with what you knew. I opted for the lumpectomy, and that's when they found that my lymph nodes had cancer. There was just so little information. They handed you a brochure. And you didn't know survivors then.

I trained for the Walks with a team for the first few years. I walked with the team. They were so supportive; some are still in my life as very dear friends. It can be difficult to do a Walk alone, but with a team, you can learn: from blister care, to how to hydrate, the importance of electrolytes, safety things, and listening to your body to make sure you're okay.

At lunch during a Walk one day, I sat beside someone who said to me, "I'm looking for someone like me—someone who's been diagnosed with Stage 2 breast cancer and has survived." That was me. And then I met someone who's a 33-year survivor, and that helped me. Both times we hugged and cried with each other. I always think of these people when I walk.

Years ago I met a couple and she had breast cancer. They always walked together. Then the wife passed, but the husband continued doing the Walks. He always carried her sneakers.

An Avon Walk is uplifting and empowering. It is not a race. There are no first or last prizes. It's all about talking and meeting people and hearing about their experiences. An Avon Walk is one of the best ways to give back.

"I carry a list of names with me on each Walk. I ask my donors if they have anyone they'd like me to walk in honor of. This year I had 300 names with me."

Judy Cherry

**SURVIVOR, AND
9-CITY AVON
WALKER**

Mom's Rice Pudding

Makes 8 servings
Prep Time: 15 minutes • *Baking Time: 2 hours and 40 minutes*

1 cup long-grain
white rice

9 cups milk

1-2 cups sugar,
according to your
taste preference

2 tsp. vanilla

NOTES:

• In order to avoid a
glutinous mess, please
follow these directions
exactly! No skimping!

• Some people like to
add raisins, but we feel
that is sacrilege and
never add raisins or
cinnamon! This is a true
farmhouse rice pudding.

1. Preheat oven to 350°.

2. Wash rice until water runs clear.

3. Put rice in greased 3-quart baking dish.

4. Pour in all the milk. Stir well. Place
   in oven.

5. Stir the milk and rice every 30 minutes
   until rice is soft, about 2 hours total.

6. Stir in 1 cup sugar. Taste. Add more
   sugar if you wish.

7. Bake for another 30 minutes.

8. Stir in vanilla.

9. Bake for 10 more minutes.

10. Allow to cool to room temperature,
    or chill, before serving.

*"This is my
all-time favorite
dish. And this is
our whole family's
favorite rice
pudding.
I had to stand over
my mom to get it!"*

Grammy Bair's Manhattan Clam Chowder

Makes 4-6 servings • Prep time: 20 minutes • Cooking Time: 2 hours

3 large russet potatoes, peeled and cubed

2 large onions, peeled and chopped

32-oz. (4 cups) chicken stock

20-oz. can diced tomatoes, undrained

large can chopped clams, undrained

3 Tbsp. poultry seasoning

1 Tbsp. Worcestershire sauce

1. Put all ingredients except clams into large stockpot. Bring to a boil.

2. Reduce heat. Cover and cook for 90 minutes.

3. Add clams. Simmer for another 5 minutes until clams are heated through.

NOTES:

• This is great to serve over pancakes—a favorite of our family!

• The chowder is even better on the second day.

"This is my grandma's recipe. I had to interview her to get the recipe since she doesn't have it written down. She does everything 'by eye,' so I had to go home and measure to make sure I had everything right! Interviewing her for this was a real treat."

Judy Cherry

SURVIVOR, AND 9-CITY AVON WALKER

A breast cancer diagnosis takes your breath away. I had found a lump and had done research, and I thought I was somewhat prepared if the diagnosis came, although no one really expects to hear it. But all of that research went out the window when I heard the words.

My husband and I went home and I said, "I'm going to have a mastectomy"—30 minutes after getting the diagnosis. And he said, "It's your life and it's your breast." My husband showed extraordinary ability to support me. He allowed me—and this is huge—to make decisions freely with no judgment.

I needed to be really clear with friends and family that I did not want them to start treating me differently. I wanted to keep things normal, with as few awkward moments as possible.

My friends were good about asking if there was anything I couldn't eat or couldn't do. Once, after they started to bring me things, I had a really bad week. Because my friend had brought me meals,

Judy Cherry with Patrick Dempsey.

I called and asked her if she could fix supper one night. She had opened the door, and so it was easier for me to ask because she had already given me unsolicited help. I believed that she really did want to do all she could for me.

Probably the biggest thing now is that I want to make a difference. After I did my first Avon Walk, I realized that I had experienced one of the most empowering weekends of my life.

For two days, absolutely everyone—regardless of our differences—was all together as one positive community. I had never had an experience like that before.

In the year of my second Walk, I realized that I would have to do the Walk alone, and I wasn't sure I could do that. So I posted a message on the Avon message board, asking if there were any other solo walkers. Thirty-five of us found each other—and we each found walking partners.

We formed Solo Strutters, and I became team leader. None of the members had walking partners. And of course we couldn't train together because we were from all over the country.

I am now 54 walks later. That sense of community is still vitally important to me.

"Now we have a Solo Strutters team in all of the Avon Walk cities. We give people who are walking alone a 'Walk family' within the Walk. We're a mixture of newbies and veterans. The veterans take care of the new ones. Everyone needs a little help getting over the fear of doing the first Walk, just like breast cancer requires getting over fear."

Tips for Helping Breast Cancer Patients

SUGGESTIONS FROM BREAST CANCER SURVIVORS:

Make a specific offer of help to the person with breast cancer. A general offer, such as, "Just let me know how I can help," will likely not result in a request.

1. Line up friends or family members to accompany the patient to each of her chemo or radiation treatments.

   • Prior to each session, send an email to the patient, telling her who will pick her up that day, wait with her, and return her to her home.

   • Orient those accompanying the patient about what to expect: the approximate length of the treatment, the response of the patient to the treatment (it will likely make her sleepy, so don't feel pressure to entertain or talk constantly), her needs (create as relaxed and comforting an atmosphere as you can.)

2. If you're a breast cancer survivor, offer to suggest a list of questions she may want to ask her doctors. Be sensitive and diplomatic, of course, but because of your own experience, you may know of areas needing discussion of which her family or other friends are unaware.

3. Volunteer to go along to doctor appointments and keep notes for the patient. All of the medical terminology and options to consider can be nearly over-whelming for a patient who is alone. And it can help to have someone to talk to afterwards as she tries to digest all of the information.

4. Coordinate a schedule for providing meals to the patient.

- Be sure to check with the patient first, asking for any dietary restrictions and food preferences, as well as the best time of day to deliver the food, the appropriate quantity, and whether the food should be brought hot or cold.

- Ask if she likes meals brought daily, or every other day, or less frequently. (Too much food can be almost as overwhelming as too little.)

- Urge those who supply meals to use containers that do not need to be returned, thus relieving the patient of a possible burden.

- Volunteer to take a meal once a week or once a month.

5. Pick up the patient's grocery list, or offer her a shared grocery list app that you can both access. Then go get her groceries. Ask if she'd like you to put them away when you deliver them.

6. Ask if you may do her laundry.

7. Ask if you may take her kids for an afternoon or evening.

8. Ask if you may clean her bathrooms. She probably won't ask anyone to do this, but she'll find it hard to refuse your genuine offer.

9. Be ready to talk about your life if the patient asks you.

A Word of Explanation:

While for ease of reading we have referred to the patient as "she" throughout this section, it is important to remember that men are also breast cancer patients and survivors, and each of these tips apply to men as well.

Craig Shniderman

**MEAL PROVIDER,
AND AVON WALKER**

• • • • • • • • • • • • •

Craig Shniderman is Executive Director of Food & Friends, which prepares 1.3 million meals each year and delivers them to persons with breast cancer and with HIV/AIDS in Washington D.C. and neighboring counties in Maryland and Virginia.

Pink Edition Sugar Cookies

Makes 2 dozen cookies
Prep Time: 20 minutes   •   Baking Time: 8-10 minutes for each baking sheet

2 sticks (1 cup) butter, softened

2 cups granulated sugar

3 eggs

2 tsp. vanilla

4 cups flour

2 tsp. baking soda

½ tsp. salt

2 tsp. red food coloring

1. Preheat oven to 325°.

2. Cream butter and sugar until well blended.

3. Stir in eggs and vanilla. Mix until well blended.

4. Combine flour, baking soda, and salt in a separate bowl.

5. Mix dry ingredients into wet ingredients until fully incorporated.

6. Stir in food coloring until well blended.

7. Drop by heaping teaspoonsful onto parchment-paper-covered baking sheet.

8. Bake 8-10 minutes.

"Our staff at Food & Friends makes between 5,000-6,000 of these cookies for the Avon Walk in Washington, D.C. Chef Devine developed the recipe especially for this event, and we give them to all of the walkers and staff during those days."

Beef Burgundy *(pictured on page 37)*

Serves 6-8 • Prep Time: 30 minutes • Cooking/Braising Time: 2½-3 hours

3 lbs. boneless beef chuck,
cut into 2" pieces

salt to taste

pepper to taste

flour

2 Tbsp. olive oil

2 carrots, peeled and cut
into 1" pieces

2 celery ribs, cut into 1" pieces

1 medium onion, peeled and diced

½ lb. white button mushrooms,
de-stemmed and quartered

3 garlic cloves, chopped

2 Tbsp. tomato paste

2 Tbsp. balsamic vinegar

2 cups dry red wine

2 small bay leaves

1 thyme sprig

1½ cups beef broth

1½ cups water

1. Preheat oven to 350°. Place rack in middle of oven.

2. Mix salt, pepper, and flour in large bowl. Stir in meat until each piece is well covered.

3. Heat oil in a 4- to 6-qt. Dutch oven, or other heavy pot that is oven-safe. Brown meat without crowding the pot. Do in 2 or 3 batches so beef browns and doesn't simply steam.

4. As meat browns, remove to platter. Tent with foil.

5. When all meat is browned, add carrots, celery, onion, mushrooms, and garlic to pot. Reduce heat to medium. Cook, stirring occasionally, until vegetables are also well browned, about 10 minutes.

6. Add tomato paste to vegetables. Continue stirring an additional 2 minutes.

7. Add vinegar and cook 2 more minutes.

8. Stir in wine, bay leaves, and thyme. Boil until liquid is reduced by about ⅔, about 10 minutes.

9. Add broth and water to pot, along with browned beef and any juices from platter. Stir. Over medium heat, bring to a simmer.

10. Cover and braise in 350° oven until meat is very tender, about 2-2½ hours.

11. At Food & Friends, we serve this over egg noodles with a side of broccoli. It's also good with roasted or mashed potatoes and your favorite crusty bread.

"This recipe for Beef Burgundy is a long-standing favorite of our Food & Friends' clients. It is hearty and satisfying, providing lots of protein and veggies. It is all about technique when making beef stew, so allow plenty of time for braising. Thanks to Executive Chef Mark Locraft of Food & Friends for developing this recipe."

Craig Shniderman

MEAL PROVIDER, AND AVON WALKER

Craig Shniderman (center)
receives Avon Foundation's check for Food & Friends
at the Closing Ceremony of the Washington D.C. Walk.

Our client services at Food & Friends work closely with a breast cancer patient's caregivers to make sure that the food we're preparing fits the patient's overall treatment program. And we consider the patient's food preferences, too.

Most of the women we serve have children, but they may be single moms. So we provide food for their families, too. We try to understand people within their own particular settings. First and foremost, we want clients to know they are not alone, that we're on their team.

I am now a 9-time Walker in the Washington D.C. Walk. I walk one day (of the multiple-day walk) in drag. My drag name is Miss Ivanna Beat Breast Cancer.

At some point it crossed my mind that I could support and encourage the participants by becoming part of the entertainment. Humor is a useful intervention for stress, fatigue, and big life challenges.

One day I was standing next to a couple who looked a little amused and frightened by my costume. I introduced myself and Food & Friends, and the woman's eyes filled with tears. "You're taking care of my daughter," she said. It was a magical moment. I thought, this is sublime.

My favorite part of the Walks is the Opening Ceremony. It's emotionally intense. It has an almost spiritual atmosphere for me. I find the Walks to be a kind of metaphor for having been diagnosed with breast cancer. It's dark (the Opening Ceremony happens before sunrise); we're all a little worried about making it through to the end. Each of us feels alone, and yet we know, too, that we're part of a group. We're each filled with expectations, with worry, with a sense of opportunity. And then you find strengths— and weaknesses—within yourself that you didn't know you had as you move along in the Walk.

I have a wife and three daughters. Ivanna Beat Breast Cancer is for them and for the great spirits, living and gone, with whom I've shared the road on the Walks and others who each day await the Avon Pink Ribbon Delivery Service of Food & Friends.

"Most of the women we serve live in families. Most have children, but they may be single moms. So we provide food for their families, too."

Craig Shniderman, (right) at the Washinton D.C. Walk as "Ivanna Beat Breast Cancer."

Beef Burgundy (recipe on page 35).

Dr. Sheryl G.A. Gabram

RESEARCHER

• • • • • • • • • • • • •

Dr. Sheryl G.A. Gabram is Surgeon-in-Chief at Grady Memorial Hospital in Atlanta, Georgia and Professor of Surgery at Emory University School of Medicine. She is Deputy Director of the Georgia Cancer Center for Excellence and Director of the Avon Comprehensive Breast Center, both at Grady.

Chunky Vegetable Chili

——— ✦ ———

Makes 4-6 servings • Prep Time: 15 minutes
Cooking Time: 5½-6 hours • Ideal Slow-Cooker Size: 4-qt.

1 medium onion, chopped

2 ribs celery, diced

1 carrot, diced

3 cloves garlic, minced

2 15-oz. cans Great Northern beans, rinsed and drained

1 cup water

1 cup frozen or canned corn

6-oz. can tomato paste

4-oz. can diced mild green chilies, undrained

1 Tbsp. chili powder

2 tsp. dried oregano leaves

1 tsp. salt

1. Combine all ingredients in slow cooker.

2. Cover. Cook on Low 5½-6 hours, or until vegetables are as tender as you like them.

"I'm a pescatarian who also loves vegetables!"

Dr. Sheryl G.A. Gabram

RESEARCHER

Dr. Gabram (right) meets with a patient.

In our Cancer Center, 90% of the women come alone to hear the results of their needle biopsy. If they are diagnosed with cancer, we ask if they would like a Personal Navigator to assist them in knowing what to do next. The great majority choose to have this companionship and support.

The clinic Navigators are breast cancer survivors. They are living testimonies that you can have hope and fight this disease. We are grateful to the Avon Foundation for funding the Navigator program.

We see 150-170 newly diagnosed cancer patients each year. Ninety percent are African American women who ordinarily wouldn't have access to high quality care because of poverty and little or no insurance. We offer a tailored personal plan for each patient whom we treat.

Every Monday afternoon at our Cancer Center, we hold a multi-disciplinary conference, during which the attendees—medical, surgical, and radiation oncologists, radiologists, pathologists, social workers, nurses, clinic navigators, and researchers—discuss and plan for each patient's care. We don't want to lose any patient because of fear, and that can happen because the patient doesn't know how to manage her diagnosis on top of everything else that is going on in her life.

We try to help these women understand all of the options available to them. Part of my research is making sure that we offer good quality care consistently and to all. We want to make sure that women understand and accept *all* of the treatments recommended to them.

The Avon Foundation provides grant funding for our Community Education Outreach Initiative. This program funds the clinic Navigators, along with lay navigators, who go out into the community and teach what mammography is and how to do breast self-examinations.

We also have a pilot project testing the role of survivorship navigators. After a woman completes all active therapies, she is ready for help in knowing how to go on living with her history of having had cancer. Does she need physical therapy to overcome limitations after surgical and radiation therapy? What side-effects might she have because of the drugs, and how does she manage those? What is an ideal diet? What kinds of exercise are especially beneficial? This program helps with all of that.

I want to make a difference to all women, especially to those who don't have the means or the wherewithal to pay for diagnosis or treatment. To see the survivors every week in clinic is really fulfilling work.

"Every week my patients teach me lessons of courage, and their experiences put life in perspective for me. I am so rewarded by serving this community."

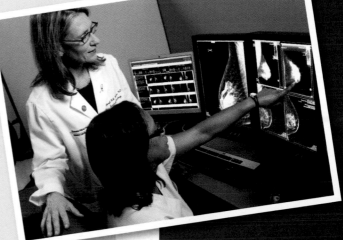

Dr. Gabram (left) in her role as a researcher.

Lillie D. Shockney

NURSE NAVIGATOR, AND A SURVIVOR

• • • • • • • • • • • • • •

Lillie D. Shockney is Administrative Director of Johns Hopkins Breast Clinical Program and Johns Hopkins Cancer Survivorship Programs in Baltimore, Maryland, an Avon Foundation Center of Excellence. She is a 20-year breast cancer survivor.

Bread Pudding

Makes 4 servings
Prep Time: 15 minutes • *Baking Time: 40-50 minutes*

4 slices lightly buttered bread of your choice, cubed

2 cups milk

2 eggs

¼ cup sugar

¼ tsp. salt

½ cup raisins

½ tsp. vanilla

1. Butter a 2-quart baking dish.

2. Place bread cubes in baking dish.

3. In a mixing bowl, beat together milk, eggs, sugar, and salt.

4. Pour mixture over bread cubes.

5. Gently stir in raisins and vanilla.

6. Place baking dish into a larger baking pan filled with hot water to a depth of ¾ inch.

7. Bake at 350° for about 40 minutes, or until pudding is firm in the center.

"My husband is the main cook in our family. He and our daughter like to make this Bread Pudding. The recipe is my mother-in-law's, whom we lost to metastatic cancer."

Lillie D. Shockney

NURSE NAVIGATOR, AND A SURVIVOR

In our cancer center, we learn to know a patient well beyond her pathology. She may be a single parent with a nine-year-old child—and now she's just been diagnosed with breast cancer. So she's more to us than a medical fact.

She may not have transportation. She may not have money for a taxi. But we do. We must know our patients well so they don't choose a treatment plan based on their other needs.

A woman may say, "I want a mastectomy," but she doesn't really. She chooses that because it's quicker and easier than a lumpectomy, with a series of radiation or chemo treatments. So we conduct a barrier assessment for each person who's been diagnosed to learn what may impact her ability to have the treatment she ought to have.

I created the Johns Hopkins Navigator program 16 years ago, and I oversee it now, along with serving as a Nurse Navigator, in addition to two other full-time Nurse Navigators. We are all three breast cancer survivors and registered nurses. In addition, we have 35 volunteers, all of whom are breast cancer survivors. One is a man. (One percent of breast cancer survivors are male.)

Lillie Shockney (left) with her mother.

We match patients with these volunteers, based on their age, life situation, stage of cancer, and the patient's treatment plan. So the patient has a "mirror partner," who's gone through the same thing. We call the program "Survivors Helping Survivors." These women give reassurance that it's possible to survive and have a vision of hope.

We also work with patients with advanced disease who are going to die. We help them to make plans for what lies ahead—making sure they have an Advance Directive, discussing ways to communicate with their kids about what's likely to happen, helping them to recognize that they are still here and are continuing to instill their values in their kids.

We instruct each partner and patient to go to a local card store and tell the manager, "This woman has Stage Four breast cancer, and we need help to select cards for our children's birthdays through age 21, their first communions, bar mitzvahs, weddings, the days when our children become grandparents." Then the woman writes what she wants to say to each child on each of those days. She gives it to her partner to give to her loved one to open on those special days.

I've gotten incredible feedback from children who've received these cards, most recently from a young woman who got one on her wedding day. She said, "My mother was right there with me that day."

"We're doing patient care here—we don't see these women just as Stage 2 breast cancer patients."

When You Join an Avon Walk for Breast Cancer, You Are "**IN IT TO END IT**"®

YOUR JOURNEY

Each Avon Walk for Breast Cancer weekend is two unforgettable days of passion, power, and pure fun. Here's a glimpse of how it all shapes up—from before you take your first step to the moment you cross the finish line. It's a journey like no other. It's a chance to change millions of lives, starting with your own.

BEFORE THE WALK

Once you register, you'll be assigned your very own Walker Coordinator. This Avon Walk staffer will be your main contact and coach and will help you develop your personal fundraising plan, connect you with local Training Walks, and help you every step of the way leading up to your Avon Walk weekend.

EVENT EVE

Event Eve, the kick-off event for the Avon Walk weekend, takes place on the Friday that launches the Walk weekend at a hotel near the event's Opening Ceremony site. This is where you officially check in for the event. You'll receive your Avon Walk wristband, get your tent assignment, turn in any last-minute donations, and celebrate the start of the Walk weekend with other walkers.

OPENING CEREMONY

The inspiring Opening Ceremony brings all Avon Walk participants together for the first time early Saturday morning. You'll connect with others, drop off your gear, fill your water bottle, stretch a little—and before you know it you'll be on the road.

WALKING

Each of the Avon Walk routes will take you through a wonderful, scenic tour of its city. You'll walk up to 26.2 miles on Day 1 and 13.1 miles on Day 2. The distance you walk is completely up to you, and you can decide that at any time. If the mileage ever starts to feel too daunting you can stop, knowing you've already made a powerful difference, and an Avon Walk crew member will be there to pick you up.

WELLNESS VILLAGE

At the end of Day 1, you'll reach Wellness Village—your home away from home for the night—where you can relax, enjoy a hot shower, a hearty dinner and maybe even a yoga class or a foot massage. You'll cap off your day with some fun and festivities before settling in to one of the two-person tents we provide. The next morning you'll wake up to a hot breakfast, and then you'll be off on the final leg of your Avon Walk. Those not wishing to camp out may easily leave the event for the evening and return the next morning to rejoin their fellow Walkers.

CLOSING CEREMONY

At the uplifting and touching Closing Ceremony, all Walkers and Crew come together one last time to celebrate their accomplishment. One of the great pleasures is watching the money you raised be awarded on Sunday to local breast cancer organizations.

THE END IS JUST THE BEGINNING

While crossing the finish line marks the end of your Avon Walk journey, it's just the beginning of the impact you'll have. Because of you, breast cancer patients will get the care they need, regardless of their ability to pay. And leading scientists and researchers will receive support in their ongoing quest for a cure.

You are **IN IT TO END IT**!

Gerie Voss

**SURVIVOR,
AND AVON WALKER**

• • • • • • • • • • • • • •

Gerie Voss is an attorney and a 10-year survivor.

Chocolate Chip Banana Bread

Makes 1 loaf of 18 slices
Prep Time: 15-20 minutes • *Baking Time: 60-65 minutes*

2 cups flour

1 cup sugar

1 tsp. baking powder

1 tsp. salt

½ tsp. baking soda

1 cup mashed ripe bananas (2 to 3 medium bananas)

½ cup shortening

2 eggs

1 cup semi-sweet mini chocolate chips

½ cup chopped nuts of your choice

1. Preheat oven to 350°. Grease bottom only of a 9" x 5" loaf pan.

2. Combine all ingredients except chocolate chips and nuts in large electric mixer bowl. Mix until well blended.

3. Stir in chocolate chips and nuts.

4. Pour batter into loaf pan.

5. Bake 60-65 minutes, or until tester inserted into center of loaf comes out clean.

6. Cool 10 minutes.

7. Remove from pan and allow to cool to room temperature on cooling rack.

*"I'm a baker.
I love this bread!"*

Gerie Voss

SURVIVOR, AND AVON WALKER

I was diagnosed a little over 10 years ago when I was 26. I had just gotten engaged to my now-husband. I was told that I had cancer in the right breast and severe atypical cells in the left breast.

Chris was my greatest support, but unfortunately, he was away when I got my diagnosis, and I had no family nearby. So to let my mind clear, I went to see "Legally Blonde" by myself, and it was great to be with people and to laugh. Chris was wonderful by phone with me that day, saying that we'll do whatever we need to do, we'll go see however many doctors we need to see. And he continued to stand by me.

Those days were very much a whirlwind. I was so worried about how I would look in my beautiful, strapless wedding dress.

Asking my sister to take over the search for bridesmaids' dresses was a very emotional conversation because I was admitting that I wouldn't be able to do everything for my wedding that I wanted to do. We were both crying. She said she'd do whatever I needed.

My father had a bit of denial about my diagnosis. I was telling him one day about doctors I was going to go see. And he said, "Why? You haven't been diagnosed with breast cancer." My mother had passed away years earlier, and he was my one parent to help me face this. But at first he was almost incapable of dealing with it himself.

I was most worried about how I would look to my husband. I was online all the time, learning about treatments that were available. My bilateral mastectomy with reconstruction happened between my diagnosis and my wedding.

Of course, no one wishes this on anyone. But the experience has changed me in such positive ways. I had the wonderfully good fortune of speaking at the Opening and Closing Ceremonies at my first Avon Walk 5 years ago. I introduced Reese Witherspoon there — and I can't tell you what that meant. She had been with me on the darkest day of my life, when I had sat in a theater watching her in "Legally Blonde." I hugged her, and she asked me how I was. I was immensely gratified to be able to tell her how she helped me.

When I was diagnosed, friends and family would say, "You should see this person or that person," but they were all a minimum of 30 years older than I was. Their concerns were not my concerns. Now I try to speak with young women who need the guidance I was looking for. Every time that I can, I tell people that breast cancer is not an old women's disease.

Gerie Voss (left) meets Reese Witherspoon, Avon Global Ambassador and Honorary Chairman of the Avon Foundation for Women, at an Avon Walk.

"I was diagnosed when I was 26. The wedding date that Chris and I had set was eight months later. I was so worried about how I would look in my beautiful strapless wedding dress. More than that, I was worried about how I would look to my husband."

Lori Viveros
PATIENT NAVIGATOR

. . . .

Lori Viveros is Program Manager of Avon Cares for Life, a program of the UCLA Jonsson Comprehensive Cancer Center, located at the Olive View - UCLA Medical Center, a public hospital in Northern Los Angeles County. The program provides hope for patients from diagnosis through treatment and beyond.

Butternut Squash Bisque

Makes 4-6 servings
Prep Time: 30 minutes • Baking/Cooking Time: 45-60 minutes

2 medium butternut squash, to yield 4 cups cubed squash

1 Tbsp. vegetable oil

1 Tbsp. unsalted butter

½ cup diced onions

¾ cup diced carrots

3 cups low-sodium chicken broth

salt to taste

pepper to taste

ground nutmeg to taste

2 oz. cream cheese (¼ of 8-oz. pkg.), cut in chunks

"This is comfort food, and I absolutely love it. Credit goes to my husband who always makes it!"

1. Cut squash in half. Remove seeds. Drizzle with oil, enough to cover cut surface. Wrap each half in foil. Lay on baking sheet.

2. Bake at 375° for 30-35 minutes, or until squash is fork-tender.

3. When cool enough to handle, peel and cube squash.

4. Heat 1Tbsp. oil and melt butter in large stockpot over medium heat.

5. Stir onion into butter and oil and cook until tender.

6. Add carrots and cubed squash to pot. Pour in chicken stock. Season to taste with salt, pepper, and nutmeg.

7. Bring to a boil. Reduce heat, and simmer until vegetables are tender.

8. In a blender or food processor, puree the soup mixture until smooth.

9. Strain soup.

10. Return to stockpot and stir in cream cheese. Heat through, but do not boil.

11. Serve warm with a dash of nutmeg.

Lori Viveros
PATIENT NAVIGATOR

Olive View has a large Latina population, so I can give back to my community and see the results of my work almost instantly. Our patients have so many barriers, including language. I was drawn to this work because I want to help women and their families at this particular time in their lives.

We start one-on-one with a patient and her family when she is diagnosed. We provide support to the medical staff, and we offer psychological and social support to the patient on behalf of the physicians. We assign a Navigator to each patient, and she connects the woman to all the resources that are available—from money to groceries to transportation. She stays with the patient the whole way through her treatment.

I started out as a Patient Navigator, and then developed the program as we took on more patients. Now I oversee three Navigators, although I still keep some patients on my caseload. I am so fulfilled when I see the Navigators making such a difference in patients' lives.

Our program continues to grow and evolve. For example, we now have a nurse practitioner managing long-term surveillance for survivors. We have a clinical research program and have incorporated

navigation into that. Before we received funding from the Avon Foundation, we had very limited opportunities for patients to participate in clinical trials. Now they can do that quite comprehensively.

Many times, for the people we see at Olive View, breast cancer isn't their biggest problem. They may have too little food today and a lot of uncertainty about enough food tomorrow, they may be homeless, they many just not have enough money. A breast cancer diagnosis on top of all of that seems almost insurmountable.

This is work of the heart. This profession, these opportunities are mission-driven. I love being part of this community. I look forward to more and more people joining this effort.

When you give so much of yourself into this kind of undertaking, this wonderful work, it's hard to keep everything balanced. I try to practice self-care; I have such a good family. When a patient passes away, I'm so glad for the support of our team. This occupation requires being able to step away, to reflect, to honor, and to keep a work-life balance.

"Many times, for the people we see, breast cancer isn't their biggest problem. This is work of the heart."

Mara Langer

TWO-TIME BREAST CANCER SURVIVOR, AND AVON WALKER

· · · · · · · · · · · · · ·

Mara Langer is a two-time breast cancer survivor and has done seven Avon Walks. She was the 2012 captain of her Avon Walk Team, Girls Gone Wild for a Cure. In total she's raised over $75,000 toward the cure.

Awesome Chicken Marinade

Makes 6 servings
Prep Time: 10 minutes • Marinating Time: 1-2 hours

½ cup fresh lemon juice (requires about **4** lemons)

½ cup low-sodium soy sauce

1 Tbsp. peeled, minced, fresh ginger

1 Tbsp. lemon pepper seasoning

2 garlic cloves, minced

6 boneless, skinless chicken breast halves

1. Combine the juice, soy sauce, ginger, lemon pepper, and garlic in a large zip-top plastic bag.

2. Add chicken to bag. Seal and shake to coat.

3. Marinate in refrigerator 1-2 hours, turning once. (Do not marinate overnight. The acid in the lemon juice tends to make the chicken mushy if it marinates that long.)

4. Remove chicken from marinade and grill, just until done.

"After my diagnosis, I started making small changes in what I eat. I watch my portions, and I try to get in some sort of exercise each day. I've now dropped all sugar and white flour, so my eating and exercise has allowed me to shed 20+ pounds. I'm now back down to my pre-baby weight and feeling great!"

Mara Langer

TWO-TIME BREAST CANCER SURVIVOR, AND AVON WALKER

Breast cancer—two powerful words! They have always been a part of my life. My mother and grandmother both died from breast cancer. I spent my childhood living next to the disease.

In the back of my mind, I always knew cancer was something that might present itself within my body. The only question was when.

In early 2004, my husband, David, and I were blessed with the birth of our beautiful daughter, Malia. Because of my strong family history, I'd begun having mammograms at the age of 30. Shortly after I stopped breast feeding, I went in for a routine mammogram. And there it was. The cancer had arrived. Because of my prior mammograms, the cancer was detected extremely early.

After several conversations with my surgeon, we decided I'd have a bi-lateral mastectomy with immediate reconstruction.

I am a poster child for early detection, and I am thankful every day.

But my story does not end there. Fast-forward two years. David and I received the news that our 12-week-old fetus was healthy and viable. We were overjoyed with happiness. Malia was 2½, and having a second child was a primary goal before, during, and after my cancer diagnosis.

One day shortly after getting the good news, David asked me if I'd felt any changes to my breasts due to the pregnancy. I decided to perform a breast self exam. As I was feeling about, I discovered a small, round thing, tucked right under my left armpit.

To say I panicked is an understatement. Days later, I was diagnosed with my second bout of breast cancer in two years. Not a metastasis, but a brand new occurrence and an aggressive one.

The question of what to do and when became critical. Unfortunately (but lucky for us) other women have been through chemo while pregnant, and I was put in contact with several of them. Through our talks, David and I both felt better about moving forward with keeping the baby and starting treatments.

Five months after my diagnosis, on my 39th birthday, our healthy baby boy, Ari Jonathan, arrived four weeks early, healthy, strong, and full of life.

After he was born, Ari accompanied me to most of my treatments. Not surprisingly, each person in the office claimed their share of the responsibility for his miraculous birth! He is a miracle baby.

"After many doctor visits—to the oncologist, the ob-gyn, the surgeon, and the peri-natal specialist—we decided I should have the tumor removed and start chemo. Yes, I was nervous, and yes, I was scared. However, I had faith that everything would work out, and it did."

Tips to Reduce Your Risk for Breast Cancer

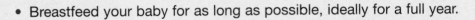

- Try to maintain a healthy weight for your body type. Avoid gaining weight as an adult.

    FACT: A weight gain of 20 or more pounds can increase an adult woman's breast cancer risk.

- Be physically active. Walk briskly or exercise for 30 minutes most days of the week.

    FACT: Exercise reduces risk of breast cancer and helps to maintain a healthy weight.

- Breastfeed your baby for as long as possible, ideally for a full year.

    FACT: Breastfeeding is healthy for babies. It may also reduce a mother's future breast cancer risk.

- Limit alcoholic beverages.

    FACT: One or more alcoholic drinks per day is associated with an increased risk of breast cancer.

- Eat leafy green vegetables and whole grains.

    FACT: Leafy greens and whole grains contain the vitamin B-9 (folate).

- Don't smoke tobacco, and don't let others smoke near you or your family at home or at work.

  FACT: Girls and young women exposed to second-hand smoke may have a higher risk of breast cancer.

- Use precaution with certain chemicals in cleaning agents and household products.

  FACT: Some chemicals may affect hormones in the body. Read labels and get more information at http://www.zerobreastcancer.org/research.html#factsheets.

- Avoid using hormone replacement therapy HRT (estrogen and progesterone combined).

  FACT: Hormone replacement therapy is associated with breast cancer. Discuss it with your doctor or nurse.

- Minimize radiation exposures, especially girls and younger women. Talk to your doctor about reducing your exposure to medical radiation.

  FACT: Girls repeatedly exposed to radiation before age 20 are at high risk for developing breast cancer.

– Adapted from Zero Breast Cancer

Critical Advances in the Fight Against Breast Cancer

Great progress has been made in breast cancer research, early detection, diagnosis, and treatment in the last 20 years since the Avon Breast Cancer Crusade was launched.

- Five-year survival rates after a breast cancer diagnosis have improved from an average of 70% in 1992 to greater than 85% today for those with access to care. For breast cancers caught early, five-year survival odds can be greater than 95%.

- Advances in breast imaging—digital mammography, ultrasound, and MRI—enable doctors to find tumors before a palpable lump can be felt.

- Surgical procedures have become less invasive, and a mastectomy is not always needed. Instead, lumpectomy plus radiation has become the standard of care in most cases.

- Research conducted over the past 20 years has enabled scientists to better understand that there are different types of breast cancer, and to develop new diagnostic tests to enable more targeted and individualized breast cancer therapies.

- Despite these advances, there is still a new diagnosis every 3 minutes. Avon is **IN IT TO END IT**, and its commitment is stronger than ever to ensure that all women have access to high-quality care.

- The Avon Breast Cancer Crusade will persevere in its effort to improve access for all women, reduce or eliminate disparities in care, understand the causes of breast cancer, and develop new prevention approaches.

GOOD NEWS, BUT NOT EQUALLY FOR ALL

Survival is improving, surgery can be less invasive in most cases, targeted therapies with fewer side-effects are available, and not every breast cancer has to be treated with harsh chemotherapy. But one recent study,* funded by the Avon Foundation, suggests these advances are not being made available to all.

The study found that African American women in 21 of the 24 largest U.S. cities had higher mortality rates from breast cancer than white women. (Similar disparities have been reported for other illnesses.) The breast cancer mortality rate for African American women has remained the same for the last 20 years. However, the rate for white women has been cut in half since 1990, due largely to advances in diagnosis and treatment.

The size of disparity varies by city, indicating that it is primarily due to a woman's access to screening and treatment services. For example, in New York the public health system is decentralized, and public hospitals are located throughout the boroughs of the city. In Chicago, only two public hospitals exist, so care is not as accessible, and only one of them offers screening mammograms. Another part of the problem is that more cancers develop at younger ages in African American women, when mammography is not as effective and is not routinely recommended.

* With the results of this new study, the Avon Foundation hopes to learn why some cities are doing better than others.

A Brief History of the Avon Foundation for Women

The Avon Foundation for Women has been working to improve the lives of women and their families since 1955. Today, it is the largest corporate-affiliated philanthropy dedicated solely to women's causes globally. Avon philanthropy focuses its current funding on breast cancer research and access to care through the Avon Breast Cancer Crusade, and on efforts to reduce domestic and gender violence through its Speak Out Against Domestic Violence program.

Avon philanthropy also responds generously in times of major disasters and emergencies. Combined, these funding programs touch the lives of millions of women across the United States and around the world.

Through 2011, Avon global philanthropy donated more than $860 million in more than 50 countries for causes most important to women.

While advances have been made, breast cancer remains the most commonly diagnosed cancer among women worldwide, and there is a new diagnosis every three minutes. Since the Avon Breast Cancer Crusade launched in 1992, Avon breast cancer programs in 58 countries have donated more than $740 million for research and advancing access to care, regardless of a person's ability to pay.

KEY AVON FOUNDATION ACHIEVEMENTS IN THE U.S. INCLUDE:

- Awarded $138 million since 2000 to support eight Avon Foundation Breast Cancer Centers of Excellence nationwide that provide exceptional research and care.

- Awarded more than 1,430 grants to community-based nonprofit breast health organizations, including support for approximately 125 organizations annually.

- Since 2011, awarded 345 grants totaling $120 million to Avon "Safety Net" hospitals and community organizations to fund patient navigation, staff, and equipment upgrades to ensure quality care for the poor or uninsured.

- Invested more than $190 million in breast cancer research, including most recently more than $25 million for 41 research projects focused on primary prevention, understanding the origin and potential causes of breast cancer, and developing new blood- or saliva-based tests for early detection.

- Educated more than 100 million women globally about the importance of breast screenings and early detection and facilitated access to mammograms for 17 million women.

- In partnership with the Dr. Susan Love Research Foundation, launched the Love/Avon Army of Women to accelerate the pace of prevention research by enlisting record numbers of women in research efforts, including healthy women who have never been diagnosed, those at risk for breast cancer, and breast cancer survivors. Through 2011 the Army of Women has recruited more than 362,000 women, launched more than 54 research studies, and had more than 53,000 Army of Women members respond to requests for volunteers.

In addition to receiving generous support from Avon Products, Inc., including all net proceeds from its sale of Avon "Pink Ribbon" products, the Foundation raises funds through a variety of events, such as the U.S. Avon Walk for Breast Cancer series, which is the Foundation's largest fund-raising source.

To learn more about the Avon Foundation, an accredited 501(c)(3) public charity, go to www.avonfoundation.org.

Ways to Get Involved and Make a Difference

1. Participate in the Avon Walk for Breast Cancer

- Register, volunteer or donate! For more information, including cities and dates, or to donate, visit www.avonwalk.org or call 888-541-WALK.

2. Visit www.avonfoundation.org for information, tools and links to:

- Host Your Own Fundraising Event

- Create a Tribute Page to Honor Someone You Love

- Shop for Breast Cancer Fundraising Products

- Shop or sell on eBay to Support the Cause

3. Volunteer

- Reach out to breast cancer organizations in your community to learn about volunteer opportunities. Many organizations could benefit from the gift of your time and talents.

4. Encourage Your Friends and Family to Buy This Book!

Welcome to the *Fix-It and Forget-It* Cooking Community!

First, a word in honor of slow cookers

Slow cookers are those ordinary workhorses that make the routine possible. They're quiet and unassuming. They need little attention once you've gotten to know the particular model (or models) you own.

They help you do what you mean to do–

- buoy up your effort to sit down daily around the table with the people you love;
- keep your food-spending in line;
- feed your household more nutritionally than if you relied on take-out or packaged meals.

Second, you're not alone

This book has a warm heart. All of the recipes come from households across the country, where they are tried and trusted and loved. Thank you to each of you who has offered your favorites–and to each of you who has tested these recipes. You exemplify the great tradition of *sharing* good recipes, rather than *possessing* them.

Phyllis Pellman Good

Make this cookbook your own

Most of the recipes in this collection are flexible and forgiving. You'll notice that most of them offer a range of cooking times; many of the recipes suggest optional ingredients.

You will also find series of recipes throughout the book that are similar. Yet these recipes differ enough from each other so that you can select the one with the ingredients which you like best, or the ingredients which you already have in your pantry.

Make this book your own. Write in it. Note the cooking time that worked for you. Star the recipe you liked. If you added or subtracted ingredients, write them in the neighboring column. Flip to the Index and put a big dot next to a recipe you especially liked. Then you can spot it at a glance when you're looking for cooking inspiration.

This is a community

The Tips spread among the recipes give you the kind of advice and encouragement your mother or good-cook-neighbor or favorite aunt might offer if s/he were cooking with you.

When you cook from this book, you're in the company of cooks everywhere who do their best to bring delicious, satisfying food to their families and friends.

May the *Fix-It and Forget-It PINK Cookbook* help make your meal preparations less harried and your dinners more satisfying! Because spending time together, after all, is among the greatest gifts we have.

Phyllis Pellman Good

Tips for Using Your Slow Cooker: A Friendly Year-Round Appliance

1. What to buy

• A good standard size for a household of four is a 4-quart slow cooker. If you often cook for more, or you like to prepare sizable roasts, turkey breasts, or chicken legs and thighs, you'll want a 6-quart cooker.

For parties or buffets, a 1½- to 2-quart size works well for dips and snacks.

• Cookers which allow you to program "On," the length of the cooking time, and "Off," are convenient. If your model doesn't include that feature, you might want to get a digital appliance timer, which gives you that option. Make sure the timer is adequate for the electrical flow that your cooker demands.

• A baking insert, a cooking rack, a temperature probe, and an insulated carrying tote are all useful additions offered with some models. Or you can buy some of them separately by going to the manufacturers' websites.

2. Learn to know your slow cooker

• Some newer slow cookers cook at a very high temperature. You can check the temperature of your slow cooker this way:
   1. Place 2 quarts of water in your slow cooker.
   2. Cover. Heat on Low 8 hours.
   3. Lift the lid. Immediately check the water temp with an accurate thermometer.
   4. The temperature of the water should be 185°F. If the temperature is higher, foods may overcook and you should reduce the overall cooking time. If the temperature is lower, your foods will probably not reach a safe temperature quickly enough, and the cooker should be discarded.

3. Maximizing what a slow cooker does best

• Slow cookers tend to work best when they're ⅔ full. You many need to increase the cooking time if you've exceeded that amount, or reduce it if you've put in less than that.

• Cut the hard veggies going into your cooker into chunks of about equal size. In other words, make your potato and carrot pieces about the same size. Then they'll be done cooking at nearly the same time. Softer veggies, like bell peppers and zucchini, cook faster, so they don't need to be cut as small. But again, keep them similar in size to each other so they finish together.

• Because raw vegetables are notoriously tough customers in a slow cooker, layer them over the bottom and around the sides of the cooker, as much as possible. That puts them in more direct contact with the heat.

• There are consequences to lifting the lid on your slow cooker while it's cooking. To compensate for the lost heat, you should plan to add 15-20 minutes of cooking time for each time the lid was lifted off.

On the other hand, moisture gathers in a slow cooker as it works. To allow that to cook off, or to thicken the cooking juices, take the lid off during the last half hour of cooking time.

• Use only the amount of liquid called for in a recipe. In contrast to an oven or a stovetop, a slow cooker tends to draw juices out of food and then harbor it.

Of course, if you sense that the food in your cooker is drying out, or browning excessively before it finishes cooking, you may want to add ½ cup of *warm* liquid to the cooker.

• Important variables to remember that don't show up in recipes:
  · The fuller your slow cooker, the longer it will take its contents to cook.
  · The more densely packed the cooker's contents are, the longer they will take to cook.
  · The larger the chunks of meat or vegetables, the more time they will need to cook.

4. Debunking the myths

• Slow cookers are *a handy year-round appliance*. They don't heat up a kitchen in warm weather. They allow you to escape to the pool or lake or lawn or gardens—so why not let them work for you when it's hot outdoors. A slow cooker fixes your dinner while you're at your child's soccer game, too.

So don't limit its usefulness. Remember the dozens of recipes-beyond-beef-stew in this collection!

One more thing—a slow cooker provides a wonderful alternative if your oven is full—no matter the season.

• You can overdo food in a slow cooker. If you're tempted to stretch a recipe's 6-hour stated cooking time to 8 or 10 hours, you may be disappointed in your dinner. Yes, these cookers work their magic using slow, moist heat. Yes, many dishes cook a long time. But these outfits have their limits.

For example, chicken can overcook in a slow cooker. Especially boneless, skinless breasts. But legs and thighs aren't immune either. Once they go past the falling-off-the-bone stage, they are prone to move on to deeply dry.

Cooked pasta and sour cream do best if added late in the cooking process, ideally 10 minutes before the end of the cooking time if the cooker is on high; 30 minutes before the end of the cooking time if it's on low.

5. Safety

• A working slow cooker gets hot on the outside—and I mean the outer electrical unit as well as the inner vessel. Make sure that curious and unsuspecting children or adults don't grab hold of either part. Use oven mitts when lifting any part of a hot cooker.

• To prevent a slow cooker from bubbling over, either when its sitting still on a counter, or when its traveling to a carry-in dinner, fill the cooker only ⅔ full.

If you're going to exceed that limit, pull out your second slow cooker (what—you have only one?!) and divide the contents between them.

6. Adapting stove-top or oven recipes for a slow cooker

• Many stove-top and oven recipes can be adapted for a slow cooker. If you want to experiment, use these conversion factors:
- Low (in a slow cooker) = 200°F approximately (in an oven).
- High (in a slow cooker) = 300°F approximately (in an oven).
- In a slow cooker, 2 hours on Low = 1 hour, approximately, on High.

7. More than one slow cooker?!

• If you run the food services for an active household, or if you often have guests, consider having more than one slow cooker. If you own two different sizes, you can do sides or appetizers or desserts in the smaller one. Or you may want two of similar, or the same, size so you can double the portions of your favorite dishes.

Appetizers, Snacks, and Spreads

Quick and Easy Nacho Dip

Kristina Shull, Timberville, VA

Makes 10-15 servings

Prep. Time: 15 minutes
Cooking Time: 2 hours
Ideal slow-cooker size: 3-qt.

1 lb. ground beef
dash of salt
dash of pepper
dash of onion powder
2 garlic cloves, minced,
  optional
2 16-oz. jars salsa (as hot *or* mild as you like)
15-oz. can refried beans
1½ cups sour cream
3 cups shredded cheddar cheese, *divided*

1. Brown ground beef. Drain. Add salt, pepper, onion powder, and minced garlic if you wish.

2. Combine beef, salsa, beans, sour cream, and 2 cups cheese in slow cooker.

3. Cover. Heat on Low 2 hours. Just before serving, sprinkle with 1 cup cheese.

Serving suggestion: Serve with **tortilla chips**.

Southwest Hot Chip Dip

Annabelle Unternahrer, Shipshewana, IN

Makes 15-20 servings

Prep. Time: 15 minutes
Cooking Time: 1½-4 hours
Ideal slow-cooker size: 3-qt.

1 lb. ground beef, browned, crumbled fine, and drained
2 15-oz. cans refried beans
2 10-oz. cans diced tomatoes and chilies
1 pkg. taco seasoning
1 lb. Velveeta cheese, cubed

1. Combine ground beef, beans, tomatoes, and taco seasoning in slow cooker.

2. Cover. Cook on Low 3-4 hours, or on High 1½ hours.

3. Add cheese. Stir occasionally. Heat until cheese is melted.

Serving suggestion: Serve with **tortilla chips**. *This can be a main dish when served alongside a soup.*

Prepare an appetizer in another little slow cooker and keep your guests busy with dipping into it while you finish the final prep of the main meal.

Hot Refried Bean Dip

Sharon Anders, Alburtis, PA

Makes 1½ quarts, or 12-20 servings

Prep. Time: 15 minutes
Cooking Time: 45 minutes
Ideal slow-cooker size: 3-qt.

15-oz. can refried beans,
   drained and mashed
½ lb. ground beef
3 Tbsp. bacon drippings
1 lb. American cheese,
   cubed
1-3 Tbsp. taco sauce
1 Tbsp. taco seasoning
dash of garlic salt
tortilla chips

1. In skillet, brown beans and ground beef in bacon drippings. Pour into slow cooker.

2. Stir in cheese, taco sauce, taco seasoning, and garlic salt.

3. Cover. Cook on High 45 minutes, or until cheese is melted, stirring occasionally. Turn to Low until ready to serve, up to 6 hours.

Chili-Cheese Taco Dip

Kim Stoltzfus, New Holland, PA

Makes 10-12 servings

Prep. Time: 15 minutes
Cooking Time: 1-1½ hours
Ideal slow-cooker size: 1- to 1½-qt.

1 lb. ground beef
1 can chili, without beans
1 lb. mild Mexican
   Velveeta cheese, cubed

1. Brown beef, crumble into small pieces, and drain.

2. Combine beef, chili, and cheese in slow cooker.

3. Cover. Cook on Low 1-1½ hours, or until cheese is melted, stirring occasionally to blend ingredients.

*Serving suggestion: Serve warm with **taco** or **tortilla chips**.*

Hamburger Cheese Dip

Julia Lapp, New Holland, PA

Makes 8-10 servings

Prep. Time: 20 minutes
Cooking Time: 2-3 hours
Ideal slow-cooker size: 1- to 1½-qt.

1 lb. ground beef, browned
   and crumbled into small
   pieces
½ tsp. salt
½ cup chopped green
   peppers
¾ cup chopped onion
8-oz. can tomato sauce
4-oz. can green chilies,
   chopped
1 Tbsp. Worcestershire
   sauce
1 Tbsp. brown sugar
1 lb. Velveeta cheese, cubed
1 Tbsp. paprika
red pepper to taste

1. Combine beef, salt, green peppers, onion, tomato sauce, green chilies, Worcestershire sauce, and brown sugar in slow cooker.

2. Cover. Cook on Low 2-3 hours. During the last hour, stir in cheese, paprika, and red pepper.

*Serving suggestion: Serve with **tortilla chips**.*

Variation:
   Prepare recipe using only ⅓-½ lb. ground beef.

Browning the meat, onions, and vegetables before putting them in the cooker improves their flavor, but this extra step can be skipped in most recipes. The flavor will still be good.
                                   Dorothy M. Van Deest, Memphis, TN

Chili-Cheese Dip

Ruth Hofstetter, Versailles, MO
Paula King, Harrisonburg, VA

Makes 10 servings

Prep. Time: 10 minutes
Cooking Time: 1 hour
Ideal slow-cooker size: 1- to 1½-qt.

1 lb. ground beef, browned, crumbled fine, and drained.
2 lbs. Velveeta cheese, cubed
10-oz. can tomatoes with chilies
1 tsp. Worcestershire sauce
½ tsp. chili powder

1. Combine all ingredients in slow cooker. Mix well.
2. Cover. Cook on High 1 hour, stirring occasionally until cheese is fully melted.
3. Serve immediately, or turn to Low for serving up to 6 hours later.

Serving suggestion: Serve with **tortilla** *or* **corn chips**.

Variation:
For a thicker dip, make a smooth paste of 2 Tbsp. flour mixed with 3 Tbsp. cold water. Stir into hot dip after Step 2.

Michelle's Taco Dip

Michelle Strite, Harrisonburg, VA

Makes 6-8 servings

Prep. Time: 10 minutes
Cooking Time: 2-3 hours
Ideal slow-cooker size: 2- to 3-qt.

1½ lbs. ground beef, browned, crumbled fine, and drained
1 pkg. taco seasoning mix
10-oz. jar salsa
1 lb. Velveeta cheese, cubed
¼ cup chopped onion

1. Combine all ingredients in slow cooker.
2. Cover. Heat on Low for 2-3 hours.

Serving suggestion: Serve with **tortilla chips**.

Variation:
The recipe can be made with half the amount of meat called for, if you prefer.

Karen's Nacho Dip

Karen Stoltzfus, Alto, MI

Makes 10-12 servings

Prep. Time: 10 minutes
Cooking Time: 1 hour
Ideal slow-cooker size: 3-qt.

1 lb. ground beef
2 lbs. American cheese, cubed
16-oz. jar salsa (mild, medium, *or* hot, whichever you prefer)
1 Tbsp. Worcestershire sauce

1. Brown beef, crumble into small pieces, and drain.
2. Combine beef, cheese, salsa, and Worcestershire sauce in slow cooker.
3. Cover. Cook on High 1 hour, stirring occasionally until cheese is fully melted.
4. Serve immediately, or turn to Low for serving up to 6 hours later.

Mexican Chip Dip Olé

Joy Sutter, Iowa City, IA

Makes 10-12 servings

Prep. Time: 15 minutes
Cooking Time: 2-4 hours
Ideal slow-cooker size: 4-qt.

2 lbs. ground turkey
1 large onion, chopped
15-oz. can tomato sauce
4-oz. can green chilies, chopped
3-oz. can jalapeno peppers, chopped
2 lbs. Velveeta cheese, cubed

1. Brown turkey and onion. Drain.
2. Add tomato sauce, chilies, jalapeno peppers, and cheese. Pour into slow cooker.
3. Cover. Cook on Low 4 hours, or on High 2 hours.

*Serving suggestion: Serve warm with **tortilla chips**.*

Pizza Fondue

Lisa Warren, Parkesburg, PA

Makes 8-12 servings

Prep. Time: 10 minutes
Cooking Time: 2-3 hours
Ideal slow-cooker size: 3-qt.

1 lb. ground beef
2 cans pizza sauce with cheese
8 oz. grated cheddar cheese
8 oz. grated mozzarella cheese
1 tsp. dried oregano
½ tsp. fennel seed, *optional*
1 Tbsp. cornstarch

1. Brown beef, crumble fine, and drain.
2. Combine all ingredients except in slow cooker.
3. Cover. Heat on Low 2-3 hours.

*Serving suggestion: Serve with **tortilla chips**.*

Hamburger Hot Dip

Janice Martins, Fairbank, IA

Makes 6 cups dip

Prep. Time: 15 minutes
Cooking Time: 4 hours
Ideal slow-cooker size: 1- to 1½-qt.

1 lb. ground beef

1 medium onion, chopped fine
½ tsp. salt
¼ tsp. pepper
8-oz. jar salsa
14-oz. can nacho cheese soup
8 slices Velveeta cheese

1. Brown ground beef and onions in saucepan. Drain. Season with salt and pepper.
2. Combine all ingredients in slow cooker.
3. Cover. Cook on Low 4 hours. Stir occasionally.

*Serving suggestion: Serve with **nacho chips**.*

Chili con Queso Cheese Dip

Melanie Thrower, McPherson, KS

Makes 8 servings

Prep. Time: 15 minutes
Cooking Time: 1-2 hours
Ideal slow-cooker size: 1- to 1½-qt.

1 lb. ground beef
½ cup chopped onion
1 cup Velveeta cheese, cubed
10-oz. can diced tomatoes and green chilies
12-oz. can evaporated milk
2 Tbsp. chili powder
tortilla chips

1. Brown ground beef and onion. Crumble beef into fine pieces. Drain.

2. Combine all ingredients except in slow cooker.

3. Cover. Heat on Low 1-2 hours, until cheese is melted.

Serving suggestion: Serve with **tortilla chips.**

Good 'n' Hot Dip

Joyce B. Suiter, Garysburg, NC

Makes 30-50 servings

Prep. Time: 15 minutes
Cooking Time: 1 hour
Ideal slow-cooker size: 3-qt.

1 lb. ground beef
1 lb. bulk sausage
10¾-oz. can cream of chicken soup
10¾-oz. can cream of celery soup
24-oz. jar salsa (use hot for some zing)
1 lb. Velveeta cheese, cubed

1. Brown beef and sausage, crumbling into small pieces. Drain.

2. Combine meat, soups, salsa, and cheese in slow cooker.

3. Cover. Cook on High 1 hour. Stir. Cook on Low until ready to serve.

Serving suggestion: Serve with **chips.**

Texas Queso Dip

Donna Treloar, Muncie, IN
Janie Steele, Moore, OK

Makes 2 quarts dip

Prep Time: 10 minutes
Cooking Time: 2 hours
Ideal slow-cooker size: 4-qt.

1 lb. spicy ground pork sausage, loose
2-lb. block Mexican-style Velveeta cheese, cubed
10-oz. can diced tomatoes with chilies
½ cup milk

1. Brown sausage in skillet, breaking it into small chunks as it browns.

2. Drain off drippings.

3. Combine cheese, tomatoes, and milk in slow cooker.

4. Stir in browned sausage.

5. Cover and cook 2 hours on Low.

Serving suggestion: Serve with **tortilla chips.**

Hot Cheese and Bacon Dip

Lee Ann Hazlett, Freeport, IL

Makes 6-8 servings

Prep. Time: 15 minutes
Cooking Time: 1 hour
Ideal slow-cooker size: 1- to 1½-qt.

16 slices bacon, diced
2 8-oz. pkgs. cream cheese, cubed and softened
4 cups shredded mild cheddar cheese
1 cup half-and-half
2 tsp. Worcestershire sauce
1 tsp. dried minced onion
½ tsp. dry mustard
½ tsp. salt
2-3 drops Tabasco

1. Brown and drain bacon. Set aside.

2. Mix remaining ingredients in slow cooker.

3. Cover. Cook on Low 1 hour, stirring occasionally until cheese melts.

4. Stir in bacon.

Serving suggestion: Serve with **fruit** *slices or* **French bread** *slices. (Dip fruit in* **lemon juice** *to prevent browning.)*

Championship Bean Dip

Renee Shirk, Mt. Joy, PA
Ada Miller, Sugarcreek, OH

Makes 4½ cups dip

Prep. Time: 10 minutes
Cooking Time: 2 hours
Ideal slow-cooker size: 3-qt.

15-oz. can refried beans
1 cup picante sauce
1 cup (4 oz.) shredded
   Monterey Jack cheese
1 cup (4 oz.) shredded
   cheddar cheese
¾ cup sour cream
3-oz. pkg. cream cheese,
   softened
1 Tbsp. chili powder
¼ tsp. ground cumin

1. In a bowl, combine all ingredients. Transfer to slow cooker.
2. Cover. Cook on High 2 hours, or until heated through, stirring once or twice.

Serving suggestion: Serve with **tortilla chips** *and* **salsa**.

Jeanne's Chile con Queso

Jeanne Allen, Rye, CO

Makes 15-20 servings

Prep. Time: 10 minutes
Cooking Time: 1-2 hours
Ideal slow-cooker size: 4-qt.

40-oz. can chili without beans
2 lbs. Velveeta cheese, cubed
16-oz. jar picante sauce
   (mild, medium, *or* hot,
   whichever you prefer)

1. Combine all ingredients in slow cooker.
2. Cover. Cook on Low 1-2 hours, until cheese is melted. Stir.

Serving suggestion: Serve with **tortilla chips**.

Maryann's Chili Cheese Dip

Maryann Westerberg, Rosamond, CA

Makes about 10 servings

Prep. Time: 10 minutes
Cooking Time: 2 hours
Ideal slow-cooker size: 3-qt.

---

2 lbs. Velveeta cheese, cubed
16-oz. can chili without
   beans
10-oz. can diced tomatoes
   with chilies, drained
10¾-oz. can cream of
   mushroom soup

1. Combine cheese and chili in slow cooker. Heat on Low until cheese melts, stirring occasionally.
2. Add tomatoes and soup.
3. Cover. Cook on Low 2 hours. Stir before serving.

Serving suggestion: Serve with **tortilla chips**.

Tina's Cheese Dip

Tina Houk, Clinton, MO

Makes 12 servings

Prep. Time: 5-10 minutes
Cooking Time: 1-1½ hours
Ideal slow-cooker size: 4-qt.

---

2 8-oz. pkgs. cream cheese,
   softened
3 15½-oz. cans chili
2 cups shredded cheddar *or*
   mozzarella cheese

1. Spread cream cheese in bottom of slow cooker.
2. Spread chili on top of cream cheese.
3. Top with shredded cheese.
4. Cover. Cook on Low 1-1½ hours, until shredded cheese is melted. Stir.

Serving suggestion: Serve with **tortilla chips**.

Marilyn's Chili con Queso

Marilyn Mowry, Irving, TX

Makes 2 cups dip

Prep. Time: 10-15 minutes
Cooking Time: 1-2 hours
Ideal slow-cooker size: 1½-qt.

1 Tbsp. chopped green peppers
1 Tbsp. chopped celery
1 Tbsp. chopped onions
2 Tbsp. diced tomatoes
2 tsp. chopped jalapeno pepper
½ cup water
¾ cup heavy cream
8 oz. Velveeta cheese, cubed
2 oz. cheddar cheese, shredded

1. Place first 5 ingredients in slow cooker. Add water.
2. Cover. Cook on High 1 hour, or until vegetables are tender.
3. Stir in cream and cheeses.
4. Reduce heat to Low. Cook until cheese is melted. Serve immediately, or keep warm on Low for hours.

*Serving suggestion: Serve with **tortilla chips**.*

White Queso Dip

Janie Steele, Moore, OK

Makes 10-12 servings

Prep Time: 10-15 minutes
Cooking Time: 1 hour
Ideal slow-cooker size: 2-qt.

2 8-oz. pkgs. cream cheese, either regular *or* low-fat, softened
1 cup sour cream, either regular *or* low-fat
½ tsp. hot sauce
10-oz. can Rotel tomatoes, your choice of hot *or* mild
1 tsp. cumin
4-oz. can green chilies, chopped
8-oz. pkg. grated Monterey Jack cheese, *or* grated Mexican cheese mix

1. Combine cream cheese, sour cream, and hot sauce in a bowl with a mixer until smooth.
2. Drain half the liquid off the tomatoes and discard.
3. Add tomatoes with half their juice, cumin, chilies, and grated cheese to creamy mixture. Stir to combine.
4. Pour mixture into slow cooker.
5. Turn to High until cheese melts, about 1 hour. Stir about every 15 minutes.
6. Turn to Low to keep dip warm while serving.

*Serving suggestion: Serve with **tortilla chips**.*

Short-Cut Fondue Dip

Jean Butzer, Batavia, NY

Makes 8-10 servings

Prep. Time: 10 minutes
Cooking Time: 2-2½ hours
Ideal slow-cooker size: 1½- to 2-qt.

2 10¾-oz. cans condensed cheese soup
2 cups grated sharp cheddar cheese
1 Tbsp. Worcestershire sauce
1 tsp. lemon juice
2 Tbsp. dried chopped chives

1. Combine soup, cheese, Worcestershire sauce, lemon juice, and chives in slow cooker.
2. Cover. Heat on Low 2-2½ hours. Stir until smooth and well blended.

*Serving suggestion: Serve warm dip with **celery sticks**, **cauliflower florets**, and **corn chips**.*

Chili Verde con Queso Dip

Bonita Ensenberger, Albuquerque, NM

Makes 1 quart (8-10 servings)

Prep. Time: 5 minutes
Cooking Time: 3 hours
Ideal slow-cooker size: 1½-qt.

2 10¾-oz. cans cheddar
   cheese soup
7-oz. can chopped green
   chilies
1 garlic clove, minced
½ tsp. dried cilantro leaves
½ tsp. ground cumin

1. Mix together all ingredients chips in slow cooker.
2. Cover. Cook on Low 1-1½ hours. Stir well. Cook an additional 1½ hours.

*Serving suggestion: Serve with **corn chips**.*

Variation:
   Make this a main dish by serving over baked potatoes.

Mexican Cheesecake

Janie Steele, Moore, OK

Makes 6-8 servings

Prep Time: 10-15 minutes
Cooking Time: 1 hour
Ideal slow-cooker size: 2-qt.

3 8-oz. pkgs. cream cheese,
   softened
2 eggs
2 tsp. chicken bouillon
½ cup hot water
4-oz. can green chilies,
   chopped
½-1½ tsp. chili powder,
   depending upon how
   much heat you enjoy
½ tsp., *or less*, hot sauce,
   optional
1 cup cooked chicken,
   chopped

1. Combine all ingredients in slow cooker until smooth.
2. Cook on High 1 hour.
3. Turn to Low to keep warm while serving.

*Serving suggestion: Serve with **tortilla chips** or **crackers**.*

Reuben Spread

Clarice Williams, Fairbank, IA
Julie McKenzie, Punxsutawney, PA

Makes 5 cups spread

Prep. Time: 10 minutes
Cooking Time: 1-2 hours
Ideal slow-cooker size: 3-qt.

½ lb. corned beef, shredded
   or chopped
16-oz. can sauerkraut, well
   drained
1-2 cups shredded Swiss
   cheese
1-2 cups shredded cheddar
   cheese
1 cup mayonnaise

1. Combine all ingredients in slow cooker. Mix well.
2. Cover. Cook on High 1-2 hours until heated through, stirring occasionally.
3. Turn to Low and keep warm in cooker while serving.

*Serving suggestion: Put spread on **rye bread** slices. Top individual servings with **Thousand Island dressing**, if desired.*

Note:
   Low-fat cheese and mayonnaise are not recommended for this spread.

Variation:
   Use dried beef instead of corned beef.

Cheesy New Orleans Shrimp Dip

Kelly Amos, Pittsboro, NC

Makes 3-4 cups dip

Prep. Time: 20 minutes
Cooking Time: 1 hour
Ideal slow-cooker size: 2- to 2½-qt.

1 slice bacon
3 medium onions, chopped
1 garlic clove, minced
4 jumbo shrimp, peeled and deveined
1 medium tomato, peeled and chopped
3 cups Monterey Jack cheese, shredded
4 drops Tabasco sauce
⅛ tsp. cayenne pepper
dash of black pepper

1. Cook bacon until crisp. Drain on paper towel. Crumble.
2. Sauté onion and garlic in bacon drippings. Drain on paper towel.
3. Coarsely chop shrimp.
4. Combine all ingredients in slow cooker.
5. Cover. Cook on Low 1 hour, or until cheese is melted. Thin with milk if too thick.

*Serving suggestion: Serve with **chips**.*

Broccoli Cheese Dip

Carla Koslowsky, Hillsboro, KS

Makes 6 cups dip

Prep. Time: 10 minutes
Cooking Time: 2 hours
Ideal slow-cooker size: 3- to 4-qt.

1 cup chopped celery
½ cup chopped onion
10-oz. pkg. frozen chopped broccoli, cooked
1 cup cooked rice
10¾-oz. can cream of mushroom soup
16-oz. jar cheese spread, *or* 15 slices American cheese, melted and mixed with ⅔ cup milk

1. Combine all ingredients in slow cooker.
2. Cover. Heat on Low 2 hours.

*Serving suggestion: Serve with **snack breads** or **crackers**.*

Italiano Spread

Nanci Keatley, Salem, OR

Makes 8 servings

Prep Time: 15 minutes
Cooking Time: 2-3 hours
Ideal slow-cooker size: 2-qt.

2 8-oz. pkgs. cream cheese, softened
1 cup prepared pesto
3 medium tomatoes, chopped
1 cup mozzarella cheese, shredded
½ cup Parmesan cheese, shredded
2 Tbsp. olive oil

1. Spread cream cheese on bottom of slow cooker.
2. Spread pesto over cream cheese.
3. Add a layer of chopped tomatoes over cream cheese and pesto.
4. Sprinkle cheeses on top of tomatoes.
5. Drizzle olive oil over top.
6. Cook on Low 2-3 hours or until cheese is melted.

*Serving suggestion: Spread on **crackers** or slices of **Italian bread**.*

When I use mushrooms or green peppers in the slow cooker, I usually stir them in during the last hour so they don't get too mushy.
Trudy Kutter, Corfu, NY

Slow-Cooked Salsa

Joleen Albrecht, Gladstone, MI

Makes 8 ½ cups

Prep Time: 15-20 minutes
Cooking Time: 2½-3 hours
Ideal slow-cooker size: 3-qt.

10 fresh Roma, *or* plum, tomatoes, chopped coarsely
2 garlic cloves, minced
1 onion, chopped
2 jalapeno peppers
¼ cup cilantro leaves
½ tsp. salt

1. Place tomatoes, garlic, and onion in slow cooker.
2. Remove stems from jalapenos. Remove seeds, too, if you prefer a milder flavor. Chop jalapenos. Stir into slow cooker.
3. Cover. Cook on High 2½-3 hours, or until vegetables are softened.
4. Allow to cool.
5. When cooled, combine cooked mixture with cilantro and salt in a blender or food processor. Blend or process to the consistency that you like.

Roasted Pepper and Artichoke Spread

Sherril Bieberly, Sauna, KS

Makes 3 cups, or about 12 servings

Prep. Time: 10 minutes
Cooking Time: 1 hour
Ideal slow-cooker size: 1- to 1½-qt.

1 cup grated Parmesan cheese
½ cup mayonnaise
8-oz. pkg. cream cheese, softened
1 garlic clove, minced
14-oz. can artichoke hearts, drained and chopped finely
⅓ cup finely chopped roasted red bell peppers (from 7¼-oz. jar)

1. Combine Parmesan cheese, mayonnaise, cream cheese, and garlic in food processor. Process until smooth. Place mixture in slow cooker.
2. Add artichoke hearts and red bell pepper. Stir well.
3. Cover. Cook on Low 1 hour. Stir again.

*Serving suggestion: Use as spread for **crackers**, cut-up **fresh vegetables**, or **snack-bread** slices.*

Baked Brie with Cranberry Chutney

Amymarlene Jensen, Fountain, CO

Makes 8-10 servings

Prep. Time: 5-10 minutes
Cooking Time: 4 hours
Ideal slow-cooker size: 1- to 1½-qt.

1 cup fresh, *or* dried, cranberries
½ cup brown sugar
⅓ cup cider vinegar
2 Tbsp. water, *or* orange juice
2 tsp. minced crystallized ginger
¼ tsp. cinnamon
⅛ tsp. ground cloves
oil
8-oz. round of Brie cheese
1 Tbsp. sliced almonds, toasted

1. Mix together cranberries, brown sugar, vinegar, water or juice, ginger, cinnamon, and cloves in slow cooker.
2. Cover. Cook on Low 4 hours. Stir once near the end to see if it is thickening. If not, remove top, turn heat to High, and cook 30 minutes without lid.
3. Put cranberry chutney in covered container and chill for up to 2 weeks. When ready to serve, bring to room temperature.
4. Brush ovenproof plate with vegetable oil, place

unpeeled Brie on plate, and bake uncovered at 350° for 9 minutes, until cheese is soft and partially melted. Remove from oven.

5. Top with at least half the chutney and garnish with almonds.

*Serving suggestion: Serve with **crackers**.*

Peach Chutney

Jan Mast, Lancaster, PA

Makes 8 cups

Prep Time: 10 minutes
Cooking Time: 5-8 hours
Ideal slow-cooker size: 4-qt.

2 29-oz. cans (about 6 cups) peaches, diced
1 cup raisins
1 small onion, chopped
1 garlic clove, minced
1 Tbsp. mustard seed
1 tsp. dried red chilies, chopped
¼ cup crystallized ginger, chopped
1 tsp. salt
¾ cup vinegar
½ cup brown sugar

1. Combine all ingredients in slow cooker.
2. Cover. Cook on Low 4-6 hours.
3. Remove lid. Stir chutney. Cook on High, uncovered, an additional 1-2 hours.

Note:

This is a great accompaniment to curried chicken or lamb.

Artichokes

Susan Yoder Graber, Eureka, IL

Makes 4 servings

Prep. Time: 10 minutes
Cooking Time: 2-10 hours
Ideal slow-cooker size: 4-qt.

4 artichokes
1 tsp. salt
2 Tbsp. lemon juice

1. Wash and trim artichokes by cutting off the stems flush with the bottoms of the artichokes and by cutting ¾-1 inch off the tops. Stand upright in slow cooker.
2. Mix together salt and lemon juice and pour over artichokes. Pour in water to cover ¾ of artichokes.
3. Cover. Cook on Low 8-10 hours or on High 2-4 hours.

*Serving suggestion: Serve with melted **butter**. Pull off individual leaves and dip bottom*

of each into butter. Strip the individual leaf of the meaty portion at the bottom of each leaf.

Curried Almonds

Barbara Aston, Ashdown, AR

Makes 4 cups nuts

Prep. Time: 5 minutes
Cooking Time: 3-4½ hours
Ideal slow-cooker size: 3-qt.

2 Tbsp. melted butter
1 Tbsp. curry powder
½ tsp. seasoned salt
1 lb. blanched almonds

1. Combine butter with curry powder and seasoned salt.
2. Pour over almonds in slow cooker. Mix to coat well.
3. Cover. Cook on Low 2-3 hours. Turn to High. Uncover cooker and cook 1-1½ hours.

Serving suggestion: Serve hot or cold.

If you're having guests, and those dinners that require last-minute attention drive you crazy, do your side-dish vegetables in your small slow cooker. They won't demand any of your attention until they're ready to be served.

All-American Snack

Doris M. Coyle-Zipp, South Ozone Park, NY
Melissa Raber, Millersburg, OH
Ada Miller, Sugarcreek, OH
Nanci Keatley, Salem, OR

Makes 3 quarts snack mix

Prep. Time: 10 minutes
Cooking Time: 3 hours
Ideal slow-cooker size: 4-qt.

3 cups thin pretzel sticks
4 cups Wheat Chex
4 cups Cheerios
12-oz. can salted peanuts
¼ cup melted butter, *or*
    margarine
1 tsp. garlic powder
1 tsp. celery salt
½ tsp. seasoned salt
2 Tbsp. grated Parmesan
    cheese

1. Combine pretzels, cereal, and peanuts in large bowl.
2. Melt butter. Stir in garlic powder, celery salt, seasoned salt, and Parmesan cheese. Pour over pretzels, cereal, and peanuts. Toss until well mixed.
3. Pour into large slow cooker. Cover. Cook on Low 2½ hours, stirring every 30 minutes. Remove lid and cook another 30 minutes on Low.

Serving suggestion: Serve warm or at room temperature. Store in tightly covered container.

Variations:

1. Use 3 cups Wheat Chex (instead of 4 cups) and 3 cups Cheerios (instead of 4 cups). Add 3 cups Corn Chex.

Marcia S. Myer
Manheim, PA

2. Alter the amounts of pretzels, cereal, and peanuts to reflect your preferences.

Chili Nuts

Barbara Aston, Ashdown, AR

Makes 5 cups nuts

Prep. Time: 5 minutes
Cooking Time: 2-2½ hours
Ideal slow-cooker size: 3-qt.

¼ cup melted butter
2 12-oz. cans cocktail
    peanuts
1⅝-oz. pkg. chili seasoning
    mix

1. Pour butter over nuts in slow cooker. Sprinkle in dry chili mix. Toss together.
2. Cover. Heat on Low 2-2½ hours. Turn to High. Remove lid and cook 10-15 minutes.

Serving suggestion: Serve warm or cool.

Hot Caramel Dip

Marilyn Yoder, Archbold, OH

Makes about 3 cups dip

Prep. Time: 5 minutes
Cooking Time: none
Ideal slow-cooker size: 2½-qt.

½ cup butter
½ cup light corn syrup
1 cup brown sugar
1 can sweetened condensed
    milk

1. Mix together all ingredients except apples in saucepan. Bring to boil.
2. Pour into slow cooker. Set on Low.

Serving suggestion: Dip fresh **apple slices** *into hot caramel.*

Variation:

Add ½ cup peanut butter to dip.

Rhonda's Apple Butter

Rhonda Burgoon, Collingswood, NJ

Makes about 2 pints apple butter

Prep. Time: 15 minutes
Cooking Time: 12-14 hours
Ideal slow-cooker size: 2½- to 3-qt.

4 lbs. apples
2 tsp. cinnamon
½ tsp. ground cloves

1. Peel, core, and slice apples. Place in slow cooker.
2. Cover. Cook on High 2-3 hours. Reduce to Low and cook 8 hours. Apples should be a rich brown and be cooked down by half.
3. Stir in spices. Cook on High 2-3 hours with lid off. Stir until smooth.
4. Pour into freezer containers and freeze, or into sterilized jars and seal.

Shirley's Apple Butter

Shirley Sears, Tiskilwa, IL

Makes 6-10 pints apple butter

Prep. Time: 30 minutes
Cooking Time: 13-15 hours
Ideal slow-cooker size: 7-qt.

4 qts. finely chopped tart apples
2¾ cups sugar
2¾ tsp. cinnamon
¼ tsp. ground cloves
⅛ tsp. salt

1. Pour apples into slow cooker.
2. Combine remaining ingredients. Drizzle over apples.
3. Cover. Cook on High 3 hours, stirring well with a large spoon every hour. Reduce heat to Low and cook 10-12 hours, until butter becomes thick and dark in color. Stir occasionally with strong wire whisk for smooth butter.
4. Freeze or pour into sterilized jars and seal.

Charlotte's Apple Butter

Charlotte Fry, St. Charles, MO

Makes 5 pints apple butter

Prep. Time: 15 minutes
Cooking Time: 14-18 hours
Ideal slow-cooker size: 6- to 6½-qt.

3 quarts Jonathan, *or* Winesap, apples
2 cups apple cider
2½ cups sugar
1 tsp. star anise, *optional*
2 Tbsp. lemon juice
2 cinnamon sticks

1. Peel, core, and chop apples. Combine with apple cider in large slow cooker.
2. Cover. Cook on Low 10-12 hours.
3. Stir in sugar, star anise if you wish, lemon juice, and cinnamon sticks.
4. Cover. Cook on High 2 hours. Stir. Remove lid and cook on High 2-4 hours more, until thickened.
5. Pour into sterilized jars and seal.

If there is too much liquid in your cooker, stick a toothpick under the edge of the lid to tilt it slightly and to allow the steam to escape. Carol Sherwood, Batavia, NY

Dolores' Apple Butter

Dolores Metzler, Mechanicsburg, PA

Makes 3 quarts apple butter

Prep. Time: 5 minutes
Cooking Time: 8-10 hours
Ideal slow-cooker size: 5½- to 6-qt.

3 quarts unsweetened
  applesauce
3 cups sugar (*or sweeten to*
  taste)
2 tsp. cinnamon
1 tsp., *or less*, ground cloves

1. Combine all ingredients
in large slow cooker.
2. Cover. Cook on High 8-10
hours. Remove lid during last
4 hours. Stir occasionally.

Lilli's Apple Butter

Lilli Peters, Dodge City, KS

Makes about 2 pints apple butter

Prep. Time: 5 minutes
Cooking Time: 14-15 hours
Ideal slow-cooker size: 4-qt.

7 cups unsweetened
  applesauce
2 cups apple cider
1½ cups honey
1 tsp. cinnamon

½ tsp. ground cloves
½ tsp. allspice

1. Combine all ingredients
in slow cooker. Mix well with
whisk.
2. Cook on Low 14-15 hours.

Peach or Apricot Butter

Charlotte Shaffer, East Earl, PA

Makes 6 8-oz. jars butter

Prep. Time: 10 minutes
Cooking Time: 8-10 hours
Ideal slow-cooker size: 4-qt.

4 29-oz. cans peaches, *or*
  apricots
2¾-3 cups sugar
2 tsp. cinnamon
1 tsp. ground cloves

1. Drain fruit. Remove pits.
Purée in blender. Pour into
slow cooker.
2. Stir in remaining ingredients.
3. Cover. Cook on High 8-10
hours. Remove cover during
last half of cooking. Stir
occasionally.

Note:
  Spread on bread, or use
as a topping for ice cream or
toasted pound cake.

Pear Butter

Dorothy Miller, Gulfport, MI

Makes 6 pints pear butter

Prep. Time: 5 minutes
Cooking Time: 8-10 hours
Ideal slow-cooker size: 4-qt.

8 cups pear sauce
3 cups brown sugar
1 Tbsp. lemon juice
1 Tbsp. cinnamon

1. Combine all ingredients
in slow cooker.
2. Cover. Cook on High
10-12 hours.

Note:
  To make pear sauce, peel,
core, and slice 12 large pears.
Place in slow cooker with ¾
cup water. Cover and cook on
Low 8-10 hours, or until very
soft. Stir to blend.

Breakfast Foods

Welsh Rarebit

Sharon Timpe, Mequon, WI

Makes 6-8 servings

Prep. Time: 5 minutes
Cooking Time: 1½-2½ hours
Ideal slow-cooker size: 4-qt.

12-oz. can beer
1 Tbsp. dry mustard
1 tsp. Worcestershire sauce
½ tsp. salt
⅛ tsp. black, *or* white, pepper
1 lb. American cheese, cubed
1 lb. sharp cheddar cheese, cubed

1. In slow cooker, combine beer, mustard, Worcestershire sauce, salt, and pepper.
2. Cover and cook on High 1-2 hours, until mixture boils.

3. Add cheese, a little at a time, stirring constantly until all the cheese melts.
4. Heat on High 20-30 minutes with cover off, stirring frequently.

*Serving suggestion: Serve hot over toasted **English muffins** or over toasted **bread** cut into triangles. Garnish with strips of crisp **bacon** and **tomato** slices.*

Note:

   This is a good dish for brunch with fresh fruit, juice, and coffee. Also makes a great lunch or late-night light supper. Serve with a tossed green salad, especially fresh spinach and orange slices with a vinaigrette dressing.

When taking your hot slow cooker full of food in your car remove the lid and cover the crock with plastic wrap. Replace the lid to seal.   Sue Hamilton, Minooka, IL

Cheese Souffle Casserole

Iva Schmidt, Fergus Falls, MN

Makes 6 servings

Prep. Time: 15 minutes
Cooking Time: 3-4 hours
Ideal slow-cooker size: 3- to 4-qt.

8 slices bread (crusts removed), cubed, *or* torn into squares
2 cups (8 oz.) grated cheddar, Swiss, *or* American, cheese
1 cup cooked, chopped ham
4 eggs
1 cup light cream, *or* milk
1 cup evaporated milk
¼ tsp. salt
1 Tbsp. parsley
paprika

1. Lightly grease slow cooker. Alternate layers of bread and cheese and ham.
2. Beat together eggs, milk, salt, and parsley. Pour over bread in slow cooker.
3. Sprinkle with paprika.
4. Cover and cook on Low 3-4 hours. (The longer cooking time yields a firmer, dryer dish.)

Breakfast Casserole

Shirley Hinh, Wayland, IA

Makes 8-10 servings

Prep. Time: 15 minutes
Cooking Time: 3 hours
Ideal slow-cooker size: 4-qt.

6 eggs, beaten
1 lb. little smokies (cocktail wieners), *or* 1½ lbs. bulk sausage, browned and drained
1½ cups milk
1 cup shredded cheddar cheese
8 slices bread, torn into pieces
1 tsp. salt
½ tsp. dry mustard
1 cup shredded mozzarella cheese

1. Mix together all ingredients except mozzarella cheese. Pour into greased slow cooker.
2. Sprinkle mozzarella cheese over top.
3. Cover and cook 2 hours on High, and then 1 hour on Low.

Egg and Cheese Bake

Evie Hershey, Atglen, PA

Makes 6 servings

Prep. Time: 15 minutes
Cooking Time: 4-6 hours
Ideal slow-cooker size: 4-qt.

3 cups toasted bread cubes
1½ cups shredded cheese fried, crumbled bacon, *or* ham chunks, *optional*
6 eggs, beaten
3 cups milk
¾ tsp. salt
¼ tsp. pepper

1. Combine bread cubes, cheese, and meat in greased slow cooker.
2. Mix together eggs, milk, salt, and pepper. Pour over bread.
3. Cook on Low 4-6 hours.

Slow-Cooker Eggs and Ham

Dot Hess, Willow Street, PA

Makes 8 servings

Prep Time: 15 minutes
Cooking Time: 8-9 hours
Ideal slow-cooker size: 6 qt.

32-oz. bag frozen hash browns
1½-2 cups cheddar cheese, shredded
1 lb. cooked ham, cubed
1 medium onion, chopped
12 eggs
1 cup milk
1 tsp. salt
1 tsp. pepper

1. Divide potatoes, cheese, ham, and onion into thirds.
2. Spray cooking spray over interior of slow cooker.
3. Make three 4-part layers (potatoes on bottom, onion on top) in slow cooker.
4. In a mixing bowl, beat eggs, milk, salt, and pepper together. Pour over layers in slow cooker.
5. Cover and cook on Low 8-9 hours.

Variations:
1. For extra flavor, use Monterey Jack, jalapeno, or extra-sharp cheddar cheese, instead of a mild cheddar.
2. To add kick, substitute garlic powder for salt.

Veronica Sabo
Shelton, CT

Egg and Broccoli Casserole

Joette Droz, Kalona, IA

Makes 6 servings

Prep. Time: 15 minutes
Cooking Time: 2½-3 hours
Ideal slow-cooker size: 4-qt.

24-oz. carton small-curd cottage cheese
10-oz. pkg. frozen chopped broccoli, thawed and drained
2 cups (8 oz.) shredded cheddar cheese
6 eggs, beaten
⅓ cup flour
¼ cup melted butter, *or* margarine
3 Tbsp. finely chopped onion
½ tsp. salt

1. Combine first 8 ingredients. Pour into greased slow cooker.
2. Cover and cook on High 1 hour. Stir. Reduce heat to Low. Cover and cook 2½-3 hours, or until temperature reaches 160° and eggs are set.

*Serving suggestion: Sprinkle with shredded **cheese**, if desired, and serve.*

Easy Spinach Quiche

Sue Hamilton, Minooka, IL

Makes 6 servings

Prep Time: 15 minutes
Cooking Time: 3 hours
Ideal slow-cooker size: 4- to 5-qt, oval-shaped

2 pkgs. flat refrigerated pie dough
5 eggs
1 cup spinach dip
4 oz. prosciutto, diced
4 oz. pepper jack cheese, diced

1. Press pie crusts into cold slow cooker. Overlap seams by ¼ inch, pressing to seal. Tear off pieces to fit up the sides, pressing pieces together at seams.
2. Cover. Cook on High 1½ hours.
3. Beat eggs in a mixing bowl. Stir in spinach dip, prosciutto, and cheese. Pour into hot crust.
4. Cover. Cook on High 1½ hours, or until filling is set.
5. Let stand 5 minutes before serving.

Don't peek. It takes 15-20 minutes for the cooker to regain lost steam and return to the right temperature.

Janet V. Yocum, Elizabethtown, PA

Baked Oatmeal

Ellen Ranck, Gap, PA

Makes 4-6 servings

Prep. Time: 10 minutes
Cooking Time: 2½-3 hours
Ideal slow-cooker size: 3-qt.

⅓ cup oil
½ cup sugar
1 large egg, beaten
2 cups dry quick oats
1½ tsp. baking powder
½ tsp. salt
¾ cup milk

1. Pour the oil into the slow cooker to grease bottom and sides.
2. Add remaining ingredients. Mix well.
3. Bake on Low 2½-3 hours.

Apple Oatmeal

Frances B. Musser, Newmanstown, PA

Makes 4-5 servings

Prep. Time: 10 minutes
Cooking Time: 5-6 hours
Ideal slow-cooker size: 2-qt.

2 cups milk
2 Tbsp. honey
1 Tbsp. butter (no substitute!)
¼ tsp. salt
½ tsp. cinnamon
1 cup dry old-fashioned oats
1 cup chopped apples
½ cup chopped walnuts
2 Tbsp. brown sugar

1. Mix together all ingredients in greased slow cooker.
2. Cover. Cook on Low 5-6 hours.

Serving suggestion: Serve with milk or ice cream.

Variation:
Add ½ cup light *or* dark raisins to mixture.

Jeanette Oberholtzer
Manheim, PA

Cook your favorite "Plum Pudding" recipe in a can set inside a slow cooker on a metal rack or trivet. Pour about 2 cups warm water around it. The water helps steam the pudding. Cover the can tightly with foil to help keep the cake dry. Cover the cooker with its lid. Cook on High.
Eleanor J. Ferreira, North Chelmsford, MA

Breads

Healthy Whole Wheat Bread

Esther Becker, Gordonville, PA

Makes 8 servings

Prep. Time: 20 minutes
Cooking Time: 2½-3 hours
Ideal slow-cooker size: 5- to 6-qt.

2 cups warm reconstituted powdered milk
2 Tbsp. vegetable oil
¼ cup honey, *or* brown sugar
¾ tsp. salt
1 pkg. yeast
2½ cups whole wheat flour
1¼ cups white flour

1. Mix together milk, oil, honey or brown sugar, salt, yeast, and half the flour in electric mixer bowl. Beat with mixer for 2 minutes. Add remaining flour. Mix well.

2. Place dough in well-greased bread or cake pan that will fit into your cooker. Cover with greased tin foil. Let stand for 5 minutes. Place in slow cooker.

3. Cover cooker and bake on High 2½-3 hours. Remove pan and uncover. Let stand for 5 minutes. Serve warm.

Corn Bread From Scratch

Dorothy M. Van Deest, Memphis, TN

Makes 6 servings

Prep. Time: 15 minutes
Cooking Time: 2-3 hours
Ideal slow-cooker size: 6-qt.

1¼ cups flour
¾ cup yellow cornmeal
¼ cup sugar
4½ tsp. baking powder
1 tsp. salt
1 egg, slightly beaten
1 cup milk
⅓ cup melted butter, *or* oil

1. In mixing bowl sift together flour, cornmeal, sugar, baking powder, and salt. Make a well in the center.

2. Pour egg, milk, and butter into well. Mix into the dry mixture until just moistened.

3. Pour mixture into a greased 2-quart mold. Cover with a plate. Place on a trivet or rack in the bottom of slow cooker.

4. Cover. Cook on High 2-3 hours.

Broccoli Corn Bread

Winifred Ewy, Newton, KS

Makes 8 servings

Prep. Time: 15 minutes
Cooking Time: 6 hours
Ideal slow-cooker size: 3- to 4-qt.

1 stick margarine, melted
10-oz. pkg. chopped
   broccoli, cooked and
   drained
1 onion, chopped
1 box corn bread mix
4 eggs, well beaten
8 oz. cottage cheese
1¼ tsp. salt

1. Combine all ingredients.
Mix well.

2. Pour into greased slow
cooker. Cook on Low 6 hours,
or until toothpick inserted in
center comes out clean.

*Serving suggestion: Serve
like spoon bread, or invert the
pot, remove bread, and cut into
wedges.*

Old-Fashioned Gingerbread

Mary Ann Westerberg, Rosamond, CA

Makes 6-8 servings

Prep. Time: 15 minutes
Cooking Time: 2½-3 hours
Ideal slow-cooker size: 4-qt.

½ cup butter, softened
½ cup sugar
1 egg
1 cup light molasses
2½ cups flour
1½ tsp. baking soda
1 tsp. ground cinnamon
2 tsp. ground ginger
½ tsp. ground cloves
½ tsp. salt
1 cup hot water

1. Cream together butter
and sugar. Add egg and
molasses. Mix well.

2. Stir in flour, baking soda,
cinnamon, ginger, cloves, and
salt. Mix well.

3. Add hot water. Beat well.

4. Pour batter into greased
and floured 2-pound coffee
can.

5. Place can in cooker.
Cover top of can with 8 paper
towels. Cover cooker and bake
on High 2½-3 hours.

*Serving suggestion: Serve
with **applesauce**. Top with*

Lemon Bread

Ruth Ann Gingrich, New Holland, PA

Makes 6 servings

Prep. Time: 15 minutes
Cooking Time: 2-2¼ hours
Ideal slow-cooker size: 4-qt.

½ cup shortening
¾ cup sugar
2 eggs, beaten
1⅔ cups flour
1⅔ tsp. baking powder
½ tsp. salt
½ cup milk
½ cup chopped nuts
grated peel from 1 lemon

Glaze:
¼ cup powdered sugar
juice of 1 lemon

1. Cream together shortening
and sugar. Add eggs. Mix well.

2. Sift together flour, baking
powder, and salt. Add flour
mixture and milk alternately
to shortening mixture.

3. Stir in nuts and lemon
peel.

4. Spoon batter into well-
greased 2-pound coffee can
and cover with well-greased
tin foil. Place in cooker set on
High for 2-2¼ hours, or until
done. Remove bread from
coffee can.

5. Mix together powdered
sugar and lemon juice. Pour
over loaf.

*Serving suggestion: Serve
plain or with **cream cheese**.*

A slow cooker provides enough warmth to raise dough.
Donna Barnitz, Jenks, OK

All-American Snack,
page 84

Slow-Cooked Salsa,
page 82

Healthy Whole Wheat Bread,
page 91

Soups, Stews, and Chilis

Nancy's Vegetable Beef Soup

Nancy Graves, Manhattan, KS

Makes 6-8 servings

Prep. Time: 10 minutes
Cooking Time: 8 hours
Ideal slow-cooker size: 5- to 6-qt.

2-lb. roast, cut into bite-sized
    pieces, *or* 2 lbs. stewing
    meat
15-oz. can corn
15-oz. can green beans
1-lb. bag frozen peas
40-oz. can stewed tomatoes
5 beef bouillon cubes
Tabasco to taste
2 tsp. salt

1. Combine all ingredients
in slow cooker. Do not drain
vegetables.

2. Add water to fill slow
cooker to within 3 inches of top.

3. Cover. Cook on Low 8
hours, or until meat is tender
and vegetables are soft.

Variation:

Add 1 large onion, sliced, 2
cups sliced carrots, and ¾ cup
pearl barley to mixture before
cooking.

Frances' Hearty Vegetable Soup

Frances Schrag, Newton, KS

Makes 10 servings

Prep. Time: 15 minutes
Cooking Time: 8 hours
Ideal slow-cooker size: 3- to 4-qt.

1-lb. round steak, cut into
    ½-inch pieces

14½-oz. can diced tomatoes
3 cups water
2 potatoes, peeled and cubed
2 onions, sliced
3 celery ribs, sliced
2 carrots, sliced
3 beef bouillon cubes
½ tsp. dried basil
½ tsp. dried oregano
1 tsp. salt
¼ tsp. pepper
1½ cups frozen mixed
    vegetables, *or* your choice
    of frozen vegetables

1. Combine first 3 ingredients in slow cooker.

2. Cover. Cook on High 6
hours.

3. Add remaining ingredi-
ents. Cover and cook on High
2 hours more, or until meat
and vegetables are tender.

Variation:

Cut salt back to ½ tsp.
Increase dried basil to 1 tsp.
and dried oregano to 1 tsp.

Tracy Clark, Mt. Crawford, VA

"Absent Cook" Stew

Kathy Hertzler, Lancaster, PA

Makes 5-6 servings

Prep. Time: 15 minutes
Cooking Time: 10-12 hours
Ideal slow-cooker size: 3- to 4-qt.

2 lbs. stewing beef, cubed
2-3 carrots, sliced
1 onion, chopped
3 large potatoes, cubed
3 ribs celery, sliced
10¾-oz. can tomato soup
1 soup can water
1 tsp. salt
dash of pepper
2 Tbsp. vinegar

1. Combine all ingredients in slow cooker.
2. Cover. Cook on Low 10-12 hours.

Anona's Beef Vegetable Soup

Anona M. Teel, Bangor, PA

Makes 6 servings

Prep. Time: 15 minutes
Cooking Time: 8-10 hours
Ideal slow-cooker size: 6½-qt.

1-1½-lb. soup bone
1 lb. stewing beef cubes
1½ qts. cold water
1 Tbsp. salt
¾ cup diced celery
¾ cup diced carrots
¾ cup diced potatoes
¾ cup diced onion
1 cup frozen mixed vegetables of your choice
1-lb. can tomatoes
⅛ tsp. pepper
1 Tbsp. chopped dried parsley

1. Put all ingredients in slow cooker.
2. Cover. Cook on Low 8-10 hours. Remove bone before serving.

Ruby's Vegetable Beef Soup

Ruby Stoltzfus, Mount Joy, PA

Makes 8-10 servings

Prep. Time: 15 minutes
Cooking Time: 3-8 hours
Ideal slow-cooker size: 4½- to 5-qt.

1 lb. beef cubes
1 cup beef broth
1½ cups chopped cabbage
1½ cups stewed tomatoes, undrained
1½ cups frozen, *or* canned, corn
1½ cups frozen peas
1½ cups frozen green beans
1½ cups sliced carrots
¾ tsp. salt
¼-½ tsp. pepper

1. Combine all ingredients in slow cooker.
2. Cover. Cook on Low 6-8 hours, or High 3-4 hours.

Healthy Beef Stew

Trudy Kutter, Corfu, NY

Makes 6-8 servings

Prep Time: 20-30 minutes
Cooking Time: 8-9 hours
Ideal slow-cooker size: 5- to 6-qt.

1½ lbs. potatoes, peeled or not, and cut into small cubes
1 medium onion, chopped
8-oz. bag baby carrots
2 cups fresh mushrooms, sliced
14½-oz. can diced tomatoes
10½-oz. can beef broth
⅓ cup flour
1 Tbsp. Worcestershire sauce
1-2 tsp. sugar, according to your taste preference
1 tsp. marjoram leaves
¼ tsp. pepper
1 lb. stewing beef

1. Mix all ingredients in slow cooker except beef.
2. Stir in beef.
3. Cover. Cook on Low 8-9 hours, or until vegetables and beef are tender.
4. Stir well before serving.

Variation:

Add 1-2 cloves minced garlic and 1-lb. pkg. frozen green beans to Step 1, if you wish. The addition of the green beans may mean you need to use a 6- or 7-quart slow cooker.

Rebecca Meyerkorth, Wamego, KS

Kim's Vegetable Beef Soup

Kim McEuen, Lincoln University, PA

Makes 8-10 servings

Prep. Time: 15 minutes
Cooking Time: 4-14 hours
Ideal slow-cooker size: 4- to 5-qt.

1-2 lbs. beef shanks, *or* short ribs
1-lb. can tomatoes
2 carrots, sliced
3 ribs celery, sliced
2 medium onions, chopped
2 medium potatoes, chopped
3 cups water
1 tsp. salt
4-6 whole peppercorns
5 beef bouillon cubes
10-oz. pkg. frozen mixed vegetables, *or* its equivalent of your favorite frozen, fresh, *or* canned vegetables

1. Combine all ingredients in slow cooker. Mix well.
2. Cover. Cook on Low 12-14 hours, or High 4-6 hours.

Note:

I have a scrap vegetable container which I keep in the freezer. When I have too much of a fresh vegetable I throw it in this container and freeze it. When the container gets full, I make soup.

Variation:

To increase the proportion of vegetables, add another 10-oz. pkg. of vegetables.

Lilli's Vegetable Beef Soup

Lilli Peters, Dodge City, KS

Makes 10-12 servings

Prep. Time: 20-25 minutes
Cooking Time: 8-10 hours
Ideal slow-cooker size: 4- to 5-qt.

3 lbs. stewing meat, cut in 1-inch pieces
2 Tbsp. oil
4 potatoes, cubed
4 carrots, sliced
3 ribs celery, sliced
14-oz. can diced tomatoes
14-oz. can Italian tomatoes, crushed
2 medium onions, chopped
2 wedges cabbage, sliced thinly
2 beef bouillon cubes
2 Tbsp. fresh parsley
1 tsp. seasoned salt
1 tsp. garlic salt
½ tsp. pepper
water

1. Brown meat in oil in skillet. Drain.
2. Combine all ingredients except water in large slow cooker. Cover with water.
3. Cover. Cook on Low 8-10 hours.

Jeanne's Vegetable Beef Borscht

Jeanne Heyerly, Chenoa, IL

Makes 8 servings

Prep. Time: 20 minutes
Cooking Time: 8-10 hours
Ideal slow-cooker size: 5-qt.

1-lb. beef roast, cooked and cubed
half a head of cabbage, sliced thin
3 medium potatoes, diced
4 carrots, sliced
1 large onion, diced
1 cup tomatoes, diced
1 cup corn
1 cup green beans
2 cups beef broth
2 cups tomato juice
¼ tsp. garlic powder
¼ tsp. dill seed
2 tsp. salt
½ tsp. pepper
water

1. Mix together all ingredients except water. Add water to fill slow cooker three-quarters full.
2. Cover. Cook on Low 8-10 hours.

*Serving suggestion: Top individual servings with **sour cream**.*

Variation:

Add 1 cup diced, cooked red beets during the last half hour of cooking.

Easy Vegetable Soup

Janet Batdorf, Harrisburg, PA

Makes 10 servings

Prep Time: 15-25 minutes
Cooking Time: 14½ hours
Ideal slow-cooker size: 6-qt.

3-lb. beef roast
water
2 lbs. frozen vegetables of
    your choice
1½ cups chopped cabbage
1 small onion, chopped
24-oz. jar, *or* 3 cups,
    spaghetti sauce

1. Place beef in slow-cooker. Cover with water.
2. Cover. Cook on Low overnight, or for approximately 8 hours, until tender.
3. Remove meat and allow broth to cool.
4. Skim fat from cooled broth.
5. Return broth to slow cooker. Add frozen vegetables, cabbage, onion, and spaghetti sauce to broth.
6. Cover. Cook on High approximately 6 hours, or until vegetables are done to your liking.
7. Cut cooked roast into small pieces. Return to broth and vegetable mix.
8. Cook until mixture is hot, about 30 more minutes.

Winter's Night Beef Soup

Kimberly Jensen, Bailey, CO

Makes 8-12 servings

Prep. Time: 25 minutes
Cooking Time: 6½ hours
Ideal slow-cooker size: 5-qt.

1-lb. boneless chuck, cut in
    ½-inch cubes
1-2 Tbsp. oil
28-oz. can tomatoes
2 carrots, sliced
2 ribs celery, sliced
1 small onion, coarsely
    chopped
4 cups water
½ cup red wine
4 beef bouillon cubes
2 tsp. garlic powder
1 tsp. pepper
1 tsp. dry oregano
½ tsp. dry thyme
1 bay leaf
¼-½ cup couscous

1. Brown beef cubes in oil in skillet.
2. Place vegetables in bottom of slow cooker. Add beef.
3. Combine all other ingredients in separate bowl except couscous. Pour over ingredients in slow cooker.
4. Cover. Cook on Low 6 hours. Stir in couscous. Cover and cook 30 minutes.

Variation:
    Add zucchini or mushrooms to the rest of the vegetables before cooking.

Sharon's Vegetable Soup

Sharon Wantland, Menomonee Falls, WI

Makes 6-8 servings

Prep. Time: 25 minutes
Cooking Time: 8 hours
Ideal slow-cooker size: 5½- to 6-qt.

46-oz. can tomato juice
5 beef bouillon cubes
4 celery ribs, sliced
4 large carrots, sliced
1 onion, chopped
¼ head of cabbage,
    chopped
1-lb. can green beans
2 cups water
1 lb. beef stewing meat,
    browned
4-oz. can sliced mushrooms

1. Combine all ingredients in slow cooker.
2. Cover. Cook on Low 8 hours, or until meat and vegetables are tender.

Fill the cooker no more than two-thirds full and no less than half-full.

Rachel Kauffman, Alto, MI

Old-Fashioned Vegetable Beef Soup

Pam Hochstedler, Kalona, IA

Makes 8-10 servings

Prep. Time: 25 minutes
Cooking Time: 6-9 hours
Ideal slow-cooker size: 4-qt.

1-2 lbs. beef short ribs
2 qts. water
1 tsp. salt
1 tsp. celery salt
1 small onion, chopped
1 cup diced carrots
½ cup diced celery
2 cups diced potatoes
1-lb. can whole kernel corn, undrained
1-lb. can diced tomatoes and juice

1. Combine meat, water, salt, celery salt, onion, carrots, and celery in slow cooker.
2. Cover. Cook on Low 4-6 hours.
3. Debone meat, cut into bite-sized pieces, and return to pot.
4. Add potatoes, corn, and tomatoes.
5. Cover and cook on High 2-3 hours.

Texican Chili

Becky Oswald, Broadway, VA

Makes 15 servings

Prep. Time: 20 minutes
Cooking Time: 9-10 hours
Ideal slow-cooker size: 5- to 6-qt.

8 bacon strips, diced
2½ lbs. beef stewing meat, cubed
28-oz. can stewed tomatoes
14½-oz. can stewed tomatoes
2 8-oz. cans tomato sauce
16-oz. can kidney beans, rinsed and drained
2 cups sliced carrots
1 medium onion, chopped
1 cup chopped celery
½ cup chopped green pepper
¼ cup minced fresh parsley
1 Tbsp. chili powder
1 tsp. salt
½ tsp. ground cumin
¼ tsp. pepper

1. Cook bacon in skillet until crisp. Drain on paper towel.
2. Brown beef in bacon drippings in skillet.
3. Combine all ingredients in slow cooker.
4. Cover. Cook on Low 9-10 hours, or until meat is tender. Stir occasionally.

Chipotle Chili

Karen Ceneviva, Seymour, CT

Makes 8 servings

Prep Time: 10-15 minutes
Cooking Time: 4-9 hours
Ideal slow-cooker size: 3½-qt.

16-oz. jar chipotle chunky salsa
1 cup water
2 tsp. chili powder
1 large onion, chopped
2 lbs. stewing beef, cut into ½-inch pieces
19-oz. can red kidney beans, rinsed and drained

1. Stir all ingredients together in slow cooker.
2. Cover. Cook on High 4-5 hours or on Low 8-9 hours, until beef is fork-tender.

Forgotten Minestrone

Phyllis Attig, Reynolds, IL

Makes 8 servings

Prep. Time: 15 minutes
Cooking Time: 7½–9½ hours
Ideal slow-cooker size: 7-qt.

1 lb. beef stewing meat
6 cups water
28-oz. can tomatoes, diced, undrained
1 beef bouillon cube
1 medium onion, chopped
2 Tbsp. minced dried parsley
1½ tsp. salt
1½ tsp. dried thyme
½ tsp. pepper
1 medium zucchini, thinly sliced
2 cups finely chopped cabbage
16-oz. can garbanzo beans, drained
1 cup uncooked small elbow, *or* shell, macaroni

1. Combine beef, water, tomatoes, bouillon, onion, parsley, salt, thyme, and pepper.
2. Cover. Cook on Low 7-9 hours, or until meat is tender.
3. Stir in zucchini, cabbage, beans, and macaroni. Cover and cook on High 30-45 minutes, or until vegetables are tender.

Serving suggestion: Sprinkle individual servings with grated **Parmesan cheese.**

Slow-Cooker Minestrone

Dorothy Shank, Sterling, IL

Makes 8 servings

Prep. Time: 10 minutes
Cooking Time: 4-12 hours
Ideal slow-cooker size: 4- to 5-qt.

3 cups water
1½ lbs. stewing meat, cut into bite-sized pieces
1 medium onion, diced
4 carrots, diced
14½-oz. can tomatoes
2 tsp. salt
10-oz. pkg. frozen mixed vegetables, *or* your choice of frozen vegetables
1 Tbsp. dried basil
½ cup dry vermicelli
1 tsp. dried oregano

1. Combine all ingredients in slow cooker. Stir well.
2. Cover. Cook on Low 10-12 hours, or on High 4-5 hours.

Serving suggestion: Top individual servings with grated **Parmesan cheese.**

Hearty Alphabet Soup

Maryann Markano, Wilmington, DE

Makes 5-6 servings

Prep. Time: 10 minutes
Cooking Time: 6½-8½ hours
Ideal slow-cooker size: 4-qt.

½ lb. beef stewing meat, *or* round steak, cubed
14½-oz. can stewed tomatoes
8-oz. can tomato sauce
1 cup water
1 envelope dry onion soup mix
10-oz. pkg. frozen vegetables, partially thawed
½ cup uncooked alphabet noodles

1. Combine meat, tomatoes, tomato sauce, water, and soup mix in slow cooker.
2. Cover. Cook on Low 6-8 hours. Turn to High.
3. Stir in vegetables and noodles. Add more water if mixture is too dry and thick.
4. Cover. Cook on High 30 minutes, or until vegetables are tender.

Liquids don't boil down in a slow cooker. At the end of the cooking time, remove the cover, set dial on High and allow the liquid to evaporate, if the dish is soup-ier than you want.

John D. Allen, Rye, CO

Tasty Meatball Stew

Barbara Hershey, Lititz, PA

Makes 8 servings

Prep Time: 1 hour (includes preparing and baking meatballs)
Cooking Time: 4-5 hours
Ideal slow-cooker size: 4- to 6-qt.

Meatballs:
2 lbs. lean ground beef
2 eggs, beaten
2 Tbsp. dried onion
⅔ cup dried bread crumbs
½ cup milk
1 tsp. salt
¼ tsp. pepper
1 tsp. Dijon mustard
2 tsp. Worcestershire sauce

Stew:
6 medium potatoes,
    unpeeled if you wish,
    and diced fine
1 large onion, sliced
8 medium carrots, sliced
4 cups vegetable juice
1 tsp. basil
1 tsp. dried oregano
½ tsp. salt
½ tsp. pepper

1. In a bowl, thoroughly mix meatball ingredients together. Form into 1-inch balls.

2. Place meatballs on a lightly greased jelly-roll pan. Bake at 400° for 20 minutes.

3. Meanwhile, to make stew, prepare potatoes, onion, and carrots. Place in slow cooker.

4. When finished baking, remove meatballs from pan. Blot dry with paper towels to remove excess fat.

5. Place meatballs on top of vegetables in slow cooker.

6. In a large bowl, combine vegetable juice and seasonings. Pour over meatballs and vegetables in slow cooker.

7. Cover cooker. Cook on High 4-5 hours, or until vegetables are tender.

Tips:

1. You can speed up the preparation of this dish by using frozen meatballs, either your own, or store-bought ones.

2. If you will be gone more hours than the time required to cook the slow-cooker dish that you want to make, you can cook that recipe in your slow-cooker overnight on Low. I've done this many times. In the morning I put the slow-cooker insert, now full of the cooked food, into the refrigerator. When I get home, I reheat the food in my microwave.

Ground-Beef Stew

Kim Stoltzfus, Parksburg, PA

Makes 12 servings

Prep Time: 30-35 minutes
Cooking Time: 4-6 hours
Ideal slow-cooker size: 3½-qt.

1 lb. ground beef
6 medium potatoes, peeled
    or not, and cubed
16-oz. pkg. baby carrots
3 cups water
2 Tbsp. dry onion soup mix
1 garlic clove, minced
1 tsp. Italian seasoning
1-1½ tsp. salt
¼ tsp. pepper
¼ tsp. garlic powder
6-oz. can Italian tomato
    paste
10¾-oz. can tomato soup

1. In a skillet, cook beef over medium heat until no longer pink. Drain off drippings.

2. Combine potatoes, carrots, water, dry soup mix, garlic and seasonings in slow cooker.

3. Add beef. Mix well.

4. Cover. Cook 4-5 hours, or until vegetables are cooked to your liking.

5. Stir in tomato paste and soup.

6. Cover. Cook an additional hour, or until heated through.

Tip:

You can add the tomato paste and tomato soup with the rest of the ingredients, if that is more convenient.

Quick and Easy Italian Vegetable Beef Soup

Lisa Warren, Parkesburg, PA

Makes 8-10 servings

Prep. Time: 15 minutes
Cooking Time: 6-8 hours
Ideal slow-cooker size: 6-qt.

1 lb. ground beef, *or* turkey, browned and drained
3 carrots, sliced
4 potatoes, peeled and cubed
1 small onion, diced
1 tsp. garlic powder
1 tsp. Italian seasoning
¾ tsp. salt
¼ tsp. pepper
15-oz. can diced Italian tomatoes, *or* 2 fresh tomatoes, chopped
6-oz. can Italian-flavored tomato paste
4½ cups water
1 quart beef broth

1. Combine all ingredients in slow cooker.
2. Cover. Cook on High 6-8 hours, or until potatoes and carrots are tender.

Stick-to-Your-Ribs Veggie Soup

Judy Govotsos, Frederick, MD

Makes 12 servings

Prep Time: 15-30 minutes
Cooking Time: 4-5 hours
Ideal slow-cooker size: 5- to 6-qt.

1 lb. lean ground beef
2 cups onion, chopped
2 cups celery, chopped
2 1-lb. pkgs. frozen mixed vegetables of your choice
2 14 ½-oz. cans Italian-style stewed tomatoes, undrained
1 tsp. black pepper
2 beef bouillon cubes
½ lb. shredded coleslaw
2 medium potatoes, unpeeled and chopped very fine
6 cups water, *or* more if needed

1. Brown ground beef in skillet over medium-high heat. Add onion and celery to skillet and sauté until tender.
2. Place frozen vegetables, tomatoes, pepper, bouillon cubes, coleslaw, potatoes, and water in slow cooker. Mix together well.
3. Stir in browned beef mixture.
4. Cover. Cook on Low 4-5 hours, or until vegetables are done to your liking.

Note:
This soup tastes great even as leftovers.

Hearty Beef and Cabbage Soup

Carolyn Mathias, Williamsville, NY

Makes 8 servings

Prep. Time: 15 minutes
Cooking Time: 3½-4 hours
Ideal slow-cooker size: 5-qt.

1 lb. ground beef
1 medium onion, chopped
40-oz. can tomatoes
2 cups water
15-oz. can kidney beans
1 tsp. salt
½ tsp. pepper
1 Tbsp. chili powder
½ cup chopped celery
2 cups thinly sliced cabbage

1. Sauté beef in skillet. Drain.
2. Combine all ingredients except cabbage in slow cooker.
3. Cover. Cook on Low 3 hours. Add cabbage. Cook on High 30-60 minutes longer.

Hamburger Soup with Barley

Becky Oswald, Broadway, VA

Makes 10 servings

Prep. Time: 15 minutes
Cooking Time: 3-8 hours
Ideal slow-cooker size: 5½-qt.

1 lb. ground beef
1 medium onion, chopped
3 14½-oz. cans beef
   consomme
28-oz. can diced, *or*
   crushed, tomatoes
3 carrots, sliced
3 celery ribs, sliced
8 Tbsp. barley
1 bay leaf
1 tsp. dried thyme
1 Tbsp. dried parsley
1 tsp. salt
½ tsp. pepper

1. Brown beef and onion in skillet. Drain.
2. Combine all ingredients in slow cooker.
3. Cover. Cook on High 3 hours, or Low 6-8 hours.

Vegetable Soup with Potatoes

Annabelle Unternahrer, Shipshewana, IN

Makes 6-8 servings

Prep. Time: 15 minutes
Cooking Time: 4-12 hours
Ideal slow-cooker size: 6-qt.

1 lb. hamburger, browned
   and drained
2 15-oz. cans diced
   tomatoes
2 carrots, sliced *or* cubed
2 onions, sliced *or* cubed
2 potatoes, diced
1-2 garlic cloves, minced
12-oz. can V8 vegetable
   juice
1½-2 cups sliced celery
2 tsp. beef stock
   concentrate, *or* 2 beef
   bouillon cubes
2-3 cups vegetables (cauliflower, peas, corn, limas,
   or your choice of leftovers
   from your freezer)

1. Combine all ingredients in slow cooker.
2. Cover. Cook on Low 12 hours, or High 4-6 hours.

Note:
   If using leftover vegetables that are precooked, add during last hour if cooking on Low, or during last half hour if cooking on High.

Variation:
   Use 3 cups pre-cooked dried beans or lentils instead of hamburger.

Hamburger Lentil Soup

Juanita Marner, Shipshewana, IN

Makes 8 servings

Prep. Time: 20 minutes
Cooking Time: 4-10 hours
Ideal slow-cooker size: 5-qt.

1 lb. ground beef
½ cup chopped onions
4 carrots, diced
3 ribs celery, diced
1 garlic clove, minced, *or* 1
   tsp. garlic powder
1 qt. tomato juice
1 Tbsp. salt
2 cups dry lentils, washed
   with stones removed
1 qt. water
½ tsp. dried marjoram
1 Tbsp. brown sugar

1. Brown ground beef and onion in skillet. Drain.
2. Combine all ingredients in slow cooker.
3. Cover. Cook on Low 8-10 hours, or High 4-6 hours.

Vegetable Soup with Noodles

Glenda S. Weaver, New Holland, PA

Makes 6 servings

Prep. Time: 15 minutes
Cooking Time: 2-6 hours
Ideal slow-cooker size: 4-qt.

2 beef bouillon cubes
1 pint water
1 onion, chopped
1 lb. ground beef
¼ cup ketchup
1 tsp. salt
⅛ tsp. celery salt
½ cup uncooked noodles
12-16-oz. pkg. frozen mixed
    vegetables, *or* vegetables
    of your choice
1 pint tomato juice

1. Dissolve bouillon cubes in water.
2. Brown onion and beef in skillet. Drain.
3. Combine all ingredients in slow cooker.
4. Cover. Cook on Low 6 hours, or on High 2-3 hours, until vegetables are tender.

Dottie's Creamy Steak Soup

Debbie Zeida, Mashpee, MA

Makes 4-6 servings

Prep. Time: 15 minutes
Cooking Time: 8-10 hours
Ideal slow-cooker size: 4-qt.

1 lb. ground beef
half a large onion, chopped
12-oz. can V8 vegetable
    juice
2-3 medium potatoes, diced
10¾-oz. can cream of
    mushroom soup
10¾-oz. can cream of celery
    soup
16-oz. pkg. frozen mixed
    vegetables, *or* your choice
    of frozen vegetables
2 tsp. salt
½-¾ tsp. pepper

1. Sauté beef and onions in skillet. Drain.
2. Combine all ingredients in slow cooker.
3. Cover. Cook on Low 8-10 hours.

With vehicles now having power supply plugs in their trunks and elsewhere, and with 110-volt plug-in converters, you can cook as you travel to parties. Just be sure that your plug, adaptor, and cord are adequate for the electricity needed to power the cooker.

Sue Hamilton, Minooka, IL

Steak Soup

Ilene Bontrager, Arlington, KS
Deb Unternahrer, Wayland, IA

Makes 10-12 servings

Prep. Time: 20 minutes
Cooking Time: 4-12 hours
Ideal slow-cooker size: 4- to 5-qt.

2 lbs. coarsely ground
    chuck, browned and
    drained
5 cups water
1 large onion, chopped
4 ribs celery, chopped
3 carrots, sliced
2 14½-oz. cans diced
    tomatoes
10-oz. pkg. frozen mixed
    vegetables
5 Tbsp. beef-based
    granules, *or* 5 beef
    bouillon cubes
½ tsp. pepper
½ cup melted butter
½ cup flour
2 tsp. salt

1. Combine chuck, water, onion, celery, carrots, tomatoes, mixed vegetables, beef granules, and pepper in slow cooker.
2. Cover. Cook on Low 8-12 hours, or High 4-6 hours.
3. One hour before serving, turn to High. Make a paste of melted butter and flour. Stir until smooth. Pour into slow cooker and stir until well blended. Add salt.
4. Cover. Continue cooking on High until thickened.

Taco Soup with Black Beans

Alexa Slonin, Harrisonburg, VA

Makes 6-8 servings

Prep. Time: 15 minutes
Cooking Time: 4-6 hours
Ideal slow-cooker size: 5-qt.

1 lb. ground beef, browned and drained
28-oz. can crushed tomatoes
15¼-oz. can corn, undrained
15-oz. can black beans, undrained
15½-oz. can red kidney beans, undrained
1 envelope dry Hidden Valley Ranch Dressing mix
1 envelope dry taco seasoning
1 small onion, chopped

1. Combine all ingredients in slow cooker.
2. Cover. Cook on Low 4-6 hours.

*Serving suggestion: Garnish individual servings with **tortilla** or **corn chips**, shredded **cheese**, and **sour cream**.*

Three Bean Taco Soup

Colleen Heatwole, Burton, MI

Makes 10-12 servings

Prep Time: 30 minutes
Cooking Time: 4-6 hours
Ideal slow-cooker size: 4- to 5-qt.

1 lb. lean ground beef
1 large onion, chopped
15½-oz. can pinto beans, undrained
15½-oz. can black beans, undrained
15½-oz. can red kidney beans, undrained
28-oz., *or* 32-oz., can crushed tomatoes
15¼-oz. can corn, undrained
1-2 envelopes dry ranch dressing mix, according to your taste preference
1-2 envelopes dry taco seasoning mix, according to your taste preference

1. Brown ground beef in a skillet. Add onion and cook until translucent.
2. Combine sautéed ingredients with all other ingredients in slow cooker.
3. Cover. Cook on Low 4-6 hours.

*Serving suggestion: If you wish, top individual servings with **hot sauce**, raw chopped **onions**, and grated **cheddar cheese**.*

Taco Soup with Pinto Beans

Janie Steele, Moore, OK

Makes 10-12 servings

Prep. Time: 15 minutes
Cooking Time: 4 hours
Ideal slow-cooker size: 6½-qt.

1 lb. ground beef
1 large onion, chopped
3 14-oz. cans pinto beans
14-oz. can tomatoes with chilies
14½-oz. can chopped tomatoes
15-oz. can tomato sauce
1 pkg. dry Hidden Valley Ranch Dressing mix
1 pkg. dry taco seasoning
15¼-oz. can corn, drained

1. Brown beef and onions in skillet. Drain.
2. Combine all ingredients in slow cooker.
3. Cover. Cook on Low 4 hours, or until ingredients are heated through.

Sante Fe Soup with Melted Cheese

Carla Koslowsky, Hillsboro, KS

Makes 8 servings

Prep. Time: 15 minutes
Cooking Time: 3 hours
Ideal slow-cooker size: 4-qt.

1 lb. Velveeta cheese, cubed
1 lb. ground beef, browned
  and drained
15¼-oz. can corn,
  undrained
15-oz. can kidney beans,
  undrained
14½-oz. can diced tomatoes
  with green chilies
14½-oz. can stewed
  tomatoes
2 Tbsp. dry taco seasoning

1. Combine all ingredients
in slow cooker.
2. Cover. Cook on High 3
hours.

Serving suggestion: Serve with
corn chips *as a side, or dip* **soft**
tortillas *in individual servings*
in soup bowls.

Taco Soup with Whole Tomatoes

Marla Folkerts, Holland, OH

Makes 6-8 servings

Prep. Time: 15 minutes
Cooking Time: 4-6 hours
Ideal slow-cooker size: 5-qt.

1 lb. ground beef
½ cup chopped onions
28-oz. can whole tomatoes
  with juice
14-oz. can kidney beans
  with juice
17-oz. can corn with juice
8-oz. can tomato sauce
1 pkg. dry taco seasoning
1-2 cups water
salt to taste
pepper to taste

1. Brown beef and onions in
skillet. Drain.
2. Combine all ingredients
in slow cooker.
3. Cover. Cook on Low 4-6
hours.

Serving suggestion: Ladle into
bowls. Top with grated **cheddar**
cheese *and serve with* **taco** *or*
corn chips.

Taco Soup with Pork and Beans

Beth Shank, Wellman, IA

Makes 6 servings

Prep. Time: 15 minutes
Cooking Time: 4-6 hours
Ideal slow-cooker size: 5-qt.

1 lb. ground beef
half a small onion, finely
  diced
1 envelope dry taco
  seasoning
2 Tbsp. brown sugar
⅛ tsp. red cayenne pepper
15-oz. can kidney beans,
  drained
15-oz. can whole kernel
  corn, drained
15-oz. can pork and beans
46-oz. can tomato juice

1. Brown beef and onion in
skillet. Drain. Place in slow
cooker.
2. Stir in taco seasoning,
brown sugar, and pepper. Add
beans, corn, pork and beans,
and tomato juice. Mix well.
3. Cover. Cook on Low 4-6
hours.

Serving suggestion: Garnish
individual servings with **taco**
chips, *shredded* **cheese**, *and a*
dollop of **sour cream**.

Taco Soup with Pizza Sauce

Barbara Kuhns, Millersburg, OH

Makes 8-10 servings

Prep. Time: 15 minutes
Cooking Time: 3-4 hours
Ideal slow-cooker size: 6-qt.

2 lbs. ground beef, browned
1 small onion, chopped and sautéed in ground beef drippings
¾ tsp. salt
½ tsp. pepper
1½ pkgs. dry taco seasoning
1 qt. pizza sauce
1 qt. water

1. Combine ground beef, onion, salt, pepper, taco seasoning, pizza sauce, and water in 5-quart, or larger, slow cooker.
2. Cover. Cook on Low 3-4 hours.

*Serving suggestion: Top individual servings with **tortilla chips**, shredded **mozzarella cheese**, and **sour cream**.*

Variation:

Add 15-oz. can black beans and 4-oz. can chilies to mixture before cooking. (Be sure to use one very large cooker, or two medium-sized cookers.)

Easy Chili

Sheryl Shenk, Harrisonburg, VA

Makes 10-12 servings

Prep. Time: 15 minutes
Cooking Time: 3-8 hours
Ideal slow-cooker size: 6-qt.

1 lb. ground beef
1 onion, chopped
1 green pepper, chopped
1½ tsp. salt
1 Tbsp. chili powder
2 tsp. Worcestershire sauce
29-oz. can tomato sauce
3 16-oz. cans kidney beans, drained
14½-oz. can crushed, *or* stewed, tomatoes
6-oz. can tomato paste

1. Brown meat in skillet. Add onion and green pepper halfway through browning process. Drain. Pour into slow cooker.
2. Stir in remaining ingredients.
3. Cover. Cook on High 3 hours, or Low 7-8 hours.

*Serving suggestion: Serve in bowls topped with shredded **cheddar cheese**. This chili can also be served over cooked **rice**.*

Berenice's Favorite Chili

Berenice M. Wagner, Dodge City, KS

Makes 6 servings

Prep. Time: 20 minutes
Cooking Time: 5-12 hours
Ideal slow-cooker size: 5½-qt.

2 16-oz. cans red kidney beans, drained
2 14½-oz. cans diced tomatoes
2 lbs. coarsely ground beef, browned and drained
2 medium onions, coarsely chopped
1 green pepper, coarsely chopped
2 garlic cloves, minced
2-3 Tbsp. chili powder
1 tsp. pepper
2½ tsp. salt

1. Combine all ingredients in slow cooker in order listed. Stir once.
2. Cover. Cook on Low 10-12 hours, or High 5-6 hours.

Variations:

1. Top individual servings with green onion, sour cream, and cheese.

Judy Govotsus
Monrovia, MD

2. Increase proportion of tomatoes in chili by adding 8-oz. can tomato sauce before cooking.

Bernice A. Esau
North Newton, KS

Trail Chili

Jeanne Allen, Rye, CO

Makes 8-10 servings

Prep. Time: 15 minutes
Cooking Time: 4½-6½ hours
Ideal slow-cooker size: 4- to 5-qt.

---

2 lbs. ground beef
1 large onion, diced
28-oz. can diced tomatoes
2 8-oz. cans tomato purée
1, *or* 2, 16-oz. cans kidney
 beans, undrained
4-oz. can diced green chilies
1 cup water
2 garlic cloves, minced
2 Tbsp. mild chili powder
2 tsp. salt
2 tsp. ground cumin
1 tsp. pepper

1. Brown beef and onion in skillet. Drain. Place in slow cooker on High.
2. Stir in remaining ingredients. Cook on High 30 minutes.
3. Reduce heat to Low. Cook 4-6 hours.

Serving suggestion: Top individual servings with shred-ded **cheese**. *Serve with* **taco chips**.

Best Bean Chili

Carolyn Baer, Conrath, WI

Makes 6 servings

Prep Time: 20-30 minutes
Cooking Time: 5-6 hours
Ideal slow-cooker size: 4- to 5-qt.

---

1 lb. lean ground beef
1½ cups chopped onion
1 cup chopped green bell
 pepper
1 tsp. minced garlic
1-3 Tbsp. chili powder,
 according to your taste
 preference
1-2 tsp. ground cumin, also
 according to your taste
 preference
15-oz. can red kidney beans,
 rinsed and drained
15-oz. can pinto beans,
 rinsed and drained
3 14½-oz. cans diced
 Italian-, *or* Mexican-,
 seasoned tomatoes
2 Tbsp. brown sugar
1 tsp. unsweetened cocoa
 powder
soy sauce, *optional*
ground ginger, *optional*

1. Spray large skillet with cooking spray. Brown beef in skillet over medium heat.
2. Add onions, bell pepper, and garlic to skillet. Cook until just-tender.
3. Transfer contents of skillet to slow cooker.
4. Add seasonings, beans, tomatoes, sugar and cocoa powder.
5. Cover. Cook on Low 5-6 hours.

Tip:
 Offer a sprinkle of soy sauce and/or ground ginger with individual servings to enhance the flavor of the chili.

Judy's Chili Soup

Judy Buller, Bluffton, OH

Makes 6 servings

Prep. Time: 15 minutes
Cooking Time: 7-8 hours
Ideal slow-cooker size: 4-qt.

---

1 lb. ground beef
1 onion, chopped
10¾-oz. can condensed
 tomato soup
16-oz. can kidney beans,
 drained
1 qt. tomato juice
⅛ tsp. garlic powder
1 Tbsp. chili powder
½ tsp. pepper
½ tsp. ground cumin
½ tsp. salt

1. Brown hamburger and onion in skillet. Drain.
2. Combine all ingredients in slow cooker. Mix well.
3. Cover. Cook on Low 7-8 hours.

Variation:
 Use ground venison instead of ground beef.

Chili con Carne

Donna Conto, Saylorsburg, PA

Makes 8 servings

Prep. Time: 15 minutes
Cooking Time: 5-6 hours
Ideal slow-cooker size: 4-qt.

1 lb. ground beef
1 cup chopped onions
¾ cup chopped green peppers
1 garlic clove, minced
14½-oz. can tomatoes, cut up
16-oz. can kidney beans, drained
8-oz. can tomato sauce
2 tsp. chili powder
½ tsp. dried basil

1. Brown beef, onion, green pepper, and garlic in saucepan. Drain.
2. Combine all ingredients in slow cooker.
3. Cover. Cook on Low 5-6 hours.

Serving suggestion: Serve in **bread bowl**.

Variation:
Add 16-oz. can pinto beans, ¼ tsp. salt, and ¼ tsp. pepper in Step 2.

Alexa Slonin, Harrisonburg, VA

Quick and Easy Chili

Nan Decker, Albuquerque, NM

Makes 4 servings

Prep. Time: 20 minutes
Cooking Time: 4-5 hours
Ideal slow-cooker size: 3- to 4-qt.

1 lb. ground beef
1 onion, chopped
16-oz. can stewed tomatoes
11½-oz. can hot V8 juice
2 15-oz. cans pinto beans
¼ tsp. cayenne pepper
½ tsp. salt
1 Tbsp. chili powder

1. Crumble ground beef in microwave-safe casserole. Add onion. Microwave, covered, on High 15 minutes. Drain. Break meat into pieces.
2. Combine all ingredients in slow cooker.
3. Cook on Low 4-5 hours.

Serving suggestion: Garnish with **sour cream**, *chopped* **green onions**, *grated* **cheese**, *and sliced ripe* **olives**.

Cindy's Chili

Cindy Krestynick, Glen Lyon, PA

Makes 4-6 servings

Prep. Time: 10 minutes
Cooking Time: 4-6 hours
Ideal slow-cooker size: 6-qt.

1 lb. ground beef, browned and drained
3 15½-oz. cans chili beans (hot *or* mild)
28-oz. can stewed tomatoes, chopped
1 rib celery, chopped
4 cups tomato juice
½ tsp. garlic salt
½ tsp. chili powder
¼ tsp. pepper
¼ tsp. Tabasco sauce

1. Combine all ingredients in large slow cooker.
2. Cover. Cook on Low 4-6 hours.

Be careful about adding liquids to food in a slow cooker. Foods have natural juices in them, and unlike oven cooking which is dry, food juices remain in the slow cooker as the food cooks. Ann Sunday McDowell, Newtown, PA

Ed's Chili

Marie Miller, Scotia, NY

Makes 4-6 servings

Prep. Time: 15 minutes
Cooking Time: 2-2½ hours
Ideal slow-cooker size: 4-qt.

1 lb. ground beef
1 pkg. dry taco seasoning
    mix
half a 12-oz. jar salsa
16-oz. can kidney beans,
    undrained
15-oz. can black beans,
    undrained
14½-oz. can diced
    tomatoes, undrained
pinch of sugar

1. Brown ground beef in skillet. Drain.

2. Combine all ingredients in slow cooker.

3. Cover. Heat on High until mixture comes to boil. Reduce heat to Low. Simmer 1½ hours.

4. To reduce liquids, continue cooking uncovered.

*Serving suggestion: Top individual servings with choice of shredded **cheese**, chopped **onions**, a dollop of **sour cream**, diced fresh **tomatoes**, **guacamole**, and sliced black **olives**.*

Pirate Stew

Nancy Graves, Manhattan, KS

Makes 4-6 servings

Prep. Time: 15 minutes
Cooking Time: 6 hours
Ideal slow-cooker size: 4-qt.

¾ cup sliced onion
1 lb. ground beef
¼ cup uncooked, long-grain
    rice
3 cups diced raw potatoes
1 cup diced celery
2 cups canned kidney
    beans, drained
1 tsp. salt
⅛ tsp. pepper
¼ tsp. chili powder
¼ tsp. Worcestershire sauce
1 cup tomato sauce
½ cup water

1. Brown onions and ground beef in skillet. Drain.

2. Layer ingredients in slow cooker in order given.

3. Cover. Cook on Low 6 hours, or until potatoes and rice are cooked.

Variation:

Add a layer of 2 cups sliced carrots between potatoes and celery.

Katrine Rose, Woodbridge, VA

Corn Chili

Gladys Longacre, Susquehanna, PA

Makes 4-6 servings

Prep. Time: 15 minutes
Cooking Time: 5-6 hours
Ideal slow-cooker size: 4-qt.

1 lb. ground beef
½ cup chopped onions
½ cup chopped green
    peppers
½ tsp. salt
⅛ tsp. pepper
¼ tsp. dried thyme
14½-oz. can diced tomatoes
    with Italian herbs
6-oz. can tomato paste,
    diluted with 1 can water
2 cups frozen whole kernel
    corn
16-oz. can kidney beans
1 Tbsp. chili powder

1. Sauté ground beef, onions, and green peppers in deep saucepan. Drain and season with salt, pepper, and thyme.

2. Stir in tomatoes, tomato paste, and corn. Heat until corn is thawed. Add kidney beans and chili powder. Pour into slow cooker.

3. Cover. Cook on Low 5-6 hours.

*Serving suggestion: Top individual servings with dollops of **sour cream**, or sprinkle with shredded **cheese**.*

In place of ground meat in a recipe, use vegetarian burgers. Cut them up, and you won't need to brown the meat.

Sue Hamilton, Minooka, IL

White Bean Chili

Tracey Stenger, Gretna, LA

Makes 10-12 servings

Prep. Time: 20 minutes
Cooking Time: 8-10 hours
Ideal slow-cooker size: 7-qt.

1 lb. ground beef, browned and drained
1 lb. ground turkey, browned and drained
3 bell peppers, chopped
2 onions, chopped
4 garlic cloves, minced
2 14½-oz. cans chicken, *or* vegetable, broth
15½-oz. can butter beans, rinsed and drained
15-oz. can black-eyed peas, rinsed and drained
15-oz. can garbanzo beans, rinsed and drained
15-oz. can navy beans, rinsed and drained
4-oz. can chopped green chilies
2 Tbsp. chili powder
3 tsp. ground cumin
2 tsp. dried oregano
2 tsp. paprika
1½-2 tsp. salt
½ tsp. pepper

1. Combine all ingredients in slow cooker.
2. Cover. Cook on Low 8-10 hours.

Lotsa-Beans Chili

Jean Weller, State College, PA

Makes 12-15 servings

Prep. Time: 25 minutes
Cooking Time: 8-9 hours
Ideal slow-cooker size: 5-qt.

1 lb. ground beef
1 lb. bacon, diced
½ cup chopped onions
½ cup brown sugar
½ cup sugar
½ cup ketchup
2 tsp. dry mustard
1 tsp. salt
½ tsp. pepper
2 15-oz. cans green beans, drained
2 14½-oz. cans baked beans
2 15-oz. cans butter beans, drained
2 16-oz. cans kidney beans, rinsed and drained

1. Brown ground beef and bacon in skillet. Drain.
2. Combine all ingredients in slow cooker.
3. Cover. Cook on High 1 hour. Reduce heat to Low and cook 7-8 hours.

Dorothea's Slow-Cooker Chili

Dorothea K. Ladd, Ballston Lake, NY

Makes 6-8 servings

Prep. Time: 15 minutes
Cooking Time: 8-10 hours
Ideal slow-cooker size: 6½-qt.

1 lb. ground beef
1 lb. bulk pork sausage
1 large onion, chopped
1 large green pepper, chopped
2-3 ribs celery, chopped
2 15½-oz. cans kidney beans
29-oz. can tomato purée
6-oz. can tomato paste
2 cloves garlic, minced
2 Tbsp. chili powder
2 tsp. salt

1. Brown ground beef and sausage in skillet. Drain.
2. Combine all ingredients in slow cooker.
3. Cover. Cook on Low 8-10 hours.

*Serving suggestion: Top individual servings with shredded **sharp cheddar cheese**.*

Variations:
1. For extra flavor, add 1 tsp. cayenne pepper.
2. For more zest, use mild or hot Italian sausage instead of regular pork sausage.

Crab Soup

Susan Alexander, Baltimore, MD

Makes 10 servings

Prep. Time: 20 minutes
Cooking Time: 8-10 hours
Ideal slow-cooker size: 5-qt.

1 lb. carrots, sliced
½ bunch celery, sliced
1 large onion, diced
2 10-oz. bags frozen mixed
  vegetables, *or* your choice
  of frozen vegetables
12-oz. can tomato juice
1 lb. ham, cubed
1 lb. beef, cubed
6 slices bacon, chopped
1 tsp. salt
¼ tsp. pepper
1 Tbsp. Old Bay seasoning
1 lb. claw crabmeat

1. Combine all ingredients except seasonings and crabmeat in large slow cooker. Pour in water until cooker is half-full.
2. Add spices. Stir in thoroughly. Put crab on top.
3. Cover. Cook on Low 8-10 hours.
4. Stir well and serve.

Special Seafood Chowder

Dorothea K. Ladd, Ballston Lake, NY

Makes 8-10 servings

Prep. Time: 15 minutes
Cooking Time: 6 hours
Ideal slow-cooker size: 4½- to 5-qt.

½ cup chopped onions
2 Tbsp. butter
1 lb. fresh, *or* frozen, cod,
  or haddock
4 cups diced potatoes
15-oz. can creamed corn
½ tsp. salt
dash pepper
2 cups water
1 pint half-and-half

1. Sauté onions in butter in skillet until transparent but not brown.
2. Cut fish into ¾-inch cubes. Combine fish, onions, potatoes, corn, seasonings, and water in slow cooker.
3. Cover. Cook on Low 6 hours, until potatoes are tender.
4. Add half-and-half during last hour.

Variation:
To cut milk fat, use 1 cup half-and-half and 1 cup skim milk, instead of 1 pint half-and-half.

Manhattan Clam Chowder

Joyce Slaymaker, Strasburg, PA
Louise Stackhouse, Benton, PA

Makes 8 servings

Prep. Time: 15 minutes
Cooking Time: 8-10 hours
Ideal slow-cooker size: 3½-qt.

¼ lb. salt pork, *or* bacon,
  diced and fried
1 large onion, chopped
2 carrots, thinly sliced
3 ribs celery, sliced
1 Tbsp. dried parsley flakes
28-oz. can tomatoes
½ tsp. salt
2, *or* 3, 8-oz. cans clams
  with liquid
2 whole peppercorns
1 bay leaf
1½ tsp. dried crushed
  thyme
3 medium potatoes, cubed

1. Combine all ingredients in slow cooker.
2. Cover. Cook on Low 8-10 hours.

Chicken Clam Chowder

Irene Klaeger, Inverness, FL

Makes 10-12 servings

Prep. Time: 20-25 minutes
Cooking Time: 3-8 hours
Ideal slow-cooker size: 4-qt.

1 lb. bacon, diced
¼ lb. ham, cubed
2 cups chopped onions
2 cups diced celery
½ tsp. salt
¼ tsp. pepper
2 cups diced potatoes
2 cups cooked, diced chicken
4 cups chicken broth
2 bottles clam juice, *or*
  2 cans clams with juice
1-lb. can whole kernel corn
  with liquid
¾ cup flour
4 cups milk
4 cups shredded cheddar,
  or Jack, cheese
½ cup whipping cream (not
  whipped)
2 Tbsp. fresh parsley

1. Sauté bacon, ham, onions, and celery in skillet until bacon is crisp and onions and celery are limp. Add salt and pepper.
2. Combine all ingredients in slow cooker except flour, milk, cheese, cream, and parsley.
3. Cover. Cook on Low 6-8 hours, or on High 3-4 hours.

4. Whisk flour into milk. Stir into soup, along with cheese, whipping cream, and parsley. Cook one more hour on High.

Chicken Broth

Ruth Conrad Liechty, Goshen, IN

Makes about 6 cups broth

Prep. Time: 10 minutes
Cooking Time: 4-5 hours
Ideal slow-cooker size: 4-qt.

bony chicken pieces from
  2 chickens
1 onion, quartered
3 whole cloves, *optional*
3 ribs celery, cut up
1 carrot, quartered
1½ tsp. salt
¼ tsp. pepper
4 cups water

1. Place chicken in slow cooker.
2. Stud onion with cloves. Add to slow cooker with other ingredients.
3. Cover. Cook on High 4-5 hours.
4. Remove chicken and vegetables. Discard vegetables. Debone chicken. Cut up meat and add to broth. Use as stock for soups.

Chicken Rice Soup

Karen Ceneviva, Seymour, CT

Makes 8 servings

Prep Time: 15 minutes
Cooking Time: 4-8 hours
Ideal slow-cooker size: 3½-qt.

½ cup wild rice, uncooked
½ cup long-grain rice,
  uncooked
1 tsp. vegetable oil
1 lb. boneless, skinless
  chicken breasts, cut into
  ¾-inch cubes
5¼ cups chicken broth
1 cup celery (about 2 ribs),
  chopped in ½-inch thick
  pieces
1 medium onion, chopped
2 tsp. dried thyme leaves
¼ tsp. red pepper flakes

1. Mix wild and white rice with oil in slow cooker.
2. Cover. Cook on High 15 minutes.
3. Add chicken, broth, vegetables, and seasonings.
4. Cover. Cook 4-5 hours on High or 7-8 hours on Low.

Tip:
A dollop of sour cream sprinkled with finely chopped scallions on top of each individual serving bowl makes a nice finishing touch.

Chicken Noodle Soup

Beth Shank, Wellman, IA

Makes 6-8 servings

Prep. Time: 10 minutes
Cooking Time: 4-6 hours
Ideal slow-cooker size: 5-qt.

2 tsp. chicken bouillon granules, *or* 2 chicken bouillon cubes
5 cups hot water
46-oz. can chicken broth
2 cups cooked chicken
1 tsp. salt
4 cups homestyle noodles, uncooked
⅓ cup thinly sliced celery, lightly pre-cooked in microwave
⅓ cup shredded, *or* chopped, carrots

1. Dissolve bouillon in water. Pour into slow cooker.
2. Add remaining ingredients. Mix well.
3. Cover. Cook on Low 4-6 hours.

Brown Jug Soup

Dorothy Shank, Sterling, IL

Makes 10-12 servings

Prep. Time: 15-20 minutes
Cooking Time: 10-12 hours
Ideal slow-cooker size: 7-qt.

10½-oz. can chicken broth
4 chicken bouillon cubes
1 qt. water
2 cups diced celery
2 cups diced onions
4 cups diced potatoes
3 cups diced carrots
10-oz. pkg. frozen whole kernel corn
2 10¾-oz. cans cream of chicken soup
½ lb. Velveeta cheese, cubed

1. Combine all ingredients except cheese in slow cooker.
2. Cover. Cook on Low 10-12 hours, or until vegetables are tender.
3. Just before serving, add cheese. Stir until cheese is melted. Serve.

Chicken Corn Soup

Eleanor Larson, Glen Lyon, PA

Makes 4-6 servings

Prep. Time: 15 minutes
Cooking Time: 8-9 hours
Ideal slow-cooker size: 4-qt.

2 whole boneless, skinless chicken breasts, cubed
1 onion, chopped
1 garlic clove, minced
2 carrots, sliced
2 ribs celery, chopped
2 medium potatoes, cubed
1 tsp. mixed dried herbs
⅓ cup tomato sauce
12-oz. can cream-style corn
14-oz. can whole kernel corn
3 cups chicken stock
¼ cup chopped Italian parsley
1 tsp. salt
¼ tsp. pepper

1. Combine all ingredients except parsley, salt, and pepper in slow cooker.
2. Cover. Cook on Low 8-9 hours, or until chicken is tender.
3. Add parsley and seasonings 30 minutes before serving.

Here's a real time-saver from our house: Brown large quantities (10 lbs.) of ground beef, seasoned with onion, basil, and oregano to taste. Drain and cool. Freeze in pint freezer containers. The meat is readily available with no prep time or cleanup needed when preparing a slow cooker recipe or casserole that calls for browned ground beef.
Dale and Shari Mast, Harrisonburg, VA

Chicken Corn Chowder

Janie Steele, Moore, OK

Makes 6-8 servings

Prep Time: 10-15 minutes (with pre-cooked chicken)
Cooking Time: 1½ hours
Ideal slow-cooker size: 3- to 4-qt.

2 8-oz. pkgs. cream cheese
2 cups evaporated milk
14½-oz. can tomatoes with green chilies
1 lb. frozen corn
4 boneless, skinless chicken breast halves, cooked and chopped
12 oz. cheddar cheese, shredded, *divided*
salt to taste
pepper to taste
hot sauce to taste, *optional*

1. Combine cream cheese, milk, tomatoes with chilies, and corn in slow cooker.

2. Cover. Cook on Low 1 hour.

3. Stir in chicken. Cover. Cook 30 more minutes, or until heated through.

3. Stir in ⅔ of shredded cheese. Cover. Continue cooking until cheese is melted.

4. Add salt and pepper to taste and hot sauce to taste if you wish.

*Serving suggestion: Garnish individual serving bowls with remaining shredded **cheddar cheese**.*

Chicken Barley Chili

Colleen Heatwole, Burton, MI

Makes 10 servings

Prep Time: 20 minutes
Cooking Time: 6-8 hours
Ideal slow-cooker size: 6-qt.

2 14½-oz. cans tomatoes
16-oz. jar salsa
1 cup quick-cooking barley, uncooked
3 cups water
14½-oz. can chicken broth
15½-oz. can black beans, rinsed and drained
3 cups cooked chicken, *or* turkey, cubed
15¼-oz. can whole-kernel corn, undrained
1-3 tsp. chili powder, depending on how hot you like your chili
1 tsp. cumin

1. Combine all ingredients in slow cooker.

2. Cover. Cook on Low 6-8 hours, or until barley is tender.

*Serving suggestion: Serve in individual soup bowls topped with **sour cream** and shredded **cheese**.*

Chili, Chicken, Corn Chowder

Jeanne Allen, Rye, CO

Makes 6-8 servings

Prep. Time: 15 minutes
Cooking Time: 4 hours
Ideal slow-cooker size: 4-qt.

1 large onion, diced
1 garlic clove, minced
1 rib celery, finely chopped
¼ cup oil
2 cups frozen, *or* canned, corn
2 cups cooked, deboned, diced chicken
4-oz. can diced green chilies
½ tsp. black pepper
2 cups chicken broth
salt to taste
1 cup half-and-half

1. In saucepan, sauté onion, garlic, and celery in oil until limp.

2. Stir in corn, chicken, and chilies. Sauté for 2-3 minutes.

3. Combine all ingredients except half-and-half in slow cooker.

4. Cover. Heat on Low 4 hours.

5. Stir in half-and-half before serving. Do not boil, but be sure cream is heated through.

White Chili

Esther Martin, Ephrata, PA

Makes 8 servings

Prep. Time: 15 minutes
Cooking Time: 4-10 hours
Ideal slow-cooker size: 5-qt.

3 15-oz. cans Great
  Northern beans, drained
8 oz. cooked and shredded
  chicken breasts
1 cup chopped onions
1½ cups chopped yellow,
  red, *or* green, bell
  peppers
2 jalapeno chili peppers,
  stemmed, seeded, and
  chopped, *optional*
2 garlic cloves, minced
2 tsp. ground cumin
½ tsp. salt
½ tsp. dried oregano
3½ cups chicken broth

1. Combine all ingredients
in slow cooker.
2. Cover. Cook on Low 8-10
hours, or on High 4-5 hours.

*Serving suggestion: Ladle into
bowls and top individual servings with **sour cream**, shredded
cheddar cheese, and **tortilla
chips**.*

Southwest Chicken and White Bean Soup

Karen Ceneviva, Seymour, CT

Makes 6 servings

Prep Time: 15 minutes
Cooking Time: 4-10 hours
Ideal slow-cooker size: 3½-qt.

1 Tbsp. vegetable oil
1 lb. boneless, skinless
  chicken breasts, cut into
  1-inch cubes
1¾ cups chicken broth
1 cup chunky salsa
3 cloves garlic, minced
2 Tbsp. cumin
15½-oz. can small white
  beans, drained and
  rinsed
1 cup frozen corn
1 large onion, chopped

1. Heat oil in 10-inch skillet
over medium to high heat.
Add chicken and cook until it
is well browned on all sides.
Stir frequently to prevent
sticking.
2. Mix broth, salsa, garlic,
cumin, beans, corn, and onion
in slow cooker. Add chicken.
Stir well.
3. Cover. Cook 8-10 hours
on Low or 4-5 hours on High.

Chicken Tortilla Soup

Becky Harder, Monument, CO

Makes 6-8 servings

Prep. Time: 5-10 minutes
Cooking Time: 8 hours
Ideal slow-cooker size: 4- to 5-qt.

4 chicken breast halves
2 15-oz. cans black beans,
  undrained
2 15-oz. cans Mexican
  stewed tomatoes, *or* Rotel
  tomatoes
1 cup salsa (mild, medium,
  or hot, whichever you
  prefer)
4-oz. can chopped green
  chilies
14½-oz. can tomato sauce

1. Combine all ingredients
in large slow cooker.
2. Cover. Cook on Low 8
hours.
3. Just before serving,
remove chicken breasts and
slice into bite-sized pieces. Stir
into soup.

*Serving suggestion: To serve,
put a handful of **tortilla chips**
in each individual soup bowl.
Ladle soup over chips. Top with
shredded **cheese**.*

*If you use ground herbs and spices, add them during
the last hour of cooking.* Darlene Raber, Wellman, IA

114

Tex-Mex Chicken Chowder

Janie Steele, Moore, OK

Makes 8-10 servings

Prep. Time: 20 minutes
Cooking Time: 4½-6½ hours
Ideal slow-cooker size: 5-qt.

1 cup chopped onions
1 cup thinly sliced celery
2 garlic cloves, minced
1 Tbsp. oil
1½ lbs. boneless, skinless chicken breasts, cubed
32-oz. can chicken broth
1 pkg. country gravy mix
2 cups milk
16-oz. jar chunky salsa
32-oz. bag frozen hash brown potatoes
4½-oz. can chopped green chilies
8 oz. Velveeta cheese, cubed

1. Combine onions, celery, garlic, oil, chicken, and broth in 5-quart or larger slow cooker.
2. Cover. Cook on Low 2½ hours, until chicken is no longer pink.
3. In separate bowl, dissolve gravy mix in milk. Stir into chicken mixture. Add salsa, potatoes, chilies, and cheese and combine well. Cook on Low 2-4 hours, or until potatoes are fully cooked.

Chicken and Ham Gumbo

Barbara Tenney, Delta, PA

Makes 4 servings

Prep. Time: 20 minutes
Cooking Time: 6-8 hours
Ideal slow-cooker size: 4-qt.

1½ lbs. boneless, skinless chicken thighs
1 Tbsp. oil
10-oz. pkg. frozen okra
½ lb. smoked ham, cut into small chunks
1½ cups coarsely chopped onions
1½ cups coarsely chopped green peppers
2 *or* 3 10-oz. cans cannellini beans, drained
6 cups chicken broth
2 10-oz. cans diced tomatoes with green chilies
2 Tbsp. chopped fresh cilantro

1. Cut chicken into bite-sized pieces. Cook in oil in skillet until no longer pink.
2. Run hot water over okra until pieces separate easily.
3. Combine all ingredients but cilantro in slow cooker.
4. Cover. Cook on Low 6-8 hours. Stir in cilantro before serving.

Variations:
1. Stir in ½ cup long-grain, dry rice with rest of ingredients.

2. Add ¾ tsp. salt and ¼ tsp. pepper with other ingredients.

Easy Southern Brunswick Stew

Barbara Sparks, Glen Burnie, MD

Makes 10-12 servings

Prep. Time: 10 minutes
Cooking Time: 6½-8½ hours
Ideal slow-cooker size: 4-qt.

2-3 lbs. pork butt
17-oz. can white corn
14-oz. bottle ketchup
2 cups diced, cooked potatoes
10-oz. pkg. frozen peas
2 10¾-oz. cans tomato soup
hot sauce to taste
salt to taste
pepper to taste

1. Place pork in slow cooker.
2. Cover. Cook on Low 6-8 hours. Remove meat from bone and shred.
3. Combine all ingredients in slow cooker.
4. Cover. Bring to boil on High. Reduce heat to Low and simmer 30 minutes.

Joy's Brunswick Stew

Joy Sutter, Iowa City, IA

Makes 8 servings

Prep. Time: 10 minutes
Cooking Time: 4 hours
Ideal slow-cooker size: 4-qt.

1 lb. boneless, skinless chicken breasts, cut into bite-sized pieces
2 potatoes, thinly sliced
10¾-oz. can tomato soup
16-oz. can stewed tomatoes
10-oz. pkg. frozen corn
10-oz. pkg. frozen lima beans
3 Tbsp. onion flakes
¼ tsp. salt
⅛ tsp. pepper

1. Combine all ingredients in slow cooker.
2. Cover. Cook on High 2 hours. Reduce to Low and cook 2 hours.

Variation:
For more flavor, add 1, *or* 2, bay leaves during cooking.

Brunswick Soup Mix

Joyce B. Suiter, Garysburg, NC

Makes 14 servings

Prep. Time: 10-15 minutes
Cooking Time: 7 hours
Ideal slow-cooker size: 5-qt.

1 large onion, chopped
4 cups frozen, cubed, hash browns, thawed
4 cups chopped, cooked chicken, *or* 2 20-oz. cans canned chicken
14½-oz. can diced tomatoes
15-oz. can tomato sauce
15¼-oz. can corn
15¼-oz. can lima beans, drained
2 cups chicken broth
½ tsp. salt
½ tsp. pepper
¼ tsp. Worcestershire sauce
¼ cup sugar

1. Combine all ingredients in large slow cooker.
2. Cover. Cook on High 7 hours.
3. Cool and freeze in 2-cup portions.
4. To use, empty 1 frozen portion into saucepan with small amount of liquid: tomato juice, V8 juice, or broth. Cook slowly until soup mixture thaws. Stir frequently, adding more liquid until of desired consistency.

Oriental Turkey Chili

Kimberly Jensen, Bailey, CO

Makes 6 servings

Prep. Time: 20 minutes
Cooking Time: 6 hours
Ideal slow-cooker size: 4-qt.

2 cups yellow onions, diced
1 small red bell pepper, diced
1 lb. ground turkey, browned
2 Tbsp. minced gingerroot
3 cloves garlic, minced
¼ cup dry sherry
¼ cup hoisin sauce
2 Tbsp. chili powder
1 Tbsp. corn oil
2 Tbsp. soy sauce
1 tsp. sugar
2 cups canned whole tomatoes
16-oz. can dark red kidney beans, undrained

1. Combine all ingredients in slow cooker.
2. Cover. Cook on Low 6 hours.

Serving suggestion: Serve topped with **chow mein noodles** *or over cooked* **white rice**.

Note:
If you serve this chili over rice, this recipe will yield 10-12 servings.

Turkey Chili

Dawn Day, Westminster, CA

Makes 6-8 servings

Prep. Time: 10-15 minutes
Cooking Time: 8-9 hours
Ideal slow-cooker size: 3½- to 4-qt.

1 large chopped onion
2-3 Tbsp. oil
1 lb. ground turkey
½ tsp. salt
3 Tbsp. chili powder
6-oz. can tomato paste
3 1-lb. cans small red beans
   with liquid
1 cup frozen corn

1. Sauté onion in oil in skillet until transparent. Add turkey and salt and brown lightly in skillet.
2. Combine all ingredients in slow cooker. Mix well.
3. Cover. Cook on Low 8-9 hours.

Note:
Ground beef can be used in place of turkey.

Variation:
Serve over rice, topped with shredded cheddar cheese and sour cream.

Chili Sans Cholesterol

Dolores S. Kratz, Souderton, PA

Makes 4 servings

Prep. Time: 15 minutes
Cooking Time: 6 hours
Ideal slow-cooker size: 2½-qt.

1 lb. ground turkey
½ cup chopped celery
½ cup chopped onions
8-oz. can tomatoes
14-oz. can pinto beans
14½-oz. can diced tomatoes
½ tsp., *or more*, chili
   powder
½ tsp. salt
dash pepper

1. Sauté turkey in skillet until browned. Drain.
2. Combine all ingredients in slow cooker.
3. Cover. Cook on Low 6 hours.

Leftover Turkey Soup

Janie Steele, Moore, OK

Makes 8-10 servings

Prep. Time: 10 minutes
Cooking Time: 2-3 hours
Ideal slow-cooker size: 4-qt.

1 small onion, chopped
1 cup chopped celery
1 Tbsp. oil
2-3 cups diced turkey
1 cup cooked rice
leftover gravy, *or*
   combination of leftover
   gravy and chicken broth

1. Sauté onion and celery in oil in saucepan until translucent.
2. Combine all ingredients in slow cooker, adding gravy and/or broth until the desired consistency is reached.
3. Cover. Cook on Low for at least 2-3 hours, or until heated through.

If you're in a rush, you can skip browning the meat if the recipe calls for that.
Why do it at all? If you're working with ground beef, browning it in a skillet allows the drippings to emerge. You can drain them off before putting the browned beef into the cooker, thus reducing the fat content of your finished dish.
If you're working with a roast, browning it deepens the flavor of the finished dish.

Italian Vegetable Soup

Patti Boston, Newark, OH

Makes 4-6 servings

Prep. Time: 15 minutes
Cooking Time: 4¾-9¼ hours
Ideal slow-cooker size: 2½-qt.

3 small carrots, sliced
1 small onion, chopped
2 small potatoes, diced
2 Tbsp. chopped parsley
1 garlic clove, minced
3 tsp. beef bouillon
  granules, *or* 3 beef
  bouillon cubes
1¼ tsp. dried basil
½ tsp. salt
¼ tsp. pepper
16-oz. can red kidney
  beans, undrained
3 cups water
14½-oz. can stewed
  tomatoes, with juice
1 cup diced, cooked ham

1. Layer carrots, onions, potatoes, parsley, garlic, beef bouillon, basil, salt, pepper, and kidney beans in slow cooker. Do not stir. Add water.

2. Cover. Cook on Low 8-9 hours, or on High 4½-5½ hours, until vegetables are tender.

3. Stir in tomatoes and ham. Cover and cook on High 10-15 minutes.

Chet's Trucker Stew

Janice Muller, Derwood, MD

Makes 8 servings

Prep. Time: 15 minutes
Cooking Time: 2-3 hours
Ideal slow-cooker size: 4- to 5-qt.

1 lb. bulk pork sausage,
  cooked and drained
1 lb. ground beef, cooked
  and drained
31-oz. can pork and beans
16-oz. can light kidney
  beans
16-oz. can dark kidney
  beans
14½-oz. can waxed beans,
  drained
14½-oz. can lima beans,
  drained
1 cup ketchup
1 cup brown sugar
1 Tbsp. spicy prepared
  mustard

1. Combine all ingredients in slow cooker.

2. Cover. Simmer on High 2-3 hours.

Spicy Potato Soup

Sharon Kauffman, Harrisonburg, VA

Makes 6-8 servings

Prep. Time: 15 minutes
Cooking Time: 5-10 hours
Ideal slow-cooker size: 4-qt.

1 lb. ground beef, *or* bulk
  sausage, browned
4 cups cubed, peeled
  potatoes
1 small onion, chopped
3 8-oz. cans tomato sauce
2 tsp. salt
1½ tsp. pepper
½-1 tsp. hot pepper sauce
water

1. Combine all ingredients except water in slow cooker. Add enough water to cover ingredients.

2. Cover. Cook on Low 8-10 hours, or on High 5 hours, until potatoes are tender.

Milk products such as cream, milk, and sour cream can curdle and separate when cooked for a long period. Add them during the last 10 minutes if cooking on High, or during the last 20-30 minutes if cooking on Low.

Mrs. J. E. Barthold, Bethlehem, PA

Marilyn Yoder, Archbold, OH

Corn Chowder with Sausage

Janie Steele, Moore, OK

Makes 8-10 servings

Prep Time: 30 minutes
Cooking Time: 2 hours
Ideal slow-cooker size: 4-qt.

1 lb. sausage of your choice, cut into ¾-inch-thick slices
½ cup water, *or* more
½-⅓ cup flour, for thickening
1 cup water
4 large potatoes, peeled and cubed
2 14-oz. cans chicken broth
1 stick (½ cup) butter, cut into slices
2 cups sweet corn, freshly grated, *or* sweet frozen nibblets, *or* canned corn, drained
1 cup onion, chopped
2 cups heavy cream
1 quart milk
salt to taste
pepper to taste
hot sauce, *optional*

1. Cook sausage in skillet with water over medium to high heat. Cover. Stir meat frequently until browned. Add more water if needed so meat doesn't stick and burn.
2. Remove sausage from skillet. Set aside and keep warm.
3. Stir flour into sausage drippings in skillet over low heat. Add 1 cup water. Stir until water comes to a boil and thickens. Add gravy to sausage.
4. Place potatoes and chicken broth in slow cooker. Cover. Cook on High until tender, about 1½ hours.
5. Stir sausage and gravy into cooked potatoes in slow cooker. Add butter, corn, and onions. Continue cooking until onion is tender, about 30 more minutes on High.
6. Add cream, milk, salt, pepper, and hot sauce if you wish, for final 10 minutes of cooking.

Sausage White Bean Soup

Christie Anne Detamore-Hunsberger
Harrisonburg, VA

Makes 8 servings

Prep Time: 20-30 minutes
Cooking Time: 3-3½ hours
Ideal slow-cooker size: 4-qt.

1 lb. Italian turkey sausage, sweet *or* hot, cut in ½-inch-thick slices
½ cup water, *or* more
1 large onion, diced
2 cloves garlic, minced
4 carrots, grated
3 stalks celery, chopped
2-2½ quarts chicken broth
3-4 tsp. low-sodium chicken broth powder
1 tsp. vegetable seasoning blend, your choice, but without salt
½ tsp. dried oregano
¼ tsp. pepper
2-3 cans white beans, rinsed and drained
2 cups frozen spinach, thawed

1. Brown sausage in a skillet in ½ cup water over medium to high heat. Cover. Check and stir after 10 minutes or so to make sure sausage isn't cooking dry and burning. Add more water if needed and continue stirring until browned on all sides.
2. Remove sausage to slow cooker, reserving drippings.
3. Sauté onion, garlic, carrots, and celery in drippings in skillet until tender. Place vegetables in slow cooker.
4. Add chicken broth, powder, all seasonings, and beans. Stir well.
5. Cook on Low 3 hours.
6. Squeeze excess liquid out of thawed spinach. Add to slow cooker for the last 20-30 minutes of cooking time.

*Serving suggestion: Garnish with **parsley**.*

Turkey Bean Chili

Christie Anne Detamore-Hunsberger
Harrisonburg, VA

Makes 6-8 servings

Prep Time: 15-30 minutes
Cooking Time: 4-6 hours
Ideal slow-cooker size: 3- to 4-qt.

1 lb. bulk turkey sausage
1 onion, diced
2 ribs celery, diced
3 14½-oz. cans beans—red,
    black, pinto, *or* any
    combination, rinsed and
    drained
1 quart stewed, *or* whole,
    tomatoes, chopped
4 Tbsp. tomato paste
½ tsp. oregano
1 tsp. Worcestershire sauce
½ tsp. cumin
4 tsp. chili powder
½ tsp. basil
½ tsp. garlic powder
1 cup water

1. Brown sausage in skillet.
Remove sausage to slow
cooker. Reserve drippings.
   2. Sauté onion and celery in
drippings in skillet.
   3. Add sautéed vegetables,
beans, tomatoes, tomato paste,
seasonings, and water to slow
cooker. Stir well.
   4. Cover. Cook on Low 4-6
hours.

*Serving suggestion: In
addition to serving this in soup
bowls, you can also serve it as a
topping for baked **potatoes**.*

Hearty Potato Sauerkraut Soup

Kathy Hertzler, Lancaster, PA

Makes 6-8 servings

Prep. Time: 15-20 minutes
Cooking Time: 10-12 hours
Ideal slow-cooker size: 4-qt.

4 cups chicken broth
10¾-oz. can cream of
    mushroom soup
16-oz. can sauerkraut,
    rinsed and drained
8 oz. fresh mushrooms, sliced
1 medium potato, cubed
2 medium carrots, peeled
    and sliced
2 ribs celery, chopped
2 lbs. Polish kielbasa
    (smoked), cubed
2½ cups chopped, cooked
    chicken
2 Tbsp. vinegar
2 tsp. dried dillweed
1½ tsp. pepper

1. Combine all ingredients
in large slow cooker.
   2. Cover. Cook on Low
10-12 hours.
   3. If necessary, skim fat
before serving.

Sauerkraut Soup

Barbara Tenny, Delta, PA

Makes 8 servings

Prep. Time: 15 minutes
Cooking Time: 2-8 hours
Ideal slow-cooker size: 6½-qt.

1 lb. smoked Polish
    sausage, cut into ½-inch
    pieces
5 medium potatoes, cubed
2 large onions, chopped
2 large carrots, cut into
    ¼-inch slices
42-45-oz. can chicken broth
32-oz. can *or* bag
    sauerkraut, rinsed and
    drained
6-oz. can tomato paste

1. Combine all ingredients
in large slow cooker. Stir to
combine.
   2. Cover. Cook on High 2
hours, and then on Low 6-8
hours.

*Serving suggestion: Serve with
rye bread.*

*I often start the slow cooker on High until I'm
ready for work, then switch it to Low as I go out the
door. It may only be 45 minutes to 1 hour on High,
but I feel it starts the cooking process faster, thus
preserving flavor.*
                                    Evie Hershey, Atglen, PA

Kielbasa Soup

Bernice M. Gnidovec, Streator, IL

Makes 8 servings

Prep. Time: 10 minutes
Cooking Time: 12 hours
Ideal slow-cooker size: 8-qt.

16-oz. pkg. frozen mixed
  vegetables, *or* your choice
  of vegetables
6-oz. can tomato paste
1 medium onion, chopped
3 medium potatoes, diced
1½ lbs. kielbasa, cut into
  ¼-inch pieces
4 qts. water

1. Combine all ingredients
in large slow cooker.
2. Cover. Cook on Low 12
hours.

*Serving suggestion: Garnish
individual servings with fresh
parsley.*

Ruth's
Split Pea Soup

Ruth Conrad Liechty, Goshen, IN

Makes 6-8 servings

Prep. Time: 15 minutes
Cooking Time: 12 hours
Ideal slow-cooker size: 4-qt.

1 bag (2¼ cups) dry split peas

1 lb. bulk sausage, browned
  and drained
6 cups water
2 medium potatoes, diced
1 onion, chopped
½ tsp. dried marjoram, *or*
  thyme
½ tsp. pepper

1. Wash and sort dried peas,
removing any stones. Then
combine all ingredients in
slow cooker.
2. Cover. Cook on Low 12
hours.

Sally's
Split Pea Soup

Sally Holzem, Schofield, WI

Makes 8 servings

Prep. Time: 15 minutes
Cooking Time: 8-10 hours
Ideal slow-cooker size: 5-qt.

1-lb. pkg. split peas
1 ham hock
1 carrot, diced
1 onion, diced
1 rib celery, diced
2 qts. water
¼ tsp. pepper
1 bay leaf
2 whole allspice
3 potatoes, diced
1 tsp. sugar

1. Wash and sort split peas,
removing any stones. Then
combine ingredients in slow
cooker.

2. Cover. Cook on Low 8-10
hours.
3. Remove ham bone. Cut
meat off and dice. Return
meat to soup. Stir through.
4. Remove bay leaf before
serving.

Kelly's
Split Pea Soup

Kelly Amos, Pittsboro, NC

Makes 8 servings

Prep. Time: 10 minutes
Cooking Time: 8-9 hours
Ideal slow-cooker size: 4½-qt.

2 cups dry split peas
2 qts. water
2 onions, chopped
2 carrots, peeled and sliced
4 slices Canadian bacon,
  chopped
2 Tbsp. chicken bouillon
  granules, *or* 2 chicken
  bouillon cubes
1 tsp. salt
¼-½ tsp. pepper

1. Combine all ingredients
in slow cooker.
2. Cover. Cook on Low 8-9
hours.

Variation:
For a creamier soup,
remove half of soup when
done and purée. Stir back into
rest of soup.

Curried Pork and Pea Soup

Kathy Hertzler, Lancaster, PA

Makes 6-8 servings

Prep. Time: 15 minutes
Cooking Time: 4-12 hours
Ideal slow-cooker size: 4-qt.

1½-lb. boneless pork
   shoulder roast
1 cup yellow, *or* green, split
   peas, rinsed and drained
½ cup finely chopped
   carrots
½ cup finely chopped
   celery
½ cup finely chopped
   onions
49½-oz. can (approximately
   6 cups) chicken broth
2 tsp. curry powder
½ tsp. paprika
¼ tsp. ground cumin
¼ tsp. pepper
2 cups torn fresh spinach

   1. Trim fat from pork and
cut pork into ½-inch pieces.
   2. Combine split peas,
carrots, celery, and onions in
slow cooker.
   3. Stir in broth, curry
powder, paprika, cumin, and
pepper. Stir in pork.
   4. Cover. Cook on Low
10-12 hours, or on High 4
hours.
   5. Stir in spinach. Serve
immediately.

Karen's Split Pea Soup

Karen Stoltzfus, Alto, MI

Makes 6 servings

Prep. Time: 15 minutes
Cooking Time: 7 hours
Ideal slow-cooker size: 5-qt.

2 carrots
2 ribs celery
1 onion
1 parsnip
1 leek (reserve 3 inches of
   green)
1 ripe tomato
1 ham hock
1¾ cups (1 lb.) dried split
   peas, washed, with stones
   removed
2 Tbsp. olive oil
1 bay leaf
1 tsp. dried thyme
4 cups chicken broth
4 cups water
1 tsp. salt
¼ tsp. pepper
2 tsp. chopped fresh parsley

   1. Cut all vegetables into
¼-inch pieces and place in
slow cooker. Add remaining
ingredients except salt, pepper,
and parsley.
   2. Cover. Cook on High 7
hours.
   3. Remove ham hock. Shred
meat from bone and return
meat to pot.
   4. Season soup with salt and
pepper. Stir in parsley. Serve
immediately.

Dorothy's Split Pea Soup

Dorothy M. Van Deest, Memphis, TN

Makes 6-8 servings

Prep. Time: 20 minutes
Cooking Time: 8-10 hours
Ideal slow-cooker size: 5-qt.

2 Tbsp. butter, *or*
   margarine
1 cup minced onions
8 cups water
2 cups (1 lb.) green split
   peas, washed and stones
   removed
4 whole cloves
1 bay leaf
¼ tsp. pepper
1 ham hock
1 cup finely minced celery
1 cup diced carrots
⅛ tsp. dried marjoram
1 tsp. salt
⅛ tsp. dried savory

   1. Combine all ingredients
in slow cooker.
   2. Cover. Cook on Low 8-10
hours.
   3. Remove ham bone
and bay leaf before serving.
Debone meat, cut into bite-
sized pieces, and return to
soup. Stir in and serve.

Variation:
   For a thick soup, uncover
soup after 8-10 hours and turn
heat to High. Simmer, stirring
occasionally, until the desired
consistency is reached.

Rosemarie's Pea Soup

Rosemarie Fitzgerald, Gibsonia, PA
Shirley Sears, Tiskilwa, IL

Makes 4-6 servings

Prep. Time: 15 minutes
Cooking Time: 6-12 hours
Ideal slow-cooker size: 4½-qt.

2 cups dried split peas
4 cups water
1 rib celery, chopped
1 cup chopped potatoes
1 large carrot, chopped
1 medium onion, chopped
¼ tsp. dried thyme, *or* marjoram
1 bay leaf
½ tsp. salt
1 garlic clove
½ tsp. dried basil

1. Combine all ingredients in slow cooker.
2. Cover. Cook on Low 8-12 hours, or on High 6 hours, until peas are tender.

Variations:

For increased flavor, use chicken broth instead of water. Stir in curry powder, coriander, or red pepper flakes to taste.

French Market Soup

Ethel Mumaw, Berlin, OH

Makes 2½ quarts soup

Prep. Time: 10 minutes
Cooking Time: 10 hours
Ideal slow-cooker size: 4-qt.

2 cups dry bean mix, washed with stones removed
2 quarts water
1 ham hock
1 tsp. salt
¼ tsp. pepper
16-oz. can tomatoes
1 large onion, chopped
1 garlic clove, minced
1 chili pepper, chopped, *or* 1 tsp. chili powder
¼ cup lemon juice

1. Combine all ingredients in slow cooker.
2. Cover. Cook on Low 8 hours. Turn to High and cook an additional 2 hours, or until beans are tender.
3. Debone ham, cut meat into bite-sized pieces, and stir back into soup.

Nine Bean Soup with Tomatoes

Violette Harris Denney, Carrollton, GA

Makes 8-10 servings

Prep. Time: 10 minutes
Soaking Time: 8 hours or overnight
Cooking Time: 8 hours
Ideal slow-cooker size: 6½-qt.

2 cups dry nine-bean soup mix
1 lb. ham, diced
1 large onion, chopped
1 garlic clove, minced
½-¾ tsp. salt
2 qts. water
16-oz. can tomatoes, undrained and chopped
10-oz. can tomatoes with green chilies, undrained

1. Sort and wash bean mix. Place in slow cooker. Cover with water 2 inches above beans. Let soak overnight. Drain.
2. Add ham, onion, garlic, salt, and 2 quarts fresh water.
3. Cover. Cook on Low 7 hours.
4. Add remaining ingredients and continue cooking on Low another hour. Stir occasionally.

Note:

Bean Soup mix is a mix of barley pearls, black beans, red beans, pinto beans, navy beans, Great Northern beans, lentils, split peas, and black-eyed peas.

Calico Ham and Bean Soup

Esther Martin, Ephrata, PA

Makes 6-8 servings

Prep. Time: 20 minutes
Cooking Time: 4-10 hours
Ideal slow-cooker size: 4½-qt.

1 lb. dry bean mix, rinsed
  and drained, with stones
  removed
6 cups water
2 cups cubed cooked ham
1 cup chopped onions
1 cup chopped carrots
1 tsp. dried basil
1 tsp. dried oregano
¾ tsp. salt
¼ tsp. pepper
2 bay leaves
6 cups water
1 tsp. liquid smoke,
  optional

1. Combine beans and 6 cups water in large saucepan. Bring to boil, reduce heat, and simmer uncovered for 10 minutes. Drain, discarding cooking water, and rinse beans.

2. Combine all ingredients in slow cooker.

3. Cover. Cook on Low 8-10 hours, or High 4-5 hours. Discard bay leaves before serving.

Healthy Bean Soup

Karen Ceneviva, Seymour, CT

Makes 6 servings

Prep Time: 20-30 minutes
Cooking Time: 6-7 hours
Ideal slow-cooker size: 5-qt.

1½ cups dry great northern
  beans
3 cups parsnips, chopped
2 cups carrots, chopped
1 cup onion, chopped
2 gloves garlic, minced
5 cups water
1½ lbs. smoked ham hock,
  or ham shanks
2 tsp. salt
½ tsp. pepper
⅛-¼ tsp. hot sauce

1. Wash dried beans. Place beans in a large stockpot. Cover them with water.

2. Bring to a boil. Turn off heat. Allow beans to sit for 10 minutes.

3. Drain off water. Place beans in slow cooker.

4. Add parsnips, carrots, onion, and garlic to slow cooker.

5. Add water, ham, salt, pepper, and hot sauce to slow cooker. Stir well.

6. Cover. Cook on High 6-7 hours, or until vegetables and meat are tender.

7. Remove meat from cooker and allow to cool enough to handle. Debone.

8. Cut meat into bite-size pieces and return to slow cooker. Heat through.

Northern Bean Soup

Patricia Howard, Albuquerque, NM

Makes 6-8 servings

Prep. Time: 15 minutes
Soaking Time: 8 hours or overnight
Cooking Time: 12-14 hours
Ideal slow-cooker size: 4-qt.

1 lb. dry Northern beans
1 lb. ham
2 medium onions, chopped
half a green pepper,
  chopped
1 cup chopped celery
16-oz. can diced tomatoes
4 carrots, peeled and
  chopped
4-oz. can green chili
  peppers
1 tsp. garlic powder
1-2 qts. water
2-3 tsp. salt

1. Wash beans. Cover with water and soak overnight. Drain. Pour into slow cooker.

2. Dice ham into 1-inch pieces. Add to beans.

3. Stir in remaining ingredients.

4. Cover. Cook on High 2 hours, then on Low 10-12 hours, or until beans are tender.

Easy Lima Bean Soup

Barbara Tenney, Delta, PA

Makes 8-10 servings

Prep. Time: 15 minutes
Soaking Time: overnight
Cooking Time: 8-10 hours
Ideal slow-cooker size: 8-qt.

1-lb. bag large dry lima beans
1 large onion, chopped
6 ribs celery, chopped
3 large potatoes, cut in
    ½-inch cubes
2 large carrots, cut in
    ¼-inch rounds
2 cups ham, *or* sausage, *or*
    kielbasa
1 Tbsp. salt
1 tsp. pepper
2 bay leaves
3 quarts water, *or*
    combination water and
    beef broth

1. Sort beans. Soak overnight. Drain.
2. Combine all ingredients in slow cooker.
3. Cover. Cook on Low 8-10 hours.

Variation:
For extra flavor, add 1 tsp. dried oregano before cooking.

Vegetable Bean Soup

Kathi Rogge, Alexandria, IN

Makes 6-8 servings

Prep. Time: 10 minutes
Cooking Time: 5-8 hours
Ideal slow-cooker size: 5-qt.

6 cups cooked beans: navy,
    pinto, Great Northern, etc.
1 meaty ham bone
1 cup cooked ham, diced
¼ tsp. garlic powder
1 small bay leaf
1 cup cubed potatoes
1 cup chopped onions
1 cup chopped celery
1 cup chopped carrots
water

1. Combine all ingredients except water in slow cooker. Add water to about 2½ inches from top.
2. Cover. Cook on Low 5-8 hours.
3. Remove bay leaf before serving.

Navy Bean Soup

Joyce Bowman, Lady Lake, FL

Makes 8 servings

Prep. Time: 5 minutes
Soaking Time: 8 hours or overnight
Cooking Time: 8-10 hours
Ideal slow-cooker size: 5-qt.

1 lb. dry navy beans
8 cups water
1 onion, finely chopped
2 bay leaves
½ tsp. ground thyme
½ tsp. nutmeg
2 tsp. salt
½ tsp. lemon pepper
3 garlic cloves, minced
1 ham hock, *or* 1 lb. ham
    pieces

1. Soak beans in water overnight. Strain out stones, but reserve liquid.
2. Combine all ingredients in slow cooker.
3. Cover. Cook on Low 8-10 hours. Debone meat and cut into bite-sized pieces. Set ham aside.
4. Purée three-fourths of soup in blender in small batches. When finished blending, stir in meat.

Variation:
Add small chunks of cooked potatoes when stirring in ham pieces after blending.

I find that adding ¼-½ cup of a burgundy or Chablis wine to most soup and stew recipes brings out the flavor of the other seasonings.
        Joyce Kant, Rochester, NY

Caribbean-Style Black Bean Soup

Sheryl Shenk, Harrisonburg, VA

Makes 8-10 servings

Prep. Time: 10 minutes
Soaking Time: 8 hours or overnight
Cooking Time: 4-10 hours
Ideal slow-cooker size: 5-qt.

1 lb. dried black beans,
   washed and stones
   removed
3 onions, chopped
1 green pepper, chopped
4 cloves garlic, minced
1 ham hock, *or* ¾ cup
   cubed ham
1 Tbsp. oil
1 Tbsp. ground cumin
2 tsp. dried oregano
1 tsp. dried thyme
1 Tbsp. salt
½ tsp. pepper
3 cups water
2 Tbsp. vinegar

1. Soak beans overnight in 4 quarts water. Drain.

2. Combine beans, onions, green pepper, garlic, ham, oil, cumin, oregano, thyme, salt, pepper, and 3 cups fresh water. Stir well.

3. Cover. Cook on Low 8-10 hours, or on High 4-5 hours.

4. For a thick soup, remove half of cooked bean mixture and purée until smooth in blender or mash with potato masher. Return to cooker. If you like a soupier soup, leave as is.

5. Add vinegar and stir well. Debone ham, cut into bite-sized pieces, and return to soup.

*Serving suggestion: Serve in soup bowls with a dollop of **sour cream** in the middle of each individual serving, topped with fresh **cilantro**.*

Slow-Cooker Black Bean Chili

Mary Seielstad, Sparks, NV

Makes 8 servings

Prep. Time: 10 minutes
Cooking Time: 6-8 hours
Ideal slow-cooker size: 4½-qt.

1-lb. pork tenderloin, cut
   into 1-inch chunks
16-oz. jar thick, chunky
   salsa
3 15-oz. cans black beans,
   rinsed and drained
½ cup chicken broth
1 medium red bell pepper,
   chopped
1 medium onion, chopped
1 tsp. ground cumin
2-3 tsp. chili powder
1-1½ tsp. dried oregano

1. Combine all ingredients in slow cooker.

2. Cover. Cook on Low 6-8 hours, or until pork is tender.

*Serving suggestion: Garnish individual servings with **sour cream**.*

Katelyn's Black Bean Soup

Katelyn Bailey, Mechanicsburg, PA

Makes 4-6 servings

Prep. Time: 10 minutes
Cooking Time: 6-8 hours
Ideal slow-cooker size: 4-qt.

⅓ cup chopped onions
1 garlic clove, minced
1-2 Tbsp. oil
2 15½-oz. cans black beans,
   undrained
1 cup water
1 chicken bouillon cube
½ cup diced, cooked,
   smoked ham
½ cup diced carrots
1 dash, *or* more, cayenne
   pepper
1-2 drops, *or* more, Tabasco
   sauce

1. Sauté onion and garlic in oil in saucepan.

2. Purée or mash contents of one can of black beans. Add to sautéed ingredients.

3. Combine all ingredients except sour cream in slow cooker.

4. Cover. Cook on Low 6-8 hours.

*Serving suggestion: Add dollop of **sour cream** to each individual bowl before serving.*

Baked Bean Soup

Maryann Markano, Wilmington, DE

Makes 5-6 servings

Prep. Time: 10 minutes
Cooking Time: 4-6 hours
Ideal slow-cooker size: 2½-qt.

28-oz. can baked beans
6 slices browned bacon, chopped
2 Tbsp. bacon drippings
2 Tbsp. finely chopped onions
14½-oz. can stewed tomatoes
1 Tbsp. brown sugar
1 Tbsp. vinegar
1 tsp. seasoning salt

1. Combine all ingredients in slow cooker.
2. Cover. Cook on Low 4-6 hours.

Mjeodrah or Esau's Lentil Soup

Dianna Milhizer, Springfield, VA

Makes 8 servings

Prep. Time: 15 minutes
Cooking Time: 6-8 hours
Ideal slow-cooker size: 4-qt.

1 cup chopped carrots
1 cup diced celery
2 cups chopped onions
1 Tbsp. olive oil, *or* butter
2 cups brown rice
1 Tbsp. olive oil, *or* butter
6 cups water
1 lb. lentils, washed and drained

1. Sauté carrots, celery, and onions in 1 Tbsp. oil in skillet. When soft and translucent place in slow cooker.
2. Brown rice in 1 Tbsp. oil until dry. Add to slow cooker.
3. Stir in water and lentils.
4. Cover. Cook on High 6-8 hours.

*Serving suggestion: Serve 1 cup each in individual soup bowls. Cover each with a serving of fresh garden salad (**lettuce**, **spinach** leaves, chopped **tomatoes**, minced **onions**, chopped **bell peppers**, sliced **olives**, sliced **radishes**). Pour favorite **vinaigrette** over all.*

Sweet Potato Lentil Soup

Joleen Albrecht, Gladstone, MI

Makes 6 servings

Prep Time: 10-15 minutes
Cooking Time: 6 hours
Ideal slow-cooker size: 4-qt.

4 cups vegetable broth
3 cups (about 1¼ lbs.) sweet potatoes, peeled and cubed
3 medium carrots, chopped
1 medium onion, chopped
4 cloves garlic, minced
1 cup dried lentils, rinsed
½ tsp. ground cumin
¼ tsp. salt
¼ tsp. cayenne pepper
¼ tsp. ground ginger
¼ cup fresh cilantro, minced, *or* 1-2 Tbsp. dried cilantro

1. Combine all ingredients in slow cooker.
2. Cover. Cook on Low 6 hours, or until vegetables are done to your liking.

Sweet Potato Chowder

Carol Eberly, Harrisonburg, VA

Makes 12 servings

Prep Time: 20-25 minutes
Cooking Time: 8 hours
Ideal slow-cooker size: 4- to 5-qt.

1 celery rib, chopped
2 Tbsp. butter, melted
2 14½-oz. cans chicken broth
2 cups water
2 tsp. chicken bouillon
  granules
4 medium red potatoes,
  peeled, if you wish, and
  cubed
1 large sweet potato, peeled,
  if you wish, and cubed
2 cups ham, fully cooked
  and cubed
¼ cup chopped onion
½ tsp. garlic powder, *or*
  1 clove garlic, minced
½ tsp. seasoning salt
½ tsp. dried oregano
½ tsp. parsley flakes
¼ tsp. pepper
¼ tsp. crushed red pepper
  flakes
¼ cup flour
2 cups milk

1. Mix all ingredients except flour and milk in slow cooker.
2. Cover. Cook 8 hours on Low.
3. One hour before end of cooking time, combine milk and flour in a small bowl, or

place in covered jar and shake, until smooth. Stir into hot soup.

Sweet Potato Soup

Janie Steele, Moore, OK

Makes 4 servings

Prep Time: 30 minutes (including time to cook sweet potatoes)
Cooking Time: 1 hour
Ideal slow-cooker size: 4-qt.

2 *or* 3 large sweet potatoes,
  baked, peeled, and cubed
1½ cups chicken broth,
  divided
1 Tbsp. butter
1 Tbsp. flour
¼ tsp. ground ginger
1 cup evaporated milk

1. Combine cooked sweet potatoes and ¾ cup broth in blender. Blend on high until mixture is smooth.
2. Place butter, flour, and ginger in slow cooker. Turn cooker to High and add milk gradually.
3. Cook, stirring frequently, until thickened.
4. Add sweet potato mixture from blender. Add remaining chicken broth. Stir until smooth.
5. Cover. Cook on High until heated through, about 1 hour.

*Serving suggestion: Garnish each individual serving with a scattering of chopped **pecans**.*

French Onion Soup

Jenny R. Unternahrer, Wayland, IA
Janice Yoskovich, Carmichaels, PA

Makes 10 servings

Prep. Time: 20 minutes
Cooking Time: 5-7 hours
Ideal slow-cooker size: 6½-qt.

8-10 large onions, sliced
½ cup butter, *or* margarine
6 10½-oz. cans condensed
  beef broth
1½ tsp. Worcestershire
  sauce
3 bay leaves

1. Sauté onions in butter until crisp-tender. Transfer to slow cooker.
2. Add broth, Worcestershire sauce, and bay leaves.
3. Cover. Cook on Low 5-7 hours, or until onions are tender. Discard bay leaves.

*Serving suggestion: Ladle into bowls. Top each with a slice of toasted **French bread** and some grated **Parmesan** and/or **mozzarella cheese**.*

Note:
  For a more intense beef flavor, add one beef bouillon cube, or use home-cooked beef broth instead of canned broth.

Cider and Pork Stew

Veronica Sabo, Shelton, CT

Makes 5 servings

Prep Time: 15 minutes
Cooking Time: 7-9 hours
Ideal slow-cooker size: 3½-qt.

2 medium (about 1¼ lbs.)
 sweet potatoes, peeled,
 if you wish, and cut into
 ¾-inch pieces
3 small carrots, peeled and
 cut into ½-inch-thick slices
1 cup onions, chopped
1-2-lb. boneless pork
 shoulder, cut into 1-inch
 cubes
1 large Granny Smith
 apple, peeled, cored and
 coarsely chopped
¼ cup flour
¾ tsp. salt
½ tsp. dried sage
½ tsp. thyme
½ tsp. pepper
1 cup apple cider

1. Layer sweet potatoes,
carrots, onions, pork, and
apple in slow cooker.
2. Combine flour, salt, sage,
thyme, and pepper in medium
bowl.
3. Add cider to flour and
spice mix. Stir until smooth.
4. Pour over meat and
vegetables in slow cooker.
5. Cover. Cook on Low
7-9 hours, or until meat and
vegetables are tender.

Sandy's Potato Soup

Sandra D. Thony, Jenks, OK

Makes 8-10 servings

Prep Time: 15 minutes
Cooking Time: 9 hours
Ideal slow-cooker size: 7-qt.

8 large potatoes, cubed
2 medium onions, chopped
3 Tbsp. butter, *or*
 margarine
½-1 lb. bacon, cooked crisp,
 drained, and crumbled
3 chicken bouillon cubes
2 Tbsp. dried parsley
6 cups water
2 cups milk
½ cup flour
¼ cup water
1 tsp. salt
¼-½ tsp. pepper

1. Combine all ingredients
except flour, ¼ cup water,
salt, and pepper in large slow
cooker.
2. Cover. Cook on High
6 hours, and then on Low 3
hours.
3. Make paste out of flour
and water. Stir into soup one
hour before serving. Season
with salt and pepper.

Variations:
1. Make Cheesy Potato Soup
by adding ¼ lb. cubed Velveeta,
or your choice of cheese, during
last hour of cooking.

2. For added richness, use
1 cup whole milk and 1 cup
evaporated milk.

German Potato Soup

Lee Ann Hazlett, Freeport, IL

Makes 6-8 servings

Prep Time: 15-20 minutes
Cooking Time: 4-10 hours
Ideal slow-cooker size: 5-qt.

1 onion, chopped
1 leek, trimmed and diced
2 carrots, diced
1 cup chopped cabbage
¼ cup chopped fresh parsley
4 cups beef broth
1 lb. potatoes, diced
1 bay leaf
1-2 tsp. black pepper
1 tsp. salt, *optional*
½ tsp. caraway seeds,
 optional
¼ tsp. nutmeg
½ cup sour cream
1 lb. bacon, cooked and
 crumbled

1. Combine all ingredients
except sour cream and bacon.
2. Cover. Cook on Low 8-10
hours, or High 4-5 hours.
3. Remove bay leaf. Use
a slotted spoon to remove
potatoes. Mash potatoes and
mix with sour cream. Return to
slow cooker. Stir in. Add bacon
and mix together thoroughly.

Potato Soup

Jeanne Hertzog, Bethlehem, PA
Marcia S. Myer, Manheim, PA
Rhonda Lee Schmidt, Scranton, PA
Mitzi McGlynchey, Downingtown, PA
Vera Schmucker, Goshen, IN
Kaye Schnell, Falmouth, MA
Elizabeth Yoder, Millersburg, OH

Makes 8-10 servings

Prep. Time: 15 minutes
Cooking Time: 3-12 hours
Ideal slow-cooker size: 5½-qt.

6 potatoes, peeled and cubed
2 leeks, chopped
2 onions, chopped
1 rib celery, sliced
4 chicken bouillon cubes
1 Tbsp. dried parsley flakes
5 cups water
1 Tbsp. salt
pepper to taste
⅓ cup butter
13-oz. can evaporated milk

1. Combine all ingredients except milk in slow cooker.
2. Cover. Cook on Low 10-12 hours, or High 3-4 hours. Stir in milk during last hour.
3. If desired, mash potatoes before serving.

*Serving suggestion: Garnish with chopped **chives**.*

Variations:
1. Add one carrot, sliced, to vegetables before cooking.
2. Instead of water and bouillon cubes, use 4-5 cups chicken stock.

Black-Eyed Pea and Vegetable Chili

Julie Weaver, Reinholds, PA

Makes 4-6 servings

Prep. Time: 20 minutes
Cooking Time: 4-8 hours
Ideal slow-cooker size: 4-qt.

1 cup finely chopped onions
1 cup finely chopped carrots
1 cup finely chopped red, *or* green, pepper, *or* mixture of two
1 garlic clove, minced
4 tsp. chili powder
1 tsp. ground cumin
2 Tbsp. chopped cilantro
14½-oz. can diced tomatoes
3 cups cooked black-eyed beans, *or* 2 15-oz. cans black-eyed beans, drained
4-oz. can chopped green chilies
¾ cup orange juice
¾ cup water, *or* broth
1 Tbsp. cornstarch
2 Tbsp. water

1. Combine all ingredients except cornstarch, 2 Tbsp. water, cheese, and cilantro.
2. Cover. Cook on Low 6-8 hours, or High 4 hours.
3. Dissolve cornstarch in water. Stir into soup mixture 30 minutes before serving.

Serving suggestion: Garnish individual servings with shredded **cheddar cheese** *and* chopped **cilantro**.

Veggie Chili

Wanda Roth, Napoleon, OH

Makes 6 servings

Prep. Time: 15 minutes
Cooking Time: 3-8 hours
Ideal slow-cooker size: 5-qt.

2 qts. whole, *or* diced, tomatoes, undrained
6-oz. can tomato paste
½ cup chopped onions
½ cup chopped celery
½ cup chopped green peppers
2 garlic cloves, minced
1 tsp. salt
1½ tsp. ground cumin
1 tsp. dried oregano
¼ tsp. cayenne pepper
3 Tbsp. brown sugar
15-oz. can garbanzo beans

1. Combine all ingredients except beans in slow cooker.
2. Cook on Low 6-8 hours, or High 3-4 hours. Add beans one hour before serving.

Variation:
If you prefer a less tomatoey taste, substitute 2 vegetable bouillon cubes and 1 cup water for tomato paste.

Beans and Tomato Chili

Becky Harder, Monument, CO

Makes 6-8 servings

Prep. Time: 5 minutes
Cooking Time: 4-8 hours
Ideal slow-cooker size: 4½-qt.

15-oz. can black beans, undrained
15-oz. can pinto beans, undrained
16-oz. can kidney beans, undrained
15-oz. can garbanzo beans, undrained
2 14½-oz. cans stewed tomatoes and juice
1 pkg. prepared chili seasoning

1. Pour beans, including their liquid, into slow cooker.
2. Stir in tomatoes and chili seasoning.
3. Cover. Cook on Low 4-8 hours.

*Serving suggestion: Serve with **crackers**, and top with grated **cheddar cheese**, sliced **green onions**, and **sour cream**, if desired.*

Variation:
Add additional cans of white beans or 1 tsp. dried onion.

Vegetarian Soups

Vegetarian Chili

Connie Johnson, Loudon, NH

Makes 6 servings

Prep. Time: 15 minutes
Cooking Time: 6-8 hours
Ideal slow-cooker size: 5-qt.

3 garlic cloves, minced
2 onions, chopped
1 cup textured vegetable protein (TVP)
1-lb. can beans of your choice, drained
1 green bell pepper, chopped
1 jalapeno pepper, seeds removed, chopped
28-oz. can diced Italian tomatoes
1 bay leaf
1 Tbsp. dried oregano
½-1 tsp. salt
¼ tsp. pepper

1. Combine all ingredients in slow cooker.
2. Cover. Cook on Low 6-8 hours.

Black Bean Soup

Colleen Heatwole, Burton, MI

Makes 8 servings

Prep Time: 20-30 minutes
Cooking Time: 4½-9 hours
Ideal slow-cooker size: 5- to 6-qt.

3 medium carrots, halved and sliced thin
2 celery ribs, diced fine
1 medium onion, chopped fine
4 cloves garlic, minced
2 14½-oz. cans vegetable broth
2 15-oz. can black beans, undrained
15½-oz. can red kidney beans, undrained
2 15-oz. cans crushed tomatoes, *or* 1 quart canned tomatoes
1½ tsp. dried basil
½ tsp. dried oregano
½ tsp. cumin
1 tsp. chili powder
½ tsp. salt

1. Combine all ingredients in slow cooker.
2. Cover. Cook on Low 4½-9 hours, or until vegetables are done to your liking.

Variations:
1. This is good with a garnish of sour cream and/or grated cheddar cheese on each individual serving.
2. This works well as a topping over cooked rice.

Be sure vegetables are thinly sliced or chopped because they cook slowly in a slow cooker. *Marilyn Yoder, Archbold, OH*

Lotsa Beans Vegetarian Chili

Joleen Albrecht, Gladstone, MI

Makes 8 servings

Prep. Time: 10-15 minutes
Cooking Time: 2-4 hours
Ideal slow-cooker size: 5-qt.

15½-oz. can kidney beans,
  rinsed and drained
15½-oz. can garbanzo beans,
  rinsed and drained
16-oz. can vegetarian baked
  beans
19-oz. can black bean soup
15-oz. can whole-kernel
  corn, drained
14½-oz. can chopped
  tomatoes
1 green bell pepper, chopped
1 onion, chopped
2 ribs celery, chopped
2 cloves garlic, chopped
1 Tbsp. chili powder
1 Tbsp. dried oregano
1 Tbsp. dried parsley
1 Tbsp. dried basil
1½ tsp. Tabasco, *optional*

1. Combine all beans, soup,
and all vegetables in slow
cooker.
  2. Stir in all seasonings.
  3. Cover. Cook on High 2-3
hours, or on Low 4 hours.

*Serving suggestion: If you
wish, garnish individual servings
of chili with **sour cream**,
shredded **cheddar cheese**,
and **tortilla chips**.*

Hearty Black Bean Soup

Della Yoder, Kalona, IA

Makes 6-8 servings

Prep. Time: 15 minutes
Cooking Time: 9-10 hours
Ideal slow-cooker size: 4-qt.

3 medium carrots, halved
  and thinly sliced
2 celery ribs, thinly sliced
1 medium onion, chopped
4 cloves garlic, minced
20-oz. can black beans,
  drained and rinsed
2 14½-oz. cans vegetable
  broth
15-oz. can crushed
  tomatoes
1½ tsp. dried basil
½ tsp. dried oregano
½ tsp. ground cumin
½ tsp. chili powder
½ tsp. hot pepper sauce

1. Combine all ingredients
in slow cooker.
  2. Cover. Cook on Low 9-10
hours.

*Serving suggestion: This may
be served over cooked **rice**.*

Variation:
  If you prefer a thicker soup,
use only 1 can broth.

Black Bean and Corn Soup

Joy Sutter, Iowa City, IA

Makes 6-8 servings

Prep. Time: 10 minutes
Cooking Time: 5-6 hours
Ideal slow-cooker size: 4-qt.

2 15-oz. cans black beans,
  drained and rinsed
14½-oz. can Mexican
  stewed tomatoes,
  undrained
14½-oz. can diced
  tomatoes, undrained
11-oz. can whole-kernel
  corn, drained
4 green onions, sliced
2-3 Tbsp. chili powder
1 tsp. ground cumin
½ tsp. dried, minced garlic

1. Combine all ingredients
in slow cooker.
  2. Cover. Cook on High 5-6
hours.

Variations:
  1. Use 2 cloves fresh garlic,
minced, instead of dried garlic.
  2. Add 1 large rib celery,
sliced thinly, and 1 small
green pepper, chopped.

Tuscan Garlicky Bean Soup

Sara Harter Fredette, Williamsburg, MA

Makes 8-10 servings

Prep. Time: 10 minutes
Soaking Time: 1 hour
Cooking Time: 8-10 hours
Ideal slow-cooker size: 4-qt.

1 lb. dry Great Northern, *or* other dry white, beans
1 qt. water
1 qt. vegetable broth
2 garlic cloves, minced
4 Tbsp. chopped parsley
olive oil
2 tsp. salt
½ tsp. pepper

1. Place beans in large soup pot. Cover with water and bring to boil. Cook 2 minutes. Remove from heat. Cover pot and allow to stand for 1 hour. Drain, discarding water.

2. Combine beans, 1 quart fresh water, and broth in slow cooker.

3. Sauté garlic and parsley in olive oil in skillet. Stir into slow cooker. Add salt and pepper.

4. Cover. Cook on Low 8-10 hours, or until beans are tender.

Bean Soup

Joyce Cox, Port Angeles, WA

Makes 10-12 servings

Prep. Time: 10 minutes
Cooking Time: 5½-13 hours
Ideal slow-cooker size: 4-qt.

1 cup dry Great Northern beans
1 cup dry red beans, *or* pinto beans
4 cups water
28-oz. can diced tomatoes
1 medium onion, chopped
2 Tbsp. vegetable bouillon granules, *or* 4 bouillon cubes
2 garlic cloves, minced
2 tsp. Italian seasoning, crushed
9-oz. pkg. frozen green beans, thawed

1. Soak and rinse dried beans.

2. Combine all ingredients except green beans in slow cooker.

3. Cover. Cook on High 5½-6½ hours, or on Low 11-13 hours.

4. Stir green beans into soup during last 2 hours.

Veggie Stew

Ernestine Schrepfer, Trenton, MO

Makes 10-15 servings

Prep. Time: 15 minutes
Cooking Time: 9-11 hours
Ideal slow-cooker size: 8-qt.

5-6 potatoes, cubed
3 carrots, cubed
1 onion, chopped
½ cup chopped celery
2 cups canned diced, *or* stewed, tomatoes
3 vegetable bouillon cubes dissolved in 3 cups water
1½ tsp. dried thyme
½ tsp. dried parsley
½ cup brown rice, uncooked
1 lb. frozen green beans
1 lb. frozen corn
15-oz. can butter beans
46-oz. can V8 juice

1. Combine potatoes, carrots, onion, celery, tomatoes, broth, thyme, parsley, and rice in 8-quart cooker, or two medium-sized cookers.

2. Cover. Cook on High 2 hours. Purée one cup of mixture and add back to slow cooker to thicken the soup.

3. Stir in beans, corn, butter beans, and juice.

4. Cover. Cook on High 1 more hour, then reduce to Low and cook 6-8 more hours.

Don't have enough time? A lot of dishes can be made in less time by increasing the temperature to High and cooking the dish for about half the time as is necessary on Low.

Jenny R. Unternahrer, Wayland, IA

Southwestern Soup

Evelyn L. Ward, Greeley, CO

Makes 4 servings

Prep. Time: 10-20 minutes
Cooking Time: 6-8 hours
Ideal slow-cooker size: 4-qt.

Soup:
2 14-oz. cans vegetable broth
½ cup sliced carrots
½ cup diced onions
1 cup diced potatoes
1 garlic clove, minced
8-oz. can, *or* 1 cup home-
    canned, crushed tomatoes
1 Tbsp. Worcestershire sauce
salsa to taste

Garnishes:
grated cheese
diced avocados
diced green peppers
diced cucumbers
2¼-oz. can sliced ripe olives
6-oz. fresh mushrooms,
    sliced and sautéed in
    butter
6-oz. can cooked and peeled
    tiny shrimp
1 cup green onion, sliced
3 hard-cooked eggs,
    chopped
1 cup diced tomatoes
sour cream

1. Combine broth, carrots, onions, potatoes, garlic, tomatoes, and Worcestershire sauce in slow cooker. Cook on Low 6-8 hours.

2. Before serving, stir in salsa, sampling as you go to get the right balance of flavors.

*Serving suggestion: Serve the soup in bowls, allowing guests to add **garnishes** of their choice.*

Heart Happy Tomato Soup

Anne Townsend, Albuquerque, NM

Makes 6 servings

Prep. Time: 10 minutes
Cooking Time: 5-8 hours
Ideal slow-cooker size: 3½-qt.

46-oz. can tomato juice
8-oz. can tomato sauce
½ cup water
1 Tbsp. bouillon granules
1 sprig celery leaves, chopped
half an onion, thinly sliced
½ tsp. dried basil
2 Tbsp. sugar
1 bay leaf
½ tsp. whole cloves

1. Combine all ingredients in greased slow cooker. Stir well.
2. Cover. Cook on Low 5-8 hours. Remove bay leaf and cloves before serving.

Note:
If you prefer a thicker soup, add ¼ cup instant potato flakes. Stir well and cook 5 minutes longer.

Vegetarian Minestrone Soup

Connie Johnson, Loudon, NH

Makes 6 servings

Prep. Time: 15 minutes
Cooking Time: 6-8 hours
Ideal slow-cooker size: 4-qt.

6 cups vegetable broth
2 carrots, chopped
2 large onions, chopped
3 ribs celery, chopped
2 garlic cloves, minced
1 small zucchini, cubed
1 handful fresh kale,
    chopped
½ cup dry barley
1 can chickpeas, *or* white
    kidney beans, drained
1 Tbsp. parsley
½ tsp. dried thyme
1 tsp. dried oregano
28-oz. can crushed Italian
    tomatoes
1 tsp. salt
¼ tsp. pepper

1. Combine all ingredients in slow cooker.
2. Cover. Cook on Low 6-8 hours, or until vegetables are tender.

*Serving suggestion: Sprinkle individual servings with grated **cheese**.*

Joyce's Minestrone

Joyce Shackelford, Green Bay, WI

Makes 6 servings

Prep. Time: 15 minutes
Cooking Time: 4-16 hours
Ideal slow-cooker size: 4- to 5-qt.

3½ cups vegetable broth
28-oz. can crushed tomatoes
2 medium carrots, thinly sliced
½ cup chopped onion
½ cup chopped celery
2 medium potatoes, thinly sliced
1-2 garlic cloves, minced
16-oz. can red kidney beans, drained
2 oz. thin spaghetti, broken into 2-inch pieces
2 Tbsp. parsley flakes
2-3 tsp. dried basil
1-2 tsp. dried oregano
1 bay leaf

1. Combine all ingredients in slow cooker.
2. Cover. Cook on High 4-6 hours, or on Low 10-16 hours.
3. Remove bay leaf. Serve.

Vegetarian Minestrone Soup with Pasta

Joleen Albrecht, Gladstone, MI

Makes 10 servings

Prep Time: 20 minutes
Cooking Time: 6-8 hours
Ideal slow-cooker size: 5-qt.

15½-oz. can kidney beans, rinsed and drained
15½-oz. can garbanzo beans, rinsed and drained
4 medium tomatoes, chopped
2 medium carrots, chopped
1 medium zucchini, halved and chopped
1½ cups shredded cabbage
2 ribs celery, chopped
6 cups vegetable broth
1¼ tsp. Italian seasoning
1 tsp. salt
¼ tsp. pepper
2 cups cooked elbow macaroni

1. Combine beans, vegetables, broth, and seasonings in slow cooker.
2. Cover. Cook on Low 6-8 hours, or until vegetables are done to your liking.
3. Stir in cooked macaroni and heat through.

*Serving suggestion: Serve, topping each individual bowl with ½ Tbsp. grated **Parmesan** cheese.*

Grace's Minestrone Soup

Grace Ketcham,
Marietta, GA

Makes 8 servings

Prep. Time: 15 minutes
Cooking Time: 8 hours
Ideal slow-cooker size: 4- to 5-qt.

¾ cup dry elbow macaroni
2 qts. vegetable broth
2 large onions, diced
2 carrots, sliced
half a head of cabbage, shredded
½ cup celery, diced
1-lb. can tomatoes
½ tsp. salt
½ tsp. dried oregano
1 Tbsp. minced parsley
¼ cup each frozen corn, peas, and lima beans
¼ tsp. pepper

1. Cook macaroni according to package directions. Set aside.
2. Combine all ingredients except macaroni in large slow cooker.
3. Cover. Cook on Low 8 hours. Add macaroni during last 30 minutes of cooking time.

*Serving suggestion: Garnish individual servings with grated **Parmesan** or **Romano** cheese.*

Salsa Soup

Sue Hamilton, Minooka, IL

Makes 6 servings

Prep. Time: 5 minutes
Cooking Time: 4-6 hours
Ideal slow-cooker size: 4-qt.

3 cups (26 oz.) corn-black
   bean mild salsa
6 cups vegetable broth
¼ cup white long-grain rice,
   uncooked

1. Combine all ingredients
in slow cooker.
2. Cover. Cook on Low 4-6
hours, or until rice is tender.

Winter Squash and White Bean Stew

Mary E. Herr, Three Rivers, MI

Makes 6 servings

Prep. Time: 15 minutes
Cooking Time: 3-4 hours
Ideal slow-cooker size: 4-qt.

1 cup chopped onions
1 Tbsp. olive oil
½ tsp. ground cumin
¼ tsp. salt
¼ tsp. cinnamon
1 garlic clove, minced
3 cups peeled, butternut
   squash, cut into ¾-inch
   cubes

1½ cups vegetable broth
19-oz. can cannellini beans,
   drained
14½-oz. can diced
   tomatoes, undrained
1 Tbsp. chopped fresh cilantro

1. Combine all ingredients
in slow cooker.
2. Cover. Cook on High
1 hour. Reduce heat to Low
and heat 2-3 hours.

Variations:
1. Beans can be puréed in
blender and added during the
last hour.
2. Eight ounces dried beans
can be soaked overnight,
cooked until soft, and used in
place of canned beans.

Black Bean and Butternut Chili

Colleen Heatwole, Burton, MI

Makes 10 servings

Prep Time: 20 minutes
Cooking Time: 4-5 hours
Ideal slow-cooker size: 5-qt.

1 medium onion, chopped
1 medium red bell pepper,
   chopped
3 cloves garlic, minced
2 Tbsp. olive oil
3 cups vegetable broth
2 15-oz. can black beans,
   rinsed and drained
5 cups butternut, *or*

buttercup, squash, peeled
   and cubed
14½-oz. can crushed
   tomatoes
2 tsp. dried parsley flakes
1½ tsp. dried oregano
1½ tsp. cumin
1 tsp. chili powder
½ tsp. salt

1. In large skillet, sauté
onion, red pepper, and garlic
in olive oil until tender.
2. Combine sautéed ingredients with all other ingredients
in slow cooker.
3. Cover. Cook on Low 4-5
hours, or until vegetables are
done to your liking.

Lentil and Squash Soup

Colleen Heatwole, Burton, MI

Makes 6 servings

Prep Time: 10-20 minutes
Cooking Time: 4 hours
Ideal slow-cooker size: 5-qt.

1 cup onion, chopped
2 cloves garlic, minced
1 Tbsp. olive oil
4 cups vegetable broth
3 cups (about 1¼ lbs.)
   butternut, *or* buttercup,
   squash, peeled and cubed
1 cup carrots, chopped
1 cup dried lentils, rinsed
1 tsp. dried oregano
½ tsp. salt

1 tsp. dried basil
2 4½-oz. cans diced
   tomatoes

1. Sauté onion and garlic in olive oil in skillet.
2. Combine sautéed ingredients with all other ingredients in slow cooker.
3. Cover. Cook on Low 4 hours, or until lentils and vegetables are tender.

Cheese and Corn Chowder

Loretta Krahn, Mt. Lake, MN

Makes 8 servings

Prep. Time: 10 minutes
Cooking Time: 5-7 hours
Ideal slow-cooker size: 4-qt.

¾ cup water
½ cup chopped onions
1½ cups sliced carrots
1½ cups chopped celery
1 tsp. salt
½ tsp. pepper
15¼-oz. can whole kernel
   corn, drained
15-oz. can cream-style corn
3 cups milk
1½ cup grated cheddar
   cheese

1. Combine water, onions, carrots, celery, salt, and pepper in slow cooker.
2. Cover. Cook on High 4-6 hours.

3. Add corn, milk, and cheese. Heat on High 1 hour, and then turn to Low until you are ready to eat.

Corn Chowder

Charlotte Fry, St. Charles, MO
Jeanette Oberholtzer, Manheim, PA

Makes 4 servings

Prep. Time: 15 minutes
Cooking Time: 6-7 hours
Ideal slow-cooker size: 3½- to 4-qt.

2 Tbsp. oil
½ cup chopped onions
2 cups diced, peeled
   potatoes
2 10-oz. pkgs. frozen corn
16-oz. can cream-style corn
1 Tbsp. sugar
1 tsp. Worcestershire sauce
1 tsp. seasoned salt
¼ tsp. pepper
1 cup water

1. Place oil in skillet.
2. Add onions and potatoes to skillet and sauté for 5 minutes. Drain.
3. Combine all ingredients in slow cooker. Mix well.
4. Cover. Cook on Low 6-7 hours.

Variations:
1. To make Clam Corn Chowder, drain and add 2 cans minced clams during last hour of cooking.

2. Substitute 1 quart home-frozen corn for the store-bought frozen and canned corn.

Cream of Broccoli Soup

Barb Yoder, Angola, IN

Makes 6-8 servings

Prep. Time: 10-15 minutes
Cooking Time: 3-4 hours
Ideal slow-cooker size: 4-qt.

1 small onion, chopped
oil
20-oz. pkg. frozen broccoli
2 10¾-oz. cans cream of
   celery soup
10¾-oz. can cream of
   mushroom soup
1 cup grated American
   cheese
2 soup cans milk

1. Sauté onion in oil in skillet until soft.
2. Combine all ingredients in slow cooker.
3. Cover. Cook on Low 3-4 hours.

Broccoli-Cheese Soup

Darla Sathre, Baxter, MN

Makes 8 servings

Prep. Time: 10 minutes
Cooking Time: 8-10 hours
Ideal slow-cooker size: 4-qt.

2 16-oz. pkgs. frozen chopped broccoli
2 10¾-oz. cans cheddar cheese soup
2 12-oz. cans evaporated milk
¼ cup finely chopped onions
½ tsp. seasoned salt
¼ tsp. pepper
sunflower seeds, *optional*
crumbled bacon, *optional*

1. Combine all ingredients except sunflower seeds and bacon in slow cooker.
2. Cover. Cook on Low 8-10 hours.
3. Garnish with sunflower seeds and bacon, if you wish.

Broccoli-Cheese with Noodles Soup

Carol Sherwood, Batavia, NY

Makes 8 servings

Prep. Time: 15 minutes
Cooking Time: 4 hours
Ideal slow-cooker size: 4-qt.

2 cups cooked noodles
10-oz. pkg. frozen chopped broccoli, thawed
3 Tbsp. chopped onions
2 Tbsp. butter
1 Tbsp. flour
2 cups cubed, processed cheese
½ tsp. salt
5½ cups milk

1. Cook noodles just until soft in saucepan while combining rest of ingredients in slow cooker. Mix well.
2. Drain cooked noodles and stir into slow cooker.
3. Cover. Cook on Low 4 hours.

Double Cheese Cauliflower Soup

Zona Mae Bontrager, Kokomo, IN

Makes 6 servings

Prep. Time: 15 minutes
Cooking Time: 2-3 hours
Ideal slow-cooker size: 3½- to 4-qt.

4 cups (1 small head) cauliflower pieces
2 cups water
8-oz. pkg. cream cheese, cubed
5 oz. American cheese spread
½ cup potato flakes, *or* buds

1. Combine cauliflower and water in saucepan. Bring to boil. Set aside.
2. Heat slow cooker on Low. Add cream cheese and cheese spread. Pour in cauliflower and water. Stir to be sure the cheese is dissolved and mixed through the cauliflower.
3. Add potato flakes. Mix well.
4. Cover. Cook on Low 2-3 hours.

In place of ground meat in a recipe, use vegetarian burgers. Cut them up, and you won't need to brown the meat.
Sue Hamilton, Minooka, IL

Main Dishes

Beef Stew

Wanda S. Curtin, Bradenton, FL
Paula King, Harrisonburg, VA
Miriam Nolt, New Holland, PA
Jean Shaner, York, PA
Mary W. Stauffer, Ephrata, PA
Alma Z. Weaver, Ephrata, PA
Audrey Kneer, Willamsfield, IL

Makes 6 servings

Prep Time: 15 minutes
Cooking Time: 3-10 hours
Ideal slow-cooker size: 4½-qt.

2 lbs. beef chuck, cubed
¼-½ cup flour
1½ tsp. salt
½ tsp. black pepper
1 tsp. paprika
3½ Tbsp. quick-cooking
  raw tapioca
1 tsp. Worcestershire sauce
2 cups beef broth
half garlic clove, minced
1 bay leaf
4 carrots, sliced, *or* 1-lb. bag

whole baby carrots
2 onions, chopped
1 rib celery, sliced
3 potatoes, diced
2 cups tomatoes, diced

1. Place meat in slow cooker.
2. Combine flour, salt, pepper, paprika, and tapioca in small bowl. Stir into meat until coated thoroughly.
3. Gently stir in remaining ingredients. Mix well.
4. Cover. Cook on Low 8-10 hours, or on High 3-4 hours.
5. Stir before serving.

Herbed Beef Stew

Carol Findling, Princeton, IL

Makes 6-8 servings

Prep. Time: 15 minutes
Cooking Time: 4-12 hours
Ideal slow-cooker size: 4-qt.

1-lb. beef round roast, cubed
4 Tbsp. seasoned flour*
1½ cups beef broth
1 tsp. Worcestershire sauce
1 garlic clove
1 bay leaf
4 carrots, sliced
3 potatoes, cubed
2 onions, diced
1 rounded tsp. fresh thyme,
  or ½ tsp. dried thyme
1 rounded tsp. chopped fresh
  basil, *or* ½ tsp. dried basil
1 Tbsp. fresh parsley, *or*
  1 tsp. dried parsley
1 rounded tsp. fresh marjoram,
  or 1 tsp. dried marjoram

1. Put meat in slow cooker. Add seasoned flour. Toss with meat. Stir in remaining ingredients. Mix well.
2. Cover. Cook on High 4-6 hours, or Low 10-12 hours.

* Seasoned Flour
  1 cup flour
  1 tsp. salt
  1 tsp. paprika
  ¼ tsp. pepper

Beef Stew Olé

Andrea O'Neil, Fairfield, CT

Makes 6-8 servings

Prep. Time: 15 minutes
Cooking Time: 7-8 hours
Ideal slow-cooker size: 4-qt.

4 carrots, cubed
4 potatoes, peeled and cubed
1 onion, quartered
1½ lbs. beef stewing meat, cubed
8-oz. can tomato sauce
1 pkg. dry taco seasoning mix
2 cups water, *divided*
1½ Tbsp. cornstarch
2 tsp. salt
¼ tsp. pepper

1. Layer first four ingredients in slow cooker. Add tomato sauce.
2. Combine taco seasoning with 1½ cups water. Stir cornstarch into remaining ½ cup water until smooth. Stir into rest of water with taco seasoning. Pour over ingredients in slow cooker.
3. Sprinkle with salt and pepper.
4. Cover. Cook on Low 7-8 hours.

Serving suggestion: Serve over rice.

Variation:

If those eating at your table are cautious about spicy food, choose a mild taco seasoning mix and add 1 tsp. sugar to the seasonings.

Sturdy Pot Roast

Carole Whaling, New Tripoli, PA

Makes 8 servings

Prep. Time: 15 minutes
Cooking Time: 10-12 hours
Ideal slow-cooker size: 5- to 6-qt.

4 medium potatoes, cubed
4 carrots, sliced
1 onion, sliced
3-4-lb. rump roast, *or* pot roast, cut into serving-size pieces
1 tsp. salt
½ tsp. pepper
1 bouillon cube
½ cup boiling water

1. Put vegetables and meat in slow cooker. Stir in salt and pepper.
2. Dissolve bouillon cube in water, then pour over other ingredients.
3. Cover. Cook on Low 10-12 hours.

Tangy Swiss Steak

Marilyn Mowry, Irving, TX

Makes 4-6 servings

Prep. Time: 20 minutes
Cooking Time: 3-10 hours
Ideal slow-cooker size: 3½- to 4-qt.

3-4 Tbsp. flour
½ tsp. salt
¼ tsp. pepper
1½ tsp. dry mustard
1½-2 lbs. round steak
oil
1 cup sliced onions
1 lb. carrots
14½-oz. can whole tomatoes
1 Tbsp. brown sugar
1½ Tbsp. Worcestershire sauce

1. Combine flour, salt, pepper, and dry mustard.
2. Cut steak into serving pieces. Dredge in flour mixture. Brown on both sides in oil in saucepan. Place in slow cooker.
3. Add onions and carrots.
4. Combine tomatoes, brown sugar, and Worcestershire sauce. Pour into slow cooker.
5. Cover. Cook on Low 8-10 hours, or High 3-5 hours.

Round Steak Casserole

Gladys High, Ephrata, PA

Makes 6 servings

Prep. Time: 15 minutes
Cooking Time: 4-10 hours
Ideal slow-cooker size: 4½- to 5-qt.

2 lbs. round steak, cut ½-inch thick
1 tsp. salt
¼ tsp. pepper
1 onion, thinly sliced
3-4 potatoes, pared and quartered

16-oz. can French-style
  green beans, drained
1 clove garlic, minced
10¾-oz. can tomato soup
14½-oz. can tomatoes

1. Season roast with salt and pepper. Cut into serving pieces and place in slow cooker.
2. Add onion, potatoes, green beans, and garlic. Top with soup and tomatoes.
3. Cover and cook on Low 8-10 hours, or High 4-5 hours. Remove cover during last half hour if too much liquid has collected.

Hearty Slow-Cooker Stew

Trudy Kutter, Corfu, NY

Makes 6-8 servings

Prep. Time: 15 minutes
Cooking Time: 8-10 hours
Ideal slow-cooker size: 6½-qt.

2 lbs. boneless beef, cubed
4-6 celery ribs, sliced
6-8 carrots, sliced
6 potatoes, cubed
2 onions, sliced
28-oz. can tomatoes
¼ cup minute tapioca
1 tsp. salt
¼ tsp. pepper
½ tsp. dried basil, *or* oregano
1 garlic clove, pressed, *or* minced

1. Combine all ingredients in slow cooker.
2. Cover. Cook on Low 8-10 hours.

Variation:
Add 2 10½-oz. cans beef gravy and ½ cup water in place of the tomatoes. Reduce tapioca to 2 Tbsp.

Tuscan Beef Stew

Karen Ceneviva, Seymour, CT

Makes 8 servings

Prep Time: 5-10 minutes
Cooking Time: 4-9 hours
Ideal slow-cooker size: 3½-qt.

10½-oz. can tomato soup
10½-oz. can beef broth
½ cup water
1 tsp. dry Italian seasoning
½ tsp. garlic powder
14½-oz. can Italian diced
  tomatoes
3 large carrots (¾ lb.), cut
  into 1-inch pieces
2 lbs. stewing beef, cut into
  1-inch cubes
2 15½-oz. cans white kidney
  (cannellini) beans, rinsed
  and drained

1. Mix all ingredients, except beans, in slow-cooker.
2. Cover. Cook on High 4-5 hours, or on Low 8-9 hours, or until vegetables and beef are tender.

3. Stir in beans. Cover. Cook on High for final 10 minutes of cooking time.

Judy's Beef Stew

Judy Koczo, Plano, IL
L. Jean Moore, Pendleton, IN
Judy Wantland, Menominee Falls, WI

Makes 4-6 servings

Prep Time: 10 minutes
Cooking Time: 5-12 hours
Ideal slow-cooker size: 5-qt.

2 lbs. stewing meat, cubed
5 carrots, sliced
1 onion, diced
3 ribs celery, diced
5 potatoes, cubed
28-oz. can stewed tomatoes
⅓-½ cup quick-cooking raw
  tapioca
2 tsp. salt
½ tsp. black pepper

1. Combine all ingredients in slow cooker.
2. Cover. Cook on Low 10-12 hours or on High 5-6 hours.

Variations:
1. Add 1 whole clove and 2 bay leaves to stew before cooking.
L. Jean Moore, Pendleton, IN

2. Add 1 cup frozen peas 1 hour before end of cooking time.
Judy Wantland, Menomonee Falls, WI

Herby Beef Stew

Tracy Supcoe, Barclay, MD

Makes 6 servings

Prep. Time: 20 minutes
Cooking Time: 5-12 hours
Ideal slow-cooker size: 5½-qt.

⅔ cup flour
1½ tsp. salt
¼ tsp. pepper
1-2 lbs. stewing meat, cubed
oil
14½-oz. can diced tomatoes
8-oz. can tomato sauce
14½-oz. can beef broth
2 Tbsp. Worcestershire
  sauce
1 bay leaf
2 tsp. Kitchen Bouquet
2 Tbsp. dried parsley
1 tsp. Hungarian sweet
  paprika
4 celery heart ribs, chopped
5 mushrooms, sliced
3 potatoes, cubed
3 cloves garlic, minced
1 large onion, chopped

1. Combine flour, salt, and pepper in bowl. Dredge meat in seasoned flour, then brown in oil in saucepan. Place meat in slow cooker.

2. Combine remaining ingredients in bowl. Pour over meat and mix well.

3. Cover. Cook on High 5-6 hours, or Low 10-12 hours. Stir before serving.

Venison or Beef Stew

Frances B. Musser, Newmanstown, PA

Makes 6 servings

Prep. Time: 15 minutes
Cooking Time: 8-9 hours
Ideal slow-cooker size: 4-qt.

1½ lbs. venison, *or* beef, cubes
2 Tbsp. oil
1 medium onion, chopped
4 carrots, peeled and cut
  into 1-inch pieces
1 rib celery, cut into 1-inch
  pieces
4 medium potatoes, peeled
  and quartered
12-oz. can whole tomatoes,
  undrained
10½-oz. can beef broth
1 Tbsp. Worcestershire sauce
1 Tbsp. parsley flakes
1 bay leaf
2½ tsp. salt
¼ tsp. pepper
2 Tbsp. quick-cooking tapioca

1. Brown meat cubes in skillet in oil over medium heat. Transfer to slow cooker.

2. Add remaining ingredients. Mix well.

3. Cover. Cook on Low 8-9 hours.

Variations:

1. Substitute 1½ tsp. garlic salt and 1 tsp. salt for 2½ tsp. salt.

2. For added color and flavor, add 1 cup frozen peas 5 minutes before end of cooking time.

Layered Herby Stew

Elizabeth L. Richards, Rapid City, SD

Makes 8 servings

Prep. Time: 15 minutes
Cooking Time: 6 hours
Ideal slow-cooker size: 4½-qt.

2½ lbs. lean beef chuck,
  cubed
1 medium to large onion,
  cut in 1-inch pieces
8-12 small red potatoes, *or*
  potato chunks
4-6 carrots, cut in 1-inch
  pieces
2 large ribs celery, cut in
  1-inch pieces
2 Tbsp. Worcestershire
  sauce
¼ cup red wine, *or* water
3 Tbsp. brown sugar
1 tsp. salt
½ tsp. pepper
⅛ tsp. allspice
¼ tsp. dried marjoram
¼ tsp. dried thyme
2 bay leaves
6 Tbsp. minute tapioca
  (use only 5 Tbsp. if using
  water instead of red wine)
28-oz. can diced tomatoes

1. Layer all ingredients in slow cooker in order given.

2. Cover. Cook on High 6 hours.

*Serving suggestion: Garnish with **parsley** immediately before serving.*

Waldorf Astoria Stew

Mary V. Warye, West Liberty, OH

Makes 6-8 servings

Prep. Time: 10 minutes
Cooking Time: 7-9 hours
Ideal slow-cooker size: 6-qt.

3 lbs. beef stewing meat, cubed
1 medium onion, chopped
1 cup celery, sliced
2 cups carrots, sliced
4 medium potatoes, cubed
1 Tbsp. sugar
1 Tbsp. salt
½ tsp. pepper
3 Tbsp. minute tapioca
10¾-oz. can tomato soup
⅓ cup water

1. Layer meat, onion, celery, carrots, and potatoes in slow cooker. Sprinkle with seasonings and tapioca. Add soup and water.
2. Cover. Cook on Low 7-9 hours.

Pungent Beef Stew

Grace Ketcham, Marietta, GA

Makes 4-6 servings

Prep. Time: 15 minutes
Cooking Time: 10-12 hours
Ideal slow-cooker size: 4½-qt.

2 lbs. beef chuck, cubed

1 tsp. Worcestershire sauce
1 garlic clove, minced
1 medium onion, chopped
2 bay leaves
½ tsp. salt
½ tsp. paprika
¼ tsp. pepper
dash of ground cloves, *or* allspice
6 carrots, quartered
4 potatoes, quartered
2 ribs celery, chopped
10¾-oz. can tomato soup
½ cup water

1. Combine all ingredients in slow cooker.
2. Cover. Cook on Low 10-12 hours.

Donna's Beef Stew

Donna Treloar, Gaston, IN

Makes 6 servings

Prep. Time: 15 minutes
Cooking Time: 8-10 hours
Ideal slow-cooker size: 6-qt.

2 lbs. beef, cubed
4-5 potatoes, cubed
4-5 carrots, sliced
3 ribs celery, sliced
2 onions, chopped
1 Tbsp. sugar
2 tsp. salt
¼-½ tsp. pepper
2 Tbsp. instant tapioca
3 cups V8, *or* tomato, juice

1. Place meat and vegetables in slow cooker. Sprinkle

with sugar, salt, pepper, and tapioca. Toss lightly. Pour juice over top.
2. Cover. Cook on Low 8-10 hours.

Variation:
Add 10-oz. pkg. frozen succotash or green beans.

Venison Swiss Steak

Dede Peterson, Rapid City, SD

Makes 6 servings

Prep. Time: 15 minutes
Cooking Time: 7½-8½ hours
Ideal slow-cooker size: 3½-qt.

flour
2 tsp. salt
½ tsp. pepper
2 lbs. round venison steak
oil
2 onions, sliced
2 ribs celery, diced
1 cup carrots, diced
2 cups fresh, *or* stewed, tomatoes
1 Tbsp. Worcestershire sauce

1. Combine flour, salt, and pepper. Dredge steak in flour mixture. Brown in oil in skillet. Place in slow cooker.
2. Add remaining ingredients.
3. Cover. Cook on Low 7½-8½ hours.

Venison Steak

Eleanor Glick, Bird-In-Hand, PA

Makes 4-6 servings

Prep Time: 15-20 minutes
Cooking Time: 5 hours
Ideal slow-cooker size: 2-qt.

1 Tbsp. olive oil
1-lb. tenderloin steak, cubed
1 large onion, chopped
½ tsp. garlic salt
½ tsp. garlic powder
1 large bell pepper, diced
1 tsp. soy sauce
1 Tbsp. brown sugar
1 Tbsp. chili powder
1 cup V8, *or* home-canned tomato, juice

1. In a skillet, brown steak and onion in oil with garlic salt and powder.
2. Add chopped pepper, soy sauce, brown sugar, and chili powder to slow cooker.
3. Transfer steak and onion to slow-cooker.
4. Pour juice over top.
5. Cover. Cook 5 hours on Low.

Tip:
Cube meat while it's partially frozen and you'll find it's easier to cut.

Swiss Steak

Wanda S. Curtin, Bradenton, FL
Jeanne Hertzog, Bethlehem, PA

Makes 6 servings

Prep. Time: 15 minutes
Cooking Time: 3-10 hours
Ideal slow-cooker size: 4-qt.

1½ lbs. round steak, about ¾-inch thick
2-4 tsp. flour
½-1 tsp. salt
¼ tsp. pepper
1 medium onion, sliced
1 carrot, chopped
1 rib celery, chopped
14½-oz. can diced tomatoes, *or* 15-oz. can tomato sauce

1. Cut steak into serving pieces.
2. Combine flour, salt, and pepper. Dredge meat in seasoned flour.
3. Place onions in bottom of slow cooker. Add meat. Top with carrots and celery and cover with tomatoes.
4. Cover. Cook on Low 8-10 hours, or High 3-5 hours.

Serving suggestion: Serve over **noodles** *or* **rice.**

Jacqueline's Swiss Steak

Jacqueline Stafl, East Bethany, NY

Makes 4 servings

Prep. Time: 10 minutes
Cooking Time: 8-10 hours
Ideal slow-cooker size: 4-qt.

1½ lbs. round steak
2-4 Tbsp. flour
½ lb. sliced carrots, *or* 1 lb. baby carrots
1 pkg. dry onion soup mix
8-oz. can tomato sauce
½ cup water

1. Cut steak into serving-size pieces. Dredge in flour.
2. Place carrots in bottom of slow cooker. Top with steak.
3. Combine soup mix, tomato sauce, and water. Pour over all.
4. Cover. Cook on Low 8-10 hours.

Serving suggestion: Serve over mashed **potatoes.**

A slow cooker is perfect for less tender meats such as a round steak. Because the meat is cooked in liquid for hours, it turns out tender and juicy.

Carolyn Baer, Conrath, WI
Barbara Sparks, Glen Burnie, MD

Margaret's Swiss Steak

Margaret Rich, North Newton, KS

Makes 6 servings

Prep. Time: 15 minutes
Cooking Time: 9¼ hours
Ideal slow-cooker size: 4-qt.

1 cup chopped onions
½ cup chopped celery
2-lb. ½-inch thick round
   steak
¼ cup flour
3 Tbsp. oil
1 tsp. salt
¼ tsp. pepper
16-oz. can diced tomatoes
¼ cup flour
½ cup water

1. Place onions and celery in bottom of slow cooker.
2. Cut steak in serving-size pieces. Dredge in ¼ cup flour. Brown on both sides in oil in saucepan. Place in slow cooker.
3. Sprinkle with salt and pepper. Pour tomatoes on top.
4. Cover. Cook on Low 9 hours. Remove meat from cooker and keep warm.
5. Turn heat to High. Blend together ¼ cup flour and water. Stir into sauce in slow cooker. Cover and cook 15 minutes.

Serving suggestion: Serve gravy with steak.

Nadine and Hazel's Swiss Steak

Nadine Martinitz, Salina, KS
Hazel L. Propst, Oxford, PA

Makes 6-8 servings

Prep. Time: 20 minutes
Cooking Time: 6-8 hours
Ideal slow-cooker size: 6-qt.

3-lb. round steak
⅓ cup flour
2 tsp. salt
½ tsp. pepper
3 Tbsp. shortening
1 large onion, *or more,*
   sliced
1 large pepper, *or more,*
   sliced
14½-oz. can stewed
   tomatoes, *or 3-4 fresh
   tomatoes, chopped*
water

1. Sprinkle meat with flour, salt, and pepper. Pound both sides. Cut into 6 or 8 pieces. Brown meat in shortening over medium heat on top of stove, about 15 minutes. Transfer to slow cooker.
2. Brown onion and pepper. Add tomatoes and bring to boil. Pour over steak. Add water to completely cover steak.
3. Cover. Cook on Low 6-8 hours.

Variation:

To add some flavor, stir in your favorite dried herbs when beginning to cook the steak, or add fresh herbs in the last hour of cooking.

Beef, Tomatoes, and Noodles

Janice Martins, Fairbank, IA

Makes 8 servings

Prep. Time: 10 minutes
Cooking Time: 6-8 hours
Ideal slow-cooker size: 4-qt.

1½ lbs. stewing beef, cubed
¼ cup flour
2 cups stewed tomatoes (if
   you like tomato chunks),
   *or 2 cups crushed
   tomatoes (if you prefer a
   smoother gravy)*
1 tsp. salt
¼-½ tsp. pepper
1 medium onion, chopped
water

1. Combine meat and flour until cubes are coated. Place in slow cooker.
2. Add tomatoes, salt, pepper, and onion. Add water to cover.
3. Cover. Simmer on Low 6-8 hours.

*Serving suggestion: Serve over cooked **noodles**.*

Spanish Round Steak

Shari Jensen, Fountain, CO

Makes 4-6 servings

Prep. Time: 10 minutes
Cooking Time: 8 hours
Ideal slow-cooker size: 4-qt.

1 small onion, sliced
1 green bell pepper, sliced
   in rings
1 rib celery, chopped
2 lbs. round steak
2 Tbsp. chopped fresh
   parsley, *or* 2 tsp. dried
   parsley
1 Tbsp. Worcestershire
   sauce
1 Tbsp. dry mustard
1 Tbsp. chili powder
2 cups canned tomatoes
2 tsp. dry, minced garlic
½ tsp. salt
¼ tsp. pepper

1. Put half of onion, green pepper, and celery in slow cooker.
2. Cut steak into serving-size pieces. Place steak pieces in slow cooker.
3. Put remaining onion, green pepper, and celery over steak.
4. Combine remaining ingredients. Pour over meat.
5. Cover. Cook on Low 8 hours.

*Serving suggestion: Serve over **noodles** or **rice**.*

Slow-Cooked Pepper Steak

Carolyn Baer, Conrath, WI
Ann Driscoll, Albuquerque, NM

Makes 6-8 servings

Prep. Time: 15 minutes
Cooking Time: 6¼-7¼ hours
Ideal slow-cooker size: 4-qt.

1½-2 lbs. beef round steak,
   cut in 3-inch by 1-inch
   strips
2 Tbsp. oil
¼ cup soy sauce
1 garlic clove, minced
1 cup chopped onions
1 tsp. sugar
½ tsp. salt
¼ tsp. pepper
¼ tsp. ground ginger
2 large green peppers, cut
   in strips
4 tomatoes cut into eighths,
   or 16-oz. can diced
   tomatoes
½ cup cold water
1 Tbsp. cornstarch

1. Brown beef in oil in saucepan. Transfer to slow cooker.
2. Combine soy sauce, garlic, onions, sugar, salt, pepper, and ginger. Pour over meat.
3. Cover. Cook on Low 5-6 hours.
4. Add green peppers and tomatoes. Cook 1 hour longer.
5. Combine water and cornstarch to make paste. Stir into slow cooker. Cook

on High until thickened, about 10 minutes.

*Serving suggestion: Serve over **rice** or **noodles**.*

Pepper Steak Oriental

Donna Lantgen, Rapid City, SD

Makes 6 servings

Prep. Time: 10 minutes
Cooking Time: 6-8 hours
Ideal slow-cooker size: 2½-qt.

1-lb. round steak, sliced thin
3 Tbsp. soy sauce
½ tsp. ground ginger
1 garlic clove, minced
1 green pepper, thinly sliced
4-oz. can mushrooms,
   drained, *or* 1 cup fresh
   mushrooms
1 onion, thinly sliced
½ tsp. crushed red pepper

1. Combine all ingredients in slow cooker.
2. Cover. Cook on Low 6-8 hours.

*Serving suggestion: Serve as steak sandwiches topped with **provolone cheese**, or over **rice**.*

Note:
   Round steak is easier to slice into thin strips if it is partially frozen when cut.

Powerhouse Beef Roast with Tomatoes, Onions, and Peppers

Donna Treloar, Gaston, IN

Makes 5-6 servings

Prep. Time: 15 minutes
Cooking Time: 8-10 hours
Ideal slow-cooker size: 4- to 5-qt.

3-lb. boneless chuck roast
1 garlic clove, minced
1 Tbsp. oil
2-3 onions, sliced
2-3 sweet green and red
    peppers, sliced
16-oz. jar salsa
2 14½-oz. cans Mexican-
    style stewed tomatoes

1. Brown roast and garlic in oil in skillet. Place in slow cooker.
2. Add onions and peppers.
3. Combine salsa and tomatoes and pour over ingredients in slow cooker.
4. Cover. Cook on Low 8-10 hours.
5. Slice meat to serve.

Variation:
Make Beef Burritos with the leftovers. Shred the beef and heat with remaining peppers, onions, and ½ cup of the broth. Add 1 Tbsp. chili powder, 2 tsp. cumin, and

salt to taste. Heat thoroughly. Fill warm flour tortillas with mixture and serve with sour cream, salsa, and guacamole.

Steak San Morco

Susan Tjon, Austin, TX

Makes 4-6 servings

Prep. Time: 5-10 minutes
Cooking Time: 6-10 hours
Ideal slow-cooker size: 4-qt.

2 lbs. stewing meat, cubed
1 envelope dry onion soup
    mix
29-oz. can peeled, *or*
    crushed, tomatoes
1 tsp. dried oregano
garlic powder to taste
2 Tbsp. oil
2 Tbsp. wine vinegar

1. Layer meat evenly in bottom of slow cooker.
2. Combine soup mix, tomatoes, spices, oil, and vinegar in bowl. Blend with spoon. Pour over meat.
3. Cover. Cook on High 6 hours, or Low 8-10 hours.

Pat's Meat Stew

Pat Bishop, Bedminster, PA

Makes 4-5 servings

Prep. Time: 15 minutes
Cooking Time: 4-10 hours
Ideal slow-cooker size: 4½- to 5-qt.

1-2 lbs. beef roast, cubed
2 tsp. salt
¼ tsp. pepper
2 cups water
2 carrots, sliced
2 small onions, sliced
4-6 small potatoes, cut up
    in chunks, if desired
¼ cup quick-cooking
    tapioca
1 bay leaf
10-oz. pkg. frozen peas, *or*
    mixed vegetables

1. Brown beef in saucepan. Place in slow cooker.
2. Sprinkle with salt and pepper. Add remaining ingredients except frozen vegetables. Mix well.
3. Cover. Cook on Low 8-10 hours, or on High 4-5 hours. Add vegetables during last 1-2 hours of cooking.

If I want to have a hot dish at noon time on Sunday, I bake a casserole on Saturday. Then on Sunday morning I put it into a slow cooker, turn it on High for 30 minutes before I leave, and then switch it to cook on Low while I'm at church.

Ruth Hershey, Paradise, PA

Ernestine's Beef Stew

Ernestine Schrepfer, Trenton, MO

Makes 5-6 servings

Prep. Time: 10 minutes
Cooking Time: 7-8 hours
Ideal slow-cooker size: 4-qt.

1½ lbs. stewing meat, cubed
2¼ cups tomato juice
10½-oz. can consomme
1 cup chopped celery
2 cups sliced carrots
4 Tbsp. quick-cooking tapioca
1 medium onion, chopped
¾ tsp. salt
¼ tsp. pepper

1. Combine all ingredients in slow cooker.
2. Cover. Cook on Low 7-8 hours. (Do not peek.)

Beef Stew with Vegetables

Joyce B. Suiter, Garysburg, NC

Makes 8 servings

Prep. Time: 10 minutes
Cooking Time: 8-10 hours
Ideal slow-cooker size: 5-qt.

3 lbs. stewing beef, cubed
1 cup water
1 cup red wine
1.2-oz. envelope beef-mushroom soup mix
2 cups diced potatoes
1 cup thinly sliced carrots
10-oz. pkg. frozen peas and onions

1. Layer all ingredients in order in slow cooker.
2. Cover. Cook on Low 8-10 hours.

Note:
You may increase all vegetable quantities with good results!

Becky's Beef Stew

Becky Harder, Monument, CO

Makes 6-8 servings

Prep. Time: 10 minutes
Cooking Time: 6-8 hours
Ideal slow-cooker size: 5-qt.

1½ lbs. beef stewing meat, cubed
2 10-oz. pkgs. frozen vegetables—carrots, corn, peas
4 large potatoes, cubed
1 bay leaf
1 onion, chopped
15-oz. can stewing tomatoes of your choice—Italian, *or* Mexican, *or* regular
8-oz. can tomato sauce
2 Tbsp. Worcestershire sauce
1 tsp. salt
¼ tsp. pepper

1. Put meat on bottom of slow cooker. Layer frozen vegetables and potatoes over meat.
2. Mix remaining ingredients together in large bowl and pour over other ingredients.
3. Cover. Cook on Low 6-8 hours.

Sweet-Sour Beef and Vegetables

Jo Haberkamp, Fairbank, IA

Makes 6 servings

Prep. Time: 10 minutes
Cooking Time: 4-6 hours
Ideal slow-cooker size: 4½-qt.

2 lbs. round steak, cut in 1-inch cubes
2 Tbsp. oil
2 8-oz. cans tomato sauce
2 tsp. chili powder
2 cups sliced carrots
2 cups small white onions
1 tsp. paprika
¼ cup sugar
1 tsp. salt
⅓ cup vinegar
½ cup light molasses
1 large green pepper, cut in 1-inch pieces

1. Brown steak in oil in saucepan.
2. Combine all ingredients in slow cooker.
3. Cover. Cook on High 4-6 hours.

Gone-All-Day Casserole

Beatrice Orgish, Richardson, TX

Makes 12 servings

Prep. Time: 10-15 minutes
Cooking Time: 6-8 hours
Ideal slow-cooker size: 5-qt.

1 cup uncooked wild rice, rinsed and drained
1 cup chopped celery
1 cup chopped carrots
2 4-oz. cans mushrooms, drained
1 large onion, chopped
1 clove garlic, minced
½ cup slivered almonds
3 beef bouillon cubes
2½ tsp. seasoned salt
2-lb. boneless round steak, cut into 1-inch cubes
3 cups water

1. Place ingredients in order listed in slow cooker.
2. Cover. Cook on Low 6-8 hours or until rice is tender. Stir before serving.

Variations:
1. Brown beef in saucepan in 2 Tbsp. oil before putting in slow cooker for deeper flavor.
2. Add a bay leaf and 4-6 whole peppercorns to mixture before cooking. Remove before serving.
3. Substitute chicken legs and thighs (skin removed) for beef.

Santa Fe Stew

Jeanne Allen, Rye, CO

Makes 4-6 servings

Prep. Time: 20 minutes
Cooking Time: 4½-6½ hours
Ideal slow-cooker size: 4-qt.

2 lbs. sirloin, *or* stewing meat, cubed
1 large onion, diced
2 garlic cloves, minced
2 Tbsp. oil
1½ cups water
1 Tbsp. dried parsley flakes
2 beef bouillon cubes
1 tsp. ground cumin
½ tsp. salt
3 carrots, sliced
14½-oz. can diced tomatoes
14½-oz. can green beans, drained, *or* 1 lb. frozen green beans
14½-oz. can corn, drained, *or* 1 lb. frozen corn
4-oz. can diced green chilies
3 zucchini squash, diced, *optional*

1. Brown meat, onion, and garlic in oil in saucepan until meat is no longer pink. Place in slow cooker.
2. Stir in remaining ingredients.
3. Cover. Cook on High 30 minutes. Reduce heat to Low and cook 4-6 hours.

Full-Flavored Beef Stew

Stacy Petersheim, Mechanicsburg, PA

Makes 6 servings

Prep. Time: 10 minutes
Cooking Time: 8 hours
Ideal slow-cooker size: 5-qt.

2-lb. beef roast, cubed
2 cups sliced carrots
2 cups diced potatoes
1 medium onion, sliced
1½ cups peas
2 tsp. quick-cooking tapioca
1 Tbsp. salt
½ tsp. pepper
8-oz. can tomato sauce
1 cup water
1 Tbsp. brown sugar

1. Combine beef and vegetables in slow cooker. Sprinkle with tapioca, salt, and pepper.
2. Combine tomato sauce and water. Pour over ingredients in slow cooker. Sprinkle with brown sugar.
3. Cover. Cook on Low 8 hours.

Variation:
Add peas one hour before cooking time ends to keep their color and flavor.

One hour on High equals about 2 to 2½ hours on Low.

Rachel Kauffman, Alto, MI

Slow-Cooker Stew with Vegetables

Ruth Shank, Gridley, IL

Makes 8-10 servings

Prep. Time: 15 minutes
Cooking Time: 4-14 hours
Ideal slow-cooker size: 7-qt.

3-4-lb. beef round steak,
　or beef roast, cubed
⅓ cup flour
1 tsp. salt
½ tsp. pepper
3 carrots, sliced
1-2 medium onions, cut
　into wedges
4-6 medium potatoes, cubed
4-oz. can sliced mushrooms,
　drained
10-oz. pkg. frozen mixed
　vegetables
10½-oz. can condensed beef
　broth
½ cup water
2 tsp. brown sugar
14½-oz. can, *or* 1 pint,
　tomato wedges with juice
¼ cup flour
¼ cup water

1. Toss beef cubes with
⅓ cup flour, salt, and pepper
in slow cooker.

2. Combine all vegetables
except tomatoes. Add to meat.

3. Combine beef broth, ½ cup
water, and brown sugar. Pour
over meat and vegetables. Add
tomatoes and stir carefully.

4. Cover. Cook on Low 10-14
hours, or on High 4-5½ hours.

5. One hour before serving,
mix together ¼ cup flour and
¼ cup water. Stir into slow
cooker. Turn to High. Cover
and cook remaining time.

Note:
　For better color, add half of
the frozen vegetables (partly
thawed) during the last hour.

Beef with Mushrooms

Doris Perkins, Mashpee, MA

Makes 4-6 servings

Prep. Time: 15 minutes
Cooking Time: 3 hours
Ideal slow-cooker size: 2½-qt.

1½ lbs. stewing beef, cubed
4-oz. can mushroom pieces,
　drained (save liquid)
half a garlic clove, minced
¾ cup sliced onions
3 Tbsp. shortening
1 beef bouillon cube
1 cup hot water
8-oz. can tomato sauce
2 tsp. sugar
2 tsp. Worcestershire sauce
1 tsp. dried basil
1 tsp. dried oregano
½ tsp. salt
⅛ tsp. pepper

1. Brown meat, mushrooms,
garlic, and onions in shortening in skillet.

2. Dissolve bouillon cube in
hot water. Add to meat mixture.

3. Stir in mushroom liquid
and rest of ingredients. Mix
well. Pour into slow cooker.

4. Cover. Cook on High 3
hours, or until meat is tender.

*Serving suggestion: Serve over
cooked **noodles**, **spaghetti**, or
rice.*

Easy Company Beef

Joyce B. Suiter, Garysburg, NC

Makes 8 servings

Prep. Time: 5 minutes
Cooking Time: 10 hours
Ideal slow-cooker size: 4-qt.

3 lbs. stewing beef, cubed
10¾-oz. can cream of
　mushroom soup
7-oz. jar mushrooms,
　undrained
½ cup red wine
1 envelope dry onion soup
　mix

1. Combine all ingredients
in slow cooker.

2. Cover. Cook on Low 10
hours.

*Serving suggestion: Serve over
noodles, **rice**, or **pasta**.*

Savory Beef Pot Roast

Alexa Slonin, Harrisonburg, VA

Makes 8-10 servings

Prep. Time: 15 minutes
Cooking Time: 10-12 hours
Ideal slow-cooker size: 4-qt.

12 oz. whole tiny new potatoes, *or* 2 medium potatoes, cubed, *or* 2 medium sweet potatoes, cubed
8 small carrots, cut in small chunks
2 small onions, cut in wedges
2 ribs celery, cut up
2½-3 lb. beef chuck, *or* pot roast
2 Tbsp. cooking oil
¾ cup water, *or* dry wine, *or* tomato juice
1 Tbsp. Worcestershire sauce
1 tsp. instant beef bouillon granules
1 tsp. dried basil

1. Place vegetables in bottom of slow cooker.
2. Brown roast in oil in skillet. Place on top of vegetables.
3. Combine water, Worcestershire sauce, bouillon, and basil. Pour over meat and vegetables.
4. Cover. Cook on Low 10-12 hours.

All-Day Roast

Moreen Weaver, Bath, NY

Makes 8-10 servings

Prep Time: 15-20 minutes
Cooking Time: 7-9 hours
Ideal slow-cooker size: 6-qt.

3-4 carrots, cut in 1-inch chunks
4-5 medium potatoes, cut in 1-inch chunks
1 lb. frozen, *or* fresh, green beans
1 large onion, cut in wedges
1½ cups water
3-5-lb. beef roast
2 cloves garlic, minced
salt to taste
pepper to taste
10¾-oz. can cream of mushroom soup
2-3 Tbsp. Worcestershire sauce
1 pkg. dry onion soup mix, beef, *or* mushroom, flavor

1. Place vegetables and water into slow cooker.
2. Place beef roast on top of vegetables.
3. Sprinkle garlic over meat, followed by salt and pepper to taste.
4. Spoon cream of mushroom soup over seasoned meat.
5. Gently pour Worcestershire sauce over soup.
6. Sprinkle with dry onion soup mix.
7. Cover. Cook on High 5-6 hours.

8. Reset temperature to Low. Continue cooking 2-3 more hours, or until vegetables and meat are fork-tender, but not dry or mushy.

Pot Roast

Janet L. Roggie, Linville, NY

Makes 6-8 servings

Prep. Time: 10 minutes
Cooking Time: 10-12 hours
Ideal slow-cooker size: 4-qt.

3 potatoes, thinly sliced
2 large carrots, thinly sliced
1 onion, thinly sliced
1 tsp. salt
½ tsp. pepper
3-4-lb. pot roast
½ cup water

1. Put vegetables in bottom of slow cooker. Stir in salt and pepper. Add roast. Pour in water.
2. Cover. Cook on Low 10-12 hours.

Variations:
1. Add ½ tsp. dried dill, a bay leaf, and ½ tsp. dried rosemary for more flavor.
2. Brown roast on all sides in saucepan in 2 Tbsp. oil before placing in cooker.

Debbie Zeida
Mashpee, MA

Easy Pot Roast and Veggies

Tina Houk, Clinton, MO
Arlene Wiens, Newton, KS

Makes 6 servings

Prep. Time: 5-10 minutes
Cooking Time: 6-8 hours
Ideal slow-cooker size: 6-qt.

3-4-lb. chuck roast
4 medium-sized potatoes,
  cubed
4 medium-sized carrots,
  sliced, *or* 1 lb. baby carrots
2 celery ribs, sliced thin,
  optional
1 envelope dry onion soup
  mix
3 cups water

1. Put roast, potatoes, carrots, and celery in slow cooker.
2. Add onion soup mix and water.
3. Cover. Cook on Low 6-8 hours.

Variations:
1. To add flavor to the broth, stir 1 tsp. Kitchen Bouquet, ½ tsp. salt, ½ tsp. black pepper, and ½ tsp. garlic powder into water before pouring over meat and vegetables.
Bonita Ensenberger, Albuquerque, NM

2. Before putting roast in cooker, sprinkle it with the dry soup mix, patting it on so it adheres.
Betty Lahman, Elkton, VA

3. Add one bay leaf and 2 cloves minced garlic to Step 2.
Susan Tjon, Austin, TX

Easy Roast

Lisa Warren, Parkesburg, PA

Makes 6-8 servings

Prep. Time: 5 minutes
Cooking Time: 8 hours
Ideal slow-cooker size: 4-qt.

3-4-lb. beef roast
1 envelope dry onion soup
  mix
14½-oz. can stewed tomatoes,
  or seasoned tomatoes

1. Place roast in slow cooker. Cover with onion soup and tomatoes.
2. Cover. Cook on Low 8 hours.

Rump Roast and Vegetables

Kimberlee Greenawalt, Harrisonburg, VA

Makes 6-8 servings

Prep. Time: 15 minutes
Cooking Time: 5-12 hours
Ideal slow-cooker size: 4- to 5-qt.

1½ lbs. small potatoes
  (about 10), *or* medium
  potatoes (about 4), halved
2 medium carrots, cubed
1 small onion, sliced
10-oz. pkg. frozen lima beans
1 bay leaf
2 Tbsp. quick-cooking
  tapioca
2-2½-lb. boneless beef
  round rump, *or* round
  tip, *or* pot roast
2 Tbsp. oil
10¾-oz. can condensed
  vegetable beef soup
¼ cup water
¼ tsp. pepper

1. Place potatoes, carrots, and onion in slow cooker. Add frozen beans and bay leaf. Sprinkle with tapioca.
2. Brown roast on all sides in oil in skillet. Place over vegetables in slow cooker.
3. Combine soup, water, and pepper. Pour over roast.
4. Cover. Cook on Low 10-12 hours, or High 5-6 hours.
5. Discard bay leaf before serving.

Beef Roast with Mushroom Barley

Sue Hamilton, Minooka, IL

Makes 4-6 servings

Prep Time: 5 minutes
Cooking Time: 6-8 hours
Ideal slow-cooker size: 6-qt.

---

1 cup pearl barley (not quick-cook)
½ cup onion, diced
6½-oz. can mushrooms, undrained
1 tsp. garlic, minced
1 tsp. Italian seasoning
¼ tsp. black pepper
2-3 lbs. beef chuck roast
1¾ cups beef broth

1. Put barley, onion, mushrooms with liquid, and garlic in slow cooker.

2. Sprinkle seasoning and pepper over top.

3. Add roast. Pour broth over all.

4. Cover. Cook 6-8 hours on Low, or until meat is fork-tender and barley is also tender.

*Serving suggestion: Serve this with mashed **potatoes**. They'll benefit from the delicious broth in this dish.*

Hearty New England Dinner

Joette Droz, Kalona, IA

Makes 6-8 servings

Prep. Time: 10 minutes
Cooking Time: 8-10 hours
Ideal slow-cooker size: 5-qt.

---

2 medium carrots, sliced
1 medium onion, sliced
1 celery rib, sliced
3-lb. boneless chuck roast
½ tsp. salt
¼ tsp. pepper
1 envelope dry onion soup mix
2 cups water
1 Tbsp. vinegar
1 bay leaf
half a small head of cabbage, cut in wedges
3 Tbsp. melted margarine, or butter
2 Tbsp. flour
1 Tbsp. dried, minced onion
2 Tbsp. prepared horseradish
½ tsp. salt

1. Place carrots, onion, and celery in slow cooker. Place roast on top. Sprinkle with ½ tsp. salt and pepper. Add soup mix, water, vinegar, and bay leaf.

2. Cover. Cook on Low 7-9 hours. Remove beef and keep warm. Just before serving, cut into pieces or thin slices.

3. Discard bay leaf. Add cabbage to juice in slow cooker.

4. Cover. Cook on High 1 hour, or until cabbage is tender.

5. Melt margarine in saucepan. Stir in flour and onion. Add 1½ cups liquid from slow cooker. Stir in horseradish and ½ tsp. salt. Bring to boil. Cook over low heat until thick and smooth, about 2 minutes. Return to cooker and blend with remaining sauce in cooker.

*Serving suggestion: Serve over or alongside **meat** and **vegetables**.*

When adapting range-top recipes to slow cooking, reduce the amount of onion you normally use because the onion flavor gets stronger during slow cooking.

Beatrice Orgish, Richardson, TX

153

Autumn Brisket

Karen Ceneviva, Seymour, CT

Makes 8 servings

Prep Time: 20-30 minutes
Cooking Time: 4-9 hours
Ideal slow-cooker size: 6-qt.

3-lb. boneless beef brisket
salt to taste
pepper to taste
1 lb. head cabbage, cut into
    wedges
1 large (¾ lb.) sweet potato,
    peeled and cut into
    1-inch pieces
1 large onion, cut in wedges
salt to taste
pepper to taste
1 medium Granny Smith
    apple, cored and cut into
    8 wedges
2 10¾-oz. cans cream of
    celery soup
1 cup water
2 tsp. caraway seeds, *optional*

1. Place brisket in slow
cooker.
2. Shake salt and pepper
over meat to taste.
3. Top with cabbage, sweet
potato, and onion.
4. Season to taste with salt
and pepper.
5. Place apple wedges over
vegetables.
6. In a medium bowl
combine soup, water, and
caraway seeds if you wish.
7. Spoon mixture over
brisket and vegetables.

8. Cover. Cook on High 4-5
hours, or on Low 8-9 hours,
or until brisket and vegetables
are fork-tender, but not dry or
mushy.

Easy Beef Stew

Connie Johnson, Loudon, NH

Makes 6 servings

Prep. Time: 10 minutes
Cooking Time: 6-8 hours
Ideal slow-cooker size: 5-qt.

1 lb. stewing beef
1 cup cubed turnip
2 medium potatoes, cubed
1 large onion, sliced
1 garlic clove, minced
2 large carrots, sliced
½ cup green beans, cut up
½ cup peas
1 bay leaf
½ tsp. dried thyme
1 tsp. chopped parsley
2 Tbsp. tomato paste
2 Tbsp. celery leaves
½ tsp. salt
¼ tsp. pepper
1 qt., *or* 2 14½-oz. cans,
    beef broth

1. Place all ingredients
except broth in slow cooker.
Pour broth over all.
2. Cover. Cook on Low 6-8
hours.

Pot Roast
with Mushrooms

Julie McKenzie, Punxsutawney, PA

Makes 8 servings

Prep. Time: 10 minutes
Cooking Time: 10-12 hours
Ideal slow-cooker size: 4-qt.

3-lb. rump roast
½ envelope dry onion soup
    mix
1 small onion, sliced
4-oz. can mushrooms with
    liquid
⅓ cup dry red wine
⅓ cup water
1 garlic clove, minced
1 bay leaf
½ tsp. dried thyme
2 Tbsp. chopped fresh basil,
    or 1 tsp. dried basil

1. Combine all ingredients
in slow cooker.
2. Cover. Cook on Low
10-12 hours.

Variations:
1. Add ½ tsp. salt, if desired.
2. Mix 3 Tbsp. cornstarch
into ½ cup cold water. At
the end of the cooking time
remove bay leaf and discard.
Remove meat to serving
platter and keep warm. Stir
dissolved cornstarch into hot
liquid in slow cooker. Stir until
absorbed. Cover and cook on
High 10 minutes, until sauce
thickens. Serve over top or
alongside sliced meat.

Pot Roast with Gravy and Vegetables

Irene Klaeger, Inverness, FL
Jan Pembleton, Arlington, TX

Makes 4-6 servings

Prep. Time: 10-15 minutes
Cooking Time: 4-10 hours
Ideal slow-cooker size: 5½-qt.

3-4-lb. bottom round, *or* rump, *or* arm roast
2-3 tsp. salt
½ tsp. pepper
2 Tbsp. flour
¼ cup cold water
1 tsp. Kitchen Bouquet, *or* gravy browning seasoning sauce
1 garlic clove, minced
2 medium onions, cut in wedges
4-6 medium potatoes, cubed
2-4 carrots, quartered
1 green pepper, sliced

1. Place roast in slow cooker. Sprinkle with salt and pepper.
2. Make paste of flour and cold water. Stir in kitchen bouquet and spread over roast.
3. Add garlic, onions, potatoes, carrots, and green pepper.
4. Cover. Cook on Low 8-10 hours, or High 4-5 hours.
5. Taste and adjust seasonings before serving.

Round Steak Casserole with Carrots

Cheryl Bartel, Hillsboro, KS
Barbara Walker, Sturgis, SD

Makes 4-6 servings

Prep. Time: 10-15 minutes
Cooking Time: 9 hours
Ideal slow-cooker size: 6-qt.

2-lb. ½-inch-thick round steak
½ tsp. garlic salt
1 tsp. salt
¼-½ tsp. pepper
1 onion, thinly sliced
3-4 potatoes, quartered
3-4 carrots, sliced
14½-oz. can French-style green beans, drained, *or* 1 lb. frozen green beans
10¾-oz. can tomato soup
14½-oz. can stewed tomatoes

1. Cut meat into serving-size pieces, place in slow cooker, stir in seasonings, and mix well.
2. Add onion, potatoes, carrots, and green beans. Top with soup and tomatoes.
3. Cover. Cook on High 1 hour. Reduce heat to Low and cook 8 hours, or until done. Remove cover during last half hour if there is too much liquid.

"Smothered" Steak

Susan Yoder Graber, Eureka, IL

Makes 6 servings

Prep. Time: 10 minutes
Cooking Time: 8 hours
Ideal slow-cooker size: 4-qt.

1½-lb. chuck, *or* round, steak, cut into strips
⅓ cup flour
½ tsp. salt
¼ tsp. pepper
1 large onion, sliced
1-2 green peppers, sliced
14½-oz. can stewed tomatoes
4-oz. can mushrooms, drained
2 Tbsp. soy sauce
10-oz. pkg. frozen French-style green beans

1. Layer steak in bottom of slow cooker. Sprinkle with flour, salt, and pepper. Stir well to coat steak.
2. Add remaining ingredients. Mix together gently.
3. Cover. Cook on Low 8 hours.

Serving suggestion: Serve over rice.

Variations:
1. Use 8-oz. can tomato sauce instead of stewed tomatoes.
2. Substitute 1 Tbsp. Worcestershire sauce in place of soy sauce.

Mary E. Martin, Goshen, IN

Veal and Peppers

Irma H. Schoen, Windsor, CT

Makes 4 servings

Prep. Time: 10 minutes
Cooking Time: 4-7 hours
Ideal slow-cooker size: 4-qt.

1½ lbs. boneless veal, cubed
3 green peppers, quartered
2 onions, thinly sliced
½ lb. fresh mushrooms, sliced
1 tsp. salt
½ tsp. dried basil
2 cloves garlic, minced
28-oz. can tomatoes

1. Combine all ingredients in slow cooker.
2. Cover. Cook on Low 7 hours, or on High 4 hours.

Serving suggestion: Serve over **rice** *or* **noodles**.

Variation:
Use boneless, skinless chicken breast, cut into chunks, instead of veal.

Beef and Beans

Robin Schrock, Millersburg, OH

Makes 8 servings

Prep. Time: 10 minutes
Cooking Time: 6½-8½ hours
Ideal slow-cooker size: 4-qt.

1 Tbsp. prepared mustard
1 Tbsp. chili powder
½ tsp. salt
¼ tsp. pepper
1½-lb. boneless round steak, cut into thin slices
2 14½-oz. cans diced tomatoes, undrained
1 medium onion, chopped
1 beef bouillon cube, crushed
16-oz. can kidney beans, rinsed and drained

1. Combine mustard, chili powder, salt, and pepper. Add beef slices and toss to coat. Place meat in slow cooker.
2. Add tomatoes, onion, and bouillon.
3. Cover. Cook on Low 6-8 hours.
4. Stir in beans. Cook 30 minutes longer.

Serving suggestion: Serve over **rice**.

Forget It Pot Roast

Mary Mitchell, Battle Creek, MI

Makes 6 servings

Prep. Time: 10 minutes
Cooking Time: 8-9 hours
Ideal slow-cooker size: 5-qt.

6 potatoes, quartered
6 carrots, sliced
3-3½-lb. chuck roast
1 envelope dry onion soup mix
10¾-oz. can cream of mushroom soup
2-3 Tbsp. flour
¼ cup cold water

1. Place potatoes and carrots in slow cooker. Add meat. Top with soups.
2. Cover. Cook on Low 8-9 hours.
3. To make gravy, remove meat and vegetables to serving platter and keep warm. Pour juices into saucepan and bring to boil. Mix 2-3 Tbsp. flour with ¼ cup cold water until smooth. Stir into juices in pan until thickened.

Serving suggestion: Serve gravy over meat and vegetables, or alongside.

Trim as much visible fat from meat as possible before placing it in the slow cooker in order to avoid greasy gravy.

Carolyn Baer, Conrath, WI

Ham 'n' Cola
page 211

*Slow-Cooked
Cabbage
Rolls,
page 187*

*Fruity
Baked Bean
Casserole,
page 281*

Beef Stew Bourguignonne

Jo Haberkamp, Fairbank, IA

Makes 6 servings

Prep. Time: 15 minutes
Cooking Time: 10¼-12¼ hours
Ideal slow-cooker size: 4-qt.

2 lbs. stewing beef, cut in
   1-inch cubes
2 Tbsp. cooking oil
10¾-oz. can condensed
   golden cream of
   mushroom soup
1 tsp. Worcestershire sauce
⅓ cup dry red wine
½ tsp. dried oregano
2 tsp. salt
½ tsp. pepper
½ cup chopped onions
½ cup chopped carrots
4-oz. can mushroom pieces,
   drained
½ cup cold water
¼ cup flour

1. Brown meat in oil in saucepan. Transfer to slow cooker.
2. Mix together soup, Worcestershire sauce, wine, oregano, salt, pepper, onions, carrots, and mushrooms. Pour over meat.
3. Cover. Cook on Low 10-12 hours.
4. Combine water and flour. Stir into beef mixture. Turn cooker to High.

5. Cook and stir until thickened and bubbly.

Serving suggestion: Serve over noodles.

Baked Steak

Shirley Thieszen, Lakin, KS

Makes 6 servings

Prep. Time: 10 minutes
Cooking Time: 4-5 hours
Ideal slow-cooker size: 3½- to 4-qt.

2½ lbs. round steak, cut
   into 10 pieces
1 Tbsp. salt
½ tsp. pepper
oil
½ cup chopped onions
½ cup chopped green
   peppers
1 cup cream of mushroom
   soup
½ cup water

1. Season the steak with salt and pepper. Brown on both sides in oil in saucepan. Place in slow cooker.
2. Stir in onions, green peppers, mushroom soup, and water.
3. Cover. Cook on High 1 hour, and then on Low 3-4 hours.

Creamy Swiss Steak

Jo Ellen Moore, Pendleton, IN

Makes 6 servings

Prep. Time: 10 minutes
Cooking Time: 3-10 hours
Ideal slow-cooker size: 4½-qt.

1½-lb. ¾-inch thick round
   steak
2 Tbsp. flour
1 tsp. salt
¼ tsp. pepper
1 medium onion, sliced
10¾-oz. can cream of
   mushroom soup
1 carrot, chopped
1 small celery rib, chopped

1. Cut steak into serving-size pieces.
2. Combine flour, salt, and pepper. Dredge meat in flour.
3. Place onions in bottom of slow cooker. Add meat.
4. Spread cream of mushroom soup over meat. Top with carrots and celery.
5. Cover. Cook on Low 8-10 hours, or High 3-5 hours.

Saucy Round Steak Supper

Shirley Sears, Tiskilwa, IL

Makes 6-8 servings

Prep. Time: 10-15 minutes
Cooking Time: 8-9 hours
Ideal slow-cooker size: 4-qt.

2 lbs. round steak, sliced
  diagonally into ⅛-inch
  strips (reserve meat bone)
½ cup chopped onions
½ cup chopped celery
8-oz. can mushrooms,
  stems and pieces, drained
  (reserve liquid)
⅓ cup French dressing
½ cup sour cream
1 tsp. Worcestershire sauce

1. Place steak and bone
in slow cooker. Add onions,
celery, and mushrooms.

2. Combine dressing, sour
cream, Worcestershire sauce,
and mushroom liquid. Pour
over mixture in slow cooker.

3. Cover. Cook on Low 8-9
hours.

Serving suggestion: Serve over
noodles.

Succulent Steak

Betty B. Dennison, Grove City, PA

Makes 4 servings

Prep. Time: 10-15 minutes
Cooking Time: 8¼-10¼ hours
Ideal slow-cooker size: 4- to 5-qt.

¼ cup flour
½ tsp. salt
¼ tsp. pepper
¼ tsp. paprika
1½-lb. round steak, cut
  ½-¾-inch thick
2 onions, sliced
4-oz. can sliced mushrooms,
  drained
½ cup beef broth
2 tsp. Worcestershire sauce
2 Tbsp. flour
3 Tbsp. water

1. Mix together ¼ cup flour,
salt, pepper, and paprika.

2. Cut steak into 5-6 pieces.
Dredge steak pieces in seasoned flour until lightly coated.

3. Layer half of onions, half
of steak, and half of mushrooms into cooker. Repeat.

4. Combine beef broth and
Worcestershire sauce. Pour
over mixture in slow cooker.

5. Cover. Cook on Low 8-10
hours.

6. Remove steak to serving
platter and keep warm. Mix
together 2 Tbsp. flour and
water. Stir into drippings and
cook on High until thickened,
about 10 minutes.

Serving suggestion: Pour
gravy over steak and serve.

Steak Hi-Hat

Bonita Ensenberger, Albuquerque, NM

Makes 8-10 servings

Prep. Time: 10 minutes
Cooking Time: 8-9 hours
Ideal slow-cooker size: 4-qt.

10¾-oz. can cream of
  chicken soup
10¾-oz. can cream of
  mushroom soup
1½ Tbsp. Worcestershire
  sauce
½ tsp. black pepper
1 tsp. paprika
2 cups onion, chopped
1 garlic clove, minced
1 cup fresh, small, button
  mushrooms, quartered
2 lbs. round steak, cubed
1 cup sour cream

1. Combine chicken soup,
mushroom soup, Worcester-
shire sauce, pepper, paprika,
onion, garlic, and mushrooms
in slow cooker.

2. Stir in steak.

3. Cover. Cook on Low 8-9
hours.

4. Stir in sour cream during
the last 20-30 minutes.

Serving suggestion: Serve on
hot buttered ***noodles*** *sprinkled*
with ***poppy seeds***. *Garnish with*
bacon bits, *if you wish.*

Variation:
  Add 1 tsp. salt with seasonings in Step 1.

Steak Stroganoff

Marie Morucci, Glen Lyon, PA

Makes 6 servings

Prep. Time: 10 minutes
Cooking Time: 3¼-7¼ hours
Ideal slow-cooker size: 4- to 5-qt.

2 Tbsp. flour
½ tsp. garlic powder
½ tsp. pepper
¼ tsp. paprika
1¾-lb. boneless beef round
    steak
10¾-oz. can cream of
    mushroom soup
½ cup water
1 envelope dried onion
    soup mix
9-oz. jar sliced mushrooms,
    drained
½ cup sour cream
1 Tbsp. minced fresh parsley

1. Combine flour, garlic powder, pepper, and paprika in slow cooker.

2. Cut meat into 1½ by ½-inch strips. Place in flour mixture and toss until meat is well coated.

3. Add mushroom soup, water, and soup mix. Stir until well blended.

4. Cover. Cook on High 3-3½ hours, or Low 6-7 hours.

5. Stir in mushrooms, sour cream, and parsley. Cover and cook on High 10-15 minutes, or until heated through.

*Serving suggestion: Serve with **rice**.*

Venison Stroganoff

Eleanor Glick, Bird-In-Hand, PA

Makes 6-8 servings

Prep Time: 15-20 minutes
Cooking Time: 5 hours
Ideal slow-cooker size: 4-qt.

1 lb. venison, cubed
1 Tbsp. olive oil
½ tsp. garlic powder
½ tsp. garlic salt
dash of pepper
1 large onion, chopped
1 cup V8 juice
1 Tbsp. brown sugar
2-5 drops hot sauce,
    depending upon how
    much heat you like
2 Tbsp. Worcestershire
    sauce
1 small can mushrooms,
    drained
1 cup sour cream

1. Brown venison on both sides in olive oil in skillet, adding garlic powder, garlic salt, and pepper along with onion, as the meat browns.

2. Place browned meat and onions in slow cooker.

3. Add V8 juice, brown sugar, sauces, and mushrooms to meat and stir well.

4. Cover and cook 5 hours on Low, or until meat is tender but not dry.

5. Ten minutes before end of cooking time, stir in sour cream.

Scrumptious Beef

Julia Lapp, New Holland, PA

Makes 4-8 servings
(depending upon amount of beef used)

Prep. Time: 10 minutes
Cooking Time: 3-8 hours
Ideal slow-cooker size: 4-qt.

1-2 lbs. beef, cubed
½ lb. mushrooms, sliced
10½-oz. can beef broth, *or*
    1 cup water and 1 cube
    beef bouillon
1 onion, chopped
10¾-oz. can cream of
    mushroom soup
3 Tbsp. dry onion soup mix

1. Combine all ingredients in slow cooker.

2. Cover. Cook on High 3-4 hours, or on Low 7-8 hours.

*Serving suggestion: Serve over hot cooked **rice**.*

Good 'n' Easy Beef 'n' Gravy

Janice Crist, Quinter, KS

Makes 8 servings

Prep. Time: 5 minutes
Cooking Time: 10-12 hours
Ideal slow-cooker size: 4-qt.

3-lb. beef roast, cubed
1 envelope dry onion soup mix
½ cup beef broth
10¾-oz. can cream of mushroom, *or* cream of celery, soup
4-oz. can sliced mushrooms, drained

1. Combine all ingredients in slow cooker.
2. Cover. Cook on Low 10-12 hours.

Variation:
Use ½ cup sauterne instead of beef broth.
Joyce Shackelford, Green Bay, WI

Delicious, Easy Chuck Roast

Mary Jane Musser, Manheim, PA

Makes 4-8 servings

Prep. Time: 5 minutes
Cooking Time: 6-10 hours
Ideal slow-cooker size: 2½- to 4½-qt.

2-4-lb. chuck roast
salt to taste
pepper to taste
1 onion, sliced
10¾-oz. can cream of mushroom soup

1. Season roast with salt and pepper and place in slow cooker.
2. Add onion. Pour soup over all.
3. Cover. Cook on Low 8-10 hours, or on High 6 hours.

Dale and Shari's Beef Stroganoff

Dale and Shari Mast, Harrisonburg, VA

Makes 4 servings

Prep. Time: 5 minutes
Cooking Time: 4-8 hours
Ideal slow-cooker size: 2½-qt.

4 cups beef cubes
10¾-oz. can cream of mushroom soup
1 cup sour cream

1. Place beef in slow cooker. Cover with mushroom soup.
2. Cover. Cook on Low 8 hours, or High 4-5 hours.
3. Before serving stir in sour cream.

*Serving suggestion: Serve over cooked **rice**, **pasta**, or baked **potatoes**.*

Easy Dinner Surprise

Nancy Graves, Manhattan, KS

Makes 4-5 servings

Prep. Time: 5 minutes
Cooking Time: 8-10 hours
Ideal slow-cooker size: 2½-qt.

1-1½ lbs. stewing meat, cubed
10¾-oz. can cream of mushroom soup
10¾-oz. can cream of celery soup
1 pkg. dry onion soup mix
4-oz. can mushroom pieces

1. Combine all ingredients in slow cooker.
2. Cover. Cook on Low 8-10 hours.

*Serving suggestion: Serve over **rice** or baked **potatoes**.*

Variation:
Add ¼ cup finely chopped celery for color and texture.

Paul's Beef Bourguignonne

Janice Muller, Derwood, MD

Makes 4 servings

Prep. Time: 10 minutes
Marinating Time: 6-14 hours
Cooking Time: 8-10 hours
Ideal slow-cooker size: 4-qt.

3-lb. chuck roast, cubed
2 Tbsp. oil
2 10¾-oz. cans golden
 cream of mushroom soup
1 envelope dry onion soup
 mix
1 cup cooking sherry

1. Brown meat in oil in skillet. Drain. Place in slow cooker. Add remaining ingredients and cover.

2. Refrigerate 6-8 hours, or up to 14 hours, to marinate.

3. Remove from refrigerator, cover, and cook on Low 8-10 hours.

*Serving suggestion: Serve over cooked **egg noodles** or **rice**.*

Round Steak

Dorothy Hess, Willow Street, PA
Betty A. Holt, St. Charles, MO
Betty Moore, Plano, IL
Michelle Strite, Harrisonburg, VA
Barbara Tenney, Delta, PA
Sharon Timpe, Mequon, WI

Makes 4-5 servings

Prep. Time: 10 minutes
Cooking Time: 7-8 hours
Ideal slow-cooker size: 2½-qt.

2-lb. boneless round steak
oil
1 envelope dry onion soup
 mix
10¾-oz. can cream of
 mushroom soup
½ cup water

1. Cut steak into serving-size pieces. Brown in oil in saucepan. Place in slow cooker. Sprinkle with soup mix.

2. Combine soup and water. Pour over meat.

3. Cover. Cook on Low 7-8 hours.

Variation:

To make a dish lower in sodium, replace the onion soup mix and mushroom soup with 1 cup diced onions, ½ lb. sliced mushrooms, 1 Tbsp. fresh parsley, ¼ tsp. pepper, ½ tsp. dried basil, all stirred gently together. Place on top of meat in cooker. Dissolve 2 Tbsp. flour in ¾ cup cold water. Pour over vegetables and meat. Mix together. Cover and cook according to directions above.

Della Yoder, Kalona, IA

Slow-Cooker Beef

Sara Harter Fredette, Williamsburg, MA

Makes 4-6 servings

Prep. Time: 10 minutes
Cooking Time: 6-8 hours
Ideal slow-cooker size: 4-qt.

½ cup flour
2 tsp. salt
¼ tsp. pepper
2-3 lbs. stewing beef, cubed
2 Tbsp. oil
10¾-oz. can cream of
 mushroom soup
1 envelope dry onion soup
 mix
½ cup sour cream

1. Combine flour, salt, and pepper in plastic bag. Add beef in small batches. Shake to coat beef. Sauté beef in oil in saucepan. Place browned beef in slow cooker.

2. Stir in mushroom soup and onion soup mix.

3. Cover. Cook on Low 6-8 hours.

4. Stir in sour cream before serving. Heat for a few minutes.

*Serving suggestion: Serve with **noodles** or mashed **potatoes**.*

Creamy Beef Pot Roast

Julia B. Boyd, Memphis, TN

Makes 6-8 servings

Prep. Time: 5 minutes
Cooking Time: 10-12 hours
Ideal slow-cooker size: 4-qt.

3-4-lb. chuck, *or* English-cut, beef roast
1 envelope dry onion-mushroom soup mix
10¾-oz. can cream of celery soup
1 soup can water
2-3 Tbsp. flour
2-3 beef bouillon cubes
1 medium onion, chopped

1. Combine all ingredients in slow cooker.
2. Cover. Cook on Low 10-12 hours.

Variations:

Use leftover meat to make soup. Add one large can tomatoes and any leftover vegetables you have on hand.

Add spices such as minced onion, garlic powder, basil, bay leaf, celery seed.

To increase the liquid, use V8 juice and season with 1-2 tablespoons butter for a richer soup base. Cook on Low 6-12 hours.

If you wish, stir in cooked macaroni or rice just before serving.

Roast Beef

Judy Buller, Bluffton, OH

Makes 6 servings

Prep. Time: 5 minutes
Cooking Time: 6-7 hours
Ideal slow-cooker size: 4-qt.

2½-3-lb. bottom round roast
2 cups water
2 beef bouillon cubes
½ tsp. cracked pepper
¼ cup flour
½ tsp. salt
¾ cup cold water

1. Cut roast into 6-8 pieces and place in slow cooker. Add water and bouillon cubes. Sprinkle with pepper.
2. Cover. Cook on High 2 hours. Reduce heat to Low and cook 4-5 hours, or until meat is tender.
3. Dissolve flour and salt in cold water. Remove roast from cooker and keep warm. Stir flour paste into hot broth in cooker until smooth. Cover and cook on High for 5 minutes.

Serving suggestion: Serve gravy with sliced roast beef.

Roast

Tracey Yohn, Harrisburg, PA

Makes 6 servings

Prep. Time: 5 minutes
Cooking Time: 5-12 hours
Ideal slow-cooker size: 4-qt.

2-3-lb. shoulder roast
1 tsp. salt
1 tsp. pepper
1 tsp. garlic salt
1 small onion, sliced in rings
1 beef bouillon cube
1 cup boiling water

1. Place roast in slow cooker. Sprinkle with salt, pepper, and garlic salt. Place onion rings on top.
2. Dissolve bouillon cube in water. Pour over roast.
3. Cover. Cook on Low 10-12 hours, or on High 5-6 hours.

Savory Sweet Roast

Martha Ann Auker, Landisburg, PA

Makes 6-8 servings

Prep. Time: 10 minutes
Cooking Time: 12-16 hours
Ideal slow-cooker size: 4-qt.

3-4-lb. blade, *or* chuck, roast
oil

1 onion, chopped
10¾-oz. can cream of
    mushroom soup
½ cup water
¼ cup sugar
¼ cup vinegar
2 tsp. salt
1 tsp. prepared mustard
1 tsp. Worcestershire sauce

1. Brown meat in oil on
both sides in saucepan. Put in
slow cooker.
2. Blend together remaining
ingredients. Pour over meat.
3. Cover. Cook on Low
12-16 hours.

Pepsi Pot Roast

Mrs. Don Martins, Fairbank, IA

Makes 6-8 servings

Prep. Time: 5 minutes
Cooking Time: 6 hours
Ideal slow-cooker size: 4- to 5-qt.

3-4-lb. pot roast
10¾-oz. can cream of
    mushroom soup
1 envelope dry onion soup
    mix
16-oz. bottle Pepsi, *or* other
    cola

1. Place meat in slow cooker.
2. Top with mushroom soup
and onion soup mix. Pour in
Pepsi.
3. Cover. Cook on High
6 hours.

Hungarian Goulash in Sour Cream Sauce

Elaine Patton, West Middletown, PA

Makes 8 servings

Prep Time: 15 minutes
Cooking Time: 8-10 hours
Ideal slow-cooker size: 6 qt.

2 lbs. round steak, cut into
    ¾-inch cubes
1 cup onion, chopped
1 clove garlic, pressed
2 Tbsp. flour
½ tsp. salt
½ tsp. pepper
1 tsp. paprika
¼ tsp. dried thyme, crushed
1 bay leaf
14½-oz. can stewed, *or*
    diced, tomatoes
1 cup low-fat sour cream

1. Place steak cubes, onion
and garlic in slow-cooker.
2. Stir in flour and mix to
coat steak cubes and vegetables.
3. Add salt, pepper, paprika,
thyme, bay leaf, and tomatoes.
Stir well.
4. Cover. Cook on Low 8-10
hours, or until meat is tender
but not dry.
5. Add sour cream 30
minutes before end of cooking
time. Stir in thoroughly.
6. After sour cream has
been added, begin cooking
noodles on stove top.

*Serving suggestion: Serve
slow-cooker contents over
cooked **noodles**.*

Dilled Pot Roast

C.J. Slagle, Roann, IN

Makes 6 servings

Prep. Time: 5 minutes
Cooking Time: 7¼-9¼ hours
Ideal slow-cooker size: 4- to 5-qt.

3-3½-lb. beef pot roast
1 tsp. salt
¼ tsp. pepper
2 tsp. dried dillweed,
    divided
¼ cup water
1 Tbsp. vinegar
3 Tbsp. flour
½ cup water
1 cup sour cream

1. Sprinkle both sides of
meat with salt, pepper, and 1
tsp. dill. Place in slow cooker.
Add water and vinegar.
2. Cover. Cook on Low 7-9
hours, or until tender. Remove
meat from pot. Turn to High.
3. Dissolve flour in water.
Stir into meat drippings. Stir
in additional 1 tsp. dill. Cook
on High 5 minutes. Stir in sour
cream. Cook on High another
5 minutes.

*Serving suggestion: Slice meat
and serve with sour cream sauce
over top.*

Herbed Roast with Gravy

Sue Williams, Gulfport, MS

Makes 8-10 servings

Prep. Time: 5 minutes
Cooking Time: 4-10 hours
Ideal slow-cooker size: 4-qt.

4-lb. roast
2 tsp. salt
½ tsp. pepper
2 medium onions, sliced
half a can (10¾-oz.)
    condensed cheddar
    cheese soup
8-oz. can tomato sauce
4-oz. can mushroom pieces
    and stems, drained
¼ tsp. dried basil
¼ tsp. dried oregano

1. Season roast with salt and pepper. Place in slow cooker.
2. Combine remaining ingredients and pour over meat.
3. Cover. Cook on Low 8-10 hours, or on High 4-5 hours.

Serving suggestion: Serve with **gravy**.

Savory Beef Burgundy

Jacqueline Stefl, East Bethany, NY

Makes 6 servings

Prep. Time: 10 minutes
Cooking Time: 8-10 hours
Ideal slow-cooker size: 4-qt.

5 medium onions, thinly
    sliced
2 lbs. stewing meat, cubed
1½ Tbsp. flour
½ lb. fresh mushrooms,
    sliced
1 tsp. salt
¼ tsp. dried marjoram
¼ tsp. dried thyme
⅛ tsp. pepper
¾ cup beef broth
1½ cups burgundy wine

1. Place onions in slow cooker.
2. Dredge meat in flour. Put in slow cooker.
3. Add mushrooms, salt, marjoram, thyme, and pepper.
4. Pour in broth and wine.
5. Cover. Cook 8-10 hours on Low.

Serving suggestion: Serve over cooked **noodles**.

Goodtime Beef Brisket

AmyMarlene Jensen, Fountain, CO

Makes 6-8 servings

Prep. Time: 10 minutes
Cooking Time: 8-10 hours
Ideal slow-cooker size: 4- to 5-qt.

3½-4-lb. beef brisket
1 can beer
2 cups tomato sauce
2 tsp. prepared mustard
2 Tbsp. balsamic vinegar
2 Tbsp. Worcestershire
    sauce
1 tsp. garlic powder
½ tsp. ground allspice
2 Tbsp. brown sugar
1 small green, *or* red, bell
    pepper, chopped
1 medium onion, chopped
1 tsp. salt
½ tsp. pepper

1. Place brisket in slow cooker.
2. Combine remaining ingredients. Pour over meat.
3. Cover. Cook on Low 8-10 hours.
4. Remove meat from sauce. Slice very thin.

Serving suggestion: Serve on **rolls** *or over* **couscous**.

Always defrost meat or poultry before putting it into the slow cooker, or cook recipes containing frozen meats an additional 4-6 hours on Low, or 2 hours on High.

Rachel Kauffman, Alto, MI

Pot Roast with Ketchup

Judi Manos, West Islip, NY

Makes 8 servings

Prep. Time: 10-15 minutes
Cooking Time: 8¼ hours
Ideal slow-cooker size: 4-qt.

4-lb. chuck roast, *or* stewing
   meat, cubed
1 Tbsp. oil
¾ can beer
½ cup, plus 1 Tbsp., ketchup
1 onion, sliced
1½ Tbsp. flour
½ cup cold water

1. Brown meat in oil in saucepan.
2. Combine beer and ketchup in slow cooker. Stir in onion and browned meat.
3. Cover. Cook on Low 8 hours.
4. Remove meat and keep warm. Blend flour into cold water until dissolved. Stir into hot gravy until smooth.

Serving suggestion: Serve gravy and meat together.

Italian Beef

Joyce Bowman, Lady Lake, FL

Makes 10-12 servings

Prep. Time: 5 minutes
Cooking Time: 3-10 hours
Ideal slow-cooker size: 4- to 6-qt.

3-4-lb. beef roast
1 pkg. dry Italian dressing mix
12-oz. can beer

1. Place roast in slow cooker. Sprinkle with dry Italian dressing mix. Pour beer over roast.
2. Cover. Cook on Low 8-10 hours, or High 3-4 hours.

*Serving suggestion: When beef is done, shred and serve with juice on **crusty rolls**.*

Variations:

In place of beef, use pork chops or chicken legs and thighs (skin removed).

Slow-Cooker Roast Beef

Ernestine Schrepfer, Trenton, MO

Makes 6 servings

Prep. Time: 5 minutes
Cooking Time: 8-10 hours
Ideal slow-cooker size: 5-qt.

3-lb. sirloin tip roast
½ cup flour
1 envelope dry onion soup
   mix
1 envelope brown gravy mix
2 cups ginger ale

1. Coat roast with flour (reserve remaining flour). Place in slow cooker.
2. Combine soup mix, gravy mix, remaining flour, and ginger ale in bowl. Mix well. Pour over roast.
3. Cover. Cook on Low 8-10 hours.

Savory Hungarian Goulash

Audrey Romonosky, Austin, TX

Makes 5-6 servings

Prep. Time: 10 minutes
Cooking Time: 8¼ hours
Ideal slow-cooker size: 3½-qt.

2 lbs. beef chuck, cubed
1 onion, sliced
½ tsp. garlic powder
½ cup ketchup
2 Tbsp. Worcestershire
   sauce
1 Tbsp. brown sugar
½ tsp. salt
2 tsp. paprika
½ tsp. dry mustard
1 cup cold water
½ cup water
¼ cup flour

1. Place meat in slow cooker. Add onion.
2. Combine garlic powder, ketchup, Worcestershire sauce, brown sugar, salt, paprika, mustard, and 1 cup water. Pour over meat.
3. Cover. Cook on Low 8 hours.
4. Dissolve flour in ½ cup water. Stir into meat mixture. Cook on High until thickened, about 10 minutes.

*Serving suggestion: Serve over **noodles**.*

Chuck Wagon Beef

Charlotte Bull, Cassville, MO

Makes 8 servings

Prep. Time: 20 minutes
Cooking Time: 8¼-10¼ hours
Ideal slow-cooker size: 4-qt.

4-lb. boneless chuck roast
1 tsp. garlic salt
¼ tsp. black pepper
2 Tbsp. oil
6-8 garlic cloves, minced
1 large onion, sliced
1 cup water
1 bouillon cube
2-3 tsp. instant coffee
1 bay leaf, *or* 1 Tbsp. mixed
    Italian herbs
3 Tbsp. cold water
2 Tbsp. cornstarch

1. Sprinkle roast with garlic salt and pepper. Brown on all sides in oil in saucepan. Place in slow cooker.

2. Sauté garlic and onion in meat drippings in saucepan. Add water, bouillon cube, and coffee. Cook over low heat for several minutes, stirring until drippings loosen. Pour over meat in cooker.

3. Add bay leaf or herbs.

4. Cover. Cook on Low 8-10 hours, or until very tender. Remove bay leaf and discard. Remove meat to serving platter and keep warm.

5. Mix water and cornstarch together until paste forms.

Stir into hot liquid and onions in cooker. Cover. Cook 10 minutes on High, or until thickened.

Serving suggestion: Slice meat and serve with gravy over top or on the side.

Peppery Roast

Lovina Baer, Conrath, WI

Makes 8-10 servings

Prep. Time: 10 minutes
Cooking Time: 6-8 hours
Ideal slow-cooker size: 4-qt.

4-lb. beef, *or* venison, roast
1 tsp. garlic salt
1 tsp. onion salt
2 tsp. celery salt
1½ tsp. salt
2 tsp. Worcestershire sauce
2 tsp. pepper
½ cup ketchup
1 Tbsp. liquid smoke
3 Tbsp. brown sugar
1 Tbsp. dry mustard
dash of nutmeg
1 Tbsp. soy sauce
1 Tbsp. lemon juice
3 drops hot pepper sauce

1. Place roast in slow cooker.

2. Combine remaining ingredients and pour over roast.

3. Cover. Cook on High 6-8 hours.

Zippy Beef Tips

Maryann Westerberg, Rosamond, CA

Makes 6-8 servings

Prep. Time: 5-10 minutes
Cooking Time: 8 hours
Ideal slow-cooker size: 4-qt.

2 lbs. stewing meat, cubed
2 cups sliced fresh
    mushrooms
10¾-oz. can cream of
    mushroom soup
1 envelope dry onion soup
    mix
1 cup 7-Up, *or* other lemon-
    lime carbonated drink

1. Place meat and mushrooms in slow cooker.

2. Combine mushroom soup, soup mix, and soda. Pour over meat.

3. Cover. Cook on Low 8 hours.

Serving suggestion: Serve over rice.

Horseradish Beef

Barbara Nolan, Pleasant Valley, NY

Makes 6-8 servings

Prep. Time: 10 minutes
Cooking Time: 8-10 hours
Ideal slow-cooker size: 4-qt.

3-4-lb. pot roast
2 Tbsp. oil
½ tsp. salt
½ tsp. pepper
1 onion, chopped
6-oz. can tomato paste
⅓ cup horseradish sauce

1. Brown roast on all sides in oil in skillet. Place in slow cooker. Add remaining ingredients.
2. Cover. Cook on Low 8-10 hours.

Spicy Pot Roast

Jane Talso, Albuquerque, NM

Makes 6-8 servings

Prep. Time: 5-10 minutes
Cooking Time: 4-10 hours
Ideal slow-cooker size: 2½- to 4-qt.

3-4-lb. beef pot roast
salt to taste
pepper to taste
¾-oz. pkg. brown gravy mix
¼ cup ketchup
2 tsp. Dijon mustard
1 tsp. Worcestershire sauce

⅛ tsp. garlic powder
1 cup water

1. Sprinkle meat with salt and pepper. Place in slow cooker.
2. Combine remaining ingredients. Pour over meat.
3. Cover. Cook on Low 8-10 hours, or on High 4-5 hours.

Chinese Pot Roast

Marsha Sabus, Fallbrook, CA

Makes 6 servings

Prep. Time: 10-15 minutes
Cooking Time: 8¼-10¼ hours
Ideal slow-cooker size: 4-qt.

3-lb. boneless beef pot roast
2 Tbsp. flour
1 Tbsp. oil
2 large onions, chopped
salt to taste
pepper to taste
½ cup soy sauce
1 cup water
½ tsp. ground ginger

1. Dip roast in flour and brown on both sides in oil in saucepan. Place in slow cooker.
2. Top with onions, salt, and pepper.
3. Combine soy sauce, water, and ginger. Pour over meat.
4. Cover. Cook on High 10 minutes. Reduce heat to Low and cook 8-10 hours.

Serving suggestion: Slice and serve with rice.

Mexican Pot Roast

Bernice A. Esau, North Newton, KS

Makes 6-8 servings

Prep. Time: 15 minutes
Cooking Time: 10-12 hours
Ideal slow-cooker size: 4-qt.

3 lbs. beef brisket, cubed
2 Tbsp. oil
½ cup slivered almonds
2 cups mild picante sauce, *or* hot, if you prefer
2 Tbsp. vinegar
1 tsp. garlic powder
½ tsp. salt
¼ tsp. cinnamon
¼ tsp. dried thyme
¼ tsp. dried oregano
⅛ tsp. ground cloves
⅛ tsp. pepper
½-¾ cup water, as needed

1. Brown beef in oil in skillet. Place in slow cooker.
2. Combine remaining ingredients. Pour over meat.
3. Cover. Cook on Low 10-12 hours. Add water as needed.

Serving suggestion: Serve with potatoes, noodles, or rice.

French Dip

Barbara Walker, Sturgis, SD

Makes 6-8 servings

Prep. Time: 5 minutes
Cooking Time: 10-12 hours
Ideal slow-cooker size: 2½- to 4½-qt.

3-lb. rump roast
½ cup soy sauce
1 beef bouillon cube
1 bay leaf
1 tsp. dried thyme
3-4 peppercorns
1 tsp. garlic powder

1. Combine all ingredients in slow cooker. Add water to almost cover meat.
2. Cover. Cook on Low 10-12 hours.

French Dip Roast

Patti Boston, Newark, OH

Makes 8-10 servings

Prep. Time: 5-10 minutes
Cooking Time: 5-12 hours
Ideal slow-cooker size: 3½- to 4½-qt.

1 large onion, sliced
3-lb. beef bottom roast
½ cup dry white wine, *or* water
1 pkg. dry au jus gravy mix
2 cups beef broth

1. Place onion in slow cooker. Add roast.
2. Combine wine and gravy mix. Pour over roast.
3. Add enough broth to cover roast.
4. Cover. Cook on High 5-6 hours, or on Low 10-12 hours.
5. Remove meat from liquid. Let stand 5 minutes before slicing thinly across grain.

Dripped Beef

Mitzi McGlynchey, Downingtown, PA

Makes 8 servings

Prep. Time: 5 minutes
Cooking Time: 6-7 hours
Ideal slow-cooker size: 4½-qt.

3-4-lb. chuck roast
1 tsp. salt
1 tsp. seasoned salt
1 tsp. white pepper
1 Tbsp. rosemary
1 Tbsp. dried oregano
1 Tbsp. garlic powder
1 cup water

1. Combine all ingredients in slow cooker.
2. Cover. Cook on Low 6-7 hours.
3. Shred meat using two forks. Strain liquid and return liquid and meat to slow cooker.

*Serving suggestion: Serve meat and au jus over mashed **potatoes**, **noodles**, or **rice**.*

Deep Pit Beef

Kristina Shull, Timberville, VA

Makes 6-8 servings

Prep. Time: 5 minutes
Marinating Time: 8 hours minimum
Cooking Time: 6-7 hours
Ideal slow-cooker size: 5-qt.

1 tsp. garlic salt, *or* powder
1 tsp. celery salt
1 tsp. lemon pepper
1½ Tbsp. liquid smoke
2 Tbsp. Worcestershire sauce
3-4-lb. beef roast

1. Combine seasonings in small bowl. Spread over roast as a marinade. Cover tightly with foil. Refrigerate for at least 8 hours.
2. Place roast in slow cooker. Cover with marinade sauce.
3. Cover. Cook on Low 6-7 hours. Save juice for gravy and serve with roast.

Note:
This is also good served cold, along with picnic foods.

Barbecued Roast Beef

Kim Stoltzfus, New Holland, PA

Makes 10-12 servings

Prep. Time: 10 minutes
Cooking Time: 3-8 hours
Ideal slow-cooker size: 5-qt.

4-lb. chuck roast
1 cup ketchup
1 cup barbecue sauce
2 cups chopped celery
2 cups water
1 cup chopped onions
4 Tbsp. vinegar
2 Tbsp. brown sugar
2 Tbsp. Worcestershire
   sauce
1 tsp. chili powder
1 tsp. garlic powder
1 tsp. salt

1. Combine all ingredients in large bowl. Spoon into 5-quart cooker, or 2 3½-quart cookers.

2. Cover. Cook on Low 6-8 hours, or on High 3-4 hours.

*Serving suggestion: Slice meat into thin slices and serve in barbecue sauce over mashed **potatoes** or **rice**.*

Italian Roast Beef

Elsie Russett, Fairbank, IA

Makes 6-8 servings

Prep. Time: 10 minutes
Cooking Time: 8-10 hours
Ideal slow-cooker size: 5-qt.

flour
4-lb. beef rump roast
1 onion
2 garlic cloves
1 large rib celery
2-oz. salt pork, *or* bacon
1 onion, sliced

1. Lightly flour roast.

2. In blender, grind onion, garlic, celery, and salt pork together. Rub ground mixture into roast.

3. Place sliced onion in slow cooker. Place roast on top of onion.

4. Cover. Cook on Low 8-10 hours.

Diane's Gutbuster

Joyce Cox, Port Angeles, WA

Makes 10-15 servings

Prep. Time: 10 minutes
Cooking Time: 10-12 hours
Ideal slow-cooker size: 6½-qt.

5-lb. chuck roast
1 large onion, sliced
2 tsp. salt
¾ tsp. pepper
28-oz. can stewed tomatoes
1 Tbsp. brown sugar
1 cup water
half a bottle barbecue sauce
1 Tbsp. Worcestershire
   sauce

1. Combine all ingredients except barbecue sauce and Worcestershire sauce in slow cooker.

2. Cover. Cook on Low 6-7 hours. Refrigerate for at least 8 hours.

3. Shred meat and place in slow cooker. Add barbecue sauce and Worcestershire sauce.

4. Cover. Cook on Low 4-5 hours.

*Serving suggestion: Serve as main dish or in **hamburger buns**.*

Roasting bags work well in the slow cooker. Simply fill with meat and vegetables and cook as directed in slow cooker recipes. Follow manufacturer's directions for filling and sealing bags.
Charlotte Shaffer, East Earl, PA

Barbecue Brisket

Patricia Howard, Albuquerque, NM

Makes 8-10 servings

Prep. Time: 5 minutes
Marinating Time: 8 hours
Cooking Time: 8-10 hours
Ideal slow-cooker size: 5-qt.

4-5-lb. beef brisket
⅛ tsp. celery salt
¼ tsp. garlic salt
¼ tsp. onion salt
¼ tsp. salt
3 Tbsp. liquid smoke
1½ cups barbecue sauce

1. Place brisket in slow cooker.
2. Sprinkle with celery salt, garlic salt, onion salt, and salt.
3. Pour liquid smoke over brisket. Cover. Refrigerate for 8 hours.
4. Cook on Low 8-10 hours, or until tender. During last hour pour barbecue sauce over brisket.

Easy Barbecued Beef or Pork Ribs

Moreen Weaver, Bath, NY

Makes 7-8 servings

Prep Time: 5 minutes
Cooking Time: 8-9 hours
Ideal slow-cooker size: 5- to 6-qt.

beef, *or* pork, ribs to nearly fill a 5- to 6-quart slow cooker
1 *or* 2 18-oz. bottles of your favorite barbecue sauce

1. Cut ribs into pieces that lay flat in your slow cooker.
2. Pour barbecue sauce over each layer of ribs.
3. Cover. Cook 8-9 hours on Low, or until meat begins to fall off the bones.

Note:

I live on a farm, and so we have an abundance of beef and pork in our freezer. I love ribs, but I don't always have time to prepare them. One day I decided to put ribs in my slow cooker and spoon barbecue sauce over them. They cooked all day on Low. By supper-time, they were deliciously tender.

Beef Ribs

Maryann Westerberg, Rosamond, CA

Makes 8-10 servings

Prep. Time: 5 minutes
Cooking Time: 8½ hours
Ideal slow-cooker size: 4-qt.

3-4-lb. boneless beef roast, *or* short ribs
1½ cups barbecue sauce, *divided*
½ cup apricot, *or* pineapple, jam
1 Tbsp. soy sauce

1. Place ribs in baking pan.
2. Combine ¾ cup barbecue sauce, jam, and soy sauce. Pour over ribs. Bake at 450° for 30 minutes until brown.
3. Take out of oven. Layer beef and sauce used in oven in slow cooker.
4. Cover. Cook on Low 8 hours.
5. Mix remaining ¾ cup barbecue sauce with sauce from slow cooker. Pour over ribs and serve.

A slow cooker set on Low does not burn food and will not spoil a meal if cooked beyond the designated time — within an hour, that is.

Eleanor J. Ferreira, North Chelmsford, MA

Chianti-Braised Short Ribs

Veronica Sabo, Shelton, CT

Makes 4 servings

Prep Time: 30-40 minutes
Cooking Time: 6 hours
Ideal slow-cooker size: 5- to 6-qt.

8 beef short ribs on bone
(4-5 lbs.)
salt to taste
pepper to taste
1 Tbsp. vegetable oil
1 onion, finely chopped
2 cups Chianti wine
2 tomatoes, seeded and
chopped
1 tsp. tomato paste
salt to taste
pepper to taste

1. Season ribs with salt and pepper.
2. Add vegetable oil to large skillet. Brown half the ribs 7-10 minutes, turning to brown all sides. Remove to slow cooker.
3. Repeat browning with second half of ribs. Transfer to slow cooker.
4. Pour off all but one tablespoon of drippings from skillet.
5. Sauté onion in skillet, scraping up any browned bits, until slightly softened, about 4 minutes.
6. Add wine and tomatoes to skillet. Bring to a boil.
7. Carefully pour hot mixture into slow cooker.
8. Cover. Cook on Low 6 hours, or until ribs are tender.
9. Transfer ribs to serving plate and cover to keep warm.
10. Strain cooking liquid from slow cooker into a measuring cup.
11. Skim off as much fat as possible.
12. Pour remaining juice into skillet used to brown ribs. Boil sauce until reduced to one cup.
13. Stir in tomato paste until smooth.
14. Season to taste with salt and pepper.

Serving suggestion: Serve sauce over ribs or on the side.

Reuben Sandwiches

Maryann Markano, Wilmington, DE

Makes 3-4 servings

Prep. Time: 5 minutes
Cooking Time: 3-4 hours
Ideal slow-cooker size: 3½-qt.

1-lb. can sauerkraut
1 lb. sliced corned beef
brisket
¼ lb. Swiss cheese, sliced

1. Drain sauerkraut in sieve, then on paper towels until very dry. Place in bottom of slow cooker.
2. Arrange layer of corned beef slices over sauerkraut. Top with cheese slices.
3. Cover. Cook on Low 3-4 hours.

*Serving suggestion: Toast **rye bread**. Spread generously with **sandwich spread** or **Thousand Island dressing**. Spoon ingredients from slow cooker onto toasted bread, maintaining layers of sauerkraut, meat, and cheese.*

Smoky Brisket

Angeline Lang, Greeley, CO

Makes 8-10 servings

Prep. Time: 5 minutes
Cooking Time: 10-12 hours
Ideal slow-cooker size: 4½- to 5-qt.

2 medium onions, sliced
3-4-lb. beef brisket
1 Tbsp. smoke-flavored salt
1 tsp. celery seed
1 Tbsp. mustard seed
½ tsp. pepper
12-oz. bottle chili sauce

1. Arrange onions in bottom of slow cooker.
2. Sprinkle both sides of meat with smoke-flavored salt.
3. Combine celery seed, mustard seed, pepper, and chili sauce. Pour over meat.
4. Cover. Cook on Low 10-12 hours.

Easy Barbecued Venison

Tracey B. Stenger, Gretna, LA

Makes 6 servings

Prep. Time: 5 minutes
Cooking Time: 8-10 hours
Ideal slow-cooker size: 5-qt.

2-3-lb. venison, *or* beef, roast, cubed
2 large onions, sliced in rings
1-2 18-oz. bottles barbecue sauce

1. Put layer of meat and layer of onion rings in slow cooker. Drizzle generously with barbecue sauce. Repeat layers until meat and onion rings are all in place.
2. Cover. Cook on Low 8-10 hours.

*Serving suggestion: Eat with au gratin **potatoes** and a **vegetable**, or slice thin and pile into **steak rolls**, drizzled with juice.*

Note:
   To be sure venison cooks tender, marinate overnight in 1 cup vinegar and 2 Tbsp. dried rosemary. In the morning, discard marinade, cut venison into cubes, and proceed with recipe.

Old World Sauerbraten

C.J. Slagle, Roann, IN
Angeline Lang, Greeley, CO

Makes 8 servings

Prep. Time: 10 minutes
Marinating Time: 24-36 hours
Cooking Time: 6¼-8¼ hours
Ideal slow-cooker size: 4-qt.

3½-4-lb. beef rump roast
1 cup water
1 cup vinegar
1 lemon, sliced but unpeeled
10 whole cloves
1 large onion, sliced
4 bay leaves
6 whole peppercorns
2 Tbsp. salt
2 Tbsp. sugar
12 gingersnaps, crumbled

1. Place meat in deep ceramic or glass bowl.
2. Combine water, vinegar, lemon, cloves, onion, bay leaves, peppercorns, salt, and sugar. Pour over meat. Cover and refrigerate 24-36 hours. Turn meat several times during marinating.
3. Place beef in slow cooker. Pour 1 cup marinade over meat.
4. Cover. Cook on Low 6-8 hours. Remove meat.
5. Strain meat juices and return to pot. Turn to High. Stir in gingersnaps. Cover and cook on High 10-14 minutes.

Serving suggestion: Slice meat. Pour finished sauce over meat.

Meatloaf Dinner

Esther Lehman, Croghan, NY

Makes 4 servings

Prep. Time: 15 minutes
Cooking Time: 9-10 hours
Ideal slow-cooker size: 4- to 5-qt.

6 potatoes, cubed
4 carrots, thinly sliced
¼ tsp. salt
1 egg, slightly beaten
1 large shredded wheat biscuit, crushed
¼ cup chili sauce
¼ cup finely chopped onion
½ tsp. salt
¼ tsp. dried marjoram
⅛ tsp. pepper
1 lb. ground beef

1. Place potatoes and carrots in slow cooker. Season with salt.
2. Combine egg, shredded wheat, chili sauce, onion, salt, marjoram, and pepper. Add ground beef. Mix well. Shape into loaf, slightly smaller in diameter than the cooker. Place on top of vegetables, not touching sides of cooker.
3. Cover. Cook on Low 9-10 hours.

Variation:
   Substitute ½ cup bread crumbs or dry oatmeal for crushed shredded wheat biscuit.

Ruth Ann's Meatloaf

Ruth Ann Hoover, New Holland, PA

Makes 4 servings

Prep. Time: 15 minutes
Cooking Time: 8-9 hours
Ideal slow-cooker size: 4-qt.

1 egg
¼ cup milk
2 slices day-old bread, cubed
¼ cup chopped onions
2 Tbsp. chopped green
  peppers
1 tsp. salt
¼ tsp. pepper
1½ lbs. ground beef
¼ cup ketchup
8 small red potatoes
4-6 medium carrots,
  cut in 1-inch chunks

1. Beat together eggs and milk.
2. Stir in bread cubes, onions, green peppers, salt, and pepper. Add beef and mix well.
3. Shape into loaf that is about an inch smaller in circumference than the inside of the slow cooker. Place loaf into slow cooker.
4. Spread top with ketchup.
5. Peel strip around the center of each potato. Place carrots and potatoes around meatloaf.
6. Cover. Cook on High 1 hour. Reduce heat to Low. Cook 7-8 hours longer.

Tracey's Italian Meatloaf

Tracey Yohn, Harrisburg, PA

Makes 8 servings

Prep. Time: 10 minutes
Cooking Time: 2½-6 hours
Ideal slow-cooker size: 4½-qt.

2 lbs. ground beef
2 cups soft bread crumbs
½ cup spaghetti sauce
1 large egg
2 Tbsp. dried onion
¼ tsp. pepper
1¼ tsp. salt
1 tsp. garlic salt
½ tsp. dried Italian herbs
¼ tsp. garlic powder
2 Tbsp. spaghetti sauce

1. Combine beef, bread crumbs, ½ cup spaghetti sauce, egg, onion, and seasonings. Shape into loaf. Place on top of foil in slow cooker. Spread 2 Tbsp. spaghetti sauce over top.
2. Cover. Cook on High 2½-3 hours, or on Low 5-6 hours.

Mary Ann's Italian Meatloaf

Mary Ann Wasick, West Allis, WI

Makes 8-10 servings

Prep. Time: 5-10 minutes
Cooking Time: 8 hours
Ideal slow-cooker size: 4½-qt.

2 lbs. ground beef
2 eggs, beaten
⅔ cup quick-cooking oats
1 envelope dry onion soup
  mix
½ cup pasta sauce (your
  favorite)
1 tsp. garlic powder
onion slices

1. Combine ground beef, eggs, oats, soup mix, pasta sauce, and garlic powder. Shape into a loaf. Place in slow cooker. Garnish top of loaf with onion slices.
2. Cover. Cook on Low 8 hours.

*Serving suggestion: Serve with **pasta** and more of the sauce that you mixed into the meatloaf.*

To remove meatloaf or other meats from your cooker, make foil handles to lift the food out. Use double strips of heavy foil to make 3 strips, each about 20" x 3". Crisscross them in the bottom of the pot and bring them up the sides in a spoke design before putting in the food.

John D. Allen, Rye, CO
Esther Lehman, Croghan, NY

Nutritious Meatloaf

Elsie Russett, Fairbank, IA

Makes 6 servings

Prep. Time: 10 minutes
Cooking Time: 3-4 hours
Ideal slow-cooker size: 4-qt.

1 lb. ground beef
2 cups finely shredded
 cabbage
1 medium green pepper,
 diced
1 Tbsp. dried onion flakes
½ tsp. caraway seeds
1 tsp. salt

1. Combine all ingredients. Shape into loaf and place on rack in slow cooker.
2. Cover. Cook on High 3-4 hours.

Meatloaf Sensation

Andrea O'Neil, Fairfield, CT

Makes 8 servings

Prep. Time: 5-10 minutes
Cooking Time: 8-10 hours
Ideal slow-cooker size: 4- to 5-qt.

2½ lbs. ground beef
half of an 8-oz. jar salsa

1 pkg. dry taco seasoning,
 divided
1 egg, slightly beaten
1 cup bread crumbs
12-oz. pkg. shredded
 Mexican-mix cheese
2 tsp. salt
½ tsp. pepper

1. Combine all ingredients, except half of taco seasoning. Mix well. Shape into loaf and place in slow cooker. Sprinkle with remaining taco seasoning.
2. Cover. Cook on Low 8-10 hours.

Barbecue Hamburger Steaks

Jeanette Oberholtzer, Manheim, PA

Makes 4 servings

Prep. Time: 5-10 minutes
Cooking Time: 4-6 hours
Ideal slow-cooker size: 4-qt.

1 lb. ground beef
1 tsp. salt
1 tsp. pepper
½ cup milk
1 cup soft bread crumbs
2 Tbsp. brown sugar
2 Tbsp. vinegar
3 Tbsp. Worcestershire
 sauce
1 cup ketchup

1. Combine beef, salt, pepper, milk, and bread crumbs. Mix well. Form into patties. Brown in saucepan and drain.
2. Combine brown sugar, vinegar, Worcestershire sauce, and ketchup in slow cooker. Add ground beef patties, pushing them down into the sauce, so that each one is well covered.
3. Cover. Cook on Low 4-6 hours.

Poor Man's Steak

Elsie Schlabach, Millersburg, OH

Makes 8-10 servings

Prep. Time: 10 minutes
Refrigeration Time: 8 hours minimum
Cooking Time: 2-3 hours
Ideal slow-cooker size: 3½-qt.

1½ lbs. ground beef
1 cup milk
¼ tsp. pepper
1 tsp. salt
1 small onion, finely
 chopped
1 cup cracker crumbs
1 tsp. brown sugar
10¾-oz. can cream of
 mushroom soup
1 soup can water

1. Mix together all ingredients except soup and water. Shape into narrow loaf. Refrigerate for at least 8 hours.
2. Slice and fry until brown in skillet.
3. Mix soup and water

together until smooth. Spread diluted soup on each piece. Place slices into cooker. Pour any remaining soup over slices in cooker.

4. Cover. Cook on Low 2-3 hours.

Beef Stroganoff

Julette Leaman, Harrisonburg, VA

Makes 6 servings

Prep. Time: 15 minutes
Cooking Time: 6-8 hours
Ideal slow-cooker size: 3½-qt.

2 lbs. ground beef
2 medium onions, chopped
2 garlic cloves, minced
6½-oz. can mushrooms
1½ cups sour cream
4 Tbsp. flour
2½ tsp. salt
¼ tsp. pepper
1 cup bouillon
3 Tbsp. tomato paste

1. In skillet, brown beef, onions, garlic, and mushrooms until meat and onions are brown. Drain. Pour into slow cooker.

2. Combine sour cream and flour. Add to mixture in slow cooker. Stir in remaining ingredients.

3. Cover. Cook on Low 6-8 hours.

*Serving suggestion: Serve over hot buttered **noodles**.*

Chili and Cheese on Rice

Dale and Shari Mast, Harrisonburg, VA

Makes 6 servings

Prep. Time: 15 minutes
Cooking Time: 4 hours
Ideal slow-cooker size: 4-qt.

1 lb. ground beef
1 onion, diced
1 tsp. dried basil
1 tsp. dried oregano
16-oz. can light red kidney beans
15½-oz. can chili beans
1 pint stewed tomatoes, drained

1. Brown ground beef and onion in skillet. Season with basil and oregano.

2. Combine all ingredients in slow cooker.

3. Cover. Cook on Low 4 hours.

*Serving suggestion: Serve over cooked **rice**. Top with grated **cheddar cheese**.*

Loretta's Spanish Rice

Loretta Krahn, Mt. Lake, MN

Makes 8 servings

Prep. Time: 15 minutes
Cooking Time: 6-10 hours
Ideal slow-cooker size: 6-qt.

2 lbs. ground beef, browned
2 medium onions, chopped
2 green peppers, chopped
28-oz. can tomatoes
8-oz. can tomato sauce
1½ cups water
2½ tsp. chili powder
2 tsp. salt
2 tsp. Worcestershire sauce
1½ cups rice, uncooked

1. Combine all ingredients in slow cooker.

2. Cover. Cook on Low 8-10 hours, or on High 6 hours.

Cut up vegetables for your slow-cooker recipe the night before and place them in ziplock bags in the refrigerator. This cuts down on preparation time in the morning.
Tracy Supcoe, Barclay, MD

A Hearty Western Casserole

Karen Ashworth, Duenweg, MO

Makes 5 servings

Prep. Time: 10 minutes
Cooking Time: 1 hour
Ideal slow-cooker size: 4-qt.

1 lb. ground beef, browned
16-oz. can whole corn, drained
16-oz. can red kidney beans, drained
10¾-oz. can condensed tomato soup
1 cup (4 oz.) Colby cheese
¼ cup milk
1 tsp. minced dry onion flakes
½ tsp. chili powder

1. Combine beef, corn, beans, soup, cheese, milk, onion, and chili powder in slow cooker.
2. Cover. Cook on Low 1 hour.

Variation:
1 pkg. (of 10) refrigerator biscuits
2 Tbsp. margarine
¼ cup yellow cornmeal

Dip biscuits in margarine and then in cornmeal. Bake 20 minutes or until brown. Top beef mixture with biscuits before serving.

Green Chili Stew

Jeanne Allen, Rye, CO

Makes 6-8 servings

Prep. Time: 20 minutes
Cooking Time: 4-6 hours
Ideal slow-cooker size: 4-qt.

1 large onion, diced
2 garlic cloves, minced
1 lb. ground sirloin
½ lb. ground pork
3 Tbsp. oil
3 cups chicken broth
2 cups water
2 4-oz. cans diced green chilies
4 large potatoes, diced
10-oz. pkg. frozen corn
1 tsp. black pepper
1 tsp. crushed dried oregano
½ tsp. ground cumin
1 tsp. salt

1. Brown onion, garlic, sirloin, and pork in oil in skillet. Cook until meat is no longer pink.
2. Combine all ingredients in slow cooker.
3. Cover. Cook on Low 4-6 hours, or until potatoes are soft.

*Serving suggestion: This recipe is excellent served with warm **tortillas** or **corn bread**.*

Cowboy Casserole

Lori Berezovsky, Salina, KS

Makes 4-6 servings

Prep. Time: 20 minutes
Cooking Time: 5-6 hours
Ideal slow-cooker size: 4½-qt.

1 onion, chopped
1½ lbs. ground beef, browned and drained
6 medium potatoes, sliced
1 clove garlic, minced
16-oz. can kidney beans
15-oz. can diced tomatoes mixed with 2 Tbsp. flour, *or* 10¾-oz. can tomato soup
1 tsp. salt
¼ tsp. pepper

1. Layer onions, ground beef, potatoes, garlic, and beans in slow cooker.
2. Spread tomatoes or soup over all. Sprinkle with salt and pepper.
3. Cover. Cook on Low 5-6 hours, or until potatoes are tender.

10-Layer Slow-Cooker Dish

Norma Saltzman, Shickley, NE

Makes 6-8 servings

Prep. Time: 20 minutes
Cooking Time: 4 hours
Ideal slow-cooker size: 5-qt.

6 medium potatoes, thinly
  sliced
1 medium onion, thinly
  sliced
salt to taste
pepper to taste
15-oz. can corn
15-oz. can peas
¼ cup water
1½ lbs. ground beef,
  browned
10¾-oz. can cream of
  mushroom soup

1. Layer 1: ¼ of potatoes, ½
of onion, salt, and pepper
2. Layer 2: ½ can of corn
3. Layer 3: ¼ of potatoes
4. Layer 4: ½ can of peas
5. Layer 5: ¼ of potatoes, ½
of onion, salt, and pepper
6. Layer 6: remaining corn
7. Layer 7: remaining
potatoes
8. Layer 8: remaining peas
and water
9. Layer 9: ground beef
10. Layer 10: soup
11. Cover. Cook on High
4 hours.

Hamburger Potatoes

Juanita Marner, Shipshewana, IN

Makes 3-4 servings

Prep. Time: 15 minutes
Cooking Time: 6-8 hours
Ideal slow-cooker size: 4-qt.

3 medium potatoes, sliced
3 carrots, sliced
1 small onion, sliced
2 Tbsp. dry rice
1 tsp. salt
½ tsp. pepper
1 lb. ground beef, browned
  and drained
1½-2 cups tomato juice, as
  needed to keep dish from
  getting too dry

1. Combine all ingredients
in slow cooker.
2. Cover. Cook on Low 6-8
hours.

Shipwreck

Betty Lahman, Elkton, VA

Makes 8 servings

Prep. Time: 15 minutes
Cooking Time: 6-8 hours
Ideal slow-cooker size: 4-qt.

1 lb. ground beef, browned
4-5 potatoes, cut in French-
  fry-like strips
1-2 onions, chopped
16-oz. can light red kidney
  beans, drained
¼ lb. Velveeta cheese, cubed
10¾-oz. can tomato soup
1½ tsp. salt
¼ tsp. pepper
butter

1. Layer in slow cooker
in this order: ground beef,
potatoes, onions, kidney
beans, and cheese. Pour soup
over top. Season with salt and
pepper. Dot with butter.
2. Cover. Cook on Low 6-8
hours.

*Serving suggestion: This is
particularly good served with
Parmesan cheese sprinkled on
top at the table.*

To prevent potatoes from darkening, slice them, then stir a mixture of 1 cup water and ½ tsp. cream of tartar into them. Drain, then place potatoes in cooker and proceed with the recipe. Dale Peterson, Rapid City, SD

Beef and Lentils

Esther Porter, Minneapolis, MN

Makes 12 servings

Prep. Time: 35 minutes
Cooking Time: 6-8 hours
Ideal slow-cooker size: 4- to 5-qt.

3 whole cloves
1 medium onion
5 cups water
1 lb. lentils
1 tsp. salt
1 bay leaf
1 lb. (*or less*) ground beef,
   browned and drained
½ cup ketchup
¼ cup molasses
2 Tbsp. brown sugar
1 tsp. dry mustard
¼ tsp. Worcestershire sauce
1 onion, finely chopped

1. Stick cloves into whole onion. Set aside.
2. In large saucepan, combine water, lentils, salt, bay leaf, and whole onion with cloves. Simmer 30 minutes.
3. Meanwhile, combine all remaining ingredients in slow cooker. Stir in simmered ingredients from saucepan. Add additional water if mixture seems dry.
4. Cover. Cook on Low 6-8 hours (check to see if lentils are tender).
Note:
   Freezes well.
Variation:
   Top with sour cream and/or salsa when serving.

Judy's Hamburger Stew

Judy Koczo, Plano, IL

Makes 6-8 servings

Prep. Time: 15 minutes
Cooking Time: 2-8 hours
Ideal slow-cooker size: 5-qt.

3 large potatoes, sliced
3 carrots, sliced
1 lb. frozen peas
1 onion, diced
2 ribs celery, sliced thin
salt to taste
pepper to taste
1½ lbs. ground beef,
   browned and drained
10¾-oz. can tomato soup
1 soup can water

1. Put vegetables in slow cooker in layers as listed. Season each layer with salt and pepper.
2. Layer beef on top of celery. Mix together soup and water. Pour over ground beef.
3. Cover. Cook on Low 6-8 hours, or on High 2-4 hours, stirring occasionally.

Variation:
   Substitute 28-oz. can whole, or diced, tomatoes in place of tomato soup and water.
   Ann Bender, Fort Defiance, VA

Taters 'n' Beef

Maryland Massey, Millington, MD

Makes 6-8 servings

Prep. Time: 20 minutes
Cooking Time: 4¼-6¼ hours
Ideal slow-cooker size: 4-qt.

2 lbs. ground beef, browned
1 tsp. salt
½ tsp. pepper
¼ cup chopped onions
1 cup canned tomato soup
6 potatoes, sliced
1 cup milk

1. Combine beef, salt, pepper, onions, and soup.
2. Place a layer of potatoes in bottom of slow cooker. Cover with a portion of the meat mixture. Repeat layers until ingredients are used.
3. Cover. Cook on Low 4-6 hours. Add milk and cook on High 15-20 minutes.

Variations:
   1. Use home-canned spaghetti sauce instead of tomato soup.
   2. Add a layer of chopped raw cabbage after each layer of sliced potatoes to add to the flavor, texture, and nutritional value of the meal.

Jeanne's Hamburger Stew

Jeanne Heyerly, Chenoa, IL

Makes 8 servings

Prep. Time: 20 minutes
Cooking Time: 8-10 hours
Ideal slow-cooker size: 4-qt.

2 lbs. ground beef
1 medium onion, chopped
1 garlic clove, minced
2 cups tomato juice
2-3 carrots, sliced
2-3 ribs celery, sliced
half a green pepper, chopped
2 cups green beans
2 medium potatoes, cubed
2 cups water
1 Tbsp. Worcestershire sauce
¼ tsp. dried oregano
¼ tsp. dried basil
¼ tsp. dried thyme
dash of hot pepper sauce
2 Tbsp. dry onion soup mix, *or* 1 beef bouillon cube
1 tsp. salt
¼ tsp. pepper

1. Brown meat and onion in saucepan. Drain. Stir in garlic and tomato juice. Heat to boiling.

2. Combine all ingredients in slow cooker.

3. Cover. Cook on Low 8-10 hours.

Variation:
Use 1 cup barley in place of potatoes.

Suit-Yourself Veggies with Beef

Carol Eberly, Harrisonburg, VA

Makes 6-8 servings

Prep Time: 20-30 minutes
Cooking Time: 6-8 hours
Ideal slow-cooker size: 4- to 5-qt.

3 cups grated raw carrots
2½ cups onions, sliced thin
6 cups grated raw potatoes
1 lb. ground beef, browned and drained
salt to taste
pepper to taste
10¾-oz. can cream of mushroom soup
1 Tbsp. Worcestershire sauce

1. Grate and slice vegetables either in the amounts above, or to suit tastes of those you're serving and size of your slow cooker.

2. Place layer of grated carrots in bottom. Season with salt and pepper.

3. Lay onion slices on top of carrots.

4. Place potatoes on top of onions. Season with salt and pepper.

5. Put hamburger on top of vegetables. Season with salt and pepper.

6. Combine soup and Worcestershire sauce in a small bowl.

7. Spoon soup mixture over all.

8. Cover. Cook 6-8 hours on Low, or until vegetables are as tender as you like them.

Supper-in-a-Dish

Martha Hershey, Ronks, PA

Makes 8 servings

Prep. Time: 20 minutes
Cooking Time: 4 hours
Ideal slow-cooker size: 4-qt.

1 lb. ground beef, browned and drained
1½ cups sliced raw potatoes
1 cup sliced carrots
1 cup peas
½ cup chopped onions
½ cup chopped celery
¼ cup chopped green peppers
1 tsp. salt
¼ tsp. pepper
10¾-oz. can cream of chicken, *or* mushroom, soup
¼ cup milk
⅔ cup grated sharp cheese

1. Layer ground beef, potatoes, carrots, peas, onions, celery, green peppers, salt, and pepper in slow cooker.

2. Combine soup and milk. Pour over layered ingredients. Sprinkle with cheese.

3. Cover. Cook on High 4 hours.

Ground Beef Casserole

Lois J. Cassidy, Willow Street, PA

Makes 6-8 servings

Prep. Time: 5-10 minutes
Cooking Time: 6-8 hours
Ideal slow-cooker size: 5-qt.

1½ lbs. ground beef
6-8 potatoes, sliced
1 medium onion, sliced
½ tsp. salt
dash of pepper
14½-oz. can cut green
    beans with juice
10¾-oz. can cream of
    mushroom soup

1. Crumble uncooked ground beef in bottom of slow cooker. Add potatoes, onion, salt, and pepper. Pour beans over all. Spread can of mushroom soup over beans.
2. Cover. Cook on Low 6-8 hours.

Variation:
   Brown the beef before putting in the slow cooker. Mix half a soup can of water with the mushroom soup before placing over beans.

Chinese Hamburger

Esther J. Yoder, Hartville, OH

Makes 8 servings

Prep. Time: 15 minutes
Cooking Time: 3-4 hours
Ideal slow-cooker size: 4-qt.

1 lb. ground beef, browned
    and drained
1 onion, diced
2 ribs celery, diced
10¾-oz. can chicken noodle
    soup
10¾-oz. can cream of
    mushroom soup
12-oz. can Chinese
    vegetables
salt to taste, about ¼-½ tsp.
pepper to taste, about ¼
    tsp.
1 green pepper, diced
1 tsp. soy sauce

1. Combine all ingredients in slow cooker.
2. Cover. Cook on High 3-4 hours.

Serving suggestion: Serve over rice.

Tater Tot Casserole

Shirley Hinh, Wayland, IA

Makes 6-8 servings

Prep. Time: 15 minutes
Cooking Time: 3 hours
Ideal slow-cooker size: 4½-qt.

32-oz. bag frozen tater tots
1 lb. ground beef, browned
½ tsp. salt
¼ tsp. pepper
2 14½-oz. cans green beans,
    drained
10¾-oz. can cream of
    mushroom soup
1 Tbsp. dried onions
¼ cup milk

1. Line slow cooker with frozen tater tots.
2. Combine remaining ingredients. Pour over potatoes.
3. Cover. Cook on High 3 hours.

*Serving suggestion: Sprinkle individual servings with your choice of grated **cheese**.*

Slow cookers come in a variety of sizes, from 2 to 8 quarts. The best size for a family of four or five is a 5- to 6-quart-size.   *Dorothy M. Van Deest, Memphis, TN*

Hash Brown Dinner

Rebecca Meyerkorth, Wamego, KS

Makes 6-8 servings

Prep Time: 15-30 minutes
Cooking Time: 4½ hours
Ideal slow-cooker size: 5-qt.

1 lb. ground beef
½ cup chopped onion
3 cups frozen hash brown
  potatoes, thawed
½ tsp. salt
½ tsp. pepper
1-lb. pkg. frozen California
  blend vegetables
10¾-oz. can cream of
  chicken soup
1 cup milk
¾ lb. cheese of your choice,
  cubed

1. Cook beef and chopped onion in skillet until browned.
2. Drain off drippings.
3. Place meat and onion mixture in lightly greased slow cooker.
4. Spoon potatoes over top of meat.
5. Sprinkle with salt and pepper.
6. Top with vegetables.
7. Combine soup and milk in a small bowl.
8. Pour over vegetables.
9. Cover. Cook on Low 4 hours.
10. Top with cheese.
11. Cover. Cook 30 minutes longer, or until cheese is melted.

Serving suggestion: Just before serving, sprinkle with **French-fried onions.**

Bean Tater Tot Casserole

Marjora Miller, Archbold, OH

Makes 6 servings

Prep. Time: 5-10 minutes
Cooking Time: 4 hours
Ideal slow-cooker size: 4-qt.

1 lb. ground beef
½ tsp. salt
¼ tsp. pepper
1 onion, chopped
1-lb. bag frozen string beans
10¾-oz. can cream of
  mushroom soup
1 cup shredded cheese
21-oz. bag. frozen tater tots

1. Crumble raw ground beef in bottom of slow cooker. Sprinkle with salt and pepper.
2. Layer remaining ingredients on beef in order listed.
3. Cover. Cook on High 1 hour. Reduce heat to Low and cook 3 hours.

Variation:

In order to reduce the calorie content of this dish, use raw shredded potatoes instead of tater tots.

Noodle Hamburger Dish

Esther J. Yoder, Hartville, OH

Makes 10 servings

Prep. Time: 20 minutes
Cooking Time: 3-4 hours
Ideal slow-cooker size: 4- to 5-qt.

1½ lbs. ground beef,
  browned and drained
1 green pepper, diced
1 qt. whole tomatoes
10¾-oz. can cream of
  mushroom soup
1 large onion, diced
1½ Tbsp. Worcestershire
  sauce
8-oz. pkg. noodles, uncooked
1 tsp. salt
¼ tsp. pepper

1. Combine all ingredients in slow cooker.
2. Cover. Cook on High 3-4 hours.

Serving suggestion: Sprinkle with shredded **cheese** *before serving.*

Meal-in-One-Casserole

Elizabeth Yoder, Millersburg, OH
Marcella Stalter, Flanagan, IL

Makes 4-6 servings

Prep. Time: 20 minutes
Cooking Time: 4 hours
Ideal slow-cooker size: 4-qt.

1 lb. ground beef
1 medium onion, chopped
1 medium green pepper, chopped
15¼-oz. can whole kernel corn, drained
4-oz. can mushrooms, drained
1 tsp. salt
¼ tsp. pepper
11-oz. jar salsa
5 cups uncooked medium egg noodles
28-oz. can diced tomatoes, undrained
1 cup shredded cheddar cheese

1. Cook beef and onion in saucepan over medium heat until meat is no longer pink. Drain. Transfer to slow cooker.
2. Top with green pepper, corn, and mushrooms. Sprinkle with salt and pepper. Pour salsa over mushrooms. Cover and cook on Low 3 hours.
3. Cook noodles according to package in separate pan. Drain and add to slow cooker after mixture in cooker has cooked for 3 hours. Top with tomatoes. Sprinkle with cheese.

4. Cover. Cook on Low 1 more hour.

Variation:
   Add uncooked noodles after salsa. Pour tomatoes and 1 cup water over all. Sprinkle with cheese. Cover and cook on Low 4 hours, or until noodles are tender.
   Nadine Martinitz, Salina, KS

Yum-e-setti

Elsie Schlabach, Millersburg, OH

Makes 6-8 servings

Prep. Time: 20 minutes
Cooking Time: 2-3 hours
Ideal slow-cooker size: 4- to 5-qt.

1½ lbs. ground beef, browned and drained
10¾-oz. can tomato soup
10¾-oz. can cream of chicken soup
8-oz. pkg. wide noodles, cooked
1 cup chopped celery, cooked tender
1 lb. frozen mixed vegetables
2 tsp. salt
½ lb. Velveeta cheese, cubed

1. Combine ground beef and tomato soup.
2. Combine chicken soup, noodles, and celery.
3. Layer beef mixture, chicken mixture, and vegetables. Sprinkle with salt. Lay cheese over top.

4. Cover. Cook on Low 2-3 hours.

Variation:
   For more bite, use shredded cheddar cheese instead of cubed Velveeta.

Shell Casserole

Jean Butzer, Batavia, NY

Makes 4-5 servings

Prep. Time: 20 minutes
Cooking Time: 2¼-3¼ hours
Ideal slow-cooker size: 4-qt.

1 lb. ground beef
1 small onion, chopped
¾ tsp. salt
¼ tsp. garlic powder
1 tsp. Worcestershire sauce
¼ cup flour
1¼ cups hot water
2 tsp. beef bouillon granules
2 Tbsp. red wine
6 oz. medium-sized shell pasta, uncooked
4-oz. can sliced mushrooms, drained
1 cup sour cream

1. Brown ground beef and onion in saucepan. Drain. Place in slow cooker.
2. Stir in salt, garlic powder, Worcestershire sauce, and flour.
3. Add water, bouillon, and wine. Mix well.

4. Cover. Cook on Low 2-3 hours.

5. Cook pasta in separate pan according to package directions. Stir cooked pasta, mushrooms, and sour cream into slow cooker. Cover. Cook on High 10-15 minutes.

Family Favorite Casserole

Lizzie Weaver, Ephrata, PA

Makes 6-8 servings

Prep. Time: 20 minutes
Cooking Time: 2-5 hours
Ideal slow-cooker size: 5½-qt.

1½ lbs. ground beef
1 onion, chopped
1½ cups diced potatoes
1½ cups sliced carrots
1½ cups peas
1½ cups macaroni, cooked
10¾-oz. can cream of celery soup
½ lb. cheddar cheese, grated
2 cups milk
1½ tsp. salt

1. Fry beef and onion in saucepan until brown. Drain.
2. Cook vegetables just until soft.
3. Combine all ingredients in slow cooker.
4. Cover. Cook on High 2 hours, or on Low 4-5 hours.

Variation:
Skip pre-cooking the

vegetables; add them raw to the slow cooker. Increase cooking time to 4 hours on High, or 8-10 hours on Low.

Add the cooked macaroni and the milk during the last 15 minutes if cooking on High, or during the last 30 minutes if cooking on Low.

Tastes-Like-Turkey

Lizzie Weaver, Ephrata, PA

Makes 6 servings

Prep. Time: 10-15 minutes
Cooking Time: 3-8 hours
Ideal slow-cooker size: 4- to 5-qt.

2 lbs. hamburger, browned
1 tsp. salt
½ tsp. pepper
2 10¾-oz. cans cream of chicken soup
10¾-oz. can cream of celery soup
4 scant cups milk
1 large pkg. bread stuffing, *or* large loaf of bread, torn in pieces

1. Combine all ingredients in large buttered slow cooker.
2. Cover. Cook on High 3 hours, or on Low 6-8 hours.

Meatball Stew

Nanci Keatley, Salem, OR
Ada Miller, Sugarcreek, OH

Makes 8 servings

Prep. Time: 20-25 minutes
Cooking Time: 4-5 hours
Ideal slow-cooker size: 4-qt.

2 lbs. ground beef
½ tsp. salt
½ tsp. pepper
6 medium potatoes, cubed
1 large onion, sliced
6 medium carrots, sliced
1 cup ketchup
1 cup water
1½ tsp. balsamic vinegar
1 tsp. dried basil
1 tsp. dried oregano
½ tsp. salt
½ tsp. pepper

1. Combine beef, ½ tsp. salt, and ½ tsp. pepper. Mix well. Shape into 1-inch balls. Brown meatballs in saucepan over medium heat. Drain.
2. Place potatoes, onion, and carrots in slow cooker. Top with meatballs.
3. Combine ketchup, water, vinegar, basil, oregano, ½ tsp. salt, and ½ tsp. pepper. Pour over meatballs.
4. Cover. Cook on High 4-5 hours, or until vegetables are tender.

Sweet and Sour Meatballs with Vegetables

Barbara Katrine Rose, Woodbridge, VA

*Makes 4-6 servings
(24 small meatballs)*

*Prep. Time: 25 minutes
Cooking Time: 3½-4½ hours
Ideal slow-cooker size: 4-qt.*

Meatballs:
1 lb. ground beef
1 cup drained, unsweetened,
    crushed pineapple
2 slices crumbled whole
    wheat bread
2 tsp. instant minced onion
2 tsp. Worcestershire sauce
¼ tsp. garlic powder
¼ tsp. dry mustard
¼ tsp. pepper

Sauce:
4 tsp. Worcestershire sauce
2 tsp. vinegar
1 tsp. dried Italian seasoning
¼ tsp. garlic powder
¼ tsp. cinnamon
¼ tsp. pepper
2 4-oz. cans sliced
    mushrooms, undrained
2 cups sliced carrots
3 cups tomato juice
4 tsp. instant minced onion
4 Tbsp. minced green peppers

1. Combine all meatball
ingredients. Shape into
meatballs, using 1 heaping
tablespoon mixture for each.

Place on rack in baking pan.
2. Bake at 350° for 30
minutes, or until done.
3. Combine all sauce
ingredients and meatballs in
slow cooker.
4. Cover. Cook on High
3-4 hours.

*Serving suggestion: Serve over
rice.*

BBQ Meatballs

Kathryn Yoder, Minot, ND

*Makes 12-15 main-dish servings,
or 20-25 appetizer servings*

*Prep. Time: 20 minutes
Cooking Time: 7-10 hours
Ideal slow-cooker size: 4-qt.*

Meatballs:
3 lbs. ground beef
5-oz. can evaporated milk
1 cup dry oatmeal (rolled,
    or instant)
1 cup cracker crumbs
2 eggs
½ cup chopped onions
½ tsp. garlic powder
2 tsp. salt
½ tsp. pepper
2 tsp. chili powder

Sauce:
2 cups ketchup
1 cup brown sugar
1½ tsp. liquid smoke
½ tsp. garlic powder
¼ cup chopped onions

1. Combine all meatball
ingredients. Shape into
walnut-sized balls. Place on
waxed paper-lined cookie
sheets. Freeze. When fully
frozen, place in plastic bag
and store in freezer until
needed.
2. When ready to use, place
frozen meatballs in slow
cooker. Cover. Cook on High
as you mix up sauce.
3. Pour combined sauce
ingredients over meatballs.
Stir.
4. Cover. Continue cooking
on High 1 hour. Stir. Turn to
Low and cook 6-9 hours.

Variation:
    Instead of using barbecue
sauce, cook meatballs with
spaghetti sauce or cream of
mushroom soup.

*The great thing about using a slow cooker in hot
weather is that it doesn't heat up your kitchen like an
oven does.*
                        Carol Peachey, Lancaster, PA

Mary Ellen's Barbecued Meatballs

Mary Ellen Wilcox, Scatia, NY

Makes about 60 small meatballs

Prep. Time: 30 minutes
Cooking Time: 5 hours
Ideal slow-cooker size: 2-qt.

Meatballs:
¾-lb. ground beef
¾ cup bread crumbs
1½ Tbsp. minced onion
½ tsp. horseradish
3 drops Tabasco sauce
2 eggs, beaten
¾ tsp. salt
½ tsp. pepper
butter

Sauce:
¾ cup ketchup
½ cup water
¼ cup cider vinegar
2 Tbsp. brown sugar
1 Tbsp. minced onion
2 tsp. horseradish
1 tsp. salt
1 tsp. dry mustard
3 drops Tabasco
dash pepper

1. Combine all meatball ingredients except butter. Shape into ¾-inch balls. Brown in butter in skillet. Place in slow cooker.

2. Combine all sauce ingredients. Pour over meatballs.

3. Cover. Cook on Low 5 hours.

Cocktail Meatballs

Irene Klaeger, Inverness, FL

Makes 6 main dish servings, or 12 appetizer servings

Prep. Time: 35 minutes
Cooking Time: 4 hours
Ideal slow-cooker size: 3½-qt.

2 lbs. ground beef
⅓ cup ketchup
3 tsp. dry bread crumbs
1 egg, beaten
2 tsp. onion flakes
¾ tsp. garlic salt
½ tsp. pepper
1 cup ketchup
1 cup packed brown sugar
6-oz. can tomato paste
¼ cup soy sauce
¼ cup cider vinegar
1-1½ tsp. hot pepper sauce

1. Combine ground beef, ⅓ cup ketchup, bread crumbs, egg, onion flakes, garlic salt, and pepper. Mix well. Shape into 1-inch meatballs. Place on jelly roll pan. Bake at 350° for 18 minutes, or until brown. Place in slow cooker.

2. Combine 1 cup ketchup, brown sugar, tomato paste, soy sauce, vinegar, and hot pepper sauce. Pour over meatballs.

3. Cover. Cook on Low 4 hours.

Great Meatballs

Judy Denney, Lawrenceville, GA

Makes 12-16 main dish-size servings, or 24 appetizer-size servings

Prep. Time: 10-15 minutes
Cooking Time: 5 hours
Ideal slow-cooker size: 5-qt.

4 lbs. ground beef
2 eggs
4 slices fresh bread, torn into bread crumbs
1½ tsp. salt
½ tsp. pepper
1 cup tomato juice
2 10-oz. jars chili sauce
2 cans whole cranberry sauce

1. Mix together beef, eggs, bread crumbs, seasonings, and tomato juice. Form into small meatballs. Place in slow cooker.

2. Pour chili sauce and cranberry sauce on top of meatballs. Stir lightly.

3. Cover. Cook on High 2 hours. Reduce heat to Low and cook 3 more hours.

Sweet and Sour Meatballs with Pineapples

Elaine Unruh, Minneapolis, MN

Makes 6-8 main-dish servings, or 20-30 appetizer servings

Prep. Time: 40-45 minutes
Cooking Time: 6 hours
Ideal slow-cooker size: 4-qt.

Meatballs:
2 lbs. ground beef
1¼ cups bread crumbs
1½ tsp. salt
1 tsp. pepper
2-3 Tbsp. Worcestershire sauce
1 egg
½ tsp. garlic salt
¼ cup finely chopped onions

Sauce:
1 can pineapple chunks, juice reserved
3 Tbsp. cornstarch
¼ cup cold water
1-1¼ cups ketchup
¼ cup Worcestershire sauce
¼ tsp. salt
¼ tsp. pepper
¼ tsp. garlic salt
½ cup chopped green peppers

1. Combine all meatball ingredients. Shape into 60-80 meatballs. Brown in skillet, rolling so all sides are browned. Place meatballs in slow cooker.

2. Pour juice from pineapples into skillet. Stir into drippings.

3. Combine cornstarch and cold water. Add to skillet and stir until thickened.

4. Stir in ketchup and Worcestershire sauce. Season with salt, pepper, and garlic salt. Add green peppers and pineapples. Pour over meatballs.

5. Cover. Cook on Low 6 hours.

Barbecued Meatballs

Esther Becker, Gordonville, PA
Ruth Shank, Gridley, IL

Makes 30 small meatballs

Prep. Time: 25-30 minutes
Cooking Time: 6-10 hours
Ideal slow-cooker size: 4-qt.

1½ cups chili sauce
1 cup grape, *or* apple, jelly
3 tsp. brown spicy mustard
1 lb. ground beef
1 egg
3 Tbsp. dry bread crumbs
½ tsp. salt

1. Combine chili sauce, jelly, and mustard in slow cooker. Mix well.

2. Cover. Cook on High while preparing meatballs.

3. Mix together remaining ingredients. Shape into 30 balls. Place in baking pan and bake at 400° for 15-20 minutes. Drain well. Spoon into slow cooker. Stir gently to coat well.

4. Cover. Cook on Low 6-10 hours.

Variations:

1. To increase flavor, add ¼ tsp. pepper, ¼ tsp. Italian spice, and a dash of garlic powder to the meatball mixture.
Sandra Thom, Jenks, OK

2. Use Italian or seasoned bread crumbs in meatball mixture. Add 1 tsp. Worcestershire sauce and 1½ Tbsp. fresh parsley to meatball mixture.
Barbara Sparks, Glen Burnie, MD

3. Make meatballs larger and serve with rice or noodles.

Party Meatballs

Marie Miller, Scotia, NY

Makes 8-10 main-dish servings

Prep. Time: 10 minutes
Cooking Time: 2-4 hours
Ideal slow-cooker size: 4-qt.

16-oz. can jellied cranberry sauce
16-oz. jar salsa
2 lbs. frozen meatballs (see recipe for making BBQ Meatballs on page 184)

1. Melt cranberry sauce in saucepan. Stir in salsa and meatballs. Bring to boil. Stir. Pour into slow cooker.

2. Cover. Cook on Low 2-4 hours.

Nancy's Meatballs

Betty Richards, Rapid City, SD

Makes 8 main-dish servings

Prep. Time: 10 minutes
Cooking Time: 6-8 hours
Ideal slow-cooker size: 5- to 6-qt.

3-4-lb. bag prepared meatballs (see recipe for making BBQ Meatballs on page 184)
3 10¾-oz. cans cream of mushroom, *or* cream of celery, soup
4-oz. can button mushrooms
16-oz. jar Cheez Whiz
1 medium onion, diced

1. Combine all ingredients in slow cooker.

2. Cover. Cook on Low 6-8 hours.

*Serving suggestion: Use as an appetizer, or as a main dish served over **noodles** or **rice**.*

Slow-Cooked Cabbage Rolls

Rebecca Meyerkorth, Wamego, KS

Makes 6 servings

Prep Time: 30-45 minutes
Cooking Time: 6-7 hours
Ideal slow-cooker size: 3-qt.

---

large head of cabbage

1 egg, beaten
8-oz. can tomato sauce
¾ cup minute rice, uncooked
½ cup green pepper, chopped
½ cup (approx. 15) crushed crackers
1 envelope dry onion soup mix
1½ lbs. ground beef, browned
46-oz. can vegetable juice

1. Cook whole head of cabbage in boiling water just until outer leaves begin to loosen. Pull off 12 large leaves. Drain well. (Use remaining leaves for another meal.)

2. Cut out thick veins from bottoms of reserved leaves.

3. Combine egg, tomato sauce, rice, green pepper, cracker crumbs, and soup mix in a bowl.

4. Crumble beef over mixture and mix well.

5. Place approximately ⅓ cup of mixture on each cabbage leaf.

6. Fold in sides, beginning from cut end.

7. Roll up completely to enclose meat.

8. Secure each roll with a toothpick.

9. Place cabbage rolls in 3-quart slow-cooker.

10. Pour vegetable juice over rolls.

11. Cover and cook on Low 6-7 hours, or until rice is fully cooked, or filling reaches 160°.

*Serving suggestion: Just before serving, sprinkle each roll with **salt** and grated **Parmesan cheese**.*

Swedish Cabbage Rolls

Jean Butzer, Batavia, NY
Pam Hochstedler, Kalona, IA

Makes 6 servings

Prep. Time: 25 minutes
Cooking Time: 7-9 hours
Ideal slow-cooker size: 2- to 4-qt.

---

12 large cabbage leaves
1 egg, beaten
¼ cup milk
¼ cup finely chopped onions
1 tsp. salt
¼ tsp. pepper
1 lb. ground beef, browned and drained
1 cup cooked rice
8-oz. can tomato sauce
1 Tbsp. brown sugar
1 Tbsp. lemon juice
1 tsp. Worcestershire sauce

1. Immerse cabbage leaves in boiling water for about 3 minutes or until limp. Drain.

2. Combine egg, milk, onions, salt, pepper, beef, and rice. Place about ¼ cup meat mixture in center of each leaf. Fold in sides and roll ends over meat. Place in slow cooker.

3. Combine tomato sauce, brown sugar, lemon juice, and Worcestershire sauce. Pour over cabbage rolls.

4. Cover. Cook on Low 7-9 hours.

Cabbage Dinner

Kathi Rogge, Alexandria, IN

Makes 6-8 servings

Prep. Time: 10 minutes
Cooking Time: 8-10 hours
Ideal slow-cooker size: 7-qt.

medium head of cabbage
6-8 medium-sized potatoes
2 lbs. smoked sausage, *or*
   turkey sausage
salt to taste
1 qt. water

1. Cut cabbage into
1-2-inch-wide wedges. Place in
slow cooker.
2. Wash and quarter
potatoes. Do not peel. Add to
cabbage in slow cooker.
3. Cut sausage into bite-
sized pieces. Add to slow
cooker. Add salt and mix well.
4. Pour water into slow
cooker.
5. Cover. Cook on High
2 hours, and then on Low
6-8 hours, or until vegetables
are tender.

Stuffed Green Peppers

Lois Stoltzfus, Honey Brook, PA

Makes 6 servings

Prep. Time: 20 minutes
Cooking Time: 3-8 hours
Ideal slow-cooker size: 5- to 6-qt.

6 large green peppers
1 lb. ground beef, browned
2 Tbsp. minced onion
1 tsp. salt
⅛ tsp. garlic powder
2 cups cooked rice
15-oz. can tomato sauce
¾ cup shredded mozzarella
cheese

1. Cut peppers in half and
remove seeds.
2. Combine all ingredients
except peppers and cheese.
3. Stuff peppers with
ground beef mixture. Place in
slow cooker.
4. Cover. Cook on Low 6-8
hours, or on High 3-4 hours.
Sprinkle with cheese during
last 30 minutes.

Stuffed Bell Peppers

Mary Puterbaugh, Elwood, IN

Makes 8 servings

Prep. Time: 20 minutes
Cooking Time: 5-11 hours
Ideal slow-cooker size: 6- to 7-qt.

2 lbs. ground beef, lightly
   browned
1 large onion, chopped
1 cup cooked rice
2 eggs, beaten
½ cup milk
½ cup ketchup
dash hot pepper sauce
2 tsp. salt
½ tsp. pepper
8 large bell peppers, capped
   and seeded

1. Combine all ingredients
except peppers. Gently pack
mixture into peppers. Place in
greased slow cooker.
2. Cover. Cook on Low
9-11 hours, or on High 5-6
hours.

You may want to revise herb amounts when using a slow cooker. Whole herbs and spices increase their flavoring power, while ground spices tend to lose some flavor. It's a good idea to season to taste before serving.

Irma H. Schoen, Windsor, CT

Spicy Lasagna

Kathy Hertzler, Lancaster, PA
L. Jean Moore, Pendleton, IN
Mary Ellen Musser, Reinholds, PA

Makes 6 servings

Prep. Time: 20 minutes
Cooking Time: 3-9 hours
Ideal slow-cooker size: 4- to 5-qt.

10-oz. pkg. lasagna noodles,
 broken into bite-sized
 pieces, cooked
1 lb. ground beef, browned
½ lb. Italian sausage, sliced
 and browned
1 onion, chopped
1 clove garlic, minced
12 oz. mozzarella cheese,
 shredded
12 oz. cottage, *or* ricotta,
 cheese
16-oz. can tomato sauce
1 tsp. dried basil
½ tsp. dried oregano
1½ Tbsp. dried parsley
 flakes
½ tsp. pepper
1½ tsp. salt

1. Combine all ingredients
in greased slow cooker.
2. Cover. Cook on Low 7-9
hours, or on High 3-5 hours.

Variation:
  Replace mix of ground beef
and sausage with 1½ lbs.
ground beef.

Helen's Lasagna

Helen King, Fairbank, IA
Clarice Williams, Fairbank, IA
Nancy Zimmerman, Loysville, PA

Makes 6-8 servings

Prep. Time: 20 minutes
Cooking Time: 4-5 hours
Ideal slow-cooker size: 6-qt.

1 lb. ground beef
1 medium onion, chopped
2 cloves garlic, minced
29-oz. can tomato sauce
1 cup water
6-oz. can tomato paste
1 tsp. salt
1 tsp. dried oregano
8-oz. pkg. lasagna noodles,
 uncooked
4 cups (16 oz.) shredded
 mozzarella cheese
1½ cups (12 oz.) small-curd
 cottage cheese
½ cup grated Parmesan cheese

1. Cook beef, onion, and
garlic together in saucepan
until browned. Drain.
2. Stir in tomato sauce,
water, tomato paste, salt, and
oregano. Mix well.
3. Spread one-fourth of
meat sauce in ungreased slow
cooker. Arrange one-third of
noodles over sauce.
4. Combine the cheeses.
Spoon one-third of cheese
mixture over noodles. Repeat
layers twice. Top with remaining meat sauce.
5. Cover. Cook on Low 4-5
hours.

Variation:
  For a fuller flavor, use 14-oz.
can tomato sauce instead of 6-oz.
can tomato paste and water.
Add ½ tsp. garlic powder, 1 tsp.
dried basil, and ¼ tsp. pepper.
  Dolores S. Kratz, Souderton, PA

Violette's Lasagna

Violette Harris Denney, Carrollton, GA

Makes 8 servings

Prep. Time: 20 minutes
Cooking Time: 5 hours
Ideal slow-cooker size: 6-qt.

8 lasagna noodles,
 uncooked, *divided*
1 lb. ground beef, *divided*
1 tsp. Italian seasoning
28-oz. jar spaghetti sauce,
 divided
⅓ cup water, *divided*
4-oz. can sliced mushrooms,
 divided
15 oz. ricotta cheese, *divided*
2 cups shredded mozzarella
 cheese, *divided*

1. Break noodles. Place half
in bottom of greased slow cooker.
2. Brown ground beef in
saucepan. Drain. Stir in Italian
seasoning. Spread half over
noodles in slow cooker.
3. Layer half of sauce and
water, half of mushrooms, half
of ricotta cheese, and half of
mozzarella cheese over beef.
Repeat layers.
4. Cover. Cook on Low 5 hours.

Rigatoni

Susan Alexander, Baltimore, MD

Makes 10 servings

Prep. Time: 20 minutes
Cooking Time: 4-5 hours
Ideal slow-cooker size: 5-qt.

28-oz. jar spaghetti sauce
12 oz. rigatoni, cooked
1-1½ lbs. ground beef,
  browned
3 cups shredded mozzarella
  cheese
½ lb. pepperoni slices
sliced mushrooms, *optional*
sliced onions, *optional*

1. In slow cooker, layer half of each ingredient in order listed. Repeat.
2. Cover. Cook on Low 4-5 hours.

Variation:
  Use 1 lb. ground beef and 1 lb. sausage.

Taco Bake

Shelia Heil, Lancaster, PA

Makes 4-6 servings

Prep Time: 10-15 minutes
Cooking Time: 1½-4 hours
Ideal slow-cooker size: 4-qt.

1 lb. ground beef
1 onion, chopped
¾ cup water
15-oz. can tomato sauce
1¼-oz. envelope taco
  seasoning
8-oz. pkg. shell macaroni,
  uncooked

1. Brown beef and onion in a skillet.
2. Drain off drippings.
3. Add water, tomato sauce, and taco seasoning.
4. Mix well.
5. Simmer 15 minutes in skillet.
6. Transfer to slow cooker.
7. Stir in uncooked macaroni.
8. Cover. Cook on High 1½ hours, or on Low 4 hours, or until macaroni are fully cooked but not mushy.

*Serving suggestion: Just before serving, top with shredded **cheddar cheese**.*

Beef Enchiladas

Jane Talso, Albuquerque, NM

Makes 12-16 servings

Prep. Time: 15 minutes
Cooking Time: 4-5 hours
Ideal slow-cooker size: 6-qt.

4-lb. boneless chuck roast
2 Tbsp. oil
4 cups sliced onions
2 tsp. salt
2 tsp. black pepper
2 tsp. cumin seeds
2 4½-oz. cans peeled, diced
  green chilies
14½-oz. can peeled, diced
  tomatoes
8 large tortillas (10-12 inch
  size)
1 lb. cheddar cheese,
  shredded
4 cups green, *or* red,
  enchilada sauce

1. Brown roast on all sides in oil in saucepan. Place roast in slow cooker.
2. Add remaining ingredients except tortillas, cheese, and sauce.
3. Cover. Cook on High 4-5 hours.
4. Shred meat with fork and return to slow cooker.
5. Warm tortillas in oven. Heat enchilada sauce. Fill each tortilla with ¾ cup beef mixture and ½ cup cheese. Roll up and serve with sauce.

Variation:

Use 2 lbs. ground beef instead of chuck roast. Brown without oil in saucepan, along with chopped onions.

Slow-Cooker Enchiladas

Lori Berezovsky, Salina, KS
Tracy Clark, Mt. Crawford, VA
Mary E. Herr and **Michelle Reineck**
Three Rivers, MI
Marcia S. Myer, Manheim, PA
Renee Shirk, Mt. Joy, PA
Janice Showalter, Flint, MI

Makes 4 servings

Prep. Time: 30 minutes
Cooking Time: 5-7 hours
Ideal slow-cooker size: 4-qt.

1 lb. ground beef
1 cup chopped onions
½ cup chopped green peppers
16-oz. can red kidney beans, rinsed and drained
15-oz. can black beans, rinsed and drained
10-oz. can diced tomatoes with green chilies, undrained
⅓ cup water
1½ tsp. chili powder
½ tsp. ground cumin
½ tsp. salt
¼ tsp. pepper
1 cup (4 ozs.) shredded sharp cheddar cheese
1 cup (4 ozs.) shredded Monterey Jack, *or* pepper Monterey Jack, cheese

6 flour tortillas (6-7 inches in diameter)

1. Cook beef, onions, and green peppers in skillet until beef is browned and vegetables are tender. Drain.
2. Add next 8 ingredients and bring to boil. Reduce heat. Cover and simmer 10 minutes.
3. Combine cheeses.
4. In slow cooker, layer about ¾ cup beef mixture, one tortilla, and about ⅓ cup cheese. Repeat layers.
5. Cover. Cook on Low 5-7 hours or until heated through.
6. To serve, reach to bottom with each spoonful to get all the layers, or carefully invert onto large platter and cut into wedges.

*Serving suggestion: Serve with **sour cream** and/or **guacamole**.*

Cheese and Chile Enchilada Olé

Donna Treloar, Muncie, IN

Makes 4 servings

Prep Time: 20-30 minutes
Cooking Time: 3-4 hours
Ideal slow-cooker size: 4-qt.

1 large onion, diced
2 cloves garlic, minced
1 Tbsp. vegetable oil

2 lbs. ground beef
1 envelope taco seasoning mix
10 ¾-oz. can cream of mushroom soup
4-oz. can green chilies, diced
12 corn tortillas, *divided*
1 cup Mexican-blend cheese, shredded, *divided*
1 cup cheddar cheese, shredded, *divided*

1. In a large skillet sauté onion and garlic in oil.
2. Add ground beef and brown.
3. Drain off drippings.
4. Add taco seasoning and mix well.
5. In a bowl, combine mushroom soup and green chilies.
6. Spray interior of cooker with cooking spray. Put about 3 Tbsp. soup mixture in bottom of slow cooker.
7. Layer in 3 tortillas, then a layer of ¼ cup soup mixture, then a layer of one-third ground beef mixture, then a layer of ½ cup of combined cheeses.
8. Repeat layers three more times.
9. Cook on Low 3-4 hours.

*Serving suggestion: Top each individual serving with **sour cream**, **salsa**, **black olives**, and **green onion**.*

Enchilada Casserole

Rebecca Meyerkorth, Wamego, KS

Makes 4 servings

Prep Time: 20 minutes
Cooking Time: 6-8 hours
Ideal slow-cooker size: 3-qt.

1 lb. ground beef
2 10-oz. cans enchilada sauce
10¾-oz. can cream of onion soup
¼ tsp. salt
8½-oz. pkg. flour tortillas, torn, *divided*
3 cups (12 ozs.) cheddar cheese, shredded, *divided*

1. In skillet, brown beef until no longer pink.
2. Drain off drippings.
3. Stir in enchilada sauce, soup, and salt.
4. Layer one-third of beef mixture into cooker. Follow that with one-third of torn tortillas, and one-third of grated cheese.
5. Repeat layers two times.
6. Cover and cook on Low 6-8 hours, or until heated through, but not dry.

Shredded Beef for Tacos

Dawn Day, Westminster, CA

Makes 6-8 servings

Prep. Time: 15 minutes
Cooking Time: 6-8 hours
Ideal slow-cooker size: 4-qt.

2-3-lb. round roast, cut into large chunks
1 large onion, chopped
3 Tbsp. oil
2 serrano chilies, chopped
3 garlic cloves, minced
1 tsp. salt
1 cup water

1. Brown meat and onion in oil. Transfer to slow cooker.
2. Add chilies, garlic, salt, and water.
3. Cover. Cook on High 6-8 hours.
4. Pull meat apart with two forks until shredded.

*Serving suggestion: Serve with fresh **tortillas**, **lettuce**, **tomatoes**, **cheese**, and **guacamole**.*

Southwestern Flair

Phyllis Attig, Reynolds, IL

Makes 8-12 servings

Prep. Time: 5 minutes
Cooking Time: 9 hours
Ideal slow-cooker size: 4-qt.

3-4-lb. chuck roast, *or* flank steak
1 envelope dry taco seasoning
1 cup chopped onions
1 Tbsp. white vinegar
1¼ cup green chilies

1. Combine meat, taco seasoning, onions, vinegar, and chilies in slow cooker.
2. Cover. Cook on Low 9 hours.
3. Shred meat with fork.

*Serving suggestion: Serve with **tortillas** and your choice of grated **cheese**, **refried beans**, shredded **lettuce**, chopped **tomatoes**, **salsa**, **sour cream**, and **guacamole**.*

Browning meat in another pan means an extra step, but it adds a lot to a recipe's appearance and flavor.

Mary Puskar, Forest Hill, MD

Tostadas

Elizabeth L. Richards, Rapid City, SD

Makes 6-10 servings

Prep. Time: 15 minutes
Cooking Time: 6 hours
Ideal slow-cooker size: 3- to 4-qt.

1 lb. ground beef, browned
2 cans refried beans
1 envelope dry taco
   seasoning mix
8-oz. can tomato sauce
½ cup water
10 tostada shells

1. Combine ground beef, refried beans, taco seasoning mix, tomato sauce, and water in slow cooker.

2. Cover. Cook on Low 6 hours.

3. Crisp tostada shells.

*Serving suggestion: Spread hot mixture on **tostada shells**. Top with shredded **lettuce**, diced **tomatoes**, shredded **cheddar cheese**, sliced **black olives**, **sour cream**, **guacamole**, and **salsa**.*

Pecos River
Red Frito Pie

Donna Barnitz, Jerks, OK

Makes 6 servings

Prep. Time: 10 minutes
Cooking Time: 8-10 hours
Ideal slow-cooker size: 4-qt.

1 large onion, chopped
   coarsely
3 lbs. coarsely ground
   hamburger
2 garlic cloves, minced
3 Tbsp. ground hot red chili
   peppers
2 Tbsp. ground mild red
   chili peppers
1½ cups water

1. Combine onion, hamburger, garlic, chilies, and water in slow cooker.

2. Cover. Cook on Low 8-10 hours. Drain.

*Serving suggestion: Serve over **corn chips**. Top with mixture of shredded **Monterey Jack** and **cheddar** cheeses.*

Nachos

Arlene Miller, Hutchinson, KS

Makes 8 servings

Prep. Time: 15 minutes
Cooking Time: 1 hour
Ideal slow-cooker size: 4-qt.

1 lb. ground beef
¼ cup diced onions
¼ cup diced green peppers
1 pint taco sauce
1 can refried beans
10¾-oz. can cream of
   mushroom soup
1 envelope dry taco
   seasoning
salt to taste
2 cups Velveeta, *or* cheddar,
   cheese

1. Brown ground beef, onions, and green peppers in saucepan. Drain.

2. Combine all ingredients in slow cooker.

3. Cover. Cook on High 1 hour, stirring occasionally until cheese is fully melted.

*Serving suggestion: Pour into serving bowl, or turn to Low to keep warm and serve from cooker with **tortilla chips**, **lettuce**, **tomatoes**, and **sour cream**.*

Mexican Corn Bread

Jeanne Heyerly, Chenoa, IL

Makes 6 servings

Prep. Time: 20 minutes
Cooking Time: 4½-6 hours
Ideal slow-cooker size: 4-qt.

16-oz. can cream-style corn
1 cup cornmeal
½ tsp. baking soda
1 tsp. salt
¼ cup oil
1 cup milk
2 eggs, beaten
½ cup taco sauce
2 cups shredded cheddar
   cheese
1 medium onion, chopped
1 garlic clove, minced
4-oz. can diced green chilies
1 lb. ground beef, lightly
   cooked and drained

1. Combine corn, cornmeal, baking soda, salt, oil, milk, eggs, and taco sauce. Pour half of mixture into slow cooker.
2. Layer cheese, onion, garlic, green chilies, and ground beef on top of cornmeal mixture. Cover with remaining cornmeal mixture.
3. Cover. Cook on High 1 hour and on Low 3½-4 hours, or only on Low 6 hours.

Tamale Pie

Jeannine Janzen, Elbing, KS

Makes 8 servings

Prep. Time: 10 minutes
Cooking Time: 4 hours
Ideal slow-cooker size: 4-qt.

¾ cup cornmeal
1½ cups milk
1 egg, beaten
1 lb. ground beef, browned
   and drained
1 envelope dry chili
   seasoning mix
16-oz. can diced tomatoes
16-oz. can corn, drained
1 cup grated cheddar
   cheese

1. Combine cornmeal, milk, and egg.
2. Stir in meat, chili seasoning mix, tomatoes, and corn until well blended. Pour into slow cooker.
3. Cover. Cook on High 1 hour, then on Low 3 hours.
4. Sprinkle with cheese. Cook another 5 minutes until cheese is melted.

Piquant French Dip

Marcella Stalter, Flanagan, IL

Makes 8 servings

Prep. Time: 5 minutes
Cooking Time: 5-6 hours
Ideal slow-cooker size: 3½-qt.

3-lb. chuck roast
2 cups water
½ cup soy sauce
1 tsp. dried rosemary
1 tsp. dried thyme
1 tsp. garlic powder
1 bay leaf
3-4 whole peppercorns

1. Place roast in slow cooker. Add water, soy sauce, and seasonings.
2. Cover. Cook on High 5-6 hours, or until beef is tender.
3. Remove beef from broth. Shred with fork. Keep warm.
4. Strain broth. Skim fat. Pour broth into small cups for dipping.

*Serving suggestion: Serve beef on **French rolls**.*

Note:
   If you have leftover broth, freeze it to use it later for gravy or as a soup base.

When I want to warm rolls to go with a slow-cooker stew, I wrap them in foil and lay them on top of the stew in the cooker until they're warm. Donna Barnitz, Jenks, OK

Carol's Italian Beef

Carol Findling, Princeton, IL

Makes 6-8 servings

Prep. Time: 5-10 minutes
Cooking Time: 4-12 hours
Ideal slow-cooker size: 4-qt.

3-4-lb. lean rump roast
2 tsp. salt, *divided*
4 garlic cloves
2 tsp. Romano, *or*
  Parmesan, cheese, *divided*
12-oz. can beef broth
1 tsp. dried oregano

1. Place roast in slow cooker. Cut 4 slits in top of roast. Fill each slit with ½ tsp. salt, 1 garlic clove, and ½ tsp. cheese.
2. Pour broth over meat. Sprinkle with oregano.
3. Cover. Cook on Low 10-12 hours, or on High 4-6 hours.
4. Remove meat and slice or shred.

Serving suggestion: Serve on **buns** *with meat juices on the side.*

Lauren's Italian Beef

Lauren Eberhard, Seneca, IL

Makes 16 servings

Prep. Time: 10 minutes
Cooking Time: 10 hours
Ideal slow-cooker size: 4- to 5-qt.

4-5-lb. boneless roast, cubed
1 medium onion, chopped
1-2 garlic cloves, minced
2-3 pkgs. dry Good Seasons Italian dressing mix
½ cup water

1. Combine first five ingredients in slow cooker.
2. Cover. Cook on Low 10 hours. Stir occasionally.
3. Slice meat into thin slices.

Serving suggestion: Pile on **steak rolls**, *top with shredded* **mozzarella cheese**, *and serve immediately.*

Tangy Barbecue Sandwiches

Lavina Hochstedler, Grand Blanc, MI
Lois M. Martin, Lititz, PA

Makes 14-18 sandwiches

Prep. Time: 10 minutes
Cooking Time: 6-7 hours
Ideal slow-cooker size: 5-qt.

3 cups chopped celery
1 cup chopped onions
1 cup ketchup
1 cup barbecue sauce
1 cup water
2 Tbsp. vinegar
2 Tbsp. Worcestershire sauce
2 Tbsp. brown sugar
1 tsp. chili powder
1 tsp. salt
½ tsp. pepper
½ tsp. garlic powder
3-4-lb. boneless chuck roast

1. Combine all ingredients except roast and buns in slow cooker. When well mixed, add roast.
2. Cover. Cook on High 6-7 hours.
3. Remove roast. Cool and shred meat. Return to sauce. Heat well.

Serving suggestion: Serve on **hamburger buns**.

Mile-High Shredded Beef Sandwiches

Miriam Christophel, Battle Creek, MI
Mary Seielstad, Sparks, NV

Makes 8 servings

Prep. Time: 20 minutes
Cooking Time: 7-9 hours
Ideal slow-cooker size: 4-qt.

3-lb. chuck roast, *or* round
    steak
2 Tbsp. oil
1 cup chopped onions
½ cup sliced celery
2 cups beef broth, *or* bouillon
1 garlic clove
1 tsp. salt
¾ cup ketchup
4 Tbsp. brown sugar
2 Tbsp. vinegar
1 tsp. dry mustard
½ tsp. chili powder
3 drops Tabasco sauce
1 bay leaf
¼ tsp. paprika
¼ tsp. garlic powder
1 tsp. Worcestershire sauce

1. In skillet brown both sides of meat in oil. Add onions and celery and sauté briefly. Transfer to slow cooker. Add broth or bouillon.
2. Cover. Cook on Low 6-8 hours, or until tender. Remove meat from cooker and cool. Shred beef.
3. Remove vegetables from cooker and drain, reserving 1½ cups broth. Combine vegetables and meat.
4. Return shredded meat and vegetables to cooker. Add broth and remaining ingredients and combine well.
5. Cover. Cook on High 1 hour. Remove bay leaf.

*Serving suggestion: Pile into 8 **sandwich rolls** and serve.*

Slow-Cooker Beef Sandwiches

Elaine Unruh, Minneapolis, MN
Winifred Ewy, Newton, KS

Makes 6-8 servings

Prep. Time: 5 minutes
Cooking Time: 8-10 hours
Ideal slow-cooker size: 4-qt.

2-3-lb. chuck roast, cubed
1 pkg. dry onion soup mix
12-oz. can cola

1. Place meat in slow cooker.
2. Sprinkle soup mix over meat. Pour cola over all.
3. Cover. Cook on Low 8-10 hours.

*Serving suggestion: Serve as roast or shred the beef, mix with sauce, and serve on **buns**.*

Variation:

Layer 4 medium potatoes, sliced, and 4 carrots, sliced, in bottom of pot. Place meat and rest of ingredients on top, and follow recipe for cooking.

Barbecue Beef

Elizabeth Yoder, Millersburg, OH

Makes 12 servings

Prep. Time: 10 minutes
Cooking Time: 6½-8½ hours
Ideal slow-cooker size: 3½-qt.

3-lb. boneless chuck roast
1 cup barbecue sauce
½ cup apricot preserves
⅓ cup chopped green
    peppers
1 small onion, chopped
1 Tbsp. Dijon mustard
2 tsp. brown sugar

1. Cut roast into quarters. Place in greased slow cooker.
2. Combine barbecue sauce, preserves, green peppers, onion, mustard, and brown sugar. Pour over roast.
3. Cover. Cook on Low 6-8 hours. Remove roast and slice thinly. Return to slow cooker. Stir gently.
4. Cover. Cook 20-30 minutes.

*Serving suggestion: Serve beef and sauce on **sandwich rolls**.*

Barbecue Beef Sandwiches

Eleanor Larson, Glen Lyon, PA

Makes 18-20 sandwiches

Prep. Time: 10 minutes
Cooking Time: 10-12 hours
Ideal slow-cooker size: 4-qt.

3½-4-lb. beef round steak, cubed
1 cup finely chopped onions
½ cup firmly packed brown sugar
1 Tbsp. chili powder
½ cup ketchup
⅓ cup cider vinegar
12-oz. can beer
6-oz. can tomato paste

1. Combine all ingredients except buns in slow cooker.
2. Cover. Cook on Low 10-12 hours.
3. Remove beef from sauce with slotted spoon. Place in large bowl. Shred with 2 forks.
4. Add 2 cups sauce from slow cooker to shredded beef. Mix well.

Serving suggestion: Pile into **buns** *and serve immediately. Reserve any remaining sauce for serving over* **pasta**, **rice**, *or* **potatoes**.

Hearty Italian Sandwiches

Rhonda Lee Schmidt, Scranton, PA
Robin Schrock, Millersburg, OH

Makes 8 servings

Prep. Time: 15 minutes
Cooking Time: 6 hours
Ideal slow-cooker size: 4-qt.

1½ lbs. ground beef
1½ lbs. bulk Italian sausage
2 large onions, chopped
2 large green peppers, chopped
2 large sweet red peppers, chopped
1 tsp. salt
1 tsp. pepper

1. In skillet brown beef and sausage. Drain.
2. Place one-third onions and peppers in slow cooker. Top with half of meat mixture. Repeat layers. Sprinkle with salt and pepper.
3. Cover. Cook on Low 6 hours, or until vegetables are tender.

Serving suggestion: With a slotted spoon, serve about 1 cup mixture on each **sandwich roll**. *Top with shredded* **Monterey Jack cheese**.

Note:

For some extra flavor, add a spoonful of salsa to each roll before topping with cheese.

Barbecued Spoonburgers

Mrs. Paul Gray, Beatrice, NE

Makes 8-10 servings

Prep. Time: 15 minutes
Cooking Time: 3-8 hours
Ideal slow-cooker size: 4-qt.

1½ lbs. ground beef
2 Tbsp. oil
½ cup chopped onions
½ cup diced celery
half a green pepper, chopped
1 Tbsp. Worcestershire sauce
½ cup ketchup
1 garlic clove, minced
1 tsp. salt
¾ cup water
⅛ tsp. pepper
½ tsp. paprika
6-oz. can tomato paste
2 Tbsp. vinegar
2 tsp. brown sugar
1 tsp. dry mustard

1. Brown beef in oil in saucepan. Drain.
2. Combine all ingredients in slow cooker.
3. Cover. Cook on Low 6-8 hours, or on High 3-4 hours.

Serving suggestion: Serve on **buns** *or over mashed* **potatoes**, **pasta**, *or* **rice**.

Sloppy Joes

Nadine Martinitz,
Salina, KS

Makes 6 servings

Prep Time: 10-15 minutes
Cooking Time: 2-6 hours
Ideal slow-cooker size: 4- to 5-qt.

---

1 lb. ground beef
1 small onion, chopped
1 small green pepper,
  chopped
14½-oz. can diced tomatoes
3 Tbsp. brown sugar
2 tsp. Worcestershire sauce
1½ tsp. ground cumin
1 tsp. chili powder
½ tsp. salt

1. Brown beef in skillet,
stirring to break into small
pieces.
2. Add onion and pepper
to meat in skillet, cooking a
few more minutes. Drain off
drippings.
3. Transfer meat mixture to
slow cooker.
4. Stir in tomatoes, brown
sugar, Worcestershire sauce,
and seasonings.
5. Cover and cook until
flavors are well blended, 2 hours
on High or 6 hours on Low.

*Serving suggestion: To serve,
fill each* **hamburger bun** *with
½ cup beef mixture.*

Jean and Tammy's Sloppy Joes

Jean Shaner, York, PA
Tammy Smoker, Cochranville, PA

Makes 12 servings

Prep. Time: 15 minutes
Cooking Time: 3-10 hours
Ideal slow-cooker size: 4-qt.

---

3 lbs. ground beef, browned
  and drained
1 onion, finely chopped
1 green pepper, chopped
2 8-oz. cans tomato sauce
¾ cup ketchup
1 Tbsp. Worcestershire
  sauce
1 tsp. chili powder
¼ tsp. pepper
¼ tsp. garlic powder

1. Combine all ingredients
except rolls in slow cooker.
2. Cover. Cook on Low 8-10
hours, or on High 3-4 hours.

Serving suggestion: Serve in
sandwich rolls.

Penny's Sloppy Joes

Penny Blosser, Beavercreek, OH

Makes 6 servings

Prep. Time: 10 minutes
Cooking Time: 1-2 hours
Ideal slow-cooker size: 2-qt.

---

1 lb. ground beef, browned
  and drained
10¾-oz. can cream of
  mushroom soup
¼ cup ketchup
1 small onion, diced

1. Combine all ingredients
in slow cooker.
2. Cover. Cook on Low 1-2
hours.

Serving suggestion: Serve on
rolls *or over baked* **potatoes.**

Nan's Sloppy Joes

Nan Decker, Albuquerque, NM

Makes 4-6 servings

Prep. Time: 10 minutes
Cooking Time: 4-5 hours
Ideal slow-cooker size: 2- to 4-qt.

---

1 lb. ground beef
1 onion, chopped
¾ cup ketchup
2 Tbsp. chili sauce
1 Tbsp. Worcestershire sauce

1 Tbsp. prepared mustard
1 Tbsp. vinegar
1 Tbsp. sugar

1. Brown beef and onion in saucepan. Drain.
2. Combine all ingredients in slow cooker.
3. Cover. Cook on Low 4-5 hours.

Serving suggestion: Serve on **whole wheat buns**.

Corned Beef

Margaret Jarrett, Anderson, IN

Makes 6-7 servings

Prep. Time: 5 minutes
Cooking Time: 4-5 hours
Ideal slow-cooker size: 5-qt.

2-3-lb. cut of marinated corned beef
2-3 garlic cloves, minced
10-12 peppercorns

1. Place meat in bottom of cooker. Top with garlic and peppercorns. Cover with water.
2. Cover. Cook on High 4-5 hours, or until tender.

Serving suggestion: Cool meat, slice thin, and use to make Reuben sandwiches along with sliced **Swiss cheese**, **sauerkraut**, *and* **Thousand Island dressing** *on toasted* **pumpernickel bread**.

Corned Beef and Cabbage

Rhoda Burgoon, Collingswood, NJ
Jo Ellen Moore, Pendleton, IN

Makes 6-8 servings

Prep. Time: 5 minutes
Cooking Time: 7-13 hours
Ideal slow-cooker size: 5- to 6-qt.

3 carrots, cut in 3-inch pieces
3-4-lb. corned beef brisket
2-3 medium onions, quartered
¾-1¼ cups water
half a small head of
  cabbage, cut in wedges

1. Layer all ingredients except cabbage in slow cooker.
2. Cover. Cook on Low 8-10 hours, or on High 5-6 hours.
3. Add cabbage wedges to liquid, pushing down to moisten. Turn to High and cook an additional 2-3 hours.

Note:
To cook more cabbage than slow cooker will hold, cook separately in skillet. Remove 1 cup broth from slow cooker during last hour of cooking. Pour over cabbage wedges in skillet. Cover and cook slowly for 20-30 minutes.

Variations:
1. Add 4 medium potatoes, halved, with the onions.
2. Top individual servings with mixture of sour cream and horseradish.
Kathi Rogge, Alexandria, IN

Eleanor's Corned Beef and Cabbage

Eleanor J. Ferreira, N. Chelmsford, MA

Makes 6 servings

Prep. Time: 10 minutes
Cooking Time: 5-12 hours
Ideal slow-cooker size: 5-qt.

2 medium onions, sliced
2½-3-lb. corned beef brisket
1 cup apple juice
¼ cup brown sugar, packed
2 tsp. finely shredded
  orange peel
6 whole cloves
2 tsp. prepared mustard
6 cabbage wedges

1. Place onions in slow cooker. Place beef on top of onions.
2. Combine apple juice, brown sugar, orange peel, cloves, and mustard. Pour over meat.
3. Place cabbage on top.
4. Cover. Cook on Low 10-12 hours, or on High 5-6 hours.

Corned Beef Dinner

Judy Ann Govotsos, Frederick, MD

Makes 4 servings

Prep Time: 15-20 minutes
Cooking Time: 8-9 hours
Ideal slow-cooker size: 5-qt.

2 medium onions, quartered
2 cloves garlic, minced
3 medium potatoes, peeled and quartered
3-4 carrots, peeled and cut into chunks
3-3½ lbs. corned beef brisket
2 bay leaves
1 cup water
1 small cabbage head, cut in wedges
1 Tbsp. prepared mustard
¼ cup brown sugar
dash ground cloves

1. Place onions, garlic cloves, potatoes, carrots, meat, bay leaves, and water into slow cooker.
2. Cover and cook 5 hours on Low.
3. Add cabbage wedges to cooker, pushing them down into broth. Continue cooking on Low another 3 hours, or until vegetables and meat are tender, but not mushy or dry.
4. In a small bowl combine mustard, brown sugar, and ground cloves.
5. Stir mixture into slow-cooker 1 hour before end of cooking time.

Slow-Cooker Pork Tenderloin

Kathy Hertzler, Lancaster, PA

Makes 6 servings

Prep Time: 5-15 minutes
Cooking Time: 4 hours
Ideal slow-cooker size: 4-qt.

2-lb. pork tenderloin, cut in half lengthwise
1 cup water
¾ cup red wine
3 Tbsp. light soy sauce
1-oz. envelope dry onion soup mix
6 cloves garlic, peeled and chopped
freshly ground pepper

1. Place pork tenderloin pieces in slow cooker. Pour water, wine, and soy sauce over pork.
2. Turn pork over in liquid several times to completely moisten.
3. Sprinkle with dry onion soup mix. Top with chopped garlic and pepper.
4. Cover. Cook on Low 4 hours.

Tip:

I mix ½ cup uncooked long-grain white rice and ½ cup uncooked brown rice in a microwavable bowl. Stir in 2½ cups water and ¾ tsp. salt. Cover. Microwave 5 minutes on high, and then 20 minutes on medium. Place finished pork on a large platter and the finished rice alongside, topped with the au jus from the meat. A green salad goes well with this to make a meal.

Cranberry-Orange Pork Roast

Barbara Aston, Ashdown, AR

Makes 6-8 servings

Prep. Time: 10 minutes
Cooking Time: 8-10 hours
Ideal slow-cooker size: 5-qt.

3-4-lb. pork roast
salt to taste
pepper to taste
1 cup ground, *or* finely chopped, cranberries
¼ cup honey
1 tsp. grated orange peel
⅛ tsp. ground cloves
⅛ tsp. ground nutmeg

1. Sprinkle roast with salt and pepper. Place in slow cooker.
2. Combine remaining ingredients. Pour over roast.
3. Cover. Cook on Low 8-10 hours.

Cranberry-Mustard Pork Roast

Phyllis Attig, Reynolds, IL
Mrs. J. E. Barthold, Bethlehem, PA
Kelly Bailey, Mechanicsburg, PA
Joyce Kaut, Rochester, NY

Makes 4-6 servings

Prep. Time: 5-10 minutes
Cooking Time: 6-8 hours
Ideal slow-cooker size: 4-qt.

2½-3-lb. boneless rolled
  pork loin roast
16-oz. can jellied cranberry
  sauce
½ cup sugar
½ cup cranberry juice
1 tsp. dry mustard
¼ tsp. ground cloves
2 Tbsp. cornstarch
2 Tbsp. cold water
1 tsp. salt

1. Place roast in slow cooker.
2. Combine cranberry sauce, sugar, cranberry juice, mustard, and cloves. Pour over roast.
3. Cover. Cook on Low 6-8 hours, or until meat is tender.
4. Remove roast and keep warm.
5. Skim fat from juices. Measure 2 cups, adding water if necessary. Pour into saucepan. Bring to boil over medium heat. Combine the cornstarch and cold water to make a paste. Stir into gravy. Cook and stir until thickened. Season with salt.
6. Serve with sliced pork.

Teriyaki Pork Roast

Janice Yoskovich, Carmichaels, PA

Makes 8 servings

Prep. Time: 5-10 minutes
Cooking Time: 7-8 hours
Ideal slow-cooker size: 4-qt.

¾ cup unsweetened apple
  juice
2 Tbsp. sugar
2 Tbsp. soy sauce
1 Tbsp. vinegar
1 tsp. ground ginger
¼ tsp. garlic powder
⅛ tsp. pepper
3-lb. boneless pork loin
  roast, halved
2½ Tbsp. cornstarch
3 Tbsp. cold water

1. Combine apple juice, sugar, soy sauce, vinegar, ginger, garlic powder, and pepper in greased slow cooker.
2. Add roast. Turn to coat.
3. Cover. Cook on Low 7-8 hours. Remove roast and keep warm.
4. In saucepan, combine cornstarch and cold water until smooth. Stir in juices from roast. Bring to boil. Cook and stir for 2 minutes, or until thickened. Serve with roast.

Savory Pork Roast

Betty A. Holt, St. Charles, MO

Makes 8-10 servings

Prep. Time: 5 minutes
Cooking Time: 7 hours
Ideal slow-cooker size: 5-qt.

4-5-lb. pork loin roast
large onion, sliced
1 bay leaf
2 Tbsp. soy sauce
1 Tbsp. garlic powder

1. Place roast and onion in slow cooker. Add bay leaf, soy sauce, and garlic powder.
2. Cover. Cook on High 1 hour and then on Low 6 hours.
3. Slice and serve.

Pork and Apricots with Mashed Sweet Potatoes

Carolyn Baer, Conrath, WI

Makes 8 servings

Prep Time: 35-40 minutes
Cooking Time: 3½-9 hours
Ideal slow-cooker size: 6-qt.

2½ lbs. sweet potatoes,
    peeled and cut into
    1½-inch-thick slices
3½-4-lb. boneless pork
    shoulder roast
1 tsp. dried tarragon, crushed
1½ tsp. fennel seed, crushed
3 cloves garlic, minced
1½ tsp. salt
1 tsp. pepper
2 Tbsp. cooking oil
12-16 oz. kielbasa, *or* other
    smoked sausage links, cut
    in half lengthwise, then
    in 2-inch pieces
14-oz. can chicken broth
¾ cup apricot nectar, *divided*
½ cup dried apricots
4 tsp. cornstarch

1. Place sweet potato slices in bottom of slow cooker.
2. Trim fat from pork roast.
3. Combine tarragon, fennel seed, garlic, salt, and pepper in small bowl.
4. Rub spice mix all over pork roast.
5. In large skillet, brown roast on all sides in hot oil.
6. Drain off drippings.
7. Place roast on top of sweet potatoes.
8. Place sausage pieces around roast in cooker.
9. Pour broth and ½ cup apricot nectar over all.
10. Cover and cook for 3½ hours on High.
11. Add dried apricots to cooker. Cover and continue cooking on High 30 more minutes.
12. With slotted spoon, transfer pork, sausage, and apricots to serving platter. Cover and keep warm.
13. Transfer sweet potatoes to a large bowl.
14. Mash with potato masher.
15. Strain cooking liquid from cooker into a glass measuring cup.
16. Skim and discard fat.
17. Reserve 2 cups liquid, adding chicken broth if necessary to make 2 cups.
18. In a small bowl, whisk together ¼ cup apricot nectar and cornstarch until smooth.
19. In a medium saucepan, combine cooking liquid and cornstarch mixture.
20. Cook and stir over medium heat until thick and bubbly.
21. Cook two minutes longer.

Serving suggestion: Serve sauce with pork and mashed sweet potatoes.

Tip:

If your ingredients are hot when you place them in your slow cooker, pre-heating your cooker will speed up the cooking time.

Pork Roast with Potatoes and Onions

Trudy Kutter, Corfu, NY

Makes 6-8 servings

Prep. Time: 15 minutes
Cooking Time: 8½ hours
Ideal slow-cooker size: 4-qt.

2½-3-lb. boneless pork loin
    roast
1 large garlic clove, slivered
5-6 potatoes, cubed
1 large onion, sliced
¾ cup broth, *or* tomato
    juice, *or* water
1½ Tbsp. soy sauce
1 Tbsp. cornstarch
1 Tbsp. cold water

1. Make slits in roast and insert slivers of garlic. Put under broiler to brown.
2. Put potatoes in slow cooker. Add half of onions. Place roast on onions and potatoes. Cover with remaining onions.
3. Combine broth and soy sauce. Pour over roast.
4. Cover. Cook on Low 8 hours. Remove roast and vegetables from liquid.
5. Combine cornstarch and water. Add to liquid in slow cooker. Turn to High until thickened.

Serving suggestion: Serve gravy over sliced meat and vegetables.

Variation:

Use sweet potatoes instead of white potatoes.

Tangy Pork Chops

Tracy Clark, Mt. Crawford, VA
Lois M. Martin, Lititz, PA
Becky Oswald, Broadway, PA

Makes 4 servings

Prep. Time: 15 minutes
Cooking Time: 5½-6½ hours
Ideal slow-cooker size: 4-qt.

4 ½-inch thick pork chops
½ tsp. salt
⅛ tsp. pepper
2 medium onions, chopped
2 celery ribs, chopped
1 large green pepper, sliced
14½-oz. can stewed tomatoes
½ cup ketchup
2 Tbsp. cider vinegar
2 Tbsp. brown sugar
2 Tbsp. Worcestershire sauce
1 Tbsp. lemon juice
1 beef bouillon cube
2 Tbsp. cornstarch
2 Tbsp. water

1. Place chops in slow cooker. Sprinkle with salt and pepper.
2. Add onions, celery, pepper, and tomatoes.
3. Combine ketchup, vinegar, brown sugar, Worcestershire sauce, lemon juice, and bouillon. Pour over vegetables.
4. Cover. Cook on Low 5-6 hours.

5. Combine cornstarch and water until smooth. Stir into slow cooker.
6. Cover. Cook on High 30 minutes, or until thickened.

Serving suggestion: Serve over rice.

Variation:

Use chunks of beef or chicken legs and thighs instead of pork.

Spicy Pork Chops

Mary Puskar, Forest Hill, MD

Makes 5 servings

Prep. Time: 15 minutes
Cooking Time: 6-8 hours
Ideal slow-cooker size: 4-qt.

5-6 center-cut loin pork chops
3 Tbsp. oil
1 onion, sliced
1 green pepper, cut in strips
8-oz. can tomato sauce
3-4 Tbsp. brown sugar
1 Tbsp. vinegar
1½ tsp. salt
1-2 tsp. Worcestershire sauce

1. Brown chops in oil in skillet. Transfer to slow cooker.
2. Add remaining ingredients to cooker.
3. Cover. Cook on Low 6-8 hours.

Serving suggestion: Serve over rice.

Barbecued Pork Steaks

Marcia S. Myer, Manheim, PA

Makes 4 servings

Prep Time: 15-20 minutes
Cooking Time: 8 hours
Ideal slow-cooker size: 5-qt.

4 pork shoulder steaks, cut ½-inch thick
1 Tbsp. oil
1 large onion, sliced
1 large green pepper, sliced
2 tomatoes, sliced
1 Tbsp. instant tapioca
½ cup barbecue sauce
¼ cup red wine
½ tsp. cumin

1. Brown steaks in hot oil in skillet.
2. In slow cooker, arrange slices of onion, green pepper, and tomato.
3. Sprinkle tapioca over vegetables.
4. Place browned pork steaks on top of vegetables.
5. In bowl combine barbecue sauce, wine, and cumin.
6. Pour over meat.
7. Cover. Cook 8 hours on Low.

Saucy Pork Chops

Bonita Ensenberger, Albuquerque, NM

Makes 4 servings

Prep. Time: 15-20 minutes
Cooking Time: 4-9 hours
Ideal slow-cooker size: 4-qt.

4 pork chops
salt to taste
pepper to taste
1 tsp. garlic powder
1 Tbsp. oil
2-2½ cups ketchup
½ cup brown sugar
1 Tbsp. hickory-flavored
  liquid smoke
1 cup onions, chopped

1. Season chops with salt, pepper, and garlic powder. Brown on both sides in oil in skillet. Drain.

2. Combine ketchup, brown sugar, and liquid smoke in bowl.

3. Place onions in slow cooker. Dip browned pork chops in sauce mixture and place on onions. Pour remaining sauce over chops.

4. Cover. Cook on Low 7-9 hours, or on High 4-5 hours.

*Serving suggestion: Makes a great meal served with **cole slaw** and oven-roasted, cut-up **root vegetables**.*

Pork Chops in Bean Sauce

Shirley Sears, Tiskilwa, IL

Makes 6 servings

Prep. Time: 15-20 minutes
Cooking Time: 7-8 hours
Ideal slow-cooker size: 5-qt.

6 pork chops
⅓ cup chopped onions
½ tsp. salt
⅓ tsp. garlic salt
⅛ tsp. pepper
28-oz. can vegetarian, *or* baked, beans
¼ tsp. hot pepper sauce
13½-oz. can crushed pineapple, undrained
⅓ cup chili sauce

1. Brown pork chops in skillet five minutes per side. Place in slow cooker.

2. Sauté onion in skillet in meat juices. Spread over pork chops.

3. Sprinkle with salt, garlic salt, and pepper.

4. Combine beans and hot sauce. Pour over chops.

5. Combine pineapple and chili sauce. Spread evenly over beans.

6. Cover. Cook on Low 7-8 hours.

Chops and Beans

Mary L. Casey, Scranton, PA

Makes 4-6 servings

Prep. Time: 15-20 minutes
Cooking Time: 4-6 hours
Ideal slow-cooker size: 4-qt.

2 1-lb. cans pork and beans
½ cup ketchup
2 slices bacon, browned and crumbled
½ cup chopped onions, sautéed
1 Tbsp. Worcestershire sauce
¼ cup firmly packed brown sugar
4-6 pork chops
2 tsp. prepared mustard
1 Tbsp. brown sugar
¼ cup ketchup
1 lemon, sliced

1. Combine beans, ½ cup ketchup, bacon, onions, Worcestershire sauce, and ¼ cup brown sugar in slow cooker.

2. Brown chops in skillet. In separate bowl, mix together 2 tsp. mustard, 1 Tbsp. brown sugar, and ¼ cup ketchup. Brush each chop with sauce, then carefully stack into cooker, placing a slice of lemon on each chop. Submerge in bean/bacon mixture.

3. Cover. Cook on Low 4-6 hours.

To get the best flavor, saute vegetables or brown meat before placing in cooker to cook.

Connie Johnson, Loudon, NH

Autumn Pork Chops

Jan Mast, Lancaster, PA

Makes 6 servings

Prep Time: 15-25 minutes
Cooking Time: 4-6 hours
Ideal slow-cooker size: 6-qt, oval-shaped

2 medium acorn squash, unpeeled
6 pork chops, trimmed of fat
¾ tsp. salt
2 Tbsp. butter, melted
¾ cup brown sugar
1 Tbsp. orange juice
½ tsp. grated orange peel
⅛ tsp. ground cloves

1. Cut each squash into 4-5 crosswise slices. Remove seeds.
2. Arrange 3 or 4 chops in slow cooker. Cover with squash slices. Top with remaining 2 or 3 chops.
3. In a small mixing bowl, combine remaining ingredients and spread over squash slices and chops.
4. Cook on Low 4 hours. Check if chops on bottom of cooker are done. If so, remove from cooker and keep warm. Place remaining chops on bottom of cooker. Cover and continue cooking until tender, up to 1-1½ hours.

Serving suggestion: Serve each chop topped with a slice or two of squash.

Italian Chops

Jan Moore, Wellsville, KS

Makes 2-4 servings

Prep. Time: 5 minutes
Cooking Time: 2-4 hours
Ideal slow-cooker size: 3½- to 4-qt.

16-oz. bottle Italian salad dressing (use less if cooking only 2 chops)
2-4 pork chops

1. Place pork chops in slow cooker. Pour salad dressing over chops.
2. Cover. Cook on Low 2-4 hours, or until tender.

Variation:
Add cubed potatoes and thinly sliced carrots and onions to meat before pouring dressing over top.

Cooker Chops

Lucille Metzler, Wellsboro, PA

Makes 4 servings

Prep. Time: 5 minutes
Cooking Time: 3-10 hours
Ideal slow-cooker size: 4-qt.

4 pork chops
10¾-oz. can cream of mushroom soup
¼ cup ketchup
2 tsp. Worcestershire sauce

1. Put chops in slow cooker.
2. Combine remaining ingredients. Pour over chops.
3. Cover. Cook on High 3-4 hours, or on Low 8-10 hours.

Variation:
Add one sliced onion to mixture.
Maryland Massey, Mellington, MD

Easy Sweet and Sour Pork Chops

Jeanne Hertzog, Bethlehem, PA

Makes 6 servings

Prep. Time: 5 minutes
Cooking Time: 7-8 hours
Ideal slow-cooker size: 4-qt.

16-oz. bag frozen Oriental vegetables, partially thawed
6 pork chops
12-oz. bottle sweet and sour sauce
½ cup water
1 cup frozen pea pods

1. Place partially thawed Oriental vegetables in slow cooker. Arrange chops on top.
2. Combine sauce and water. Pour over chops.
3. Cover. Cook on Low 7-8 hours.
4. Turn to High and add pea pods.
5. Cover. Cook on High 5 minutes.

Golden Glow Pork Chops

Pam Hochstedler, Kalona, IA

Makes 5-6 servings

Prep. Time: 5 minutes
Cooking Time: 3-4 hours
Ideal slow-cooker size: 3- to 4-qt.

5-6 pork chops
salt to taste
pepper to taste
29-oz. can cling peach
  halves, drained (reserve
  juice)
¼ cup brown sugar
½ tsp. ground cinnamon
¼ tsp. ground cloves
8-oz. can tomato sauce
¼ cup vinegar

1. Lightly brown pork chops on both sides in saucepan. Drain. Arrange in slow cooker. Sprinkle with salt and pepper.
2. Place drained peach halves on top of pork chops.
3. Combine brown sugar, cinnamon, cloves, tomato sauce, vinegar, and ¼ cup peach syrup. Pour over peaches and pork chops.
4. Cover. Cook on Low 3-4 hours.

Pork Chops and Cream Sauce

Sharon Wantland, Menomonee Falls, WI

Makes 8 servings

Prep. Time: 10 minutes
Cooking Time: 3-8 hours
Ideal slow-cooker size: 6-qt.

8 pork chops
salt to taste
pepper to taste
2 Tbsp. oil
2 10¾-oz. cans cream of
  mushroom soup
1 large onion, sliced
12-oz. can evaporated milk

1. Season pork chops with salt and pepper. Brown in oil. Drain. Transfer to slow cooker.
2. In separate bowl, whisk together mushroom soup, onion, and evaporated milk until smooth. Pour over chops.
3. Cook on High 3-4 hours, or on Low 6-8 hours.

Variations:
To increase flavor, stir ½-1 cup sour cream, or ¼ cup sherry, into mixture during last 30 minutes of cooking time.

Perfect Pork Chops

Brenda Pope, Dundee, OH

Makes 2 servings

Prep. Time: 15 minutes
Cooking Time: 3-4 hours
Ideal slow-cooker size: 3-qt.

2 small onions
2 ¾-inch thick boneless,
  center loin pork chops,
  frozen
fresh ground pepper to taste
1 chicken bouillon cube
¼ cup hot water
2 Tbsp. prepared mustard
  with white wine

1. Cut off ends of onions and peel. Cut onions in half crosswise to make 4 thick wheels. Place in bottom of slow cooker.
2. Sear both sides of frozen chops in heavy skillet. Place in cooker on top of onions. Sprinkle with pepper.
3. Dissolve bouillon cube in hot water. Stir in mustard. Pour into slow cooker.
4. Cover. Cook on High 3-4 hours.

*Serving suggestion: Serve topped with fresh **parsley sprigs** or **lemon slices**, if desired.*

Pork Chops and Mushrooms

Michele Ruvola, Selden, NY

Makes 4 servings

Prep. Time: 5 minutes
Cooking Time: 6-8 hours
Ideal slow-cooker size: 4- to 5-qt.

4 boneless pork chops,
  ½-inch thick
2 medium onions, sliced
4-oz. can sliced mushrooms,
  drained
1 envelope dry onion soup
  mix
¼ cup water
10¾-oz. can golden cream
  of mushroom soup

1. Place pork chops in greased slow cooker. Top with onions and mushrooms.
2. Combine soup mix, water, and mushroom soup. Pour over mushrooms.
3. Cover. Cook on Low 6-8 hours.

Pork Chops with Mushroom Sauce

Jennifer J. Gehman, Harrisburg, PA

Makes 4-6 servings

Prep. Time: 5-10 minutes
Cooking Time: 4½-10 hours
Ideal slow-cooker size: 4- to 5-qt.

4-6 boneless thin, *or* thick,
  pork chops
10¾-oz. can cream of
  mushroom soup
¾ cup white wine
4-oz. can sliced mushrooms
2 Tbsp. quick cooking
  tapioca
2 tsp. Worcestershire sauce
1 tsp. beef bouillon
  granules, *or* 1 beef
  bouillon cube
¼ tsp. minced garlic
¾ tsp. dried thyme, *optional*

1. Place pork chops in slow cooker.
2. Combine remaining ingredients and pour over pork chops.
3. Cook on Low 8-10 hours, or on High 4½-5 hours.

Serving suggestion: Serve over rice.

Pork Chops in Vegetable Gravy

Barbara J. Fabel, Wausau, WI

Makes 3-4 servings

Prep. Time: 5 minutes
Cooking Time: 4-5 hours
Ideal slow-cooker size: 4-qt.

3 large onions, quartered,
  or sliced
3 ribs of celery, chunked, *or*
  sliced
3-4 pork chops
10¾-oz. can cream of
  mushroom, *or* cream of
  celery, soup

1. Place onions and celery in slow cooker. Wash pork chops and place on top of onions and celery. Pour soup over all.
2. Cover. Cook on High 1 hour. Reduce heat to Low and cook 3-4 hours, or until chops are tender.

Pork Chop Surprise

Jan Moore, Wellsville, KS

Makes 4 servings

Prep. Time: 15 minutes
Cooking Time: 6-8 hours
Ideal slow-cooker size: 4-qt.

4 pork chops
6 potatoes, sliced
10¾-oz. can cream of
  mushroom soup
water

1. Brown pork chops on both sides in skillet. Transfer to slow cooker.
2. Add potatoes. Pour soup over top. Add enough water to cover all ingredients.
3. Cover. Cook on High 6-8 hours.

Variation:

Combine 1 envelope dry onion soup mix with mushroom soup before pouring over chops and potatoes.

Trudy Kutter, Corfu, NY

Pork Chop Casserole

Doris Bachman, Putnam, IL

Makes 4-6 servings

Prep. Time: 10 minutes
Cooking Time: 3-8 hours
Ideal slow-cooker size: 4- to 5-qt.

4-6 pork chops
3 cups water
1 cup rice, uncooked
10¾-oz. can cream of
  mushroom soup
1 tsp. salt
1 tsp. dried parsley
¼ tsp. pepper

1. Sauté pork chops in skillet until brown. Transfer to slow cooker.
2. Mix remaining ingredients and pour over chops in cooker.
3. Cover. Cook on Low 6-8 hours, or on High 3-4 hours.

Jean's Pork Chops

Jean Weller, State College, PA

Makes 6 servings

Prep. Time: 10 minutes
Cooking Time: 3½-8 hours
Ideal slow-cooker size: 5- to 6-qt.

½ cup flour
1 Tbsp. salt
1½ tsp. dry mustard
½ tsp. garlic powder
6-8 1-inch thick pork chops
2 Tbsp. oil
15½-oz. can chicken and
  rice soup

1. Combine flour, salt, dry mustard, and garlic powder. Dredge pork chops in flour mixture. Brown in oil in skillet. Transfer to slow cooker. Add soup.
2. Cover. Cook on Low 6-8 hours, or on High 3½ hours.

Variation:

For increased flavor, step up the dry mustard to 1 Tbsp. and add 1 tsp. pepper.

Mary Puskar, Forest Hill, MD

Pork and Cabbage Dinner

Mrs. Paul Gray, Beatrice, NE

Makes 8 servings

Prep. Time: 10 minutes
Cooking Time: 5-6 hours
Ideal slow-cooker size: 4- to 5-qt.

2 lbs. pork steaks, *or* chops, *or* shoulder
¾ cup chopped onions
¼ cup chopped fresh parsley, *or* 2 Tbsp. dried parsley
4 cups shredded cabbage
1 tsp. salt
⅛ tsp. pepper
½ tsp. caraway seeds
⅛ tsp. allspice
½ cup beef broth
2 cooking apples, cored and sliced ¼-inch thick

1. Place pork in slow cooker. Layer onions, parsley, and cabbage over pork.
2. Combine salt, pepper, caraway seeds, and allspice. Sprinkle over cabbage. Pour broth over cabbage.
3. Cover. Cook on Low 5-6 hours.
4. Add apple slices 30 minutes before serving.

Ham and Scalloped Potatoes

Penny Blosser, Beavercreek, OH
Jo Haberkamp, Fairbank, IA
Ruth Hofstetter, Versailles, MO
Rachel Kauffman, Alto, MI
Mary E. Martin, Goshen, IN
Brenda Pope, Dundee, OH
Joyce Slaymaker, Strasburg, PA

Makes 6-8 servings

Prep. Time: 15 minutes
Cooking Time: 4-10 hours
Ideal slow-cooker size: 5-qt.

6-8 slices ham, *divided*
8-10 medium potatoes, thinly sliced, *divided*
2 onions, thinly sliced, *divided*
salt to taste
pepper to taste
1 cup grated cheddar, *or* American, cheese, *divided*
10¾-oz. can cream of celery, *or* mushroom, soup
paprika

1. Put half of ham, potatoes, and onions in slow cooker. Sprinkle with salt, pepper, and cheese. Repeat layers.
2. Spoon soup over top. Sprinkle with paprika.
3. Cover. Cook on Low 8-10 hours, or on High 4 hours.

Variation:

If you like a lot of creamy sauce with your ham and potatoes, stir ¾ soup can of milk into the soup before pouring it over the layers.

Alma Z. Weaver, Ephrata, PA

Ham and Cabbage Supper

Louise Stackhouse, Benten, PA

Makes 4 servings

Prep. Time: 5 minutes
Cooking Time: 8-10 hours
Ideal slow-cooker size: 5½- to 6-qt.

1 medium-size cabbage head, cut into quarters
4-lb. smoked picnic ham
¼ cup water

1. Place cabbage quarters in bottom of slow cooker. Place ham on top. Pour in water.
2. Cover. Cook on Low 8-10 hours.

Variation:

To cabbage quarters, add 2 sliced carrots, 1 sliced onion, 2 potatoes cut into cubes, and 2 bay leaves for additional flavor and nutrition.

Miriam's Scalloped Potatoes with Ham

Miriam Christophel, Battle Creek, MI

Makes 6 servings

Prep. Time: 15 minutes
Cooking Time: 3-7 hours
Ideal slow-cooker size: 5-qt.

6 cups raw potatoes, cut into small cubes
1 medium onion, minced
1 tsp. salt
½ lb. cooked ham, cubed
4 Tbsp. butter
4 Tbsp. flour
1 tsp. salt
2 cups milk
1½ cups shredded cheddar cheese

1. Layer potatoes, onion, 1 tsp. salt, and ham into slow cooker.
2. Melt butter in saucepan. Stir in flour and 1 tsp. salt. Cook until bubbly. Gradually add milk. Cook until smooth and thickened. Add cheese and stir until melted. Pour over potato-ham mixture, stirring lightly.
3. Cover. Cook on Low 6-7 hours, or on High 3-4 hours.

Michelle's Scalloped Potatoes and Ham

Michelle Strite, Harrisonburg, VA

Makes 6-8 servings

Prep. Time: 25 minutes
Cooking Time: 3-4 hours
Ideal slow-cooker size: 5½-qt.

6 cups cooked, shredded potatoes
4 cups diced ham
dash pepper, if desired
10¾-oz. can cream of mushroom soup
10¾-oz. can cream of celery soup
1 cup milk

1. Combine all ingredients in slow cooker.
2. Cover. Cook on Low 3-4 hours.

Potatoes and Ham

Janice Martins, Fairbank, IA

Makes 8 servings

Prep. Time: 15 minutes
Cooking Time: 6 hours
Ideal slow-cooker size: 4-qt.

5 potatoes, sliced
½ lb. ham, diced
¼ lb. Velveeta cheese, cubed
half a small onion, diced
10¾-oz. can cream of chicken soup

1. Layer potatoes, ham, cheese, and onion in slow cooker. Top with soup.
2. Cover. Cook on Low 6 hours.

Barbara's Scalloped Potatoes with Ham

Barbara Katrine Rose, Woodbridge, VA

Makes 10-12 servings

Prep. Time: 20 minutes
Cooking Time: 6-8 hours
Ideal slow-cooker size: 5-qt.

4 lbs. potatoes, sliced
1½ lbs. cooked ham, cut into ¼-inch strips
3 Tbsp. minced dried onions
2 11-oz. cans condensed cheddar cheese soup
1 cup water

1. Layer potatoes, ham, and onions in very large slow cooker.
2. Combine soup and water. Pour over layers in pot.
3. Cover. Cook on Low 6-8 hours.

Ham and Potatoes

Ruth Shank, Gridley, IL

Makes 6-8 servings

Prep. Time: 5 minutes
Cooking Time: 10-11 hours
Ideal slow-cooker size: 5½-qt.

6-8 medium red, *or* russet, potatoes, cut into chunks
2-3-lb. boneless ham
½ cup brown sugar
1 tsp. dry mustard

1. Prick potato pieces with fork. Place in slow cooker.
2. Place ham on top of potatoes. Crumble brown sugar over ham. Sprinkle with dry mustard.
3. Cover. Cook on Low 10 or more hours, until potatoes are tender.

Serving suggestion: Pour juices over ham and potatoes to serve.

Ham 'n' Cola

Carol Peachey, Lancaster, PA

Makes 8-10 servings

Prep. Time: 5 minutes
Cooking Time: 2-10 hours
Ideal slow-cooker size: 4- to 5-qt.

½ cup brown sugar
1 tsp. dry mustard
1 tsp. prepared horseradish
¼ cup cola-flavored soda
3-4-lb. precooked ham

1. Combine brown sugar, mustard, and horseradish. Moisten with just enough cola to make a smooth paste. Reserve remaining cola.
2. Rub entire ham with mixture. Place ham in slow cooker and add remaining cola.
3. Cover. Cook on Low 6-10 hours, or on High 2-3 hours.

Ham in Cider

Dorothy M. Van Deest, Memphis, TN

Makes 6-8 servings

Prep. Time: 5 minutes
Cooking Time: 8½-10½ hours
Ideal slow-cooker size: 4- to 5-qt.

3-lb. ham (or larger; whatever fits your slow cooker)
4 cups sweet cider, *or* apple juice
1 cup brown sugar
2 tsp. dry mustard
1 tsp. ground cloves
2 cups white seedless raisins

1. Place ham and cider in slow cooker.
2. Cover. Cook on Low 8-10 hours.
3. Remove ham from cider and place in baking pan.
4. Make a paste of sugar, mustard, cloves, and a little hot cider. Brush over ham. Pour a cup of juice from slow cooker into baking pan. Stir in raisins.
5. Bake at 375° for 30 minutes, until the paste has turned into a glaze.

Less tender, less expensive cuts of meat are better suited for slow cooking than expensive cuts of meat. If desired, you can brown meat on top of the stove first, for additional flavor.
Beatrice Orgish, Richardson, TX

Sweet-Sour Pork

Mary W. Stauffer, Ephrata, PA

Makes 4-6 servings

Prep. Time: 10 minutes
Cooking Time: 5-7 hours
Ideal slow-cooker size: 4-qt.

2 lbs. pork shoulder, cut in
    strips
1 green pepper, cut in strips
half a medium onion,
    thinly sliced
¾ cup shredded carrots
2 Tbsp. coarsely chopped
    sweet pickles
¼ cup brown sugar, packed
2 Tbsp. cornstarch
¼ cup water
1 cup pineapple syrup
    (reserved from pineapple
    chunks)
¼ cup cider vinegar
1 Tbsp. soy sauce
2 cups pineapple chunks

1. Place pork strips in slow
cooker.
2. Add green pepper, onion,
carrots, and pickles.
3. In bowl, mix together
brown sugar and cornstarch.
Add water, pineapple syrup,
vinegar, and soy sauce. Stir
until smooth.
4. Pour over ingredients in
slow cooker.
5. Cover. Cook on Low 5-7
hours. One hour before serving,
add pineapple chunks. Stir.

*Serving suggestion: Serve
over **buttered noodles** with an*

*additional dash of **vinegar** or
garlic to taste.*

Barbecued Spareribs

Mrs. Paul Gray, Beatrice, NE

Makes 4 servings

Prep. Time: 5 minutes
Cooking Time: 6-8 hours
Ideal slow-cooker size: 4-qt.

4-lb. country-style
    spareribs, cut into
    serving-size pieces
10¾-oz. can tomato soup
½ cup cider vinegar
½ cup brown sugar
1 Tbsp. soy sauce
1 tsp. celery seed
1 tsp. salt
1 tsp. chili powder
dash cayenne pepper

1. Place ribs in slow cooker.
2. Combine remaining
ingredients and pour over ribs.
3. Cover. Cook on Low 6-8
hours.
4. Skim fat from juices
before serving.

Tender and Tangy Ribs

Betty Moore, Plano, IL
Renee Shirk, Mount Joy, PA

Makes 2-3 servings

Prep. Time: 10 minutes
Cooking Time: 4-6 hours
Ideal slow-cooker size: 2- to 3-qt.

¾-1 cup vinegar
½ cup ketchup
2 Tbsp. sugar
2 Tbsp. Worcestershire
    sauce
1 garlic clove, minced
1 tsp. dry mustard
1 tsp. paprika
½ tsp. salt
⅛ tsp. pepper
2 lbs. pork spareribs
1 Tbsp. oil

1. Combine all ingredients
except spareribs and oil in
slow cooker.
2. Brown ribs in oil in skillet. Transfer to slow cooker.
3. Cover. Cook on Low 4-6
hours.

*When adapting range-top recipes to slow cooking,
reduce the amount of onion you normally use because the
onion flavor gets stronger during slow cooking.*

Beatrice Orgish, Richardson, TX

Michele's Barbecued Ribs

Michele Ruvola, Selden, NY

Makes 8 servings

Prep. Time: 5 minutes
Cooking Time: 9-10 hours
Ideal slow-cooker size: 4-qt.

2 Tbsp. instant minced
   onion
1 tsp. crushed red pepper
½ tsp. ground cinnamon
½ tsp. garlic powder
3 lbs. pork loin back ribs,
   cut into serving-size
   pieces
1 medium onion, sliced
½ cup water
1½ cups barbecue sauce

1. Combine onion, red
pepper, cinnamon, and garlic
powder. Rub mixture into ribs.
Layer ribs and onion in slow
cooker. Pour water around
ribs.
2. Cover. Cook on Low 8-9
hours.
3. Remove ribs from slow
cooker. Drain and discard
liquid. Pour barbecue sauce
in bowl and dip ribs in sauce.
Return ribs to slow cooker.
Pour remaining sauce over
ribs.
4. Cover. Cook on Low
1 hour.

Awfully Easy Barbecued Ribs

Sara Harter Fredette, Williamsburg, MA
Colleen Konetzni, Rio Rancho, NM
Mary Mitchell, Battle Creek, MI
Audrey Romonosky, Austin, TX
Iva Schmidt, Fergus Falls, MN
Susan Tjon, Austin, TX

Makes 4-6 servings

Prep. Time: 10 minutes
Cooking Time: 6 hours
Ideal slow-cooker size: 4- to 5-qt.

3-4-lb. baby back, *or*
   country-style, spareribs
½ tsp. salt, *optional*
½ tsp. pepper, *optional*
2 onions, sliced
16-24-oz. bottle barbecue
   sauce (depending upon
   how saucy you like your
   chops)

1. Brown ribs under broiler.
Slice into serving-size pieces,
season, and place in slow
cooker.
2. Add onions and barbecue
sauce.
3. Cover. Cook on Low 6
hours.

*Serving suggestion: These are
good served with* **baked beans**
and **corn on the cob**.

Variation:
   Instead of broiling the ribs,
place them in slow cooker
with other ingredients and
cook on High 1 hour. Turn to
Low and cook 8 more hours.

Asian-Style Country Ribs

Marcia S. Myer, Manheim, PA

Makes 4 servings

Prep Time: 10 minutes
Cooking Time: 8-10 hours
Ideal slow-cooker size: 5-qt.

⅓ cup orange marmalade
2 Tbsp. ketchup
1 tsp. ground ginger
1 *or* 2 garlic cloves, crushed
   and chopped
¼ cup light soy sauce
4 lbs. meaty spare, *or*
   country-style, ribs

1. Combine all ingredients
except ribs in a bowl.
2. Brush mixture on both
sides of ribs.
3. Place coated ribs in slow
cooker.
4. Pour remaining sauce
over ribs.
5. Cover. Cook 8-10 hours
on Low, or until meat is
fall-off-the-bone tender, but
not dry.

Sharon's Barbecued Ribs

Sharon Easter, Yuba City, CA

Makes 4-6 servings

Prep. Time: 5 minutes
Cooking Time: 8 hours
Ideal slow-cooker size: 4- to 5-qt.

3-4-lb. boneless pork ribs, cut into serving-size pieces
1 cup barbecue sauce
1 cup Catalina salad dressing

1. Place ribs in slow cooker.
2. Combine barbecue sauce and salad dressing. Pour over ribs.
3. Cover. Cook on Low 8 hours.

Variation:

Add 1 garlic clove sliced thin to top of sauce before cooking.

Just Peachy Ribs

Amymarlene Jensen, Fountain, CO

Makes 4-6 servings

Prep. Time: 10 minutes
Cooking Time: 8-10 hours
Ideal slow-cooker size: 4-qt.

4-lb. boneless pork spareribs
½ cup brown sugar
¼ cup ketchup
¼ cup white vinegar
1 garlic clove, minced
1 tsp. salt
1 tsp. pepper
2 Tbsp. soy sauce
15-oz. can spiced cling peaches, cubed, with juice

1. Cut ribs in serving-size pieces and brown in broiler or in saucepan in oil. Drain. Place in slow cooker.
2. Combine remaining ingredients. Pour over ribs.
3. Cover. Cook on Low 8-10 hours.

Barbecued Ribs

Moreen Weaver, Bath, NY

Makes 5 servings

Prep Time: 10-15 minutes
Cooking Time: 6-8 hours
Ideal slow-cooker size: 5- to 6-qt., oval-shaped

4-4½ lbs. spare, *or* country-style, ribs
2½ cups barbecue sauce
¾ cup cherry preserves, *or* jam
1 Tbsp. Dijon mustard
1 garlic clove, minced
1½ tsp. pepper

1. Cut ribs into serving-size pieces.
2. Place rib pieces in slow cooker.
3. Combine all other ingredients in a mixing bowl.
4. Pour sauce over ribs. If you've stacked the ribs, be sure that all are topped with sauce.
5. Cover. Cook 6-8 hours on Low, or until ribs are tender but not dry.

Sesame Pork Ribs

Joette Droz, Kalona, IA

Makes 6 servings

Prep. Time: 10 minutes
Cooking Time: 5-6 hours
Ideal slow-cooker size: 5-qt.

1 medium onion, sliced
¾ cup packed brown sugar
¼ cup soy sauce
½ cup ketchup
¼ cup honey
2 Tbsp. cider, *or* white, vinegar
3 garlic cloves, minced
1 tsp. ground ginger
¼-½ tsp. crushed red pepper flakes
5 lbs. country-style pork ribs

1. Place onions in bottom of slow cooker.
2. Combine brown sugar, soy sauce, ketchup, honey, vinegar, garlic, ginger, and red pepper flakes in large bowl. Add ribs and turn to coat. Place on top of onions in slow cooker. Pour sauce over meat.
3. Cover. Cook on Low 5-6 hours.

*Serving suggestion: Place ribs on serving platter. Sprinkle with toasted **sesame seeds** and chopped **green onions**. Serve sauce on the side.*

Barbecued Pork and Beef Sandwiches

Nanci Keatley, Salem, OR

Makes 12 servings

Prep Time: 15-30 minutes
Cooking Time: 8 hours
Ideal slow-cooker size: 6- to 7-qt.

1 cup onion, finely chopped
2 cups green pepper, finely chopped
6-oz. can tomato paste
½ cup brown sugar
¼ cup cider vinegar
1 Tbsp. chili powder
1 tsp. salt
2 tsp. Worcestershire sauce
1 tsp. dry mustard
1 tsp. hot sauce
1½ lbs. lean stewing beef
1½ lbs. lean pork cubes

1. Blend all ingredients, except beef and pork in slow cooker.
2. When thoroughly mixed, stir in beef and pork pieces.
3. Cover. Cook 8 hours on Low.
4. Stir to shred meat before serving.

Serving suggestion: Serve in **sandwich buns** *or* **pita bread***, or over* **rice***.*

Barbecued Pork

Grace Ketcham, Marietta, GA
Mary Seielstad, Sparks, NV

Makes 6 servings

Prep. Time: 15 minutes
Cooking Time: 8 hours
Ideal slow-cooker size: 4-qt.

3 lbs. pork, cubed
2 cups chopped onions
3 green peppers, chopped
½ cup brown sugar
¼ cup vinegar
6-oz. can tomato paste
1½ Tbsp. chili powder
1 tsp. dry mustard
2 tsp. Worcestershire sauce
2 tsp. salt

1. Combine all ingredients in slow cooker.
2. Cover. Cook on High 8 hours.
3. Shred meat with fork. Mix into sauce and heat through.

Serving suggestion: Serve on **hamburger buns** *with grated* **cheese** *and* **cole slaw** *on top.*

Variation:
Substitute cubed chuck roast or stewing beef for the pork, or use half beef, half pork.

Barbecued Pork in the Slow Cooker

Dawn Day, Westminster, CA

Makes 6-8 servings

Prep. Time: 10 minutes
Cooking Time: 6-8 hours
Ideal slow-cooker size: 4-qt.

2-3-lb. boneless pork roast, cubed
2 onions, chopped
12-oz. bottle barbecue sauce
¼ cup honey

1. Place meat in slow cooker. Add onions, barbecue sauce, and honey.
2. Cover. Cook on Low 6-8 hours.
3. Use 2 forks to shred meat.

Serving suggestion: Serve on **sandwich rolls** *with sauce.*

Try to have vegetable and meat pieces all cut about the same size and thickness. Mary Puskar, Forest Hill, MD

Slow-Cooked Pork Barbecue

Sharon Wantland, Menomonee Falls, WI

Makes 8 servings

Prep Time: 15-20 minutes
Cooking Time: 5-6 hours
Ideal slow-cooker size: 4-qt.

3-4-lb. boneless pork loin
  roast
1½ tsp. seasoned salt
1 tsp. garlic powder
1 cup barbecue sauce
1 cup cola, regular, *or* diet

1. Cut roast in half. Place both halves in slow cooker.
2. Sprinkle with salt and garlic powder.
3. Cover. Cook 4 hours on Low.
4. Remove meat.
5. Skim fat from broth remaining in slow cooker.
6. Shred pork using 2 forks.
7. Return shredded pork to slow cooker.
8. Combine barbecue sauce and cola in a small bowl.
9. Pour over meat.
10. Cover. Cook on High 1-2 hours, or until heated through and bubbly.

Serving suggestion: Serve on **buns**.

Pulled Pork

Janet Batdorf, Harrisburg, PA

Makes 10 servings

Prep Time: 20 minutes
Cooking Time: 9 hours
Chilling Time for broth: 4-5 hours
Ideal slow-cooker size: 5-qt.

3-lb. pork roast

Sauce:
1 cup ketchup
1 cup pork broth
2 Tbsp. Worcestershire sauce
2 Tbsp. vinegar
dash pepper
¾ tsp. salt
2 Tbsp. prepared mustard
1 large onion, chopped

1. Place pork in slow cooker.
2. Cover with water.
3. Cover. Cook overnight, or for approximately 8 hours, on Low.
4. Turn off slow cooker.
5. Remove pork and set aside.
6. Refrigerate broth.
7. Skim off fat when cold.
8. Combine sauce ingredients in slow cooker.
9. Shred pork with 2 forks.
10. Add shredded pork to sauce.
11. Turn slow cooker on Low. Heat pork in sauce for about one hour, or until ingredients are hot and bubbly.

Serving suggestion: Serve in **buns**, *or over mashed* **potatoes**, *or* **rice**, *or* **pasta**.

Pork Barbecue

Mary Sommerfeld, Lancaster, PA

Makes 8-12 sandwiches

Prep Time: 10 minutes
Cooking Time: 9-20 hours
Ideal slow-cooker size: 4- to 5-qt.

2 onions, sliced, *divided*
4-5-lb. pork roast, *or* fresh
  picnic ham
5-6 whole cloves
2 cups water

Sauce:
1 large onion, chopped
16-oz. bottle barbecue sauce

1. Put half of sliced onions in bottom of slow cooker. Add meat, cloves, and water. Cover with remaining sliced onions.
2. Cover. Cook on Low 8-12 hours.
3. Remove bone from meat. Cut up meat. Drain liquid.
4. Return meat to slow cooker. Add chopped onion and barbecue sauce.
5. Cover. Cook on High 1-3 hours, or on Low 4-8 hours, stirring two or three times.

Serving suggestion: Serve on **buns**.

Note:
This freezes well.

Shredded Pork

Sharon Easter, Yuba City, CA

Makes 4-6 servings

Prep. Time: 5 minutes
Cooking Time: 7-8 hours
Ideal slow-cooker size: 4- to 5-qt.

2-3-lb. pork butt roast, *or*
  boneless country-style
  spareribs
½-1 cup water
1 pkg. dry taco seasoning mix

1. Place meat in slow cooker. Add water and seasoning mix.
2. Cover. Cook on Low 7-8 hours. Shred meat with two forks.

Serving suggestion: Use in **tacos** *or in* **rolls**, *or use the sauce as gravy and serve over* **rice**.

Kraut and Sausage

Kathi Rogge, Alexandria, IN

Makes 4 servings

Prep. Time: 10 minutes
Cooking Time: 3-6 hours
Ideal slow-cooker size: 3½-qt.

2 16-oz. cans sauerkraut,
  drained and rinsed
2 Tbsp. dark brown sugar
1 large onion, chopped
2 strips bacon, diced

1 lb. fully-cooked sausage,
  sliced

1. Combine sauerkraut and brown sugar. Place in slow cooker. Add layers of onion, bacon, and sausage. Add enough water to cover half of sausage.
2. Cover. Cook on Low 5-6 hours, or on High 3 hours.

Melt-in-Your-Mouth Sausages

Ruth Ann Gingrich, New Holland, PA
Ruth Hershey, Paradise, PA
Carol Sherwood, Batavia, NY
Nancy Zimmerman, Loysville, PA

Makes 6-8 servings

Prep. Time: 15 minutes
Cooking Time: 6 hours
Ideal slow-cooker size: 4-qt.

2 lbs. sweet Italian sausage,
  cut into 5-inch lengths
48-oz. jar spaghetti sauce
6-oz. can tomato paste
1 large green pepper, thinly
  sliced
1 large onion, thinly sliced
1 Tbsp. grated Parmesan
  cheese
1 tsp. dried parsley, *or* 1 Tbsp.
  chopped fresh parsley
1 cup water

1. Place sausage in skillet. Cover with water. Simmer 10 minutes. Drain.
2. Combine remaining

ingredients in slow cooker. Add sausage.
3. Cover. Cook on Low 6 hours.

Serving suggestion: Serve in **buns**, *or cut sausage into bite-sized pieces and serve over cooked* **spaghetti**. *Sprinkle with more* **Parmesan cheese**.

Polish Sausage Stew

Jeanne Heyerly, Chenoa, IL
Joyce Kaut, Rochester, NY
Joyce B. Suiter, Garysburg, NC

Makes 6-8 servings

Prep. Time: 15 minutes
Cooking Time: 4-8 hours
Ideal slow-cooker size: 4- to 5-qt.

10¾-oz. can cream of celery
  soup
⅓ cup packed brown sugar
27-oz. can sauerkraut,
  drained
1½ lbs. Polish sausage, cut
  into 2-inch pieces and
  browned
4 medium potatoes, cubed
1 cup chopped onions
1 cup (4 oz.) shredded
  Monterey Jack cheese

1. Combine soup, sugar, and sauerkraut. Stir in sausage, potatoes, and onions.
2. Cover. Cook on Low 8 hours, or on High 4 hours.
3. Stir in cheese and serve.

Polish Kraut 'n' Apples

Lori Berezovsky, Salina, KS
Marie Morucci, Glen Lyon, PA

Makes 4 servings

Prep. Time: 10 minutes
Cooking Time: 3-7 hours
Ideal slow-cooker size: 3½-qt.

1 lb. fresh, *or* canned, sauerkraut, *divided*
1 lb. lean smoked Polish sausage
3 tart cooking apples, thinly sliced
½ cup packed brown sugar
¾ tsp. salt
⅛ tsp. pepper
½ tsp. caraway seeds, *optional*
¾ cup apple juice, *or* cider

1. Rinse sauerkraut and squeeze dry. Place half in slow cooker.
2. Cut sausage into 2-inch lengths and add to cooker.
3. Continue to layer remaining ingredients in slow cooker in order given. Top with remaining sauerkraut. Do not stir.
4. Cover. Cook on High 3-3½ hours, or on Low 6-7 hours. Stir before serving.

Old World Sauerkraut Supper

Josie Bollman, Maumee, OH
Joyce Bowman, Lady Lake, FL
Vera Schmucker, Goshen, IN

Makes 8 servings

Prep. Time: 15 minutes
Cooking Time: 3-8 hours
Ideal slow-cooker size: 5-qt.

3 strips bacon, cut into small pieces
2 Tbsp. flour
2 15-oz. cans sauerkraut
2 small potatoes, cubed
2 small apples, cubed
3 Tbsp. brown sugar
1½ tsp. caraway seeds
3 lbs. Polish sausage, cut into 3-inch pieces
½ cup water

1. Fry bacon until crisp. Drain, reserving drippings.
2. Add flour to bacon drippings. Blend well. Stir in sauerkraut and bacon. Transfer to slow cooker.
3. Add remaining ingredients.
4. Cover. Cook on Low 6-8 hours, or on High 3-4 hours.

Sausage Sauerkraut Supper

Ruth Ann Hoover, New Holland, PA
Robin Schrock, Millersburg, OH

Makes 10-12 servings

Prep. Time: 20 minutes
Cooking Time: 8-9 hours
Ideal slow-cooker size: 4- to 5-qt.

4 cups cubed carrots
4 cups cubed red potatoes
2 14-oz. cans sauerkraut, rinsed and drained
2½ lbs. fresh Polish sausage, cut into 3-inch pieces
1 medium onion, thinly sliced
3 garlic cloves, minced
1½ cups dry white wine, *or* chicken broth
½ tsp. pepper
1 tsp. caraway seeds

1. Layer carrots, potatoes, and sauerkraut in slow cooker.
2. Brown sausage in skillet. Transfer to slow cooker. Reserve 1 Tbsp. drippings in skillet.
3. Sauté onion and garlic in drippings until tender. Stir in wine. Bring to boil. Stir to loosen brown bits. Stir in pepper and caraway seeds. Pour over sausage.
4. Cover. Cook on Low 8-9 hours.

Kielbasa and Cabbage

Barbara McGinnis, Jupiter, FL

Makes 6 servings

Prep. Time: 15 minutes
Cooking Time: 7-8 hours
Ideal slow-cooker size: 4- to 5-qt.

1½-lb. head green cabbage, shredded
2 medium onions, chopped
3 medium red potatoes, peeled and cubed
1 red bell pepper, chopped
2 garlic cloves, minced
⅔ cup dry white wine
1½ lbs. Polish kielbasa, cut into 3-inch long links
28-oz. can cut-up tomatoes with juice
1 Tbsp. Dijon mustard
¾ tsp. caraway seeds
½ tsp. pepper
¾ tsp. salt

1. Combine all ingredients in slow cooker.
2. Cover. Cook on Low 7-8 hours, or until cabbage is tender.

Sausage, Cabbage, and Potatoes: One-Pot Dinner

Donna Treloar, Muncie, IN

Makes 6-8 servings

Prep Time: 15-30 minutes
Cooking Time: 7 hours
Ideal slow-cooker size: 4-qt.

8-10 cups shredded fresh cabbage
3 potatoes, peeled and cubed
1 large onion, chopped
dash of salt
dash of pepper
14½-oz. can chicken broth
2 lbs. kielbasa, *or* sausage of your choice, cut into serving-size pieces

1. Combine cabbage, potatoes, onion, salt, and pepper in slow cooker.
2. Add chicken broth.
3. Place sausage pieces on top.
4. Cover and cook on Low 7 hours, or until vegetables are tender.

Aunt Lavina's Sauerkraut

Pat Unternahrer, Wayland, IA

Makes 8-12 servings

Prep. Time: 10 minutes
Cooking Time: 3-6 hours
Ideal slow-cooker size: 4-qt.

2-3 lbs. smoked sausage, cut into 1-inch pieces
2 bell peppers, chopped
2 onions, sliced
½ lb. fresh mushrooms, sliced
2 Tbsp. water, *or* oil
1 qt. sauerkraut, drained
2 14½-oz. cans diced tomatoes with green peppers
1 tsp. salt
½ tsp. pepper
2 Tbsp. brown sugar

1. Place sausage in slow cooker. Heat on Low while you prepare other ingredients.
2. Sauté peppers, onions, and mushrooms in small amount of water or oil in saucepan.
3. Combine all ingredients in slow cooker.
4. Cover. Cook on Low 5-6 hours, or on High 3-4 hours.

*Serving suggestion: Serve with mashed **potatoes**.*

Be sure vegetables are thinly sliced or chopped because they cook slowly in a slow cooker.

Marilyn Yoder, Archbold, OH

Pork and Kraut

Joyce B. Suiter, Garysburg, NC

Makes 6 servings

Prep. Time: 15 minutes
Cooking Time: 10 hours
Ideal slow-cooker size: 6½-qt.

4-lb. pork loin
29-oz. can sauerkraut
¼ cup water
1 onion, sliced
1 large white potato, sliced
10¾-oz. can cheddar cheese
   soup
1 Tbsp. caraway seeds
1 large Granny Smith apple,
   peeled and sliced
salt to taste
pepper to taste

1. Brown roast on all sides in skillet. Place in slow cooker.
2. Rinse sauerkraut and drain well. Combine sauerkraut, water, onion, potato, soup, caraway seeds, and apple. Pour over roast.
3. Cover. Cook on Low 10 hours.
4. Season with salt and pepper before serving.

Note:

Apple and potato disappear into the cheese soup as they cook, making a good sauce.

Pork Roast with Sauerkraut

Gail Bush, Landenberg, PA
Barbara Hershey, Lititz, PA

Makes 8 servings

Prep Time: 5-10 minutes
Cooking Time: 7 hours
Ideal slow-cooker size: 6- to 7-qt.

2 3-lb. pork shoulder roasts
2 large cans sweet Bavarian
   sauerkraut with caraway
   seeds
¼ cup brown sugar
1 envelope dry onion soup
   mix
½-1 cup water

1. Place roasts in slow cooker.
2. Rinse and drain sauerkraut. Combine sauerkraut, brown sugar, and onion soup mix. Layer over roasts. Pour water over all.
3. Cover. Cook on Low 7 hours.

Note:

If you can't find Bavarian sauerkraut with caraway seeds, substitute with 2 large cans regular sauerkraut and 1 tsp. caraway seeds.

Pork and Sauerkraut

Carole Whaling, New Tripoli, PA

Makes 6 servings

Prep. Time: 10 minutes
Cooking Time: 3-4 hours
Ideal slow-cooker size: 5-qt.

4 large potatoes, cubed
32-oz. bag sauerkraut,
   drained
1 large onion, chopped
1 large tart apple, chopped
2 Tbsp. packed brown sugar
1 tsp. caraway seeds
1 tsp. minced garlic
½ tsp. pepper
2½-lb. boneless pork loin
   roast

1. Put potatoes in slow cooker.
2. Combine remaining ingredients, except pork, in slow cooker. Place half of the sauerkraut mixture on top of the potatoes. Add roast. Top with remaining sauerkraut mixture.
3. Cover. Cook on High 3-4 hours.

Cooked pasta and rice should be added during the last 1-1½ hours of cooking time to prevent them from disintegrating.
John D. Allen, Rye, CO

Pork and Cabbage Dinner,
page 209

Taco Bake,
page 190

Pork Spareribs with Sauerkraut

Char Hagner, Montague, MI

Makes 4-6 servings

Prep. Time: 15 minutes
Cooking Time: 4-8 hours
Ideal slow-cooker size: 4-qt.

2 small cooking apples, sliced in rings
1½-2 lbs. spareribs, cut into serving-size pieces and browned
1 qt. sauerkraut
½ cup apple cider, *or* juice
½ tsp. caraway seeds, *optional*

1. Layer apples, ribs, and sauerkraut into slow cooker. Pour on juice. Sprinkle with caraway seeds.

2. Cover. Cook on Low 8 hours, or on High 4 hours.

Country Ribs and Sauerkraut

Andrea O'Neil, Fairfield, CT

Makes 4-6 servings

Prep. Time: 15 minutes
Cooking Time: 7-8 hours
Ideal slow-cooker size: 5-qt.

2 27-oz. cans sauerkraut, drained and rinsed

2-3 lbs. country-style pork ribs, cut into serving-size pieces
6 slices bacon, browned
3-4 Tbsp. caraway seeds
2 cups water

1. Place alternating layers of sauerkraut and ribs in slow cooker, starting and ending with sauerkraut.

2. Crumble bacon and mix gently into top layer of sauerkraut. Sprinkle with caraway seeds. Pour water over all.

3. Cover. Cook on Low 7-8 hours.

Sauerkraut and Ribs

Margaret H. Moffitt, Bartlett, TN

Makes 6 servings

Prep. Time: 5-10 minutes
Cooking Time: 4½-5 hours
Ideal slow-cooker size: 3½- to 4-qt.

27-oz. can sauerkraut with juice
1 small onion, chopped
2 lbs. pork, *or* beef, ribs, cut into serving-size pieces
1 tsp. salt
¼ tsp. pepper
half a sauerkraut can of water

1. Pour sauerkraut and juice into slow cooker. Add onion.

2. Season ribs with salt and pepper. Place on top of kraut. Add water.

3. Cover. Cook on High until mixture boils. Reduce heat to Low and cook 4 hours.

*Serving suggestion: Serve with mashed **potatoes**.*

Pork Rib and Kraut Dinner

Betty A. Holt, St. Charles, MO

Makes 6-8 servings

Prep. Time: 5 minutes
Cooking Time: 3-8 hours
Ideal slow-cooker size: 5-qt.

3-4 lbs. country-style ribs
4 Tbsp. brown rice
1 Tbsp. caraway seeds
28-oz. can sauerkraut, rinsed
12-oz. can V8 juice

1. Place ingredients in slow cooker in order listed.

2. Cover. Cook on Low 6-8 hours, or on High 3-4 hours.

Variation:

To take the edge off the sour flavor of sauerkraut, stir in 3 Tbsp. mild molasses or honey before cooking.

Chops and Kraut

Willard E. Roth, Elkhart, IN

Makes 6 servings

Prep. Time: 5 minutes
Cooking Time: 6 hours
Ideal slow-cooker size: 5-qt.

1-lb. bag fresh sauerkraut
2 large Vidalia onions,
  sliced
6 pork chops

1. Make 3 layers in well-greased cooker: kraut, onions, and chops.
2. Cover. Cook on Low 6 hours.

*Serving suggestion: Serve with mashed **potatoes** and **apple-sauce** or **cranberry sauce**.*

Sauerkraut and Pork

Ethel Mumaw, Berlin, OH

Makes 6-8 servings

Prep. Time: 15 minutes
Cooking Time: 7-8 hours
Ideal slow-cooker size: 4-qt.

2 lbs. pork cutlets
2 14-oz. cans sauerkraut
2 apples, chopped
2 Tbsp. brown sugar

1. Cut pork into serving-size pieces. Brown under broiler or in 2 Tbsp. oil in skillet. Place in slow cooker.
2. Add remaining ingredients.
3. Cover. Cook on Low 7-8 hours.

Ham Hock and Sauerkraut

Bernice M. Gnidovec, Streator, IL

Makes 2 servings

Prep. Time: 10 minutes
Cooking Time: 6¼-8¼ hours
Ideal slow-cooker size: 4-qt.

2 small ham hocks, *or* pork
  chops
14-oz. can sauerkraut, rinsed
1 large potato, cubed
half a small onion, diced
1 Tbsp. butter
1 Tbsp. flour
2 Tbsp. cold water

1. Place ham hocks or chops in slow cooker. Top with sauerkraut and potato. Add enough water to cover meat, potato and sauerkraut.
2. Cover. Cook on High 4 hours, or on Low 6-8 hours.
3. Sauté onions in butter in saucepan until transparent. Stir in flour and brown. Add 2 Tbsp. cold water, stirring until thickened. Pour over ingredients in slow cooker. Cover and cook on High 5-10 minutes.

Smothered Lentils

Tracey B. Stenger, Gretna, LA

Makes 6 servings

Prep. Time: 10 minutes
Cooking Time: 8 hours
Ideal slow-cooker size: 4-qt.

2 cups dry lentils, rinsed
  and sorted
1 medium onion, chopped
½ cup chopped celery
2 garlic cloves, minced
1 cup ham, cooked and
  chopped
½ cup chopped carrots
1 cup diced tomatoes
1 tsp. dried marjoram
1 tsp. ground coriander
salt to taste
pepper to taste
3 cups water

1. Combine all ingredients in slow cooker.
2. Cover. Cook on Low 8 hours. (Check lentils after 5 hours of cooking. If they've absorbed all the water, stir in 1 more cup water.)

Green Beans and Sausage

Alma Weaver, Ephrata, PA

Makes 4-6 servings

Prep. Time: 5-10 minutes
Cooking Time: 5-6 hours
Ideal slow-cooker size: 4-qt.

1 qt. green beans, cut into
   2-inch pieces
1 carrot, chopped
1 small green pepper,
   chopped
8-oz. can tomato sauce
¼ tsp. dried thyme
½ tsp. salt
1 lb. bulk pork sausage,
   or link sausage, cut into
   1-inch pieces

1. Combine all ingredients
except sausage in slow cooker.
2. Cover. Cook on High 3-4
hours. Add sausage and cook
another 2 hours on Low.

Sausage Supreme

Jan Moore, Wellsville, KS

Makes 4 servings

Prep. Time: 10-15 minutes
Cooking Time: 8 hours
Ideal slow-cooker size: 3-qt.

1 lb. fresh sausage, cut into
   1-inch pieces and browned
2 10¾-oz. cans cream of
   mushroom soup
1 onion, chopped
4 potatoes, cubed

1. Combine all ingredients
in slow cooker.
2. Cover. Cook on Low 8
hours. If mixture becomes too
dry, stir in half a soup can or
more of water.

Variation:

   Substitute 1 can cheese
soup for 1 can cream of
mushroom soup.

Sausage and Scalloped Potato Supper

Veronica Sabo, Shelton, CT

Makes 4-5 servings

Prep Time: 10-15 minutes
Cooking Time: 5 hours
Ideal slow-cooker size: 5-qt.

5-oz. pkg. cheesy scalloped
   potatoes-with-skin-on
   potato mix
10¾-oz. can cream of
   mushroom soup
1 soup can water
1 lb. kielbasa, cooked, cut
   diagonally into 2-inch
   pieces
1 cup frozen green peas

1. Spray inside of slow
cooker with cooking spray.
2. Place uncooked potato
mix in slow cooker.
3. Mix soup and 1 soup can
of water (use empty soup can
to measure) in a small bowl.
4. Pour over potatoes in
slow cooker and mix well.
5. Lay kielbasa over potatoes.
6. Cover. Cook on Low 5
hours, or until potatoes are
tender.
7. Sprinkle peas over
potatoes and meat.
8. Cover. Cook on High
5 minutes. Turn off cooker
and allow to stand 5 minutes
before serving.

Since I work full-time, I often put my dinner into the slow cooker to cook until I get home. My three teenagers and umpire/referee husband can all get a hot nutritious meal no matter what time they get home.

Rhonda Burgoon, Collingswood, NJ

Sausage, Beans, and Rice

Janie Steele, Moore, OK

Makes 4-6 servings

Prep. Time: 10-15 minutes
Cooking Time: 2-3 hours
Ideal slow-cooker size: 4-qt.

1 lb. smoked sausage, cut in
    bite-size pieces
1 onion, chopped
1 green pepper, chopped
1 clove garlic, chopped
2 15-oz. cans kidney beans,
    drained
15-oz. can stewed tomatoes
    with juice
salt, *or* garlic powder, to
    taste
black pepper to taste

1. Combine all ingredients
in slow cooker.
2. Cook on High 2-3 hours,
or until vegetables are tender
and dish is heated through.

*Serving suggestion: Serve over
rice. Pass **hot sauce** for those
who want to add it.*

Supreme Sausage Dish

Shirley Thieszen, Lakin, KS

Makes 6 servings

Prep. Time: 20 minutes
Cooking Time: 4-5 hours
Ideal slow-cooker size: 5-qt.

1 lb. smoky wieners, cut in
    1-inch pieces
2 cups cooked macaroni
1 cup frozen peas, *or* corn
½ cup chopped onions
1 tsp. dry parsley
1 small jar chopped
    pimentos (about 3 Tbsp.)
¾ cup shredded American,
    or Velveeta, cheese
3 Tbsp. flour
¾ tsp. salt
¼ tsp. pepper
1 cup milk
1 cup water
½ Tbsp. vinegar

1. Combine wieners, maca-
roni, peas, onions, parsley, and
pimentos in greased slow cooker.
2. In saucepan, combine
cheese, flour, salt, pepper, milk,
water, and vinegar. Cook until
smooth and thickened. Pour
into slow cooker. Mix well.
3. Cover. Cook on High 1
hour, and then on Low 3-4
hours.

Variation:
    Use smoked sausage instead
of smoky wieners.

Sausage and Apples

Evelyn L. Ward, Greeley, CO

Makes 4 servings

Prep. Time: 10 minutes
Cooking Time: 4-6 hours
Ideal slow-cooker size: 3-qt.

20-oz. can apple pie filling
¼ cup water
ground nutmeg
10-oz. pkg. fully cooked and
    browned sausage patties

1. Spoon pie filling into
slow cooker. Stir in water.
Sprinkle with nutmeg. Top
with sausage.
2. Cover. Cook on Low 4-6
hours.

Spiced Hot Dogs

Tracey Yohn, Harrisburg, PA

Makes 3-4 servings

Prep. Time: 5 minutes
Cooking Time: 2 hours
Ideal slow-cooker size: 3-qt.

1 lb. hot dogs, cut in pieces
2 Tbsp. brown sugar
3 Tbsp. vinegar
½ cup ketchup
2 tsp. prepared mustard
½ cup water
½ cup chopped onions

1. Place hot dogs in slow cooker.
2. Combine all ingredients except hot dogs in saucepan. Simmer. Pour over hot dogs.
3. Cover. Cook on Low 2 hours.

Barbecued Sausage Pieces

Elizabeth Yutzy, Wauseon, OH

Makes 4-5 main-dish servings, or 8-10 snack-sized servings

Prep. Time: 10 minutes
Cooking Time: 2 hours
Ideal slow-cooker size: 1½-qt.

1 lb. smoked sausage
1 cup hickory-flavored barbecue sauce
¼ cup honey
2 Tbsp. brown sugar

1. Cut sausage in ½-inch pieces. Brown in skillet. Place in slow cooker.
2. Combine remaining ingredients. Pour over sausage.
3. Cover. Cook on Low 2 hours.

*Serving suggestion: Serve over **rice** or **noodles** as a main dish, or with toothpicks as a party snack.*

Perfection Hot Dogs

Audrey L. Kneer, Williamsfield, IL

Makes 12 servings

Prep. Time: 2 minutes
Cooking Time: 1-2 hours
Ideal slow-cooker size: 2½-qt.

12 hot dogs, *or bratwurst, or Polish sausage links*

1. Place hot dogs, or bratwurst, or sausages in slow cooker.
2. Cover. Cook on High 1-2 hours.

Beer Brats

Mary Ann Wasick, West Allis, WI

Makes 6 servings

Prep. Time: 10 minutes
Cooking Time: 6-7 hours
Ideal slow-cooker size: 3½-qt.

6 fresh bratwurst
2 garlic cloves, minced
2 Tbsp. olive oil
12-oz. can beer

1. Brown sausages and garlic in olive oil in skillet. Pierce sausage casings and cook 5 more minutes. Transfer to slow cooker.
2. Pour beer into cooker to cover sausages.
3. Cover. Cook on Low 6-7 hours.

If you're in a rush, you can skip browning the meat if the recipe calls for that. Why do it at all? If you're working with ground beef, browning it in a skillet allows the drippings to emerge. You can drain them off before putting the browned beef into the cooker, thus reducing the fat content of your finished dish. If you're working with a roast, browning it deepens the flavor of the finished dish.

Barbecued Mini-Franks

Zona Mae Bontrager, Kokomo, IN

*Makes 8-10 full-sized servings,
or 16-20 appetizer-sized servings*

Prep. Time: 10 minutes
Cooking Time: 5½ hours
Ideal slow-cooker size: 4½-qt.

1 cup finely chopped onions
1 cup ketchup
⅓ cup Worcestershire sauce
¼ cup sugar
¼ cup vinegar
4 tsp. prepared mustard
1 tsp. pepper
4 lbs. miniature hot dogs

1. Combine all ingredients except hot dogs in slow cooker.
2. Cover. Heat on High 1½ hours, or until hot. Add hot dogs.
3. Reduce heat to Low and simmer 4 hours.

Variations:
1. Add 1 Tbsp. finely chopped green pepper and 2 garlic cloves, pressed.
2. Use miniature smoked sausages instead of mini hot dogs.

Bits and Bites

Betty Richards, Rapid City, SD

Makes 12 servings

Prep. Time: 5 minutes
Cooking Time: 3-4 hours
Ideal slow-cooker size: 4-qt.

12-oz. can beer
1 cup ketchup
1 cup light brown sugar
½-1 cup barbecue sauce
1 lb. all-beef hot dogs, sliced 1½-inches thick
2 lbs. cocktail sausages

1. Combine beer, ketchup, brown sugar, and barbecue sauce. Pour into slow cooker.
2. Add hot dogs and sausages. Mix well.
3. Cover. Cook on Low 3-4 hours.

Spicy Franks

Char Hagner, Montague, MI

*Makes 4-6 full-sized servings,
or 32 appetizer-sized servings*

Prep. Time: 5 minutes
Cooking Time: 1½-4 hours
Ideal slow-cooker size: 2½-qt.

2 1-lb. pkgs. cocktail wieners
1 cup chili sauce
1 cup bottled barbecue sauce
8-oz. can jellied cranberry sauce

1. Place wieners in slow cooker.
2. In separate bowl, combine chili sauce, barbecue sauce, and cranberry sauce. Pour over wieners.
3. Cover. Cook on Low 3-4 hours, or on High 1½-2 hours.

Barbecued Hot Dogs

Jeanette Oberholtzer, Manheim, PA

Makes 8 servings

Prep. Time: 5 minutes
Cooking Time: 4½ hours
Ideal slow-cooker size: 4-qt.

1 cup apricot preserves
4 oz. tomato sauce
⅓ cup vinegar
2 Tbsp. soy sauce
2 Tbsp. honey
1 Tbsp. oil
1 tsp. salt
¼ tsp. ground ginger
2 lbs. hot dogs, cut into 1-inch pieces

1. Combine all ingredients except hot dogs in slow cooker.
2. Cover. Cook on High 30 minutes. Add hot dog pieces. Cook on Low 4 hours.

Serving suggestion: Serve over rice as a main dish, or with toothpicks as an appetizer.

Sweet and Sour Vienna Sausages

Judy Denney, Lawrenceville, GA

*Makes 10 full-sized servings,
or 20 appetizer-sized servings*

Prep. Time: 5 minutes
Cooking Time: 6 hours
Ideal slow-cooker size: 3½-qt.

**8 cans Vienna sausages,
drained**
2 cups grape jelly
2 cups ketchup

1. Put sausages in slow cooker.
2. Combine jelly and ketchup. Pour over sausages. Stir lightly. (Add more jelly and ketchup if sausages are not covered.)
3. Cover. Cook on High 1 hour, then turn to Low for 5 hours.

Variations:

Instead of Vienna sausages, use smoky links. Add 1 can pineapple chunks and juice to jelly and ketchup.

Barbecued Ham Sandwiches

Jane Steiner, Orrville, OH

Makes 4-6 full-sized servings

Prep. Time: 5-7 minutes
Cooking Time: 5 hours
Ideal slow-cooker size: 3-qt.

**1 lb. turkey ham chipped,
or chipped honey-glazed
ham**
1 small onion, finely diced
½ cup ketchup
1 Tbsp. vinegar
3 Tbsp. brown sugar

1. Place half of meat in greased slow cooker.
2. Combine other ingredients. Pour half of mixture over meat. Repeat layers.
3. Cover. Cook on Low 5 hours.

*Serving suggestion: Fill **buns** and serve.*

Ham Barbecue

Janet V. Yocum, Elizabethtown, PA

Makes 6-8 servings

Prep. Time: 5 minutes
Cooking Time: 8 hours
Ideal slow-cooker size: 3-qt.

**1 lb. boiled ham, cut into
cubes**
1 cup cola-flavored soda
1 cup ketchup

1. Place ham in slow cooker. Pour cola and ketchup over ham.
2. Cover. Cook on Low 8 hours.

*Serving suggestion: Serve in **hamburger rolls**.*

With vehicles now having power supply plugs in their trunks and elsewhere, and with 110-volt plug-in converters, you can cook as you travel to parties. Just be sure that your plug, adaptor, and cord are adequate for the electricity needed to power the cooker.

Sue Hamilton, Minooka, IL

Beef and Pork Spaghetti Sauce

Doris Perkins, Mashpee, MA

Makes 18-24 servings

Prep. Time: 30 minutes
Cooking Time: 4-5 hours
Ideal slow-cooker size: 6-qt.

¼-lb. bacon, diced
1¼-lb. ground beef
½ lb. ground pork
1 cup chopped onions
½ cup chopped green
  peppers
3 garlic cloves, minced
2 35-oz. cans Italian
  tomatoes
2 6-oz. cans tomato paste
1 cup dry red wine, *or* water
2½ tsp. dried oregano
2½ tsp. dried basil
1 bay leaf, crumbled
¾ cup water
¼ cup chopped fresh parsley
1 tsp. dried thyme
1 Tbsp. salt
¼ tsp. pepper
¼ cup dry red wine, *or* water

1. Brown bacon in skillet until crisp. Remove. Add ground beef and pork. Crumble and cook until brown. Stir in onions, green peppers, and garlic. Cook 10 minutes.

2. Pour tomatoes into slow cooker and crush with back of spoon.

3. Add all other ingredients, except ¼ cup wine, in slow cooker.

4. Cover. Bring to boil on High. Reduce heat to Low for 3-4 hours.

5. During last 30 minutes, stir in ¼ cup red wine, or water.

Sausage-Beef Spaghetti Sauce

Jeannine Janzen, Elbing, KS

Makes 16-20 servings

Prep. Time: 15 minutes
Cooking Time: 6½ hours
Ideal slow-cooker size: 5-qt.

1 lb. ground beef
1 lb. Italian sausage, sliced
2 28-oz. cans crushed
  tomatoes
¾ can (28-oz. tomato can)
  water
2 tsp. garlic powder
1 tsp. pepper
2 Tbsp. *or more* parsley
2 Tbsp. dried oregano
2 12-oz. cans tomato paste
2 12-oz. cans tomato purée

1. Brown ground beef and sausage in skillet. Drain. Transfer to large slow cooker.

2. Add crushed tomatoes, water, garlic powder, pepper, parsley, and oregano.

3. Cover. Cook on High 30 minutes. Add tomato paste and tomato purée. Cook on Low 6 hours.

Note:
Leftovers freeze well.

Italian Spaghetti Sauce

Michele Ruvola, Selden, NY

Makes 8-10 servings

Prep. Time: 20 minutes
Cooking Time: 8-9 hours
Ideal slow-cooker size: 5- to 6-qt.

2 lbs. sausage, *or* ground beef
3 medium onions, chopped
  (about 2¼ cups)
2 cups sliced mushrooms
6 garlic cloves, minced
2 14½-oz. cans diced
  tomatoes, undrained
29-oz. can tomato sauce
12-oz. can tomato paste
2 Tbsp. dried basil
1 Tbsp. dried oregano
1 Tbsp. sugar
1 tsp. salt
½ tsp. crushed red pepper
  flakes

1. Cook sausage, onions, mushrooms, and garlic in skillet over medium heat for 10 minutes. Drain. Transfer to slow cooker.

2. Stir in remaining ingredients.

3. Cover. Cook on Low 8-9 hours.

Note:
This is also a good sauce to use in lasagna.

Chunky Spaghetti Sauce

Patti Boston, Newark, OH

Makes 6 cups

Prep. Time: 15-20 minutes
Cooking Time: 3½-8 hours
Ideal slow-cooker size: 4-qt.

1 lb. ground beef, browned
   and drained
½ lb. bulk sausage,
   browned and drained
14½-oz. can Italian
   tomatoes with basil
15-oz. can Italian tomato
   sauce
1 medium onion, chopped
1 green pepper, chopped
8-oz. can sliced mushrooms
½ cup dry red wine
2 tsp. sugar
1 tsp. minced garlic

1. Combine all ingredients
in slow cooker.
2. Cover. Cook on High
3½-4 hours, or on Low 7-8
hours.

Variations:
1. For added texture and
zest, add 3 fresh, medium-
sized tomatoes, chopped, and
4 large fresh basil leaves, torn.
Stir in 1 tsp. salt and
½ tsp. pepper.
2. To any leftover sauce, add
chickpeas or kidney beans and
serve chili!

Easy-Does-It Spaghetti

Rachel Kauffman, Alto, MI
Lois Stoltzfus, Honey Brook, PA
Deb Unternahrer, Wayland, IA

Makes 8 servings

Prep. Time: 15 minutes
Cooking Time: 3¼-8¼ hours
Ideal slow-cooker size: 4-qt.

2 lbs. ground chuck,
   browned and drained
1 cup chopped onions
2 cloves garlic, minced
2 15-oz. cans tomato sauce
2-3 tsp. Italian seasoning
1½ tsp. salt
¼ tsp. pepper
2 4-oz. cans sliced
   mushrooms, drained
6 cups tomato juice
16-oz. dry spaghetti, broken
   into 4-5-inch pieces

1. Combine all ingredients
except spaghetti and cheese in
slow cooker.
2. Cover. Cook on Low 6-8
hours, or on High 3-5 hours.
Turn to High during last
30 minutes and stir in dry
spaghetti. (If spaghetti is not
fully cooked, continue cooking
another 10 minutes, checking
to make sure it is not becoming over-cooked.)

*Serving suggestion: Sprinkle
individual servings with*
Parmesan cheese.

Variation:
   Add 1 tsp. dry mustard and
½ tsp. allspice in Step 1.
   Kathy Hertzler, Lancaster, PA

Slow-Cooker Spaghetti Sauce

Lucille Amos, Greensboro, NC
Julia Lapp, New Holland, PA

Makes 6-8 servings

Prep. Time: 15 minutes
Cooking Time: 7 hours
Ideal slow-cooker size: 4-qt.

1 lb. ground beef
1 medium onion, chopped
2 14-oz. cans diced
   tomatoes, with juice
6-oz. can tomato paste
8-oz. can tomato sauce
1 bay leaf
4 garlic cloves, minced
2 tsp. dried oregano
1 tsp. salt
2 tsp. dried basil
1 Tbsp. brown sugar
½-1 tsp. dried thyme

1. Brown meat and onion in
saucepan. Drain well. Transfer
to slow cooker.
2. Add remaining ingredi-
ents.
3. Cover. Cook on Low 7
hours. If the sauce seems too
runny, remove lid during last
hour of cooking.

Mom's Spaghetti and Meatballs

Mary C. Casey, Scranton, PA

Makes 8-10 servings

Prep. Time: 20 minutes
Cooking Time: 4-5 hours
Ideal slow-cooker size: 5½-qt.

Sauce:
¼-½ cup chopped onions
3 garlic cloves, minced
2 Tbsp. oil
29-oz. can tomato purée
29-oz. can water
12-oz. can tomato paste
12-oz. can water
1 tsp. salt
1 Tbsp. sugar
2 tsp. dried oregano
¼ tsp. Italian seasoning
½ tsp. dried basil
⅛ tsp. pepper
¼ cup diced green peppers

Meatballs:
1 lb. ground beef
1 egg
2 Tbsp. water
¾ cup Italian bread crumbs
⅛ tsp. black pepper
½ tsp. salt
2 Tbsp. oil

1. Sauté onions and garlic in oil in saucepan.
2. Combine all sauce ingredients in slow cooker.
3. Cover. Cook on Low.
4. Mix together all meatball ingredients except oil. Form into small meatballs, then brown on all sides in oil in saucepan. Drain on paper towels. Add to sauce.
5. Cover. Cook on Low 4-5 hours.

Spaghetti with Meat Sauce

Esther Lehman, Croghan, NY

Makes 8-10 servings

Prep. Time: 20 minutes
Cooking Time: 8½-10½ hours
Ideal slow-cooker size: 6-qt.

1 lb. ground beef, browned
2 28-oz. cans tomatoes, *divided*
2 medium onions, quartered
2 medium carrots, cut into chunks
2 garlic cloves, minced
6-oz. can tomato paste
2 Tbsp. chopped fresh parsley
1 bay leaf
1 Tbsp. sugar
1 tsp. dried basil
¾ tsp. salt
½ tsp. dried oregano
dash pepper
2 Tbsp. cold water
2 Tbsp. cornstarch

1. Place meat in slow cooker.
2. In blender, combine 1 can tomatoes, onions, carrots, and garlic. Cover and blend until finely chopped. Stir into meat.
3. Cut up the remaining can of tomatoes. Stir into meat mixture. Add tomato paste, parsley, bay leaf, sugar, basil, salt, oregano, and pepper. Mix well.
4. Cover. Cook on Low 8-10 hours.
5. To serve, turn to High. Remove bay leaf. Cover and heat until bubbly, about 10 minutes.
6. Combine water and cornstarch. Stir into tomato mixture. Cook 10 minutes longer.

*Serving suggestion: Serve with cooked **spaghetti** and grated **Parmesan cheese**.*

Beef and Vegetables Spaghetti Sauce

Colleen Heatwole, Burton, MI

Makes 15 servings

Prep Time: 30-35 minutes
Cooking Time: 4 hours
Ideal slow-cooker size: 1 7-qt., or 2 4-qt. cookers

1½ lbs. lean ground beef, cooked and drained
3 onions, coarsely chopped
1 red bell pepper, coarsely chopped
1 green bell pepper, coarsely chopped
4 cloves garlic, minced
2 28-oz. cans diced tomatoes
14½-oz. can diced tomatoes
2 14½-oz. cans beef broth
2 Tbsp. sugar
2 tsp. dried basil, *or more*

2 tsp. dried oregano, *or more*
2 tsp. salt
2 6-oz. cans tomato paste

1. Combine all ingredients except tomato paste in slow cooker.
2. Cook for 3½ hours on High. Stir in tomato paste.
3. Cover and cook an additional 30 minutes.

Char's Spaghetti Sauce

Char Hagner, Montague, MI

Makes 16-20 servings

Prep. Time: 30 minutes
Cooking Time: 6 hours
Ideal slow-cooker size: 7-qt.

4 lbs. ground beef
2 large onions, chopped
¼-lb. bacon, cut into small squares
5 garlic cloves, minced
1 Tbsp. salt
¼ tsp. celery salt
4 10¾-oz. cans tomato soup
2 6-oz. cans tomato paste
8-oz. can mushrooms
3 green peppers, chopped

1. Brown ground beef, onions, bacon, and garlic in saucepan. Drain.
2. Combine all ingredients in large slow cooker.
3. Cover. Cook on Low 6 hours.

Creamy Spaghetti

Dale Peterson, Rapid City, SD

Makes 6 servings

Prep. Time: 25 minutes
Cooking Time: 4-6 hours
Ideal slow-cooker size: 4- to 5-qt.

1 cup chopped onions
1 cup chopped green peppers
1 Tbsp. butter, *or* margarine
28-oz. can tomatoes with juice
4-oz. can mushrooms, chopped and drained
2¼-oz. can sliced ripe olives, drained
2 tsp. dried oregano
1 lb. ground beef, browned and drained
12 oz. spaghetti, cooked and drained
10¾-oz. can cream of mushroom soup
½ cup water
2 cups (8 oz.) shredded cheddar cheese
¼ cup grated Parmesan cheese

1. Sauté onions and green peppers in butter in skillet until tender. Add tomatoes, mushrooms, olives, oregano, and beef. Simmer for 10 minutes. Transfer to slow cooker.
2. Add spaghetti. Mix well.
3. Combine soup and water. Pour over casserole. Sprinkle with cheeses.
4. Cover. Cook on Low 4-6 hours.

So-Easy Spaghetti

Ruth Ann Swartzendruber, Hydro, OK

Makes 4-6 servings

Prep. Time: 15 minutes
Cooking Time: 3½-8 hours
Ideal slow-cooker size: 4-qt.

1 lb. ground beef
½ cup diced onions
1 pkg. dry spaghetti sauce mix
8-oz. can tomato sauce
3 cups tomato juice
4 oz. dry spaghetti, broken into 4-inch pieces

1. Brown meat and onions in skillet. Drain. Transfer to greased slow cooker.
2. Add remaining ingredients, except spaghetti.
3. Cover. Cook on Low 6-8 hours, or on High 3½ hours.
4. During last hour, turn to High and add spaghetti. Stir frequently to keep spaghetti from clumping together.

Tomato Spaghetti Sauce

Jean Butzer, Batavia, NY

Makes 6 servings

Prep. Time: 10 minutes
Cooking Time: 10½-12½ hours
Ideal slow-cooker size: 2½-qt.

1 cup finely chopped onions
2 garlic cloves, minced
2 lbs. fresh tomatoes, peeled and chopped, *or* 28-oz. can tomatoes, cut up, with juice
6-oz. can tomato paste
1 Tbsp. sugar
2 tsp. instant beef bouillon granules
1 tsp. dried oregano
½ tsp. dried basil
1 large bay leaf
salt to taste
pepper to taste
4-oz. can sliced mushrooms
2 Tbsp. cornstarch
2 Tbsp. cold water

1. Combine all ingredients except mushrooms, cornstarch, and water in slow cooker.
2. Cover. Cook on Low 10-12 hours.
3. Remove bay leaf. Stir in mushrooms.
4. Combine cornstarch and water. Stir into sauce.
5. Cover. Cook on High until thickened and bubbly, about 25 minutes.

Italian Vegetable Pasta Sauce

Sherril Bieberly, Salina, KS

Makes 2½ quarts sauce

Prep. Time: 25 minutes
Cooking Time: 5-18 hours
Ideal slow-cooker size: 4- to 5-qt.

3 Tbsp. olive oil
1 cup packed chopped fresh parsley
3 ribs celery, chopped
1 medium onion, chopped
2 garlic cloves, minced
2-inch sprig fresh rosemary, *or* ½ tsp. dried rosemary
2 small fresh sage leaves, *or* ½ tsp. dried sage
32-oz. can tomato sauce
32-oz. can chopped tomatoes
1 small dried hot chili pepper
¼ lb. fresh mushrooms, sliced, *or* 8-oz. can sliced mushrooms, drained
1½ tsp. salt

1. Heat oil in skillet. Add parsley, celery, onion, garlic, rosemary, and sage. Sauté until vegetables are tender. Place in slow cooker.
2. Add tomatoes, chili pepper, mushrooms, and salt.
3. Cover. Cook on Low 12-18 hours, or on High 5-6 hours.

Variation:
Add 2 lbs. browned ground beef to olive oil and sautéed vegetables. Continue with recipe.

Louise's Vegetable Spaghetti Sauce

Louise Stackhouse, Benton, PA

Makes 4-6 servings

Prep. Time: 15 minutes
Cooking Time: 8-10 hours
Ideal slow-cooker size: 4-qt.

6-7 fresh tomatoes, peeled and crushed
1 medium onion, chopped
2 green peppers, chopped
2 cloves garlic, minced
½ tsp. dried basil
½ tsp. dried oregano
¼ tsp. salt
¼ cup sugar
6-oz. can tomato paste, *optional*

1. Combine all ingredients in slow cooker.
2. Cover. Cook on Low 8-10 hours. If the sauce is too watery for your liking, stir in a 6-oz. can of tomato paste during the last hour of cooking.

*Serving suggestion: Serve over cooked **spaghetti** or other **pasta**.*

Slow-Cooker Pizza

Marla Folkerts, Holland, OH
Ruth Ann Swartzendruber, Hydro, OK
Arlene Wiens, Newton, KS

Makes 6-8 servings

Prep. Time: 20 minutes
Cooking Time: 3-4 hours
Ideal slow-cooker size: 4- to 5-qt.

1½ lbs. ground beef, *or* bulk Italian sausage
1 medium onion, chopped
1 green pepper, chopped
half a box rigatoni, cooked
7-oz. jar sliced mushrooms, drained
3 oz. sliced pepperoni
16-oz. jar pizza sauce
10 oz. cheddar cheese, shredded
10 oz. mozzarella cheese, shredded

1. Brown ground beef and onions in saucepan. Drain.
2. Layer half of each of the following, in the order given, in slow cooker: ground beef and onions, green pepper, noodles, mushrooms, pepperoni, pizza sauce, cheddar cheese, and mozzarella cheese. Repeat layers.
3. Cover. Cook on Low 3-4 hours.

Note:
Keep rigatoni covered with sauce so they don't become dry and crunchy.

Variation:
Add a 10¾-oz. can cream of mushroom soup to the mix, putting half of it in as a layer after the first time the noodles appear, and the other half after the second layer of noodles.
Dorothy Horst, Tiskilwa, IL

Pizza in a Pot

Marianne J. Troyer, Millersburg, OH

Makes 6-8 servings

Prep. Time: 20 minutes
Cooking Time: 8-9 hours
Ideal slow-cooker size: 4-qt.

1 lb. bulk Italian sausage, browned and drained
28-oz. can crushed tomatoes
15½-oz. can chili beans
2¼-oz. can sliced black olives, drained
1 medium onion, chopped
1 small green pepper, chopped
2 garlic cloves, minced
¼ cup grated Parmesan cheese
1 Tbsp. quick-cooking tapioca
1 Tbsp. dried basil
1 bay leaf
1 tsp. salt

1. Combine all ingredients in slow cooker.
2. Cover. Cook on Low 8-9 hours.
3. Discard bay leaf. Stir well.

*Serving suggestion: Serve over **pasta**. Top with shredded **mozzarella cheese**.*

Pizza Rice

Sue Hamilton, Minooka, IL

Makes 6 servings

Prep. Time: 5 minutes
Cooking Time: 6-10 hours
Ideal slow-cooker size: 4-qt.

2 cups rice, uncooked
3 cups chunky pizza sauce
2½ cups water
7-oz. can mushrooms, undrained
4 oz. pepperoni, sliced
1 cup grated cheese

1. Combine rice, sauce, water, mushrooms, and pepperoni. Stir.
2. Cover. Cook on Low 10 hours, or on High 6 hours. Sprinkle with cheese before serving.

In recipes calling for uncooked rice, don't use minute or quick-cooking rice. Mary Puskar, Forest Hill, MD

Wild Rice Casserole

Carolyn Baer, Coranth, WI

Makes 6-8 servings

Soaking Time for rice: overnight, or 8 hours
Prep Time: 35-40 minutes
Cooking Time: 3-4 hours
Ideal slow-cooker size: 3- to 4-qt.

1 cup uncooked wild rice
½ lb. loose pork sausage
1 lb. ground beef
1 medium onion, chopped
1 cup celery, chopped
1 green pepper, chopped
2-3 medium carrots, grated
2 tsp. light soy sauce
1 tsp. Worcestershire sauce
10¾-oz. can cream of mushroom soup
10¾-oz. can cream of chicken soup
1 cup sliced mushrooms, *optional* (undrained, if using canned mushrooms)
½ cup water, *or more*

1. Wash and soak rice overnight.
2. Brown sausage and beef together in large skillet.
3. Drain off drippings. Place meat in slow cooker.
4. Drain rice.
5. Add rice, chopped onion, celery, green pepper, and carrots to slow cooker.
6. Stir in soy sauce, Worcestershire sauce, soups, and mushrooms if you wish.
7. Mix in water.
8. Cover. Cook on High 1 hour. Stir. If dish seems somewhat dry, add another ½ cup water.
9. Cover. Cook on Low 2 hours.
10. Or cook on Low a total of 4 hours.

Wild Rice Hot Dish

Barbara Tenney, Delta, PA

Makes 8-10 servings

Prep. Time: 15 minutes
Cooking Time: 4-6 hours
Ideal slow-cooker size: 4-qt.

2 cups wild rice, uncooked
½ cup slivered almonds
½ cup chopped onions
½ cup chopped celery
8-12-oz. can mushrooms, drained
2 cups cut-up chicken
6 cups chicken broth
¼-½ tsp. salt
¼ tsp. pepper
¼ tsp. garlic powder
1 Tbsp. parsley

1. Wash and drain rice.
2. Combine all ingredients in slow cooker. Mix well.
3. Cover. Cook on Low 4-6 hours, or until rice is finished. Do not remove lid before rice has cooked 4 hours.

Frances' Roast Chicken

Frances Schrag, Newton, KS

Makes 6 servings

Prep. Time: 5-10 minutes
Cooking Time: 4-10 hours
Ideal slow-cooker size: 4- to 5-qt.

3-4-lb. whole frying chicken
salt to taste
pepper to taste
½ tsp. poultry seasoning
half an onion, chopped
1 rib celery, chopped
¼ tsp. dried basil

1. Sprinkle chicken cavity with salt, pepper, and poultry seasoning. Put onion and celery inside cavity. Put chicken in slow cooker. Sprinkle with basil.
2. Cover. Cook on Low 8-10 hours, or on High 4-6 hours.

Donna's Cooked Chicken

Donna Treloar, Gaston, IN

Makes 1 chicken

Prep. Time: 5 minutes
Cooking Time: 4 hours
Ideal slow-cooker size: 4-qt.

1 onion, sliced
chicken (boneless, skinless
    breasts are the easiest,
    but any chicken pieces
    will do)
seasoned salt
pepper
minced garlic, *or* garlic
    powder

1. Layer onion in bottom of slow cooker. Add chicken and sprinkle with seasoned salt, pepper, minced garlic, or garlic powder.

2. Cook on Low 4 hours, or until done but not dry. (Time will vary according to amount of chicken and size of pieces.)

Serving suggestion: Use in stir-frys, chicken salads, or casseroles, slice for sandwiches, shred for enchiladas, or cut up and freeze for later use.

Variation:
Splash chicken with 2 Tbsp. soy sauce before cooking.

Chicken in a Pot

Carolyn Baer, Conrath, WI
Evie Hershey, Atglen, PA
Judy Koczo, Plano, IL
Mary Puskar, Forest Hill, MD
Mary Wheatley, Mashpee, MA

Makes 6 servings

Prep. Time: 10 minutes
Cooking Time: 3½-10 hours
Ideal slow-cooker size: 5-qt.

2 carrots, sliced
2 onions, sliced
2 celery ribs, cut in 1-inch
    pieces
3 lb. chicken, whole, *or*
    cut up
2 tsp. salt
½ tsp. dried coarse black
    pepper
1 tsp. dried basil
½ cup water, *or* chicken
    broth, *or* white cooking
    wine

1. Place vegetables in bottom of slow cooker. Place chicken on top of vegetables. Add seasonings and water.

2. Cover. Cook on Low 8-10 hours, or on High 3½-5 hours (use 1 cup liquid if cooking on High).

Notes:
1. To make this a full meal, add 2 medium-sized potatoes, quartered, to vegetables before cooking.

2. This is a great foundation for soups, such as chicken vegetable and chicken noodle.

Another Chicken in a Pot

Jennifer J. Gehman, Harrisburg, PA

Makes 4-6 servings

Prep. Time: 10 minutes
Cooking Time: 3½-10 hours
Ideal slow-cooker size: 4- to 5-qt.

1-lb. bag baby carrots
1 small onion, diced
14½-oz. can green beans
3-lb. whole chicken, cut
    into serving-size pieces
2 tsp. salt
½ tsp. black pepper
½ cup chicken broth
¼ cup white wine
½-1 tsp. dried basil

1. Put carrots, onion, and beans on bottom of slow cooker. Add chicken. Top with salt, pepper, broth, and wine. Sprinkle with basil.

2. Cover. Cook on Low 8-10 hours, or on High 3½-5 hours.

Savory Slow-Cooker Chicken

Sara Harter Fredette, Williamsburg, MA

Makes 4 servings

Prep. Time: 10-15 minutes
Cooking Time: 8-10 hours
Ideal slow-cooker size: 4- to 5-qt.

2½ lbs. chicken pieces, skinned
1 lb. fresh tomatoes, chopped, *or* 15-oz. can stewed tomatoes
2 Tbsp. white wine
1 bay leaf
¼ tsp. pepper
2 garlic cloves, minced
1 onion, chopped
½ cup chicken broth
1 tsp. dried thyme
1½ tsp. salt
2 cups broccoli, cut into bite-sized pieces

1. Combine all ingredients except broccoli in slow cooker.
2. Cover. Cook on Low 8-10 hours.
3. Add broccoli 30 minutes before serving.

Baked Chicken Breasts

Janice Crist, Quinter, KS
Tracy Supcoe, Barclay, MD

Makes 4-6 servings

Prep. Time: 10 minutes
Cooking Time: 8-10 hours
Ideal slow-cooker size: 2- to 3½-qt.

2-3 whole chicken breasts, halved
2 Tbsp. butter, *or* margarine
10¾-oz. can cream of chicken soup
½ cup dry sherry
1 tsp. dried tarragon, *or* rosemary, *or* both
1 tsp. Worcestershire sauce
¼ tsp. garlic powder
4-oz. can sliced mushrooms, drained

1. Place chicken breasts in slow cooker.
2. In saucepan, combine remaining ingredients. Heat until smooth and hot. Pour over chicken.
3. Cover. Cook on Low 8-10 hours.

Chicken Delicious

Janice Crist, Quinter, KS

Makes 8-12 servings

Prep. Time: 5 minutes
Cooking Time: 8-10 hours
Ideal slow-cooker size: 4-qt.

4-6 whole skinless chicken breasts, boned and halved
lemon juice
salt to taste
pepper to taste
celery salt to taste
paprika to taste
10¾-oz. can cream of mushroom soup
10¾-oz. can cream of celery soup
⅓ cup dry sherry, *or* white wine
grated Parmesan cheese

1. Season chicken with lemon juice, salt, pepper, celery salt, and paprika. Place in slow cooker.
2. Combine soups with sherry. Pour over chicken. Sprinkle with cheese.
3. Cover. Cook on Low 8-10 hours.

Serving suggestion: Serve with rice.

Use your slow cooker to cook a hen, turkey, or roast beef (in 1 cup liquid) for use in salads or casseroles. The meat can even be frozen when you put it in the slow cooker. Set the cooker on Low, and let the meat cook all night while you sleep.
Julia B. Boyd, Memphis, TN

Chicken in Wine

Mary Seielstad, Sparks, NV

Makes 4-6 servings

Prep. Time: 5 minutes
Cooking Time: 6-8 hours
Ideal slow-cooker size: 4-qt.

2-3 lbs. chicken breasts, *or* pieces
10¾-oz. can cream of mushroom soup
10¾-oz. can French onion soup
1 cup dry white wine, *or* chicken broth

1. Put chicken in slow cooker.
2. Combine soups and wine. Pour over chicken.
3. Cover. Cook on Low 6-8 hours.

Serving suggestion: Serve over ***rice, pasta,*** *or* ***potatoes.***

Sunday Chicken

Dot Hess, Willow Street, PA

Makes 12 servings

Prep Time: 20-30 minutes
Cooking Time: 7-8 hours
Ideal slow-cooker size: 6-qt.

7 lbs. chicken, cut up
paprika
salt
pepper
2 10¾-oz. cans condensed cream of celery soup
¾ cup white wine, *or* chicken broth

1. Rinse chicken in cold water.
2. Pat dry.
3. Sprinkle paprika, salt, and pepper on chicken.
4. Combine soup and wine, or broth, in a medium bowl.
5. Place half of chicken in slow cooker.
6. Spoon half of soup mixture over chicken.
7. Layer in rest of chicken.
8. Spoon rest of soup mixture over top.
9. Cover. Cook 4 hours on High. Reset cooker to Low and continue cooking, covered, 4 more hours, or until chicken is tender but not dry.

Chicken in Mushroom Gravy

Rosemarie Fitzgerald, Gibsonia, PA
Audrey L. Kneer, Williamsfield, IL

Makes 6 servings

Prep. Time: 5 minutes
Cooking Time: 7-9 hours
Ideal slow-cooker size: 4½-qt.

6 boneless, skinless chicken breast halves
salt to taste
pepper to taste
¼ cup dry white wine, *or* chicken broth
10¾-oz. can cream of mushroom soup
4-oz. can sliced mushrooms, drained

1. Place chicken in slow cooker. Season with salt and pepper.
2. Combine wine and soup. Pour over chicken. Top with mushrooms.
3. Cover. Cook on Low 7-9 hours.

Ruth's Slow-Cooker Chicken

Sara Harter Fredette, Williamsburg, MA

Makes 6 servings

Prep. Time: 5 minutes
Cooking Time: 6-8 hours
Ideal slow-cooker size: 4-qt.

6 boneless chicken breast
  halves
10¾-oz. can cream of
  mushroom soup
1 pkg. dry mushroom soup
  mix
¼-½ cup sour cream
4-oz. can mushrooms,
  drained

1. Combine chicken, soup, and soup mix in slow cooker.
2. Cover. Cook on Low 6-8 hours.
3. Just before serving, stir in sour cream and mushrooms. Reheat briefly.

Serving suggestion: Serve on ***noodles***.

Note:
  Leftover sauce makes a flavorful topping for grilled hamburgers.

Creamy Cooker Chicken

Violette Harris Denney, Carrollton, GA

Makes 6 servings

Prep. Time: 5 minutes
Cooking Time: 8 hours
Ideal slow-cooker size: 4- to 5-qt.

1 envelope dry onion soup
  mix
2 cups sour cream
10¾-oz. can cream of
  mushroom soup
6 boneless, skinless chicken
  breast halves

1. Combine soup mix, sour cream, and cream of mushroom soup in slow cooker. Add chicken, pushing it down so it is submerged in the sauce.
2. Cover. Cook on Low 8 hours.

Serving suggestion: Serve over ***rice*** *or* ***noodles***.

Mushroom Chicken

Brenda Pope, Dundee, OH

Makes 4 servings

Prep. Time: 5 minutes
Cooking Time: 8 hours
Ideal slow-cooker size: 4-qt.

1 lb. boneless, skinless
  chicken breasts
1 pkg. dry chicken gravy mix
10¾-oz. can cream of mushroom, *or* chicken, soup
1 cup white wine
8-oz. pkg. cream cheese,
  softened

1. Put chicken in slow cooker. Sprinkle gravy mix on top. In separate bowl, combine soup and wine and pour over gravy mix.
2. Cover. Cook on Low 8 hours.
3. During last 30 minutes of cooking time, stir in cream cheese. Before serving, remove chicken (keeping it warm) and whisk the sauce until smooth.

Serving suggestion: Serve chicken and sauce over ***noodles*** *or* ***rice***.

Creamy Mushroom Chicken

Patricia Howard, Albuquerque, NM

Makes 4-5 servings

Prep. Time: 5 minutes
Cooking Time: 5-6 hours
Ideal slow-cooker size: 4-qt.

2-3 lbs. chicken parts, skinned
4-oz. can mushrooms
2 10¾-oz. cans cream of
  chicken soup

1 envelope dry onion soup mix
½-1 cup chicken broth

1. Place chicken in slow cooker.
2. Combine remaining ingredients and pour over chicken.
3. Cover. Cook on Low 5-6 hours.

So You Forgot to Defrost!

Mary Seielstad, Sparks, NV

Makes 6 servings

Prep. Time: 5 minutes
Cooking Time: 10-12 hours
Ideal slow-cooker size: 4½-qt.

6 boneless, skinless frozen chicken breast halves
2 10¾-oz. cans cream of chicken soup
4-oz. can sliced mushrooms, *or* ½ cup sliced fresh mushrooms
¾ tsp. salt
¼ tsp. pepper

1. Place frozen chicken in slow cooker.
2. Mix together soup, mushrooms, salt, and pepper and pour over chicken.
3. Cover. Cook on Low 10-12 hours.

Serving suggestion: Serve over **rice**.

Continental Chicken

Jennifer J. Gehman, Harrisburg, PA
Gladys M. High, Ephrata, PA
L. Jean Moore, Pendleton, IN

Makes 4-6 servings

Prep. Time: 5-10 minutes
Cooking Time: 3-9 hours
Ideal slow-cooker size: 4½-qt.

2¼-oz. pkg. dried beef
3-4 whole chicken breasts, halved, skinned, and boned
6-8 slices bacon
10¾-oz. can cream of mushroom soup, undiluted
¼ cup sour cream
¼ cup flour

1. Arrange dried beef in bottom of slow cooker.
2. Wrap each piece of chicken with a strip of bacon. Place on top of dried beef.
3. Combine soup, sour cream, and flour. Pour over chicken.
4. Cover. Cook on Low 7-9 hours, or on High 3-4 hours.

Serving suggestion: Serve over hot buttered **noodles**.

Wanda's Chicken and Rice Casserole

Wanda Roth, Napoleon, OH

Makes 6-8 servings

Prep. Time: 10 minutes
Cooking Time: 3-4 hours
Ideal slow-cooker size: 4-qt.

1 cup long-grain rice, uncooked
3 cups water
2 tsp. chicken bouillon granules
10¾-oz can cream of chicken soup
16-oz. bag frozen broccoli
2 cups chopped, cooked chicken
¼ tsp. garlic powder
1 tsp. onion salt
1 cup grated cheddar cheese

1. Combine all ingredients in slow cooker.
2. Cook on High 3-4 hours.

Note:
If casserole is too runny, remove lid from slow cooker for 15 minutes while continuing to cook on High.

Lightly grease your slow cooker before adding ingredients. Sara Wilson, Blairstown, MO

239

Chicken and Rice Casserole

Kim Stoltzfus, Parksburg, PA

Makes 6 servings

Prep Time: 20-30 minutes
Cooking Time: 4-6 hours
Ideal slow-cooker size: 3½-qt.

10¾- oz. can cream of chicken soup
1 cup milk
¼ cup celery, finely chopped
½ cup onion, finely chopped
1 cup uncooked instant rice
½ cup peas
½ cup carrots
1 lb. uncooked chicken breast, skinned, boned, and cut into cubes
½ lb. cheddar, *or* your favorite, cheese, cubed

1. Spray inside of slow cooker with cooking spray.
2. Combine all ingredients in slow cooker, mixing well but gently.
3. Cover. Cook on Low 4-6 hours, or until rice, vegetables, and chicken are tender.
4. Stir well before serving.

Sharon's Chicken and Rice Casserole

Sharon Anders, Alburtis, PA

Makes 2 servings

Prep. Time: 5 minutes
Cooking Time: 4-6 hours
Ideal slow-cooker size: 2½-qt.

10¾-oz. can cream of celery soup
2-oz. can sliced mushrooms, undrained
½ cup raw long-grain rice
2 chicken breast halves, skinned and boned
1 Tbsp. dry onion soup mix

1. Combine soup, mushrooms, and rice in greased slow cooker. Mix well.
2. Layer chicken breasts on top of mixture. Sprinkle with onion soup mix.
3. Cover. Cook on Low 4-6 hours.

No-Peek Chicken

Elaine Patton, West Middletown, PA

Makes 8 servings

Prep Time: 15 minutes
Cooking Time: 4-6 hours
Ideal slow-cooker size: 4-qt.

10¾-oz. can cream of chicken soup
10¾-oz. can cream of celery soup
10¾-oz. can cream of mushroom
3 soup cans of regular milk (use the soup cans you've just emptied of soup)
1½ cups long-grain uncooked rice
3 lbs. chicken breast, uncooked, cut into cubes
1 envelope dry onion soup mix

1. Whisk soups and milk together in slow cooker until smooth.
2. Spread uncooked rice evenly over liquid.
3. Arrange chicken pieces over rice, pushing chicken down into liquid.
4. Sprinkle with dry onion soup mix.
5. Cover. Cook 4 hours on Low. Check to see if rice and chicken are cooked. If not, cover and continue another hour. Then check again. Cover and cook up to another hour if needed.

Fresh vegetables take longer to cook than meats, because, in a slow cooker, liquid simmers rather than boils. Remember this if you've adapted range-top recipes to slow cooking.
Beatrice Orgish, Richardson, TX

Variation:

If you wish, sprinkle rice with salt and pepper after spreading into the cooker, and sprinkle chicken with salt and pepper after adding to slow cooker.

Chicken-Vegetable Dish

Cheri Jantzen, Houston, TX

Makes 4 servings

Prep. Time: 10 minutes
Cooking Time: 5-7 hours
Ideal slow-cooker size: 4- to 5-qt.

4 skinless chicken breast halves, with bone in
15-oz. can crushed tomatoes
10-oz. pkg. frozen green beans
2 cups water, *or* chicken broth
1 cup brown rice, uncooked
1 cup sliced mushrooms
2 carrots, chopped
1 onion, chopped
½ tsp. minced garlic
½ tsp. herb-blend seasoning
¼ tsp. dried tarragon

1. Combine all ingredients in slow cooker.
2. Cover. Cook on High 2 hours, and then on Low 3-5 hours.

Scalloped Potatoes and Chicken

Carol Sommers, Millersburg, OH

Makes 6-8 servings

Prep. Time: 15 minutes
Cooking Time: 4½-5½ hours
Ideal slow-cooker size: 4-qt.

¼ cup chopped green peppers
½ cup chopped onions
1½ cups diced Velveeta cheese
7-8 medium potatoes, sliced
salt to taste
3-4 whole boneless, skinless chicken breasts
salt to taste
10¾-oz. can cream of celery soup
1 soup can milk

1. Place layers of green peppers, onions, cheese, potatoes, and a sprinkling of salt in slow cooker.
2. Sprinkle chicken breasts with salt and lay on top of potatoes.
3. Combine soup and milk and pour into slow cooker, pushing meat down into liquid.
4. Cover. Cook on High 1½ hours. Reduce temperature to Low and cook 3-4 hours. Test that potatoes are soft. If not, continue cooking on Low another hour and test again, continuing to cook until potatoes are finished.

Chicken and Vegetables

Jeanne Heyerly, Chenoa, IL

Makes 2 servings

Prep. Time: 10 minutes
Cooking Time: 8-9 hours
Ideal slow-cooker size: 4-qt.

2 medium potatoes, quartered
2-3 carrots, sliced
2 frozen chicken breasts, *or* 2 frozen drumstick/thigh pieces
salt to taste
pepper to taste
1 medium onion, chopped
2 garlic cloves, minced
1-2 cups shredded cabbage
16-oz. can chicken broth

1. Place potatoes and carrots in slow cooker. Layer chicken on top. Sprinkle with salt, pepper, onion, and garlic. Top with cabbage. Carefully pour chicken broth around edges.
2. Cover. Cook on Low 8-9 hours.

California Chicken

Shirley Sears, Tiskilwa, IL

Makes 4-6 servings

Prep. Time: 10 minutes
Cooking Time: 8½-9½ hours
Ideal slow-cooker size: 4-qt.

3-lb. chicken, quartered
1 cup orange juice
⅓ cup chili sauce
2 Tbsp. soy sauce
1 Tbsp. molasses
1 tsp. dry mustard
1 tsp. garlic salt
2 Tbsp. chopped green
  peppers
3 medium oranges, peeled
  and separated into slices,
  or 13½-oz. can mandarin
  oranges

1. Arrange chicken in slow cooker.
2. In separate bowl, combine juice, chili sauce, soy sauce, molasses, dry mustard, and garlic salt. Pour over chicken.
3. Cover. Cook on Low 8-9 hours.
4. Stir in green peppers and oranges. Heat 30 minutes longer.

Variation:
Stir 1 tsp. curry powder in with sauces and seasonings. Stir 1 small can pineapple chunks and juice in with green peppers and oranges.

Orange Chicken Leg Quarters

Kimberly Jensen, Bailey, CO

Makes 4-5 servings

Prep. Time: 15 minutes
Cooking Time: 6-7 hours
Ideal slow-cooker size: 5- to 6-qt.

4 chicken drumsticks
4 chicken thighs
1 cup strips of green and
  red bell peppers
½ cup canned chicken broth
½ cup prepared orange juice
½ cup ketchup
2 Tbsp. soy sauce
1 Tbsp. light molasses
1 Tbsp. prepared mustard
½ tsp. garlic salt
11-oz. can mandarin
  oranges
2 tsp. cornstarch
1 cup frozen peas

1. Place chicken in slow cooker. Top with pepper strips.
2. Combine broth, juice, ketchup, soy sauce, molasses, mustard, and garlic salt. Pour over chicken.
3. Cover. Cook on Low 6-7 hours.
4. Remove chicken and vegetables from slow cooker. Keep warm.
5. Measure out 1 cup of cooking sauce. Put in saucepan and bring to boil.
6. Drain oranges, reserving 1 Tbsp. juice. Stir cornstarch into reserved juice. Add to boiling sauce in pan.
7. Add peas to sauce and cook, stirring for 2-3 minutes until sauce thickens and peas are warm. Stir in oranges.

*Serving suggestion: Arrange chicken pieces on platter of cooked **white rice**, fried **cellophane noodles**, or **lo mein noodles**. Pour orange sauce over chicken and rice or noodles. Top with sliced **green onions**.*

Cranberry Chicken

Teena Wagner, Waterloo, ON

Makes 6-8 servings

Prep. Time: 5-10 minutes
Cooking Time: 4-8 hours
Ideal slow-cooker size: 4- to 5-qt.

3-4 lbs. chicken pieces
½ tsp. salt
¼ tsp. pepper
½ cup diced celery
½ cup diced onions
16-oz. can whole berry
  cranberry sauce
1 cup barbecue sauce

1. Combine all ingredients in slow cooker.
2. Cover. Bake on High for 4 hours, or on Low for 6-8 hours.

Chicken Sweet and Sour

Willard E. Roth, Elkhart, IN

Makes 8 servings

Prep. Time: 10 minutes
Cooking Time: 6½ hours
Ideal slow-cooker size: 4- to 5-qt.

4 medium potatoes, sliced
8 boneless, skinless chicken breast halves
2 Tbsp. cider vinegar
¼ tsp. ground nutmeg
1 tsp. dry basil, *or* 1 Tbsp. chopped fresh basil
2 Tbsp. brown sugar
1 cup orange juice
dried parsley flakes
17-oz. can waterpack sliced peaches, drained

1. Place potatoes in greased slow cooker. Arrange chicken on top.
2. In separate bowl, combine vinegar, nutmeg, basil, brown sugar, and orange juice. Pour over chicken. Sprinkle with parsley.
3. Cover. Cook on Low 6 hours.
4. Remove chicken and potatoes from sauce and arrange on warm platter.
5. Turn cooker to High. Add peaches and heat until warm.

Serving suggestion: Spoon peaches and sauce over chicken and potatoes. Garnish with fresh **parsley** *and* **orange slices.**

Chicken with Tropical Barbecue Sauce

Lois Stoltzfus, Honey Brook, PA

Makes 6 servings

Prep. Time: 5 minutes
Cooking Time: 3-9 hours
Ideal slow-cooker size: 4-qt.

¼ cup molasses
2 Tbsp. cider vinegar
2 Tbsp. Worcestershire sauce
2 tsp. prepared mustard
⅛-¼ tsp. hot pepper sauce
2 Tbsp. orange juice
3 whole chicken breasts, halved

1. Combine molasses, vinegar, Worcestershire sauce, mustard, hot pepper sauce, and orange juice. Brush over chicken.
2. Place chicken in slow cooker.
3. Cover. Cook on Low 7-9 hours, or on High 3-4 hours.

Fruited Barbecue Chicken

Barbara Katrine Rose, Woodbridge, VA

Makes 4-6 servings

Prep. Time: 5 minutes
Cooking Time: 4 hours
Ideal slow-cooker size: 4-qt.

29-oz. can tomato sauce
20-oz. can unsweetened crushed pineapple, undrained
2 Tbsp. brown sugar
3 Tbsp. vinegar
1 Tbsp. instant minced onion
1 tsp. paprika
2 tsp. Worcestershire sauce
¼ tsp. garlic powder
⅛ tsp. pepper
3 lbs. chicken, skinned and cubed
11-oz. can mandarin oranges, drained

1. Combine all ingredients except chicken and oranges. Add chicken pieces.
2. Cover. Cook on High 4 hours.
3. Just before serving, stir in oranges.

Serving suggestion: Serve over hot **rice.**

When using raw meat, you may want to begin by cooking it for 1-2 hours on High to avoid cooking it too slowly.
Joy Sutter, Iowa City, IA

Orange-Glazed Chicken Breasts

Leona Miller, Millersburg, OH

Makes 6 servings

Prep. Time: 5 minutes
Cooking Time: 3¼-9¼ hours
Ideal slow-cooker size: 4-qt.

6-oz. can frozen orange
    juice concentrate, thawed
½ tsp. dried marjoram
6 boneless, skinless chicken
    breast halves
¼ cup cold water
2 Tbsp. cornstarch

1. Combine orange juice and marjoram in shallow dish. Dip each breast in orange-juice mixture and place in slow cooker. Pour remaining sauce over breasts.

2. Cover. Cook on Low 7-9 hours, or on High 3½-4 hours.

3. Remove chicken from slow cooker. Turn cooker to High and cover.

4. Combine water and cornstarch. Stir into liquid in slow cooker. Place cover slightly ajar on slow cooker. Cook until sauce is thick and bubbly, about 15-20 minutes.

Serving suggestion: Serve with sauce over chicken.

Variation:

To increase "spice" in dish, add ½-1 tsp. Worcestershire sauce to orange juice-marjoram glaze.

Sweet and Sour Chicken

Bernice A. Esau, North Newton, KS

Makes 6 servings

Prep. Time: 10 minutes
Cooking Time: 8-10 hours
Ideal slow-cooker size: 4½-qt.

1½ cups sliced carrots
1 large green pepper,
    chopped
1 medium onion, chopped
2 Tbsp. quick-cooking
    tapioca
2½-3-lb. chicken, cut into
    serving-size pieces
8-oz. can pineapple chunks
    in juice
⅓ cup brown sugar
⅓ cup vinegar
1 Tbsp. soy sauce
½ tsp. instant chicken
    bouillon
¼ tsp. garlic powder
¼ tsp. ground ginger, *or* ½
    tsp. freshly grated ginger
1 tsp. salt

1. Place vegetables in bottom of slow cooker. Sprinkle with tapioca. Add chicken.

2. In separate bowl, combine pineapple, brown sugar, vinegar, soy sauce, bouillon, garlic powder, ginger, and salt. Pour over chicken.

3. Cover. Cook on Low 8-10 hours.

*Serving suggestion: Serve over cooked **rice**.*

Orange Chicken and Sweet Potatoes

Kimberlee Greenawalt, Harrisonburg, VA

Makes 6 servings

Prep. Time: 10 minutes
Cooking Time: 3-10 hours
Ideal slow-cooker size: 4-qt.

2-3 sweet potatoes, peeled
    and sliced
3 whole chicken breasts,
    halved
⅔ cup flour
1 tsp. salt
1 tsp. nutmeg
½ tsp. cinnamon
dash pepper
dash garlic powder
10¾-oz. can cream of celery,
    or cream of chicken, soup
4-oz. can sliced mushrooms,
    drained
½ cup orange juice
½ tsp. grated orange rind
2 tsp. brown sugar
3 Tbsp. flour

1. Place sweet potatoes in bottom of slow cooker.

2. Rinse chicken breasts and pat dry. Combine flour, salt, nutmeg, cinnamon, pepper, and garlic powder. Thoroughly coat chicken in flour mixture. Place on top of sweet potatoes.

3. Combine soup with remaining ingredients. Stir well. Pour over chicken breasts.

4. Cover. Cook on Low 8-10 hours, or on High 3-4 hours.

Serving suggestion: Serve over **rice.**

Easy Teriyaki Chicken

Barbara Shie, Colorado Springs, CO

Makes 5-6 servings

Prep. Time: 5 minutes
Cooking Time: 4-8 hours
Ideal slow-cooker size: 4-qt.

2-3 lbs. skinless chicken pieces
20-oz. can pineapple chunks
dash of ground ginger
1 cup teriyaki sauce

1. Place chicken in slow cooker. Pour remaining ingredients over chicken.
2. Cover. Cook on Low 6-8 hours, or on High 4-6 hours.

Salsa Chicken

Christine Lucke, Aumsville, OR

Makes 8 servings

Prep Time: 10 minutes
Cooking Time: 6-8 hours
Ideal slow-cooker size: 5-qt.

8 boneless, skinless chicken breast halves

3 cups salsa of your choice
¼ cup brown sugar

1. Place chicken in slow cooker.
2. Pour salsa over chicken. If you have to stack the chicken, be sure to spoon salsa over all layers.
3. Sprinkle brown sugar over top. Again, make sure that you've sprinkled brown sugar over all layers.
4. Cover. Cook on Low 6-8 hours, or until chicken is tender but not dry or mushy.

Zesty Chicken in Cream Sauce

Barbara Shie, Colorado Springs, CO

Makes 4-6 servings

Prep. Time: 5 minutes
Cooking Time: 6 hours
Ideal slow-cooker size: 4½-qt.

4-6 boneless, skinless chicken breast halves
12-oz. jar mushroom gravy
1 cup milk
8-oz. pkg. cream cheese, cubed
4½-oz. can chopped green chilies
1 pkg. dry Italian salad dressing

1. Combine all ingredients in slow cooker.
2. Cover. Cook on Low 6 hours.

Serving suggestion: Serve over **noodles** *or* **rice.**

Slow-Cooker Tex-Mex Chicken

Kim Stoltzfus, Parkesburg, PA

Makes 4-6 servings

Prep Time: 15-20 minutes
Cooking Time: 3-8 hours
Ideal slow-cooker size: 3½-qt.

1 lb. boneless skinless chicken breasts, cut into ¾-inch-wide strips
2 Tbsp. dry taco seasoning mix
2 Tbsp. flour
1 green pepper, cut into strips
1 red pepper, cut into strips
1 cup frozen corn
1½ cups chunky salsa

1. Toss chicken with seasoning and flour in slow cooker.
2. Gently stir in vegetables and salsa.
3. Cook on Low 6-8 hours, or on High 3-4 hours, until chicken and vegetables are cooked through but are not dry or mushy.
4. Stir before serving.

Serving suggestion: Serve topped with shredded **Mexican-style cheese.**

Creamy Chicken Italiano

Sharon Easter, Yuba City, CA
Rebecca Meyerkorth, Wamego, KS
Bonnie Miller, Cochranville, PA

Makes 4 servings

Prep. Time: 5 minutes
Cooking Time: 4 hours
Ideal slow-cooker size: 4-qt.

4 boneless, skinless chicken breast halves
1 envelope dry Italian salad dressing mix
¼ cup water
8-oz. pkg. cream cheese, softened
10¾-oz. can cream of chicken soup
4-oz. can mushroom stems and pieces, drained

1. Place chicken in slow cooker.
2. Combine salad dressing mix and water. Pour over chicken.
3. Cover. Cook on Low 3 hours.
4. Combine cheese and soup until blended. Stir in mushrooms. Pour over chicken.
5. Cover. Cook on Low 1 hour, or until chicken juices run clear.

*Serving suggestion: Serve over **noodles** or **rice**.*

Ann's Chicken Cacciatore

Ann Driscoll, Albuquerque, NM

Makes 6-8 servings

Prep. Time: 10 minutes
Cooking Time: 3-9 hours
Ideal slow-cooker size: 4-qt.

1 large onion, thinly sliced
2½-3-lb. chicken, cut up
2 6-oz. cans tomato paste
4-oz. can sliced mushrooms, drained
1 tsp. salt
¼ cup dry white wine
¼ tsp. pepper
1-2 garlic cloves, minced
1-2 tsp. dried oregano
½ tsp. dried basil
½ tsp. celery seed, *optional*
1 bay leaf

1. Place onion in slow cooker. Add chicken.
2. Combine remaining ingredients. Pour over chicken.
3. Cover. Cook on Low 7-9 hours, or on High 3-4 hours.

*Serving suggestion: Serve over **spaghetti**.*

Darla's Chicken Cacciatore

Darla Sathre, Baxter, MN

Makes 6 servings

Prep. Time: 5-10 minutes
Cooking Time: 8 hours
Ideal slow-cooker size: 4-qt.

2 onions, thinly sliced
4 boneless chicken breasts, cubed
3 garlic cloves, minced
¼ tsp. pepper
2 tsp. dried oregano
1 tsp. dried basil
1 bay leaf
2 15-oz. cans diced tomatoes
8-oz. can tomato sauce
4-oz. can sliced mushrooms

1. Place onions in bottom of slow cooker. Add remaining ingredients.
2. Cover. Cook on Low 8 hours.

*Serving suggestion: Serve over hot **spaghetti**.*

Chicken Cacciatore

Donna Lantgen, Arvada, CO

Makes 6 servings

Prep Time: 10 minutes
Cooking Time: 5-6 hours
Ideal slow-cooker size: 5-qt.

1 green pepper, chopped
1 onion, chopped
1 Tbsp. Italian seasoning
15½-oz. can tomatoes, chopped
½ cup tomato juice
6 boneless skinless chicken breast halves

1. Mix green pepper, onion, Italian seasoning, tomatoes, and tomato juice in a bowl.
2. Spread ½ cup of mixture over bottom of slow cooker.
3. Place 3 chicken breast pieces on top of vegetable mixture.
4. Spoon half the remaining vegetable mixture over those pieces.
5. Add remaining 3 pieces of meat.
6. Pour remaining mixture over chicken.
7. Cook on Low 5-6 hours, or until chicken is cooked through, but isn't dry or mushy.

Serving suggestion: Serve topped with grated mozzarella or Parmesan cheese.

Dale and Shari's Chicken Cacciatore

Dale and Shari Mast, Harrisonburg, VA

Makes 4 servings

Prep. Time: 5 minutes
Cooking Time: 3-8 hours
Ideal slow-cooker size: 5-qt.

4 chicken quarters, *or* 4 boneless, skinless chicken breast halves
15-oz. can tomato, *or* spaghetti, sauce
4-oz. can sliced mushrooms, drained
½ cup water
1 tsp. dry chicken broth granules
½ tsp. Italian seasoning

1. Place chicken in slow cooker. Pour on sauce, mushrooms, and water. Sprinkle with granules and seasoning.
2. Cover. Cook on High 3-4 hours, or on Low 6-8 hours.

Serving suggestion: Serve over rice.

Chicken Parmigiana

Brenda Pope, Dundee, OH

Makes 6 servings

Prep. Time: 10-15 minutes
Cooking Time: 6¼-8¼ hours
Ideal slow-cooker size: 4-qt.

1 egg
1 tsp. salt
¼ tsp. pepper
6 boneless, skinless chicken breast halves
1 cup Italian bread crumbs
2-4 Tbsp. butter
14-oz. jar pizza sauce
6 slices mozzarella cheese
grated Parmesan cheese

1. Beat egg, salt, and pepper together. Dip chicken into egg and coat with bread crumbs. Sauté chicken in butter in skillet. Arrange chicken in slow cooker.
2. Pour pizza sauce over chicken.
3. Cover. Cook on Low 6-8 hours.
4. Layer mozzarella cheese over top and sprinkle with Parmesan cheese. Cook an additional 15 minutes.

If you have them available, use whole or leaf herbs and spices rather than crushed or ground ones.

Barbara Sparks, Glen Burnie, MD

Easy Chicken a la King

Jenny R. Unternahrer,
Wayland, IA

Makes 4 servings

Prep. Time: 5 minutes
Cooking Time: 3-6 hours
Ideal slow-cooker size: 4-qt.

1½ lbs. boneless, skinless
  chicken breasts
10¾-oz. can cream of
  chicken soup
3 Tbsp. flour
¼ tsp. pepper
9-oz. pkg. frozen peas and
  onions, thawed and
  drained
2 Tbsp. chopped pimentos
½ tsp. paprika

1. Cut chicken into bite-sized pieces and place in slow cooker.
2. Combine soup, flour, and pepper. Pour over chicken. Do not stir.
3. Cover. Cook on High 2½ hours, or on Low 5-5½ hours.
4. Stir in peas and onions, pimentos, and paprika.
5. Cover. Cook on High 20-30 minutes.

Variation:
Add ¼-½ cup chopped green peppers to Step 2.

Sharon Brubaker
Myerstown, PA

Coq au Vin

Kimberlee Greenawalt, Harrisonburg, VA

Makes 6 servings

Prep. Time: 10-15 minutes
Cooking Time: 6¼-8¼ hours
Ideal slow-cooker size: 4- to 5-qt.

---

2 cups frozen pearl onions,
  thawed
4 thick slices bacon, fried
  and crumbled
1 cup sliced button
  mushrooms
1 garlic clove, minced
1 tsp. dried thyme leaves
⅛ tsp. black pepper
6 boneless, skinless chicken
  breast halves
½ cup dry red wine
¾ cup chicken broth
¼ cup tomato paste
3 Tbsp. flour

1. Layer ingredients in slow cooker in the following order: onions, bacon, mushrooms, garlic, thyme, pepper, chicken, wine, and broth.
2. Cover. Cook on Low 6-8 hours.
3. Remove chicken and vegetables. Cover and keep warm.
4. Ladle ½ cup cooking liquid into small bowl. Cool slightly. Turn slow cooker to High. Cover. Mix reserved liquid, tomato paste, and flour until smooth. Return mixture to slow cooker, cover, and cook 15 minutes, or until thickened.

*Serving suggestion: Serve chicken, vegetables, and sauce over **noodles**.*

Stuffed Chicken Rolls

Lois M. Martin, Lititz, PA
Renee Shirk, Mount Joy, PA

Makes 6 servings

Prep. Time: 25 minutes
Refrigeration Time: 1 hour
Cooking Time: 4-5 hours
Ideal slow-cooker size: 4-qt.

---

6 large boneless, skinless
  chicken breast halves
6 slices fully cooked ham
6 slices Swiss cheese
¼ cup flour
¼ cup grated Parmesan
  cheese
½ tsp. rubbed sage
¼ tsp. paprika
¼ tsp. pepper
¼ cup oil
10¾-oz. can cream of
  chicken soup
½ cup chicken broth

1. Flatten chicken to ⅛-inch thickness. Place ham and cheese slices on each breast. Roll up and tuck in ends. Secure with toothpick.
2. Combine flour, Parmesan cheese, sage, paprika, and pepper. Coat chicken on all sides. Cover and refrigerate for 1 hour.
3. Brown chicken in oil in skillet. Transfer to slow cooker.

4. Combine soup and broth. Pour over chicken.

5. Cover. Cook on Low 4-5 hours.

6. Remove toothpicks.

*Serving suggestion: Garnish with chopped fresh **parsley**.*

Lemon Garlic Chicken

Cindy Krestynick, Glen Lyon, PA

Makes 4 servings

Prep. Time: 15 minutes
Cooking Time: 2½-5½ hours
Ideal slow-cooker size: 2-qt.

1 tsp. dried oregano
½ tsp. seasoned salt
¼ tsp. pepper
2 lbs. chicken breast halves, skinned and rinsed
2 Tbsp. butter, *or* margarine
¼ cup water
3 Tbsp. lemon juice
2 garlic cloves, minced
1 tsp. chicken bouillon granules
1 tsp. minced fresh parsley

1. Combine oregano, salt, and pepper. Rub all of mixture into chicken. Brown chicken in butter or margarine in skillet. Transfer to slow cooker.

2. Place water, lemon juice, garlic, and bouillon cubes in skillet. Bring to boil, loosening browned bits from skillet. Pour over chicken.

3. Cover. Cook on High 2-2½ hours, or on Low 4-5 hours.

4. Add parsley and baste chicken. Cover. Cook on High 15-30 minutes, until chicken is tender.

Lemon Honey Chicken

Carolyn W. Carmichael,
Berkeley Heights, NJ

Makes 4-6 servings

Prep. Time: 5 minutes
Cooking Time: 8 hours
Ideal slow-cooker size: 4-qt.

1 lemon
1 whole roasting chicken, rinsed
½ cup orange juice
½ cup honey

1. Pierce lemon with fork. Place in chicken cavity. Place chicken in slow cooker.

2. Combine orange juice and honey. Pour over chicken.

3. Cover. Cook on Low 8 hours. Remove lemon and squeeze over chicken.

4. Carve chicken and serve.

Melanie's Chicken Cordon Bleu

Melanie Thrower, McPherson, KS

Makes 6 servings

Prep. Time: 15 minutes
Cooking Time: 4-5 hours
Ideal slow-cooker size: 4-qt.

3 whole chicken breasts, split and deboned
6 pieces thinly sliced ham
6 slices Swiss cheese
salt to taste
pepper to taste
6 slices bacon
¼ cup water
1 tsp. chicken bouillon granules
½ cup white cooking wine
1 tsp. cornstarch
¼ cup cold water

1. Flatten chicken to ⅛- to ¼-inch thickness. Place a slice of ham and a slice of cheese on top of each flattened breast. Sprinkle with salt and pepper. Roll up and wrap with strip of bacon. Secure with toothpick. Place in slow cooker.

2. Combine ¼ cup water, granules, and wine. Pour into slow cooker.

3. Cover. Cook on High 4 hours.

4. Combine cornstarch and ¼ cup cold water. Add to slow cooker. Cook until sauce thickens.

Ham and Swiss Chicken

Nanci Keatley, Salem, OR
Janice Yoskovich, Carmichaels, PA

Makes 6 servings

Prep. Time: 15 minutes
Cooking Time: 4-5 hours
Ideal slow-cooker size: 4-qt.

2 eggs, beaten
1½ cups milk
2 Tbsp. butter, melted
½ cup chopped celery
¼ cup diced onion
10 slices bread, cubed
12 thin slices deli ham, rolled up
2 cups grated Swiss cheese
2½ cups cubed cooked chicken
10¾-oz. can cream of chicken soup
½ cup milk

1. Combine eggs and milk. Add butter, celery, and onion. Stir in bread cubes. Place half of mixture in greased slow cooker. Top with half the ham, cheese, and chicken.

2. Combine soup and milk. Pour half over chicken. Repeat layers.

3. Cover. Cook on Low 4-5 hours.

Marcy's Barbecued Chicken

Marcy Engle, Harrisonburg, VA

Makes 6 servings

Prep. Time: 5-7 minutes
Cooking Time: 5 hours
Ideal slow-cooker size: 4-qt.

2 lbs. chicken pieces
¼ cup flour
1 cup ketchup
2 cups water
⅓ cup Worcestershire sauce
1 tsp. chili powder
½ tsp. salt
½ tsp. pepper
2 drops Tabasco sauce
¼ tsp. garlic salt
¼ tsp. onion salt

1. Dust chicken with flour. Transfer to slow cooker.

2. Combine remaining ingredients. Pour over chicken.

3. Cover. Cook on Low 5 hours.

Tasty Drumsticks

Trudy Kutter, Corfu, NY

Makes 5-6 servings

Prep Time: 20 minutes
Cooking Time: 6 hours
Ideal slow-cooker size: 5-qt.

3-4 lbs. chicken drumsticks, skin removed
8-oz. can tomato sauce
¼ cup soy sauce
¼ cup brown sugar
1 tsp. minced garlic
3 Tbsp. cornstarch
¼ cup cold water

1. Place drumsticks in slow cooker.

2. Combine tomato sauce, soy sauce, brown sugar, and garlic in a bowl.

3. Pour over drumsticks, making sure that each drumstick is sauced.

4. Cover. Cook on Low 6 hours, or until chicken is tender.

5. Remove chicken with tongs to a platter and keep it warm.

6. Strain juices into saucepan.

7. In a bowl combine cornstarch and water until smooth.

8. Add cornstarch mixture to saucepan.

9. Bring mixture to a boil, stirring continuously.

10. Stir for two minutes until thickened.

Serving suggestion: Serve sauce alongside, or spooned over, chicken.

Tip:
The sauce is also a tasty dip for sides, such as fries.

Oriental Chicken

Marcia S. Myer, Manheim, PA

Makes 6 servings

Prep. Time: 15 minutes
Cooking Time: 3¼-4¼ hours
Ideal slow-cooker size: 5-qt.

¼ cup flour
1½ tsp. salt
2 2½-3 lb. broiler/fryer chickens, cut up
2 Tbsp. oil
6-oz. can lemonade concentrate, thawed
2 Tbsp. brown sugar
3 Tbsp. ketchup
1 Tbsp. vinegar
2 Tbsp. cold water
2 Tbsp. cornstarch

1. Combine flour with salt. Coat chicken. Brown chicken in oil in skillet. Transfer to slow cooker.
2. Combine lemonade concentrate, brown sugar, ketchup, and vinegar. Pour over chicken.
3. Cover. Cook on High 3-4 hours.
4. Remove chicken. Pour liquid into saucepan. Return chicken to cooker and cover to keep warm. Skim fat from liquid.
5. Combine water and cornstarch. Stir into hot liquid. Cook and stir until thick and bubbly.

Serving suggestion: Serve chicken and sauce over **rice**.

Tracy's Barbecued Chicken Wings

Tracy Supcoe, Barclay, MD

Makes 8 full-sized servings

Prep. Time: 20 minutes
Cooking Time: 5-6 hours
Ideal slow-cooker size: 5-qt.

4 lbs. chicken wings
2 large onions, chopped
2 6-oz. cans tomato paste
2 large garlic cloves, minced
¼ cup Worcestershire sauce
¼ cup cider vinegar
½ cup brown sugar
½ cup sweet pickle relish
½ cup red, *or* white, wine
2 tsp. salt
2 tsp. dry mustard

1. Cut off wing tips. Cut wings at joint. Place in slow cooker.
2. Combine remaining ingredients. Add to slow cooker. Stir.
3. Cover. Cook on Low 5-6 hours.

Mary's Chicken Wings

Mary Casey, Scranton, PA

Makes 8-12 full-sized servings

Prep. Time: 10 minutes
Cooking Time: 4-6 hours
Ideal slow-cooker size: 4- to 5-qt.

3-6 lbs. chicken wings
1-3 Tbsp. oil
¾-1 cup vinegar
½ cup ketchup
2 Tbsp. sugar
2 Tbsp. Worcestershire sauce
3 garlic cloves, minced
1 Tbsp. dry mustard
1 tsp. paprika
½-1 tsp. salt
⅛ tsp. pepper

1. Brown wings in oil in skillet, or brush wings with oil and broil, watching carefully so they do not burn.
2. Combine remaining ingredients in slow cooker. Add wings. Stir gently so that they are all well covered with sauce.
3. Cover. Cook on Low 4-6 hours, or until tender.

Don't peek. It takes 15-20 minutes for the cooker to regain lost steam and return to the right temperature.

Janet V. Yocum, Elizabethtown, PA

Rosemarie's Barbecued Chicken Wings

Rosemarie Fitzgerald, Gibsonia, PA

Makes 10 full-sized servings

Prep. Time: 5 minutes
Cooking Time: 2-8 hours
Ideal slow-cooker size: 5-qt.

5 lbs. chicken wings, tips
   cut off
12-oz. bottle chili sauce
⅓ cup lemon juice
1 Tbsp. Worcestershire sauce
2 Tbsp. molasses
1 tsp. salt
2 tsp. chili powder
¼ tsp. hot pepper sauce
dash garlic powder

1. Place wings in cooker.
2. Combine remaining ingredients and pour over chicken.
3. Cover. Cook on Low 6-8 hours, or on High 2-3 hours.

Note:
   These wings are also a great appetizer, yielding about 15 appetizer-size servings.
   Take any leftover chicken off the bone and combine with leftover sauce. Serve over cooked pasta for a second meal.

Donna's Chicken Wings

Donna Conto, Saylorsburg, PA

Makes 10 full-sized servings

Prep. Time: 5 minutes
Cooking Time: 3-4 hours
Ideal slow-cooker size: 5-qt.

5 lbs. chicken wings
28-oz. jar spaghetti sauce
1 Tbsp. Worcestershire sauce
1 Tbsp. molasses
1 Tbsp. prepared mustard
1 tsp. salt
½ tsp. pepper

1. Place wings in slow cooker.
2. Combine remaining ingredients. Pour over wings and stir them gently, making sure all are covered with sauce.
3. Cover. Cook on High 3-4 hours.

Sweet Aromatic Chicken

Anne Townsend, Albuquerque, NM

Makes 4 servings

Prep. Time: 5 minutes
Cooking Time: 5-6 hours
Ideal slow-cooker size: 4-qt.

½ cup coconut milk
½ cup water
8 chicken thighs, skinned
½ cup brown sugar
2 Tbsp. soy sauce
⅛ tsp. ground cloves
2 garlic cloves, minced

1. Combine coconut milk and water. Pour into greased slow cooker.
2. Add remaining ingredients in order listed.
3. Cover. Cook on Low 5-6 hours.

Note:
   What to do with leftover coconut milk?
   1. Two or three spoonfuls over vanilla ice cream, topped with a cherry, makes a flavorful, quick dessert.
   2. Family Piña Coladas are good. Pour the coconut milk into a pitcher and add one large can pineapple juice, along with some ice cubes. Decorate with pineapple chunks and cherries.

I generally spray the inside of my slow cooker with non-stick cooking spray prior to putting my ingredients in. It helps with cleanup. Barb Yoder, Angola, IN

Chicken Casablanca

Joyce Kaut, Rochester, NY

Makes 6-8 servings

Prep. Time: 30 minutes
Cooking Time: 4½-6½ hours
Ideal slow-cooker size: 4- to 5-qt.

2 large onions, sliced
1 tsp. ground ginger
3 garlic cloves, minced
2 Tbsp. oil
3 large carrots, diced
2 large potatoes, diced
3 lbs. skinless chicken pieces
½ tsp. ground cumin
½ tsp. salt
½ tsp. pepper
¼ tsp. cinnamon
2 Tbsp. raisins
14½-oz. can chopped tomatoes
3 small zucchini, sliced
15-oz. can garbanzo beans, drained
2 Tbsp. chopped parsley

1. Sauté onions, ginger, and garlic in oil in skillet. (Reserve oil.) Transfer vegetables to slow cooker. Add carrots and potatoes.

2. Brown chicken over medium heat in reserved oil. Transfer to slow cooker. Mix gently with vegetables.

3. Combine seasonings in separate bowl. Sprinkle over chicken and vegetables. Add raisins and tomatoes.

4. Cover. Cook on High 4-6 hours.

5. Add sliced zucchini, beans, and parsley 30 minutes before serving.

*Serving suggestion: Serve over **cooked rice** or **couscous**.*

Variation:

Add ½ tsp. turmeric and ¼ tsp. cayenne pepper to Step 3.
Michelle Mann, Mt. Joy, PA

Greek Chicken

Judy Govotsus, Monrovia, MD

Makes 4-6 servings

Prep. Time: 10 minutes
Cooking Time: 5-10 hours
Ideal slow-cooker size: 6-qt.

4-6 potatoes, quartered
2-3 lbs. chicken pieces
2 large onions, quartered
1 whole bulb garlic, minced
3 tsp. dried oregano
1 tsp. salt
½ tsp. pepper
1 Tbsp. olive oil

1. Place potatoes in bottom of slow cooker. Add chicken, onions, and garlic. Sprinkle with seasonings. Top with oil.

2. Cover. Cook on High 5-6 hours, or on Low 9-10 hours.

Autumn Chicken and Veggies

Nanci Keatley, Salem, OR

Makes 6 servings

Prep Time: 20 minutes
Cooking Time: 4-6 hours
Ideal slow-cooker size: 6-qt.

2 yellow onions, chopped
2 parsnips, cut into ½-inch-thick slices
3 carrots, cut into ½-inch-thick slices
1 lb. celery root, cut into chunks
½ tsp. salt
¼-½ tsp. pepper
6 boneless chicken breast halves
salt to taste
pepper to taste
1 tsp. tarragon
1 cup chicken broth
½ cup white wine

1. Place vegetables in slow cooker. Stir in salt and pepper. Mix well.

2. Lay chicken pieces over vegetables.

3. Season with salt and pepper. Sprinkle with tarragon.

4. Pour broth and wine around the chicken pieces, so as not to disturb the seasonings.

5. Cover. Cook on Low 4-6 hours, or until vegetables and chicken are tender and done to your liking.

*Serving suggestion: Serve with mashed **potatoes** or some good **French bread**.*

Chicken with Vegetables in Gravy

Trudy Kutter, Corfu, NY

Makes 4 servings

Prep Time: 20-40 minutes
Cooking Time: 8 hours
Ideal slow-cooker size: 5-qt.

2-3 cups potatoes, cubed
2-3 cups baby carrots
1 medium onion, chopped
4 bone-in chicken breast halves
2 .87-oz. pkgs. dry chicken gravy mix
1 cup water
1 tsp. thyme
scant tsp. poultry seasoning
1 cup sour cream, *or* condensed cream soup

1. Place vegetables in slow cooker. Stir together until well mixed.
2. Put chicken on top of vegetables.
3. Mix dry gravy mix with water, thyme, and poultry seasoning in a medium bowl.
4. Pour gravy into slow cooker.
5. Cook on Low 8 hours, or until vegetables and chicken are tender and done to your liking.
6. Remove meat and vegetables to serving platter.
7. Whisk sour cream or cream soup into broth.
8. Pour over chicken and vegetables and serve.

Braised Chicken with Summer Tomatoes

Karen Ceneviva, Seymour, CT

Makes 6 servings

Prep Time: 30 minutes
Cooking Time: 3-4 hours
Ideal slow-cooker size: 6-qt.

4½-lb. chicken, cut into 8 pieces (excluding back and wings; save them for making soup another day)
salt to taste
pepper to taste
4 Tbsp. extra-virgin olive oil, *divided*
1 large yellow onion, chopped
10 cloves garlic, peeled
½ cup wine vinegar
1½ cups chicken broth
4 fresh tarragon sprigs, *or* 2 Tbsp. finely chopped fresh tarragon leaves
6-8 medium (about 3½ lbs.) tomatoes, chopped

1. Season chicken to taste with salt and pepper.
2. Place 2 Tbsp. oil in large skillet. Brown chicken, a few pieces at a time, over medium-high heat in skillet. Turn once and brown underside.
3. When both sides of each piece of chicken are browned, remove from skillet and keep warm on platter.
4. Add 2 Tbsp. oil to skillet. Stir in chopped onion. Sauté over medium heat about 8 minutes.
5. Add garlic and sauté about 5 minutes. Add vinegar and broth and simmer 1 minute.
6. Carefully pour oil/vinegar/onion/garlic mixture into slow cooker. Place chicken on top.
7. Tuck tarragon sprigs around chicken pieces, or sprinkle with chopped tarragon. Spoon chopped tomatoes over top.
8. Cover. Cook on Low 3-4 hours, or until chicken is tender.

Honeyed Chicken

Christie Anne Detamore-Hunsberger
Harrisonburg, VA

Makes 4-5 servings

Prep Time: 15 minutes
Cooking Time: 4-5 hours
Ideal slow-cooker size: 3- to 4-qt.

2 Tbsp. butter
½ cup honey
¼ cup prepared mustard
¼ tsp. salt
1 tsp. curry powder
1 whole chicken, cut up, *or* 4-5 good-sized chicken breast halves

1. Melt butter in saucepan.
2. Add honey, mustard, salt, and curry. Mix together well.
3. Place chicken in slow cooker.

4. Spoon liquid mixture over each piece of chicken.

5. Cover. Cook on Low 4-5 hours, or just until chicken is tender.

Barbara's Creole Chicken

Barbara McGinnis, Jupiter, FL

Makes 4 servings

Prep. Time: 15 minutes
Cooking Time: 6 hours
Ideal slow-cooker size: 4½-qt.

2 (.9-oz.) pkgs. dry béarnaise sauce mix
½ cup dry white wine
1 lb. boneless, skinless chicken breasts, cut into bite-sized cubes
9-oz. pkg. frozen mixed vegetables
1-lb. cooked ham, cubed
1 lb. red potatoes, cubed
1 red bell pepper, chopped
1 green bell pepper, chopped
3 shallots, minced
½ tsp. garlic powder
½ tsp. turmeric powder
½ tsp. dried tarragon

1. Combine all ingredients in slow cooker.

2. Cover. Cook on Low 6 hours.

Chicken Curry

Maricarol Magill, Freehold, NJ

Makes 4 servings

Prep. Time: 10 minutes
Cooking Time: 5¼-6¼ hours
Ideal slow-cooker size: 5-qt.

4 boneless, skinless chicken breast halves
1 small onion, chopped
2 sweet potatoes (about 1½ lbs.), cubed
⅔ cup orange juice
1 garlic clove, minced
1 tsp. chicken bouillon granules
1 tsp. salt
¼ tsp. pepper
4 tsp. curry powder
2 Tbsp. cornstarch
2 Tbsp. cold water

Toppings:
sliced green onions
shredded coconut
peanuts
raisins

1. Place chicken in slow cooker. Cover with onions and sweet potatoes.

2. Combine orange juice, garlic, chicken bouillon granules, salt, pepper, and curry powder. Pour over vegetables.

3. Cover. Cook on Low 5-6 hours.

4. Remove chicken and vegetables and keep warm.

5. Turn slow cooker to High. Dissolve cornstarch in cold water. Stir into sauce in slow cooker. Cover. Cook on High 15-20 minutes.

*Serving suggestion: Serve chicken and sauce over **rice**. Sprinkle with your choice of **toppings**.*

African Chicken Treat

Anne Townsend, Albuquerque, NM

Makes 4 servings

Prep. Time: 10 minutes
Cooking Time: 5-6 hours
Ideal slow-cooker size: 4-qt.

1½ cups water
2 tsp. chicken bouillon granules
2 ribs celery, thinly sliced
2 onions, thinly sliced
1 red bell pepper, sliced
1 green bell pepper, sliced
½ cup extra crunchy peanut butter
8 chicken thighs, skinned
crushed chili pepper of your choice

1. Combine water, chicken bouillon granules, celery, onions, and peppers in slow cooker.

2. Spread peanut butter over both sides of chicken pieces. Sprinkle with chili pepper. Place on top of ingredients in slow cooker.

3. Cover. Cook on Low 5-6 hours.

Fruited Chicken Curry

Jan Mast, Lancaster, PA

Makes 4-5 servings

Prep Time: 15 minutes
Cooking Time: 4½ -6½ hours
Ideal slow-cooker size: 6-qt.

2½-3½ lbs. chicken legs and
 thighs
¼-½ tsp. salt
¼ tsp. pepper
29-oz. can peach halves
1 Tbsp. curry powder
1 garlic clove, minced
1 Tbsp. dried onion
1 Tbsp. butter, melted
½ cup chicken broth
½ cup prunes, pitted
3 Tbsp. cornstarch
3 Tbsp. cold water

1. Place chicken pieces in slow cooker. Season with salt and pepper.

2. Drain peaches. Reserve syrup.

3. In a small bowl combine curry, garlic, dried onion, butter, and broth. Stir in ½ cup reserved peach syrup.

4. Pour curry sauce over chicken.

5. Cover. Cook on Low 4-6 hours, or until chicken is tender but not dry or mushy.

6. Remove chicken from cooker and keep warm on a platter.

7. Turn cooker to High and stir in prunes.

8. In a small bowl, dissolve cornstarch in cold water and stir until smooth. Stir into hot broth in cooker.

9. Cover. Cook on High 10-15 minutes, or until broth is slightly thickened.

10. Stir in peach halves. Cover. Heat an additional 10-15 minutes.

Serving suggestion: Serve chicken with warm fruited curry sauce.

Groundnut Stew

Cathy Boshart, Lebanon, PA

Makes 8 servings

Prep. Time: 10 minutes
Cooking Time: 3½ hours
Ideal slow-cooker size: 4-qt.

---

2 green peppers, cut into
 rings
1 medium onion, cut into
 rings
2 Tbsp. shortening
6-oz. can tomato paste
¾ cup peanut butter
3 cups chicken broth
1½ tsp. salt
1 tsp. chili powder
1 tsp. sugar
½ tsp. ground nutmeg
4 cups cubed, cooked
 chicken

Toppings:
 coconut
 peanuts
 raisins
 hard-boiled eggs, chopped
 bananas, chopped
 oranges, cut up
 eggplant, chopped
 apples, chopped
 tomatoes, chopped
 carrots, shredded
 green pepper, chopped
 onion, chopped
 pineapple, crushed

1. Cook and stir green pepper and onion rings in shortening in hot slow cooker.

2. Combine tomato paste and peanut butter. Stir into slow cooker.

3. Add broth and seasonings. Stir in chicken.

4. Cover. Cook on Low 3 hours.

*Serving suggestion: Serve over hot **rice** with your choice of **toppings**.*

Mulligan Stew

Carol Ambrose, Ripon, CA

Makes 8-10 servings

Prep. Time: 15 minutes
Cooking Time: 7 hours
Ideal slow-cooker size: 4- to 5-qt.

3-lb. stewing hen, cut up, *or* 4
 lbs. chicken legs and thighs
1½ tsp. salt
¼-lb. salt pork, *or* bacon,
 cut in 1-inch squares
4 cups tomatoes, peeled
 and sliced
2 cups fresh corn, *or* 1-lb.
 pkg. frozen corn

1 cup coarsely chopped
  potatoes
10-oz. pkg. lima beans, frozen
½ cup chopped onions
1 tsp. salt
¼ tsp. pepper
dash of cayenne pepper

1. Place chicken in very
large slow cooker. Add water
to cover. Add 1½ tsp. salt.

2. Cover. Cook on Low 2
hours. Add more water if needed.

3. Add remaining ingredients.
(If you don't have a large cooker,
divide the stew between 2
average-sized ones.) Simmer
on Low 5 hours longer.

Notes:

1. Flavor improves if stew is
refrigerated and reheated the
next day. May also be made in
advance and frozen.

2. You can debone the
chicken after the first cooking
for 2 hours. Stir chicken pieces
back into cooker with other
ingredients and continue with
directions above.

Gran's Big Potluck

Carol Ambrose, Ripon, CA

Makes 10-15 servings

Prep. Time: 20 minutes
Cooking Time: 10-12 hours
Ideal slow-cooker size: 5- to 6-qt.

2½-3 lb. stewing hen, cut
  into pieces

½ lb. stewing beef, cubed
½ lb. veal shoulder, *or*
  roast, cubed
1½ qts. water
½ lb. small red potatoes,
  cubed
½ lb. small onions, cut in half
1 cup sliced carrots
1 cup chopped celery
1 green pepper, chopped
1-lb. pkg. frozen lima beans
1 cup okra, whole *or* diced,
  fresh *or* frozen
1 cup whole kernel corn
8-oz. can whole tomatoes
  with juice
15-oz. can tomato purée
1 tsp. salt
¼-½ tsp. pepper
1 tsp. dry mustard
½ tsp. chili powder
¼ cup chopped fresh parsley

1. Combine all ingredients
except last 5 seasonings in
one very large slow cooker, or
divide between two medium-
sized ones.

2. Cover. Cook on Low
10-12 hours. Add seasonings
during last hour of cooking.

Note:

You may want to debone the
chicken and mix it back into the
cooker before serving the meal.

Marsha's Chicken Enchilada Casserole

Marsha Sabus, Fallbrook, CA

Makes 4-6 servings

Prep. Time: 30 minutes
Cooking Time: 3-4 hours
Ideal slow-cooker size: 5-qt.

1 onion, chopped
1 garlic clove, minced
1 Tbsp. oil
10-oz. can enchilada sauce
8-oz. can tomato sauce
salt to taste
pepper to taste
3 boneless chicken breast
  halves, cooked and cubed
15-oz. can ranch-style
  beans, drained
11-oz. can Mexicorn, drained
¾ lb. cheddar cheese, grated
2¼-oz. can sliced black
  olives, drained
8 corn tortillas, *divided*

1. Sauté onion and garlic in
oil in saucepan. Stir in enchilada sauce and tomato sauce.
Season with salt and pepper.

2. Ladle one-fourth of the sauce
onto the bottom of the cooker.

3. Follow that with one-third
of the chicken, one-third sauce
mixture, one-third beans, one-
third corn, one-third cheese,
and one-third black olives.

4. Top that with 2 tortillas.

5. Repeat Steps 2 through 4
three times, ending with 2 tortillas.

6. Cover. Cook on Low 3-4
hours, or until bubbly throughout.

Chicken Olé

Barb Yoder, Angola, IN

Makes 8 servings

Prep. Time: 10 minutes
Cooking Time: 4½-5½ hours
Ideal slow-cooker size: 5-qt.

10¾-oz. can cream of
  mushroom soup
10¾-oz. can cream of
  chicken soup
1 cup sour cream
2 Tbsp. grated onion
1½ cups grated cheddar
  cheese
12 flour tortillas, each torn
  into 6-8 pieces
3-4 cups cubed, cooked
  chicken
7-oz. jar salsa
½ cup grated cheddar cheese

1. In separate bowl, combine soups, sour cream, onion, and 1½ cups cheese.

2. Place one-third of each of the following in layers in slow cooker: soup mixture, torn tortillas, chicken, and salsa. Repeat layers 2 more times.

3. Cover. Cook on Low 4-5 hours. (This recipe does not respond well to cooking on High.)

4. Gently stir. Sprinkle with remaining ½ cup cheese. Cover. Cook on Low another 15-30 minutes.

*Serving suggestion: Serve with **tortilla chips** and **lettuce**.*

Chicken Enchilada Casserole

Nadine Martinitz, Salina, KS

Makes 6-8 servings

Prep Time: 20 minutes
Cooking Time: 2-6 hours
Ideal slow-cooker size: 6-qt.

1 large onion, chopped
1 Tbsp. oil
10¾-oz. can cream of
  chicken soup
10¾-oz. can cream of
  mushroom soup
2 10½-oz. cans green
  enchilada sauce
4½-oz. can green chilies, diced
1 cup sour cream
15 large flour tortillas
3½ cups cooked chicken,
  chopped
3 cups Mexican-blend
  cheese, shredded

1. In large skillet or saucepan, sauté onion in oil.

2. Add soups, enchilada sauce, chilies, and sour cream to sautéed onion. Mix together well.

3. Tear tortillas into bite-size pieces.

4. Layer ¼ of sauce into slow cooker. Top with ⅓ of chicken, ⅓ of torn tortillas, and ¼ of cheese.

5. Repeat layers two more times, ending with sauce and cheese.

6. Cover. Cook 5-6 hours on Low or 2-3 hours on High.

Chicken Tortillas

Julette Leaman, Harrisonburg, VA

Makes 4 servings

Prep. Time: 60 minutes
Cooking Time: 6-8 hours
Ideal slow-cooker size: 4- to 5-qt.

1 fryer chicken, cooked and
  cubed
10¾-oz. can cream of
  chicken soup
14½-oz. can tomatoes with
  chilies
2 Tbsp. quick-cooking
  tapioca
6-8 tortillas, torn into pieces
1 medium onion, chopped
2 cups grated cheddar
  cheese

1. Combine chicken, soup, tomatoes with chilies, and tapioca.

2. Line bottom of slow cooker with one-third tortilla pieces. Add one-third chicken mixture. Sprinkle with one-third onion and one-third cheese. Repeat layers.

3. Cover. Cook on Low 6-8 hours. (This recipe does not respond well to being cooked on High.)

*Serving suggestion: If you wish, serve with shredded **lettuce**, chopped fresh **tomatoes**, diced raw **onions**, **sour cream**, and **salsa**.*

Chicken on a Whim

Colleen Heatwole, Burton, MI

Makes 6-8 servings

Prep. Time: 10 minutes
Cooking Time: 4½ hours
Ideal slow-cooker size: 5-qt.

6 medium-sized, boneless, skinless chicken breast halves
1 small onion, sliced
1 cup dry white wine, *or* chicken broth, *or* water
15-oz. can chicken broth
2 cups water
6-oz. can sliced black olives, with juice
1 small can artichoke hearts, with juice
5 garlic cloves, minced
1 cup dry elbow macaroni, *or* small shells
1 envelope dry savory garlic soup

1. Place chicken in slow cooker. Spread onion over chicken.
2. Combine remaining ingredients, except dry soup mix, and pour over chicken. Sprinkle with dry soup.
3. Cover. Cook on Low 4½ hours.

Joyce's Chicken Tetrazzini

Joyce Slaymaker, Strasburg, PA

Makes 4 servings

Prep. Time: 10 minutes
Cooking Time: 6-8 hours
Ideal slow-cooker size: 5-qt.

2-3 cups diced cooked chicken
2 cups chicken broth
1 small onion, chopped
¼ cup sauterne, *or* white wine, *or* milk
½ cup slivered almonds
2 4-oz. cans sliced mushrooms, drained
10¾-oz. can cream of mushroom soup

1. Combine all ingredients except spaghetti and cheese in slow cooker.
2. Cover. Cook on Low 6-8 hours.

*Serving suggestion: Serve over buttered **spaghetti**. Sprinkle with grated **Parmesan cheese**.*

Variations:
1. Place spaghetti in large baking dish. Pour sauce in center. Sprinkle with Parmesan cheese. Broil until lightly browned.
2. Add 10-oz. pkg. frozen peas to Step 1.

Darlene Raber, Wellman, IA

Chicken Spaghetti

Janie Steele, Moore, OK

Makes 6-8 servings

Prep Time: 30-45 minutes
Cooking Time: 1 hour
Ideal slow-cooker size: 4-qt.

2 lbs. cooked chicken, without skin, deboned, and cut in 1-inch chunks
10-oz. pkg. dry spaghetti, cooked in chicken broth and drained
1 bell pepper, chopped
1 medium onion, chopped
10¾-oz. can mushroom soup
1 small jar pimentos, drained and chopped
14½-oz. can Mexican stewed, *or* diced, tomatoes
10¾-oz. can tomato soup
⅓ lb. cheddar, *or* your favorite, cheese, cubed
¼-lb. fresh mushrooms, sliced, *or* small can sliced mushrooms, drained, *optional*
¼ cup black olives, sliced, *optional*

1. Combine all ingredients in slow cooker.
2. Cover. Cook on High 1 hour, or until heated through.

*Serving suggestion: Serve with grated **cheese** of your choice on top.*

Chickenetti

Miriam Nolt, New Holland, PA
Ruth Hershey, Paradise, PA

Makes 10 servings

Prep. Time: 25 minutes
Cooking Time: 2-3 hours
Ideal slow-cooker size: 6- to 7-qt.

1 cup chicken broth
16-oz. pkg. spaghetti, cooked
4-6 cups cubed and cooked
    chicken, *or* turkey, breast
10¾-oz. can cream of
    mushroom soup, *or*
    cream of celery soup
1 cup water
¼ cup green peppers, chopped
½ cup diced celery
½ tsp. pepper
1 medium onion, grated
½ lb. white, *or* yellow,
    American cheese, cubed

1. Put cup of chicken broth into very large slow cooker. Add spaghetti and meat.
2. In large bowl, combine soup and water until smooth. Stir in remaining ingredients, then pour into slow cooker.
3. Cover. Cook on Low 2-3 hours.

Variations:
1. For a creamier dish, add a 10¾-oz. can cream of chicken soup to Step 2.
    Arlene Miller, Hutchinson, KS

2. Add 4½-oz. can chopped green chilies to Step 2, for more zest.

Hot Chicken Salad

Janie Steele, Moore, OK

Makes 6-8 servings

Prep Time: 15-30 minutes
Cooking Time: 1½ hours
Ideal slow-cooker size: 4-qt.

10¾-oz. can cream of
    chicken soup
10¾-oz. can cream of
    mushroom soup
1 cup mayonnaise
1 small onion, chopped
½ tsp. salt
¼-½ tsp. pepper
4 cups cooked chicken, cubed
1 can water chestnuts,
    drained and chopped
1 cup sour cream
1 cup cooked and drained
    fettuccine pasta
2 cups cheese, shredded
crushed potato chips

1. Combine soups, mayonnaise, chopped onion, salt, and pepper in slow cooker. Mix until smooth.
2. Stir in cubed chicken and water chestnuts.
3. Fold in sour cream and fettuccine.
4. Cover. Cook on High until bubbly, about 1½ hours.
5. Ten minutes before end of cooking time and before serving, sprinkle with shredded cheese and crushed potato chips. Continue cooking, uncovered.

Golden Chicken and Noodles

Sue Pennington, Bridgewater, VA

Makes 6 servings

Prep. Time: 5-7 minutes
Cooking Time: 6-7 hours
Ideal slow-cooker size: 4-qt.

6 boneless, skinless chicken
    breast halves
2 10¾-oz. cans broccoli
    cheese soup
2 cups milk
1 small onion, chopped
½-1 tsp. salt
½-1 tsp. dried basil
⅛ tsp. pepper

1. Place chicken pieces in slow cooker.
2. Combine remaining ingredients. Pour over chicken.
3. Cover. Cook on High 1 hour. Reduce heat to Low. Cook 5-6 hours.

*Serving suggestion: Serve over cooked **noodles**.*

Creamy Chicken and Carrots

Carol Eberly, Harrisonburg, VA

Makes 8 servings

Prep Time: 20 minutes
Cooking Time: 4-8 hours
Ideal slow-cooker size: 4- to 5-qt.

2 10¾-oz. cans cream of chicken soup
½ cup water
2-4 Tbsp. lemon juice, according to your taste preference
1 Tbsp. Dijon mustard
1½ tsp. garlic powder
8 large carrots, thinly sliced
8 boneless skinless chicken breast halves

1. Mix soup, water, lemon juice, mustard, garlic powder, and carrots in slow cooker.
2. Lay chicken over top of vegetables.
3. Turn chicken to coat. Push down into vegetables and sauce. Be sure that top layer of chicken is covered with sauce.
4. Cover. Cook on High 4-5 hours, or on Low 7-8 hours, or until vegetables and chicken are tender.

*Serving suggestion: Serve over cooked **noodles**.*

Chicken and Stuffing

Janice Yoskovich, Carmichaels, PA
Jo Ellen Moore, Pendleton, IN

Makes 14-16 servings

Prep. Time: 20 minutes
Cooking Time: 4½-5 hours
Ideal slow-cooker size: 8-qt.

2½ cups chicken broth
1 cup butter, *or* margarine, melted
½ cup chopped onions
½ cup chopped celery
4-oz. can mushrooms, stems and pieces, drained
¼ cup dried parsley flakes
1½ tsp. rubbed sage
1 tsp. poultry seasoning
1 tsp. salt
½ tsp. pepper
12 cups day-old bread cubes (½-inch pieces)
2 eggs
10¾-oz. can cream of chicken soup
5-6 cups cubed cooked chicken

1. Combine all ingredients except bread, eggs, soup, and chicken in saucepan. Simmer for 10 minutes.
2. Place bread cubes in large bowl.
3. Combine eggs and soup. Stir into broth mixture until smooth. Pour over bread and toss well.
4. Layer half of stuffing and then half of chicken into very large slow cooker (or two medium-sized cookers). Repeat layers.
5. Cover. Cook on Low 4½-5 hours.

One-Dish Chicken Supper

Louise Stackhouse, Benton, PA

Makes 4 servings

Prep. Time: 5 minutes
Cooking Time: 6-8 hours
Ideal slow-cooker size: 4-qt.

4 boneless, skinless chicken breast halves
10¾-oz. can cream of chicken, *or* celery, *or* mushroom, soup
⅓ cup milk
1 pkg. Stove Top stuffing mix and seasoning packet
1⅔ cups water

1. Place chicken in slow cooker.
2. Combine soup and milk. Pour over chicken.
3. Combine stuffing mix, seasoning packet, and water. Spoon over chicken.
4. Cover. Cook on Low 6-8 hours.

Sunday Chicken Stew with Dumplings

Kathy Hertzler, Lancaster, PA

Makes 6 servings

Prep Time: 1 hour
Cooking Time: 6½-7½ hours
Ideal slow-cooker size: 5-qt.

½ cup flour
1 tsp. salt
½ tsp. white pepper
3-lb. broiler/fryer chicken,
　cut up and skin removed
2 Tbsp. olive oil
3 cups chicken broth
6 large carrots, cut in
　1-inch-thick pieces
2 celery ribs, cut into
　½-inch-thick slices
1 large sweet onion, chopped
　into ½-inch-thick slices
1-2 tsp. dried rosemary
1½ cups frozen peas

Dumplings:
　1 cup flour
　½ tsp. dried rosemary,
　　crushed
　2 tsp. baking powder
　½ tsp. salt
　1 egg, beaten
　½ cup milk

1. To prepare chicken, combine flour, salt, and pepper in a large resealable plastic bag.

2. Add chicken, a few pieces at a time. Shake to coat.

3. In a large skillet, brown chicken in olive oil, a few pieces at a time.

4. As the pieces brown, remove to a platter and keep warm.

5. When all the chicken is brown, gradually add broth to skillet while bringing to a boil. Stir up the browned, flavorful bits sticking to the skillet.

6. In a 5-quart slow cooker, layer in carrots, celery, and onion.

7. Sprinkle with rosemary.

8. Add chicken. Carefully add hot broth.

9. Cover. Cook 6-7 hours on Low, or until chicken juice runs clear, vegetables are tender, and stew is bubbling.

10. Stir in peas.

11. To make the dumplings, combine flour, crushed rosemary, baking powder, and salt in a small bowl.

12. In a separate bowl combine egg and milk.

13. Stir wet ingredients into dry ingredients until just combined.

14. Drop by spoonfuls into simmering chicken mixture.

15. Cover. Cook on High 25-30 minutes, or until a toothpick inserted in dumpling comes out clean. (Try this after 25 minutes; otherwise, do not lift the cover while simmering).

Serving suggestion: Serve each person with a "scoop" of dumpling topped with vegetables and broth, with a piece of chicken on the side.

Tip:
The dumplings cook best if you use an oval, or wide, more shallow slow cooker.

Chicken and Dumplings

Elva Ever, North English, IA

Makes 8-10 servings

Prep Time: 1 hour
Cooking Time: 3 hours
Ideal slow-cooker size: 5-qt.

4 whole chicken breasts, *or*
　1 small chicken
¾ cup sliced carrots
¼ cup chopped onions
¼ cup chopped celery
1½ cups peas
4-6 Tbsp. flour
1 cup water
salt to taste
pepper to taste
buttermilk baking mix
　dumplings
paprika to taste

1. Cook chicken in water in soup pot. Cool, skin, and debone chicken. Return broth to boiling in soup pot.

2. Cook vegetables in microwave on high for 5 minutes.

3. Meanwhile, combine flour and water until smooth. Add to boiling chicken broth. Add enough extra water to make 4 cups broth, making sure gravy is fairly thick. Season with salt and pepper.

4. Combine chicken, vegetables, and gravy in slow cooker.

5. Mix dumplings as directed on baking mix box. Place dumplings on top of chicken in slow cooker.

Sprinkle with paprika.
6. Cover. Cook on High 3 hours.

Barbecue Chicken for Buns

Linda Sluiter, Schererville, IN

Makes 16-20 servings

Prep. Time: 15 minutes
Cooking Time: 8 hours
Ideal slow-cooker size: 5½-qt.

6 cups diced cooked chicken
2 cups chopped celery
1 cup chopped onions
1 cup chopped green peppers
4 Tbsp. butter
2 cups ketchup
2 cups water
2 Tbsp. brown sugar
4 Tbsp. vinegar
2 tsp. dry mustard
1 tsp. pepper
1 tsp. salt

1. Combine all ingredients in slow cooker.
2. Cover. Cook on Low 8 hours.
3. Stir chicken until it shreds.

Serving suggestion: Pile into **steak rolls** *and serve.*

Elizabeth's Hot Chicken Sandwiches

Elizabeth Yutzy, Wauseon, OH

Makes 8 servings

Prep. Time: 5 minutes
Cooking Time: 2-3 hours
Ideal slow-cooker size: 4-qt.

3 cups cubed cooked chicken
2 cups chicken broth
1 cup crushed soda crackers
¼-½ tsp. salt
dash pepper

1. Combine chicken, broth, crackers, and seasoning in slow cooker.
2. Cover. Cook on Low 2-3 hours, until mixture thickens and can be spread.

Serving suggestion: Fill **sandwich buns** *and serve while warm.*

Loretta's Hot Chicken Sandwiches

Loretta Krahn, Mt. Lake, MN

Makes 12 servings

Prep. Time: 15 minutes
Cooking Time: 2 hours
Ideal slow-cooker size: 4-qt.

8 cups cubed cooked chicken, *or* **turkey**
1 medium onion, chopped
1 cup chopped celery
2 cups mayonnaise
1 cup cubed American cheese

1. Combine all ingredients in slow cooker.
2. Cover. Cook on High 2 hours.

Serving suggestion: Serve on **buns.**

Chicken Reuben Bake

Gail Bush, Landenberg, PA

Makes 4 servings

Prep. Time: 5 minutes
Cooking Time: 6-8 hours
Ideal slow-cooker size: 4-qt.

4 boneless, skinless chicken breast halves
2-lb. bag sauerkraut, drained and rinsed
4-5 slices Swiss cheese
1¼ cups Thousand Island salad dressing
2 Tbsp. chopped fresh parsley

1. Place chicken in slow cooker. Layer sauerkraut over chicken. Add cheese. Top with salad dressing. Sprinkle with parsley.
2. Cover. Cook on Low 6-8 hours.

No-Fuss Turkey Breast

Dorothy Miller, Gulfport, MI

Makes 3-4 pints cooked meat

Prep. Time: 5 minutes
Cooking Time: 1-5 hours
Ideal slow-cooker size: 5- to 6-qt.

1 turkey breast
olive oil
1-2 Tbsp. water

1. Rub turkey breast with oil. Place in slow cooker. Add water.
2. Cover. Cook on High 1 hour, or on Low 4-5 hours.
3. Cool. Debone and cut into bite-sized pieces and store in pint-size plastic boxes in freezer. Use when cooked turkey or chicken is called for.

Turkey in a Pot

Dorothy M. Pittman, Pickens, SC

Makes 10-12 servings

Prep. Time: 5-10 minutes
Cooking Time: 6 hours
Ideal slow-cooker size: 5-qt.

4-5 lb. turkey breast (if frozen, it doesn't have to be thawed)
1 medium onion, chopped
1 rib celery, chopped

¼ cup melted margarine
salt to taste
lemon-pepper seasoning to taste
1½ cups chicken broth

1. Wash turkey breast. Pat dry. Place in greased slow cooker. Put onion and celery in cavity.
2. Pour margarine over turkey. Sprinkle with seasonings. Pour broth around turkey.
3. Cover. Cook on High 6 hours. Let stand 10 minutes before carving.

Turkey Breast

Barbara Katrine Rose, Woodbridge, VA

Makes 6-8 servings

Prep. Time: 5 minutes
Cooking Time: 3-4 hours
Ideal slow-cooker size: 5-qt.

1 large boneless turkey breast
¼ cup apple cider, *or* juice
1 tsp. salt
¼ tsp. pepper

1. Put turkey breast in slow cooker. Drizzle apple cider over turkey. Sprinkle on both sides with salt and pepper.
2. Cover. Cook on High 3-4 hours.
3. Remove turkey breast. Let stand for 15 minutes before slicing.

Onion Turkey Breast

Mary Ann Wasick, West Allis, WI

Makes 6-8 servings

Prep. Time: 5 minutes
Cooking Time: 8-10 hours
Ideal slow-cooker size: 4- to 5-qt.

4-6-lb. boneless, skinless turkey breast
1 tsp. garlic powder
1 envelope dry onion soup mix

1. Place turkey in slow cooker. Sprinkle garlic powder and onion soup mix over breast.
2. Cover. Cook on Low 8-10 hours.

*Serving suggestion: Use au jus over **rice** or **pasta**.*

Easy and Delicious Turkey Breast

Gail Bush, Landenberg, PA

Makes 4-6 servings

Prep. Time: 5 minutes
Cooking Time: 6-8 hours
Ideal slow-cooker size: 5-qt.

1 turkey breast
15-oz. can whole berry cranberry sauce
1 envelope dry onion soup mix
½ cup orange juice
½ tsp. salt
¼ tsp. pepper

1. Place turkey in slow cooker.
2. Combine remaining ingredients. Pour over turkey.
3. Cover. Cook on Low 6-8 hours.

Turkey Stew

Ruth S. Weaver, Reinholds, PA

Makes 8 servings

Prep. Time: 15 minutes
Cooking Time: 6-12 hours
Ideal slow-cooker size: 6½-qt.

2 lbs. skinless turkey thighs
1 lb., *or* 5 large, carrots, sliced
2 medium onions, chopped
8 medium potatoes, cubed
4 ribs celery, chopped
3 garlic cloves, minced
1 tsp. salt
¼ tsp. pepper
2 Tbsp. Worcestershire sauce
15-oz. can tomato sauce
2 bay leaves

1. Place turkey in large slow cooker.
2. In separate bowl, mix together carrots, onions, potatoes, celery, garlic, salt, pepper, Worcestershire sauce, tomato sauce, and bay.
3. Pour over turkey. Cover. Cook on Low 8-12 hours, or on High 6-8 hours. Remove bay leaves before serving.

From-Scratch Baked Beans

Wanda Roth, Napoleon, OH

Makes 6 servings

Prep. Time: 10 minutes
Cooking Time: 14 hours
Ideal slow-cooker size: 3½- to 4-qt.

2½ cups Great Northern dried beans
4 cups water
1½ cups tomato sauce
½ cup brown sugar
2 tsp. salt
1 small onion, chopped
½ tsp. chili powder

1. Wash and drain dry beans. Combine beans and water in slow cooker. Cook on Low 8 hours, or overnight.
2. Stir in remaining ingredients. Cook on Low 6 hours.

Put your cooker meal together the night before you want to cook it. The following morning put the mixture in the slow cooker, cover, and cook.

Sara Wilson, Blairstown, MO

New England Baked Beans

Mary Wheatley, Mashpee, MA
Jean Butzer, Batavia, NY

Makes 8 servings

Prep. Time: 20 minutes
Cooking Time: 14½–16½ hours
Ideal slow-cooker size: 5-qt.

1 lb. dried beans—Great
    Northern, pea beans, *or*
    navy beans
¼ lb. salt pork, sliced *or*
    diced
1 qt. water
1 tsp. salt
1-4 Tbsp. brown sugar,
    according to your
    preference
½ cup molasses
½-1 tsp. dry mustard,
    according to your
    preference
½ tsp. baking soda
1 onion, coarsely chopped
5 cups water

1. Wash beans and remove
any stones or shriveled beans.
2. Meanwhile, simmer
salt pork in 1 quart water
in saucepan for 10 minutes.
Drain. Do not reserve liquid.
3. Combine all ingredients
in slow cooker.
4. Cook on High until
contents come to boil. Turn
to Low. Cook 14-16 hours, or
until beans are tender.

Variations:
1. Add ½ tsp. pepper to
Step 3.
    Rachel Kauffman, Alton, MI
2. Add ¼ cup ketchup to
Step 3.
    Cheri Jantzen, Houston, TX

Mom's New England Baked Beans

Debbie Zeida, Mashpee, MA

Makes 6-8 servings

Prep. Time: 1½ hours
Cooking Time: 4-8 hours
Ideal slow-cooker size: 6-qt.

3 cups dried navy beans
9 cups water
1 medium onion, chopped
1 cup ketchup
1 cup brown sugar
1 cup water
2 tsp. dry mustard
2 Tbsp. dark molasses
1 Tbsp. salt
¼ lb. salt pork, ground *or*
    diced

1. Cook beans in water in
soup pot until softened, or
bring to boil, cover, and let
stand for 1½ hours. Drain.
Pour beans into slow cooker.
2. Stir in remaining ingredients. Mix well.
3. Cover. Cook on Low 8
hours, or on High 4 hours,
stirring occasionally.

Variation:
   Use 1 lb. dried Great
Northern beans instead of 3
cups navy beans.
    Dorothy Miller, Gulfport, MI

Barbecued Lima Beans

Hazel L. Propst, Oxford, PA

Makes 10 servings

Prep. Time: 1 hour
Soaking Time: overnight
Cooking Time: 4-10 hours
Ideal slow-cooker size: 3½-qt.

1½ lbs. dried lima beans
6 cups water
2¼ cups chopped onions
1¼ cups brown sugar
1½ cups ketchup
13 drops Tabasco sauce
1 cup dark corn syrup
1 Tbsp. salt
½ lb. bacon, diced

1. Soak washed beans in
water overnight. Do not drain.
2. Add onion. Bring to boil.
Simmer 30-60 minutes, or
until beans are tender. Drain
beans, reserving liquid.
3. Combine all ingredients
except bean liquid in slow
cooker. Mix well. Pour in
enough liquid so that beans
are barely covered.
4. Cover. Cook on Low 10
hours, or on High 4-6 hours.
Stir occasionally.

Refried Beans with Bacon

Arlene Wengerd, Millersburg, OH

Makes 8 servings

Prep. Time: 5 minutes
Cooking Time: 5 hours
Ideal slow-cooker size: 4-qt.

2 cups dried red, *or pinto,*
    beans
6 cups water
2 garlic cloves, minced
1 large tomato, peeled,
    seeded, and chopped, *or*
    1 pint tomato juice
1 tsp. salt
½ lb. bacon, *divided*

1. Combine beans, water, garlic, tomato, and salt in slow cooker.
2. Cover. Cook on High 5 hours, stirring occasionally. When the beans become soft, drain off some liquid.
3. While the beans cook, brown bacon in skillet. Drain, reserving drippings. Crumble bacon. Add half of bacon and 3 Tbsp. drippings to beans. Stir.
4. Mash or purée beans with a food processor. Fry the mashed bean mixture in the remaining bacon drippings. Add more salt to taste.

*Serving suggestion: To serve, sprinkle the remaining bacon and **shredded cheese** on top of beans.*

Variations:

1. Instead of draining off liquid, add ⅓ cup dry minute rice and continue cooking about 20 minutes. Add a dash of hot sauce and a dollop of sour cream to individual servings.
2. Instead of frying the mashed bean mixture, place several spoonfuls on flour tortillas, roll up, and serve.

Susan McClure, Dayton, VA

No Meat Baked Beans

Esther Becker, Gordonville, PA

Makes 8-10 servings

Prep. Time: 1¾ hours
Soaking Time: overnight
Cooking Time: 10-12 hours
Ideal slow-cooker size: 3½-qt.

1 lb. dried navy beans
6 cups water
1 small onion, chopped
¾ cup ketchup
¾ cup brown sugar
¾ cup water
1 tsp. dry mustard
2 Tbsp. dark molasses
1 tsp. salt

1. Soak beans in water overnight in large soup kettle. Cook beans in water until soft, about 1½ hours. Drain, discarding bean water.
2. Mix together all ingredients in slow cooker. Mix well.
3. Cover. Cook on Low 10-12 hours.

Red Beans and Rice

Margaret A. Moffitt, Bartlett, TN

Makes 8-10 servings

Prep. Time: 5 minutes
Soaking Time: 8 hours
Cooking Time: 10-12 hours
Ideal slow-cooker size: 3½- to 4-qt.

1-lb. pkg. dried red beans
water
salt pork, *or ham hocks, or*
    sausage, cut into small
    chunks
2 tsp. salt
1 tsp. pepper
3-4 cups water
6-oz. can tomato paste
8-oz. can tomato sauce
4 garlic cloves, minced

1. Soak beans for 8 hours. Drain. Discard soaking water.
2. Mix together all ingredients in slow cooker.
3. Cover. Cook on Low 10-12 hours, or until beans are soft.

Serving suggestion: Serve over rice.

Variation:

Use canned red kidney beans. Cook 1 hour on High and then 3 hours on Low.

Note:

These beans freeze well.

New Mexico Pinto Beans

John D. Allen, Rye, CO

Makes 8-10 servings

Prep. Time: 5 minutes
Soaking Time: overnight
Cooking Time: 6-10 hours
Ideal slow-cooker size: 6-qt.

2½ cups dried pinto beans
3 qts. water
½ cup ham, *or* salt pork,
   diced, *or* a small ham
   shank
2 garlic cloves, crushed
1 tsp. crushed red chili
   peppers, *optional*
salt to taste
pepper to taste

1. Sort beans. Discard pebbles, shriveled beans, and floaters. Wash beans under running water. Place in saucepan. Cover with 3 quarts water, and soak overnight.

2. Drain beans and discard soaking water. Pour beans into slow cooker. Cover with fresh water.

3. Add meat, garlic, chili, salt, and pepper. Cook on Low 6-10 hours, or until beans are soft.

Scandinavian Beans

Virginia Bender, Dover, DE

Makes 8 servings

Prep. Time: 1½-2 hours
Soaking Time: 8 hours
Cooking Time: 5-6 hours
Ideal slow-cooker size: 4- to 5-qt.

1 lb. dried pinto beans
6 cups water
12 oz. bacon, *or* 1 ham
   hock
1 onion, chopped
2-3 garlic cloves, minced
¼ tsp. pepper
1 tsp. salt
¼ cup molasses
1 cup ketchup
Tabasco to taste
1 tsp. Worcestershire sauce
¾ cup brown sugar
½ cup cider vinegar
¼ tsp. dry mustard

1. Soak beans in water in soup pot for 8 hours. Bring beans to boil and cook 1½-2 hours, or until soft. Drain, reserving liquid.

2. Combine all ingredients in slow cooker, using just enough bean liquid to cover everything. Cook on Low 5-6 hours. If using ham hock, debone, cut ham into bite-sized pieces, and mix into beans.

New Orleans Red Beans

Cheri Jantzen, Houston, TX

Makes 6 servings

Prep. Time: 1¼ hours
Cooking Time: 8-10 hours
Ideal slow-cooker size: 4-qt.

2 cups dried kidney beans
5 cups water
2 Tbsp. bacon drippings
½ lb. hot sausage, cut in
   small pieces
2 onions, chopped
2 cloves garlic, minced
1 tsp. salt

1. Wash and sort beans. In saucepan, combine beans and water. Boil 2 minutes. Remove from heat. Soak 1 hour.

2. Heat bacon drippings in skillet. Add sausage and brown slowly. Add onions and garlic and sauté until tender.

3. Combine all ingredients, including the bean water, in slow cooker.

4. Cover. Cook on Low 8-10 hours. During last 20 minutes of cooking, stir frequently and mash lightly with spoon.

*Serving suggestion: Serve over hot cooked **white rice**.*

Hot Bean Dish Without Meat

Jeannine Janzen, Elbing, KS

Makes 8-10 servings

Prep. Time: 10 minutes
Cooking Time: 3-4 hours
Ideal slow-cooker size: 4-qt.

16-oz. can kidney beans, drained
15-oz. can lima beans, drained
¼ cup vinegar
2 Tbsp. molasses
2 heaping Tbsp. brown sugar
2 Tbsp. minced onion
mustard to taste
Tabasco sauce to taste

1. Place beans in slow cooker.
2. Combine remaining ingredients. Pour over beans.
3. Cover. Cook on Low 3-4 hours.

Variation:
Add 1 lb. browned ground beef to make this a meaty main dish.

Barbecued Beans

Jane Steiner, Orrville, OH

Makes 12-15 servings

Prep. Time: 5-10 minutes
Cooking Time: 4 hours
Ideal slow-cooker size: 4-qt.

4 11-oz. cans pork and beans
¾ cup brown sugar
1 tsp. dry mustard
6 slices bacon, diced
½ cup ketchup

1. Pour 2 cans pork and beans into slow cooker.
2. Combine brown sugar and mustard. Sprinkle half of mixture over beans.
3. Cover with remaining cans of pork and beans. Sprinkle with rest of brown sugar and mustard.
4. Layer bacon over top. Spread ketchup over all.
5. Cut through bean mixture a bit before heating.
6. Cover. Cook on Low 4 hours.

Frances' Slow-Cooker Beans

Frances B. Musser, Newmanstown, PA

Makes 6-8 servings

Prep. Time: 15 minutes
Cooking Time: 4 hours
Ideal slow-cooker size: 4-qt.

½ cup ketchup
1 Tbsp. prepared mustard
½ cup brown sugar
1 small onion, chopped
1 tsp. salt
¼ tsp. ground ginger
½ cup molasses
1 lb. turkey bacon, browned and crumbled
40-oz. can Great Northern beans, drained

1. Combine all ingredients in slow cooker.
2. Cover. Cook on Low 4 hours.

If your recipe turns out to have too much liquid, remove the cover and use the High setting for about 45 minutes.
Esther Porter, Minneapolis, MN

Maple Baked Beans

Dot Hess, Willow Street, PA

Makes 20 servings

Prep. Time: 15-20 minutes
Cooking Time: 3-8 hours
Ideal slow-cooker size: 6-qt.

10 strips bacon, cooked and crumbled
½ cup onion, chopped
½ cup maple syrup
4 tsp. dry mustard
8 15-oz. cans pork and beans

1. Cook bacon until crisp. Crumble into slow cooker.

2. Add onion, maple syrup, mustard, and beans.

3. Cover and cook on Low for 3-4 hours or 6-8 hours on High.

Kelly's Baked Beans

Kelly Bailey, Mechanicsburg, PA

Makes 6 servings

Prep. Time: 15 minutes
Draining Time: overnight
Cooking Time: 6-8 hours
Ideal slow-cooker size: 4-qt.

40-oz. can Great Northern beans, juice reserved
1-lb. can Great Northern beans, juice reserved
¾ cup brown sugar
¼ cup white corn syrup
½ cup ketchup
½ tsp. salt
half a medium-sized onion, chopped

1. Drain beans overnight in colander. Save ¼ cup liquid.

2. Mix together brown sugar, corn syrup, and ketchup. Mix well. Add salt and onion.

3. Stir in beans and pour into greased slow cooker. If beans appear dry while cooking, add some of the ¼ cup reserved bean juice.

4. Cover. Cook on Low 6-8 hours.

*Serving suggestion: Crumble **bacon** over top if you wish.*

Four Beans and Sausage

Mary Seielstad, Sparks, NV

Makes 8 servings

Prep. Time: 10 minutes
Cooking Time: 4-10 hours
Ideal slow-cooker size: 5-qt.

1-lb. can Great Northern beans, drained
1-lb. can black beans, rinsed and drained
1-lb. can red kidney beans, drained
1-lb. can butter beans, drained
1½ cups ketchup
½ cup chopped onions
1 green pepper, chopped
1 lb. smoked sausage, cooked and cut into ½-inch slices
¼ cup brown sugar
2 garlic cloves, minced
1 tsp. Worcestershire sauce
½ tsp. dry mustard
½ tsp. Tabasco sauce

1. Combine all ingredients in slow cooker.

2. Cover. Cook on Low 9-10 hours, or on High 4-5 hours.

Mary Ellen's Three-Bean Dish

Mary Ellen Musser, Reinholds, PA

Makes 10-20 servings

Prep. Time: 20 minutes
Cooking Time: 4-6 hours
Ideal slow-cooker size: 7-qt.

10-oz. pkg. frozen lima
  beans, cooked
3 16-oz. cans baked beans
40-oz. can kidney beans,
  drained
1 lb. sausage links, browned
  and cut into pieces
½-lb. cooked ham, cubed
1 medium onion, chopped
8-oz. can tomato sauce
½ cup ketchup
¼ cup packed brown sugar
1 tsp. salt
½ tsp. pepper
½ tsp. prepared mustard

1. Combine lima beans,
baked beans, kidney beans,
sausage, and ham in slow
cooker.
2. In separate bowl,
combine onion, tomato sauce,
ketchup, brown sugar, salt,
pepper, and mustard and pour
into slow cooker. Mix gently.
3. Cover. Cook on Low 4-6
hours.

Sausage Bean Casserole

Juanita Marner, Shipshewana, IN

Makes 8 servings

Prep. Time: 20 minutes
Cooking Time: 2-4 hours
Ideal slow-cooker size: 5-qt.

1 lb. ground pork sausage
½ cup chopped onions
½ cup chopped green
  peppers
1 lb. cooked speckled
  butter beans
2 cups diced canned
  tomatoes
½ cup tomato sauce
¼ tsp. salt
⅛ tsp. pepper

1. Brown sausage, onions,
and green peppers in saucepan.
2. Combine all ingredients
in slow cooker.
3. Cover. Cook on High 2
hours, or on Low 4 hours.

Cajun Sausage and Beans

Melanie Thrower, McPherson, KS

Makes 4-6 servings

Prep. Time: 10 minutes
Cooking Time: 8 hours
Ideal slow-cooker size: 4-qt.

1 lb. smoked sausage, sliced
  into ¼-inch pieces
16-oz. can red beans
16-oz. can crushed
  tomatoes with green
  chilies
1 cup chopped celery
half an onion, chopped
2 Tbsp. Italian seasoning
Tabasco sauce to taste

1. Combine all ingredients
in slow cooker.
2. Cover. Cook on Low 8
hours.

Serving suggestion: Serve over
rice *or as a thick zesty soup.*

I often start the slow cooker on High until I'm ready for work, then switch it to Low as I go out the door. It may only be 45 minutes to 1 hour on High, but I feel it starts the cooking process faster, thus preserving flavor.

Evie Hershey, Atglen, PA

Sausage Bean Quickie

Ellen Ranck, Gap, PA

Makes 4 servings

Prep. Time: 10 minutes
Cooking Time: 1-10 hours
Ideal slow-cooker size: 3- to 4-qt.

4-6 cooked brown 'n' serve
   sausage links, cut into
   1-inch pieces
2 tsp. cider vinegar
2 16-oz. cans red kidney, *or*
   baked, beans, drained
7-oz. can pineapple chunks,
   undrained
2 tsp. brown sugar
3 Tbsp. flour

1. Combine sausage,
vinegar, beans, and pineapple
in slow cooker.

2. Combine brown sugar
with flour. Add to slow cooker.
Stir well.

3. Cover. Cook on Low 5-10
hours, or on High 1-2 hours.

Beans with Rice

Miriam Christophel, Battle Creek, MI

Makes 8 servings

Prep. Time: 10 minutes
Soaking Time: overnight
Prep. Time: 14-17 hours
Ideal slow-cooker size: 6-qt.

3 cups dried small red beans
8 cups water
3 garlic cloves, minced
1 large onion, chopped
8 cups fresh water
1-2 ham hocks
½-¾ cup ketchup
2 tsp. salt
pinch of pepper
1½-2 tsp. ground cumin
1 Tbsp. parsley
1-2 bay leaves

1. Soak beans overnight in
8 cups water. Drain. Place
soaked beans in slow cooker
with garlic, onion, 8 cups
fresh water, and ham hocks.

2. Cover. Cook on High
12-14 hours.

3. Take ham hocks out of
cooker and allow to cool.
Remove meat from bones. Cut
up and return to slow cooker.
Add remaining ingredients.

4. Cover. Cook on High 2-3
hours.

Serving suggestion: Serve over
***rice** with dollop of **sour cream**.*

Best Baked Beans

Nadine Martinitz, Salina, KS

Makes 8-10 servings

Prep Time: 15 minutes
Cooking Time: 2-6 hours
Ideal slow-cooker size: 6-qt.

8 strips bacon, diced
1 small onion, chopped
5 15-oz. cans pork and beans
2 Tbsp. Worcestershire sauce
⅓ cup brown sugar
½ cup molasses
½ cup ketchup
dash of ground cloves

1. Sauté bacon in skillet
until crisp. Remove bacon but
retain drippings in skillet.

2. Brown chopped onion in
drippings until translucent.

3. Combine all ingredients
in slow cooker. Stir well.

4. Cover. Cook on Low 5-6
hours, or on High 2-3 hours.

Nan's Barbecued Beans

Nan Decker, Albuquerque, NM

Makes 10-12 servings

Prep. Time: 20 minutes
Cooking Time: 4-6 hours
Ideal slow-cooker size: 3½-qt.

1 lb. ground beef
1 onion, chopped
5 cups canned baked beans
2 Tbsp. cider vinegar
1 Tbsp. Worcestershire sauce
2 Tbsp. brown sugar
½ cup ketchup

1. Brown ground beef and onion in skillet. Drain.
2. Combine all ingredients in slow cooker.
3. Cover. Cook on Low 4-6 hours.

Betty's Calico Beans

Betty Lahman, Elkton, VA

Makes 6-8 servings

Prep. Time: 15 minutes
Cooking Time: 3-4 hours
Ideal slow-cooker size: 5-qt.

1 lb. ground beef, browned and drained
14¾-oz. can lima beans
15½-oz. can pinto beans
15¼-oz. can corn

¼ cup brown sugar
1 cup ketchup
1 Tbsp. vinegar
2 tsp. prepared mustard
1 medium onion, chopped

1. Combine all ingredients in slow cooker.
2. Cover. Cook on High 3-4 hours.

Three-Bean Barbecue

Ruth Hofstetter, Versailles, MO,
Kathryn Yoder, Minot, ND

Makes 6-8 servings

Prep. Time: 25 minutes
Cooking Time: 4-6 hours
Ideal slow-cooker size: 5-qt.

1½-2 lbs. ground beef
¾ lb. bacon
1 cup chopped onions
2 31-oz. cans pork and beans
1-lb. can kidney beans, drained
1-lb. can lima beans, drained
1 cup ketchup
¼ cup brown sugar
1 Tbsp. liquid smoke
3 Tbsp. white vinegar
1 tsp. salt
dash of pepper

1. Brown beef in saucepan. Drain.
2. Fry bacon and onions in saucepan. Drain.
3. Combine all ingredients in slow cooker.

4. Cover. Cook on Low 4-6 hours.

Serving suggestion: This is good served with baked potatoes.

Carla's Baked Beans

Carla Koslowsky, Hillsboro, KS

Makes 8-10 servings

Prep. Time: 20 minutes
Cooking Time: 4-5 hours
Ideal slow-cooker size: 4-qt.

½ lb. ground beef
½ lb. bacon, chopped
1 medium onion, minced
1 tsp. salt
½ tsp. pepper
16-oz. can red kidney beans, drained
16-oz. can pork and beans, drained
15-oz. can butter, *or* green lima, beans
⅓ cup brown sugar
¼ cup sugar
¼ cup barbecue sauce
¼ cup ketchup
1 Tbsp. prepared mustard
2 Tbsp. molasses

1. Brown meats and onion in skillet. Drain.
2. Add salt, pepper, and beans. Stir in remaining ingredients. Mix well. Pour into slow cooker.
3. Cover. Cook on High 4-5 hours.

Five-Bean Hot Dish

Dede Peterson, Rapid City, SD
Judy Ann Govotsus, Frederick, MD

Makes 10 servings

Prep Time: 20 minutes
Cooking Time: 3-5 hours
Ideal slow-cooker size: 5- to 6-qt.

1 lb. ground beef
1 tsp. prepared mustard
2 tsp. vinegar
½ lb. bacon, finely diced
¾ cup brown sugar
15-oz. can lima beans, drained
1 tsp. salt
15-oz. can butter beans, drained
1 cup ketchup
16-oz. can kidney beans, drained
32-oz. can pork and beans, undrained
15-oz. can red beans, drained

1. Brown ground beef in skillet. Drain off drippings.
2. Spoon browned beef into slow cooker. Stir in mustard, vinegar, and bacon.
3. Stir in remaining ingredients. Mix well.
4. Cover. Cook on Low 3-5 hours.

Note:
These beans freeze well.

Variation:
Use a 15-oz. can garbanzo beans, drained, instead of lima beans or butter beans.

Judy Ann Govotsus, Frederick, MD

Casey's Beans

Cheryl Bartel, Hillsboro, KS

Makes 10-12 servings

Prep. Time: 20 minutes
Cooking Time: 5-6 hours
Ideal slow-cooker size: 5- to 6-qt.

½ lb. ground beef
10 slices bacon, diced
½ cup chopped onions
⅓ cup brown sugar
⅓ cup sugar, *optional*
¼ cup ketchup
¼ cup barbecue sauce
2 Tbsp. prepared mustard
2 Tbsp. molasses
½ tsp. salt
½ tsp. chili powder
½ tsp. pepper
1-lb. can kidney beans, drained
1-lb. can butter beans, drained
1-lb. can black beans, drained
1-lb. can pork and beans

1. Brown ground beef, bacon, and onion in deep saucepan. Drain.
2. Stir in remaining ingredients, except beans. Mix well. Stir in beans. Pour into slow cooker.
3. Cover. Cook on Low 5-6 hours.

Hearty Slow-Cooker Beans

Kim McEuen, Lincoln University, PA

Makes 10 servings

Prep. Time: 20 minutes
Cooking Time: 3-6 hours
Ideal slow-cooker size: 5-qt.

1 lb. ground beef
½ lb. bacon, diced
1 onion, chopped
16-oz. can red kidney beans, drained
15-oz. can butter beans, drained
15-oz. can pork and beans
15-oz. can hot chili beans
½ cup brown sugar
½ cup sugar
1 Tbsp. prepared mustard
1 Tbsp. cider vinegar
½ cup ketchup

1. Brown beef, bacon, and onion in skillet. Drain.
2. Combine all ingredients in slow cooker. Mix well.
3. Cover. Cook on High 3 hours, or on Low 5-6 hours.

Allen's Beans

John D. Allen, Rye, CO

Makes 10-12 servings

Prep. Time: 20 minutes
Cooking Time: 4-6 hours
Ideal slow-cooker size: 5-qt.

1 lb. ground beef, browned
1 large onion, chopped
15-oz. can pork and beans
15-oz. can ranch-style
  beans, drained
16-oz. can kidney beans,
  drained
1 cup ketchup
1 tsp. salt
1 Tbsp. prepared mustard
2 Tbsp. brown sugar
2 Tbsp. hickory-flavored
  barbecue sauce
½-1 lb. small smoky link
  sausages, *optional*

1. Brown ground beef
and onion in skillet. Drain.
Transfer to slow cooker set on
High.
2. Add remaining ingredi-
ents. Mix well.
3. Reduce heat to Low and
cook 4-6 hours. Use a paper
towel to absorb oil that's risen
to the top before stirring and
serving.

Crock-O-Beans

Nanci Keatley, Salem, OR

Makes 6 servings

Prep Time: 10-15 minutes
Cooking Time: 6 hours
Ideal slow-cooker size: 6-qt.

15-oz. can tomato purée
1 medium onion, chopped
2 cloves garlic, chopped
1 Tbsp. chili powder
1 Tbsp. oregano
1 Tbsp. cumin
1 Tbsp. parsley
1-2 tsp. hot sauce,
  depending upon your
  preference for heat
15-oz. can black beans,
  drained and rinsed
15-oz. can kidney beans,
  drained and rinsed
15-oz. can garbanzo beans,
  drained and rinsed
2 15-oz. cans baked beans
15-oz. can whole-kernel corn

1. Place tomato purée, onion,
garlic, and seasonings in slow
cooker. Stir together well.
2. Add each can of beans,
stirring well after each addition. Stir in corn.
3. Cover and cook on Low
6 hours.

Six-Bean Barbecued Beans

Gladys Longacre, Susquehanna, PA

Makes 15-18 servings

Prep. Time: 10-15 minutes
Cooking Time: 4-6 hours
Ideal slow-cooker size: 6-qt.

1-lb. can kidney beans,
  drained
1-lb. can pinto beans,
  drained
1-lb. can Great Northern
  beans, drained
1-lb. can butter beans,
  drained
1-lb. can navy beans,
  drained
1-lb. can pork and beans
¼ cup barbecue sauce
¼ cup prepared mustard
⅓ cup ketchup
1 small onion, chopped
1 small pepper, chopped
¼ cup molasses, *or*
  sorghum molasses
1 cup brown sugar

1. Mix together all ingredients in slow cooker.
2. Cook on Low 4-6 hours.

When you use a slow cooker for side dishes it frees up your stove top and oven. I have four slow cookers and use them all.

Colleen Heatwole, Burton, MI

Four-Bean Medley

Sharon Brubaker, Myerstown, PA

Makes 8 servings

Prep. Time: 15 minutes
Cooking Time: 6-8 hours
Ideal slow-cooker size: 4-qt.

8 bacon slices, diced and
  browned until crisp
2 medium onions, chopped
¾ cup brown sugar
½ cup vinegar
1 tsp. salt
1 tsp. dry mustard
½ tsp. garlic powder
16-oz. can baked beans,
  undrained
16-oz. can kidney beans,
  drained
15½-oz. can butter beans,
  drained
14½-oz. can green beans,
  drained
2 Tbsp. ketchup

1. Mix together all ingredients. Pour into slow cooker.
2. Cover. Cook on Low 6-8 hours.

Variation:
Make this a main dish by adding 1 lb. hamburger to the bacon, browning it along with the bacon and chopped onions in skillet, then adding that mixture to the rest of the ingredients before pouring into slow cooker.

Lauren's Calico Beans

Lauren Eberhard, Seneca, IL

Makes 12-16 servings

Prep. Time: 20 minutes
Cooking Time: 6-8 hours
Ideal slow-cooker size: 4-qt.

8 slices bacon
1 cup chopped onions
½ cup brown sugar
½ cup ketchup
2 Tbsp. vinegar
1 tsp. dry mustard
14½-oz. can green beans,
  drained
16-oz. can kidney beans,
  drained
15½-oz. can butter beans,
  drained
15½-oz. can pork and beans

1. Brown bacon in saucepan, reserving drippings. Crumble bacon. Cook onions in bacon drippings. Drain.
2. Combine all ingredients in slow cooker.
3. Cover. Cook on Low 6-8 hours.

Sweet and Sour Beans

Julette Leaman, Harrisonburg, VA

Makes 6-8 servings

Prep. Time: 30 minutes
Cooking Time: 3 hours
Ideal slow-cooker size: 4-qt.

10 slices bacon
4 medium onions, cut in rings
½-1 cup brown sugar,
  according to your
  preference
1 tsp. dry mustard
1 tsp. salt
¼ cup cider vinegar
1-lb. can green beans,
  drained
2 1-lb. cans butter beans,
  drained
27-oz. can pork and beans

1. Brown bacon in skillet and crumble. Drain all but 2 Tbsp. bacon drippings. Stir in onions, brown sugar, mustard, salt, and vinegar. Simmer 20 minutes.
2. Combine all ingredients in slow cooker.
3. Cover. Cook on Low 3 hours.

Don't have enough time? A lot of dishes can be made in less time by increasing the temperature to High and cooking the dish for about half the time as is necessary on Low.
Jenny R. Unternahrer, Wayland, IA

Mixed Slow-Cooker Beans

Carol Peachey, Lancaster, PA

Makes 6 servings

Prep. Time: 15 minutes
Cooking Time: 8-10 hours
Ideal slow-cooker size: 3½- to 4-qt.

16-oz. can kidney beans, drained
15½-oz. can baked beans
1 pint home-frozen, *or* 1-lb. pkg. frozen, lima beans
1 pint home-frozen, *or* 1-lb. pkg. frozen, green beans
4 slices bacon, browned and crumbled
½ cup ketchup
½ cup sugar
½ cup brown sugar
2 Tbsp. vinegar
salt to taste

1. Combine beans and bacon in slow cooker.
2. Stir together remaining ingredients. Add to beans and mix well.
3. Cover. Cook on Low 8-10 hours.

Lizzie's California Beans

Lizzie Weaver, Ephrata, PA

Makes 12 servings

Prep. Time: 30 minutes
Cooking Time: 2 hours
Ideal slow-cooker size: 4½-qt.

2 medium onions, cut in rings
1 cup brown sugar
1 tsp. dry mustard
1 tsp. salt
¼ cup vinegar
⅓ cup ketchup
1 lb. bacon, browned and crumbled
16-oz. can green beans, drained
40-oz. can butter beans, drained
2 16-oz. cans baked beans

1. In saucepan mix together onions, brown sugar, dry mustard, salt, vinegar, and ketchup. Simmer in covered pan for 20 minutes. Add bacon and beans.
2. Pour into slow cooker. Cover. Cook on High 2 hours.

Marcia's California Beans

Marcia S. Myer, Manheim, PA

Makes 10-12 servings

Prep. Time: 20 minutes
Cooking Time: 3 hours
Ideal slow-cooker size: 5-qt.

16-oz. can barbecue beans, *or* pork and beans
16-oz. can baked beans
16-oz. can kidney beans
14½-oz. can green beans
15-oz. can lima beans
15½-oz. can Great Northern beans
1 onion, chopped
1 tsp. prepared mustard
1 cup brown sugar
1 tsp. salt
¼ cup vinegar
½ lb. bacon, browned until crisp and crumbled

1. Drain juice from beans. Combine beans in slow cooker.
2. In saucepan, combine onion, mustard, brown sugar, salt, vinegar, and bacon. Simmer for 10 minutes. Pour sauce over beans.
3. Cover. Cook on Low 3 hours.

LeAnne's Calico Beans

LeAnne Nolt, Leola, PA

Makes 10 servings

Prep. Time: 20 minutes
Cooking Time: 2-6 hours
Ideal slow-cooker size: 4-qt.

¼-½ lb. bacon
1 lb. ground beef
1 medium onion, chopped
2-lb. can pork and beans
1-lb. can Great Northern
    beans, drained
14½-oz. can French-style
    green beans, drained
½ cup brown sugar
½ cup ketchup
½ tsp. salt
2 Tbsp. cider vinegar
1 Tbsp. prepared mustard

1. Brown bacon, ground beef, and onion in skillet until soft. Drain.
2. Combine all ingredients in slow cooker.
3. Cover. Cook on Low 5-6 hours, or on High 2-3 hours.

Mixed Bean Casserole

Margaret Rich, North Newton, KS

Makes 8 servings

Prep. Time: 10 minutes
Cooking Time: 7-8 hours
Ideal slow-cooker size: 4-qt.

3 slices bacon, cut up
2 Tbsp. grated onion
31-oz. can pork and beans
    in tomato sauce
16-oz. can kidney beans,
    drained
15-oz. can lima beans, *or*
    butter beans, drained
3 Tbsp. brown sugar, packed
½ tsp. dry mustard
3 Tbsp. ketchup

1. Combine all ingredients in slow cooker.
2. Cover. Cook on Low 7-8 hours.

Joan's Calico Beans

Joan Becker, Dodge City, KS

Makes 10-12 servings

Prep. Time: 20 minutes
Cooking Time: 3-5½ hours
Ideal slow-cooker size: 4-qt.

¼-⅓ lb. bacon, diced
½ cup chopped onions
2 16-oz. cans pork and
    beans
15-oz. can butter beans,
    drained
16-oz. can kidney beans,
    drained
½ cup packed brown sugar
½ cup ketchup
½ tsp. salt
1 tsp. dry mustard

1. Brown bacon in skillet until crisp. Drain, reserving 2 Tbsp. drippings. Cook onion in drippings until tender. Add bacon and onion to slow cooker.
2. Stir in beans, brown sugar, ketchup, salt, and mustard. Mix well.
3. Cover. Cook on Low 4½-5½ hours, or on High 3-3½ hours.

Barbara's Calico Beans

Barbara Kuhns, Millersburg, OH

Makes 12 servings

Prep. Time: 20 minutes
Cooking Time: 3-4 hours
Ideal slow-cooker size: 5-qt.

1 lb. bacon, diced
1 onion, chopped
½ cup ketchup
⅓-½ cup brown sugar, according to taste
3 Tbsp. cider vinegar
28-oz. can pork and beans, drained
16-oz. can kidney beans, drained
16-oz. can butter beans, drained

1. Brown bacon in skillet. Drain, reserving 2 Tbsp. drippings. Sauté onion in bacon drippings.
2. Mix together ketchup, sugar, and vinegar.
3. Combine all ingredients in slow cooker.
4. Cover. Cook on Low 3-4 hours.

Doris' Sweet-Sour Bean Trio

Doris Bachman, Putnam, IL

Makes 6-8 large servings

Prep. Time: 20 minutes
Cooking Time: 6-8 hours
Ideal slow-cooker size: 4-qt.

4 slices bacon
1 onion, chopped
¼ cup brown sugar
1 tsp. crushed garlic
1 tsp. salt
3 Tbsp. cider vinegar
1 tsp. dry mustard
1-lb. can lima beans, drained
1-lb. can baked beans, drained
1-lb. can kidney beans, drained

1. Cook bacon in skillet. Reserve 2 Tbsp. bacon drippings. Crumble bacon.
2. In slow cooker, combine bacon, bacon drippings, onion, brown sugar, garlic, salt, and vinegar. Add beans. Mix well.
3. Cover. Cook on Low 6-8 hours.

Carol's Calico Beans

Carol Sommers, Millersburg, OH

Makes 10-12 servings

Prep. Time: 20 minutes
Cooking Time: 4-6 hours
Ideal slow-cooker size: 5-qt.

½ lb. bacon, *or* ground beef
32-oz. can pork and beans
1-lb. can green limas, drained
16-oz. can kidney beans, drained
1-lb. can whole kernel corn, drained
1 tsp. prepared mustard
2 medium onions, chopped
¾ cup brown sugar
1 cup ketchup

1. Brown bacon or ground beef in skillet. Drain and crumble.
2. Combine beans, corn, and meat in slow cooker.
3. Combine mustard, onions, brown sugar, and ketchup. Pour over beans. Mix well.
4. Cover. Cook on Low 4-6 hours.

I spray the inside of my slow cooker with non-stick cooking spray before putting anything in it to make cleaning up a breeze.
Dot Hess, Willow Street, PA

Ethel's Calico Beans

Ethel Mumaw, Berlin, OH

Makes 6-8 servings

Prep. Time: 15 minutes
Cooking Time: 8 hours
Ideal slow-cooker size: 4-qt.

½ lb. ground beef
1 onion, chopped
½ lb. bacon, diced
½ cup ketchup
2 Tbsp. cider vinegar
½ cup brown sugar, packed
16-oz. can red kidney
  beans, drained
14½-oz. can pork and
  beans, undrained
15-oz. can butter beans,
  drained

1. Brown ground beef, onion, and bacon in skillet. Drain.
2. Combine all ingredients in slow cooker.
3. Cover. Cook on Low 8 hours.

Sara's Bean Casserole

Sara Harter Fredette, Williamsburg, MA

Makes 6 servings

Prep. Time: 10 minutes
Cooking Time: 2-4 hours
Ideal slow-cooker size: 3½-qt.

16-oz. can kidney beans,
  drained
2 1-lb. cans pork and beans
1 cup ketchup
1 Tbsp. Worcestershire sauce
1 tsp. salt
2 cups chopped onions
1 Tbsp. prepared mustard
1 tsp. cider vinegar

1. Combine all ingredients in slow cooker.
2. Cover. Cook on High 2 hours, or on Low 4 hours.

Main Dish Baked Beans

Sue Pennington, Bridgewater, VA

Makes 6-8 main-dish servings,
or 12-16 side-dish servings

Prep. Time: 15 minutes
Cooking Time: 4-8 hours
Ideal slow-cooker size: 5-qt.

1 lb. ground beef
28-oz. can baked beans
8-oz. can pineapple tidbits,
  drained
4½-oz. can sliced
  mushrooms, drained
1 large onion, chopped
1 large green pepper,
  chopped
½ cup barbecue sauce
2 Tbsp. soy sauce
1 clove garlic, minced
½ tsp. salt
¼ tsp. pepper

1. Brown ground beef in skillet. Drain. Place in slow cooker.
2. Stir in remaining ingredients. Mix well.
3. Cover. Cook on Low 4-8 hours, or until bubbly.

Serving suggestion: Serve in soup bowls.

Fruity Baked Bean Casserole

Elaine Unruh, Minneapolis, MN

Makes 6-8 servings

Prep. Time: 20 minutes
Cooking Time: 2-3 hours
Ideal slow-cooker size: 4-qt.

½ lb. bacon
3 medium onions, chopped
16-oz. can lima beans, drained
16-oz. can kidney beans, drained
2 16-oz. cans baked beans
15½-oz. can pineapple chunks
¼ cup brown sugar
¼ cup cider vinegar
¼ cup molasses
½ cup ketchup
2 Tbsp. prepared mustard
½ tsp. garlic salt
1 green pepper, chopped

1. Cook bacon in skillet. Crumble. Reserve 2 Tbsp. drippings in skillet. Place bacon in slow cooker.

2. Add onions to drippings and sauté until soft. Drain. Add to bacon in slow cooker.

3. Add beans and pineapple to cooker. Mix well.

4. Combine brown sugar, vinegar, molasses, ketchup, mustard, garlic salt, and green pepper. Mix well. Stir into mixture in slow cooker.

5. Cover. Cook on High 2-3 hours.

Apple Bean Bake

Barbara A. Yoder, Goshen, IN

Makes 10-12 servings

Prep. Time: 20 minutes
Cooking Time: 2-4 hours
Ideal slow-cooker size: 4- to 5-qt.

4 Tbsp. butter
2 large Granny Smith apples, cubed
½ cup brown sugar
¼ cup sugar
½ cup ketchup
1 tsp. cinnamon
1 Tbsp. molasses
1 tsp. salt
24-oz. can Great Northern beans, undrained
24-oz. can pinto beans, undrained
ham chunks, *optional*

1. Melt butter in skillet. Add apples and cook until tender.

2. Stir in brown sugar and sugar. Cook until they melt. Stir in ketchup, cinnamon, molasses, and salt.

3. Add beans and ham chunks. Mix well. Pour into slow cooker.

4. Cover. Cook on High 2-4 hours.

Apple-Bean Pot

Charlotte Bull, Cassville, MO

Makes 12 servings

Prep. Time: 15 minutes
Cooking Time: 3½-4½ hours
Ideal slow-cooker size: 4-qt.

53-oz. can baked beans, well drained
1 large onion, chopped
3 tart apples, peeled and chopped
½ cup ketchup, *or barbecue sauce*
½ cup firmly packed brown sugar
1 pkg. smoky cocktail sausages, *or chopped hot dogs, or chopped ham chunks, optional*

1. Place beans in slow cooker.

2. Add onions and apples. Mix well.

3. Stir in ketchup or barbecue sauce, brown sugar, and meat if you wish. Mix.

4. Cover. Heat on Low 3-4 hours, and then on High 30 minutes.

Be careful about adding liquids to food in a slow cooker. Foods have natural juices in them, and unlike oven cooking which is dry, food juices remain in the slow cooker as the food cooks. — Ann Sunday McDowell, Newtown, PA

Linda's Baked Beans

Linda Sluiter, Schererville, IN

Makes 12 servings

Prep. Time: 10 minutes
Cooking Time: 6 hours
Ideal slow-cooker size: 4½-qt.

16-oz. can red kidney
  beans, drained
15½-oz. can butter beans,
  drained
1-lb. can baked beans
¼ lb. Velveeta cheese, cubed
½ lb. bacon, diced
½ cup brown sugar
⅓ cup sugar
2 dashes Worcestershire
  sauce

1. Combine all ingredients
in slow cooker.
2. Cover. Cook on Low
6 hours. Do not stir until
nearly finished cooking.

Ann's Boston Baked Beans

Ann Driscoll, Albuquerque, MN

Makes 20 servings

Prep. Time: 15 minutes
Cooking Time: 6-8 hours
Ideal slow-cooker size: 6-qt.

1 cup raisins
2 small onions, diced
2 tart apples, diced
1 cup chili sauce
1 cup chopped ham, *or*
  crumbled bacon
2 31-oz. cans baked beans
3 tsp. dry mustard
½ cup sweet pickle relish

1. Mix together all ingredients.
2. Cover. Cook on Low
6-8 hours.

Herb Potato-Fish Bake

Barbara Sparks, Glen Burnie, MD

Makes 4 servings

Prep. Time: 20 minutes
Cooking Time: 1-2 hours
Ideal slow-cooker size: 4-qt.

10¾-oz. can cream of celery
  soup
½ cup water
1-lb. perch fillet, fresh, *or*
  thawed
2 cups cooked, diced
  potatoes, drained
¼ cup grated Parmesan
  cheese
1 Tbsp. chopped parsley
½ tsp. salt
½ tsp. dried basil
¼ tsp. dried oregano

1. Combine soup and water.
Pour half in slow cooker.
Spread fillet on top. Place
potatoes on fillet. Pour remaining
soup mix over top.
2. Combine cheese and
herbs. Sprinkle over ingredients
in slow cooker.
3. Cover. Cook on High 1-2
hours, being careful not to
overcook fish.

Vegetables do not overcook as they do when boiled on your range. Therefore, everything can go into the cooker at one time, with the exception of milk, sour cream, and cream, which should be added during the last hour.

Darlene Raber, Wellman, IA

Shrimp Jambalaya

Karen Ashworth, Duenweg, MO

Makes 6-8 servings

Prep. Time: 15 minutes
Cooking Time: 2¼ hours
Ideal slow-cooker size: 6-qt.

2 Tbsp. margarine
2 medium onions, chopped
2 green bell peppers,
   chopped
3 ribs celery, chopped
1 cup chopped cooked ham
2 garlic cloves, chopped
1½ cups minute rice
1½ cups beef broth
28-oz. can chopped tomatoes
2 Tbsp. chopped parsley
1 tsp. dried basil
½ tsp. dried thyme
¼ tsp. pepper
⅛ tsp. cayenne pepper
1 lb. shelled, deveined,
   medium-size shrimp

1. Melt margarine in slow cooker set on High. Add onions, peppers, celery, ham, and garlic. Cook 30 minutes.
2. Add rice. Cover and cook 15 minutes.
3. Add broth, tomatoes, 2 Tbsp. parsley, and remaining seasonings. Cover and cook on High 1 hour.
4. Add shrimp. Cook on High 30 minutes, or until liquid is absorbed.

*Serving suggestion: Garnish with 1 Tbsp. **parsley**.*

Jambalaya

Doris M. Coyle-Zipp, South Ozone Park, NY

Makes 5-6 servings

Prep. Time: 15 minutes
Cooking Time: 2¼- 3¾ hours
Ideal slow-cooker size: 5-qt.

3½-4-lb. roasting chicken,
   cut up
3 onions, diced
1 carrot, sliced
3-4 garlic cloves, minced
1 tsp. dried oregano
1 tsp. dried basil
1 tsp. salt
⅛ tsp. white pepper
14-oz. can crushed tomatoes
1 lb. shelled raw shrimp
2 cups cooked rice

1. Combine all ingredients except shrimp and rice in slow cooker.
2. Cover. Cook on Low 2-3½ hours, or until chicken is tender.
3. Add shrimp and rice.
4. Cover. Cook on High 15-20 minutes, or until shrimp are done.

Shrimp Marinara

Jan Mast, Lancaster, PA

Makes 4-5 servings

Prep Time: 10-15 minutes
Cooking Time: 6¼-7¼ hours
Ideal slow-cooker size: 4-qt.

6-oz. can tomato paste
2 Tbsp. dried parsley
1 clove garlic, minced
¼ tsp. pepper
½ tsp. dried basil
1 tsp. dried oregano
scant ½ tsp. salt
scant ½ tsp. garlic salt
28-oz. can diced tomatoes,
   divided
1 lb. cooked shrimp, peeled

1. In slow-cooker combine tomato paste, parsley, garlic, pepper, basil, oregano, salt, garlic salt, and half the can of diced tomatoes.
2. Cook on Low 6-7 hours.
3. Turn to High and add shrimp.
4. If you'd like the sauce to have more tomatoes, stir in remaining tomatoes from can.
5. Cover and cook an additional 15-20 minutes.

*Serving suggestion: Serve over cooked **spaghetti**, garnished with grated **Parmesan cheese** if you wish.*

Seafood Gumbo

Barbara Katrine Rose, Woodbridge, VA

Makes 10 servings

Prep. Time: 45 minutes
Cooking Time: 3-4 hours
Ideal slow-cooker size: 4- to 5-qt.

1 lb. okra, sliced
2 Tbsp. butter, melted
¼ cup butter, melted
¼ cup flour
1 bunch green onions, sliced
½ cup chopped celery
2 garlic cloves, minced
16-oz. can tomatoes and
    juice
1 bay leaf
1 Tbsp. chopped fresh
    parsley
1 fresh thyme sprig
1½ tsp. salt
½-1 tsp. red pepper
3-5 cups water, depending
    upon the consistency you
    like
1 lb. peeled and deveined
    fresh shrimp
½ lb. fresh crabmeat

1. Sauté okra in 2 Tbsp. butter until okra is lightly browned. Transfer to slow cooker.
2. Combine remaining butter and flour in skillet. Cook over medium heat, stirring constantly until roux is the color of chocolate, 20-25 minutes. Stir in green onions, celery, and garlic. Cook until vegetables are tender. Add to slow cooker.

Gently stir in remaining ingredients.
3. Cover. Cook on High 3-4 hours.

Serving suggestion: Serve over **rice.**

Seafood Medley

Susan Alexander, Baltimore, MD

Makes 10-12 servings

Prep. Time: 20 minutes
Cooking Time: 3-4 hours
Ideal slow-cooker size: 4-qt.

1 lb. shrimp, peeled and
    deveined
1 lb. crabmeat
1 lb. bay scallops
2 10¾-oz. cans cream of
    celery soup
2 soup cans milk
2 Tbsp. butter, melted
1 tsp. Old Bay seasoning
¼-½ tsp. salt
¼ tsp. pepper

1. Layer shrimp, crab, and scallops in slow cooker.
2. Combine soup and milk. Pour over seafood.
3. Mix together butter and spices and pour over top.
4. Cover. Cook on Low 3-4 hours.

Serving suggestion: Serve over **rice** *or* **noodles.**

Salmon Cheese Casserole

Wanda S. Curtin, Bradenton, FL

Makes 6 servings

Prep. Time: 5 minutes
Cooking Time: 3-4 hours
Ideal slow-cooker size: 2-qt.

14¾-oz. can salmon with
    liquid
4-oz. can mushrooms,
    drained
1½ cups bread crumbs
2 eggs, beaten
1 cup grated cheese
1 Tbsp. lemon juice
1 Tbsp. minced onion

1. Flake fish in bowl, removing bones. Stir in remaining ingredients. Pour into lightly greased slow cooker.
2. Cover. Cook on Low 3-4 hours.

Tuna Barbecue

Esther Martin, Ephrata, PA

Makes 4 servings

Prep. Time: 10 minutes
Cooking Time: 4-10 hours
Ideal slow-cooker size: 3- to 4-qt.

12-oz. can tuna, drained
2 cups tomato juice, have
   an additional ½ cup on
   standby, if needed
1 medium green pepper,
   finely chopped
2 Tbsp. onion flakes
2 Tbsp. Worcestershire sauce
3 Tbsp. vinegar
2 Tbsp. sugar
1 Tbsp. prepared mustard
1 rib celery, chopped
dash chili powder
½ tsp. cinnamon
dash of hot sauce, *optional*

1. Combine all ingredients
in slow cooker.
2. Cover. Cook on Low 8-10
hours, or on High 4-5 hours.
If mixture becomes too dry
while cooking, add ½ cup
tomato juice.

Serving suggestion: Serve on
buns.

Tuna Salad Casserole

Charlotte Fry, St. Charles, MO
Esther Becker, Gordonville, PA

Makes 4 servings

Prep. Time: 10 minutes
Cooking Time: 5-8 hours
Ideal slow-cooker size: 4-qt.

2 7-oz. cans tuna
10¾-oz. can cream of celery
   soup
3 hard-boiled eggs, chopped
½-1½ cups diced celery
½ cup diced onions
½ cup mayonnaise
¼ tsp. ground pepper
1½ cups crushed potato
   chips, *divided*

1. Combine all ingredients
except ¼ cup potato chips in
slow cooker. Top with remaining chips.
2. Cover. Cook on Low 5-8
hours.

Tempeh-Stuffed Peppers

Sara Harter Fredette, Williamsburg, MA

Makes 4 servings

Prep. Time: 20 minutes
Cooking Time: 3-8 hours
Ideal slow-cooker size: 5-qt.

4 oz. tempeh, cubed
1 garlic clove, minced
28-oz. can crushed
   tomatoes, *divided*
2 tsp. soy sauce
¼ cup chopped onions
1½ cups cooked rice
1½ cups shredded cheese
Tabasco sauce, *optional*
4 green, red, *or* yellow, bell
   peppers, tops removed
   and seeded
¼ cup shredded cheese

1. Steam tempeh 10 minutes
in saucepan. Mash in bowl
with the garlic, half the
tomatoes, and soy sauce.
2. Stir in onions, rice, 1½
cups cheese, and Tabasco
sauce. Stuff into peppers.
3. Place peppers in slow
cooker, 3 on the bottom and
one on top. Pour remaining
half of tomatoes over peppers.
4. Cover. Cook on Low 6-8
hours, or on High 3-4 hours.
Top with remaining cheese in
last 30 minutes.

*When using fresh herbs you may want to experiment
with the amounts to use, because the strength is enhanced in
the slow cooker, rather than becoming weaker.*
Annabelle Unternahrer, Shipshewana, IN

Tastes-Like-Chili-Rellenos

Roseann Wilson, Albuquerque, NM

Makes 6 servings

Prep. Time: 10 minutes
Cooking Time: 2-3 hours
Ideal slow-cooker size: 3-qt.

2 tsp. butter
2 4-oz. cans whole green chilies
½ lb. grated cheddar cheese
½ lb. grated Monterey Jack cheese
14½-oz. can stewed tomatoes
4 eggs
2 Tbsp. flour
¾ cup evaporated milk

1. Grease sides and bottom of slow cooker with butter.
2. Cut chilies into strips. Layer chilies and cheeses in slow cooker. Pour in stewed tomatoes.
3. Combine eggs, flour, and milk. Pour into slow cooker.
4. Cover. Cook on High 2-3 hours.

Barbecued Lentils

Sue Hamilton, Minooka, IL

Makes 8 servings

Prep. Time: 5 minutes
Cooking Time: 6-8 hours
Ideal slow-cooker size: 4-qt.

2 cups barbecue sauce
3½ cups water
1 lb. dry lentils
1 pkg. vegetarian hot dogs, sliced

1. Combine all ingredients in slow cooker.
2. Cover. Cook on Low 6-8 hours.

Cheryl's Macaroni and Cheese

Cheryl Bartel, Hillsboro, KS

Makes 6 servings

Prep. Time: 20 minutes
Cooking Time: 3-4 hours
Ideal slow-cooker size: 2½-qt.

8 oz. dry elbow macaroni, cooked
3-4 cups (about ¾ lb.) shredded sharp cheddar cheese, *divided*
13-oz. can evaporated milk

1½ cups milk
2 eggs
1 tsp. salt
¼ tsp. black pepper
chopped onion to taste

1. Combine all ingredients, except 1 cup cheese, in greased slow cooker. Sprinkle reserved cup of cheese over top.
2. Cover. Cook on Low 3-4 hours. Do not remove the lid or stir until the mixture has finished cooking.

Variation:

For some extra zest, add ½ tsp. dry mustard when combining all ingredients. Add thin slices of cheese to top of cooker mixture.

Dorothy M. Pittman, Pickens, SC

Macaroni and Cheese

Martha Hershey, Ronks, PA
Marcia S. Myer, Manheim, PA
LeAnne Nolt, Leola, PA
Ellen Ranck, Gap, PA
Mary Sommerfeld, Lancaster, PA
Kathryn Yoder, Minot, ND
Janie Steele, Moore, OK

Makes 6 servings

Prep Time: 30 minutes
Cooking Time: 3-4 hours
Ideal slow-cooker size: 4-qt.

8-oz. pkg. dry macaroni, cooked

2 Tbsp. oil
13-oz. can evaporated milk
(fat-free will work)
1½ cups milk
1 tsp. salt
3 cups (about ½ lb.)
shredded cheese: cheddar,
or American, *or* Velveeta,
or a combination
2-4 Tbsp. melted butter
2 Tbsp. onion, chopped fine
4 hot dogs, sliced, *optional*

1. In slow cooker, toss cooked macaroni in oil. Stir in remaining ingredients except hot dogs.

2. Cover. Cook on Low 2-3 hours.

3. Add hot dogs if you wish. Cover. Cook 1 hour longer on Low (whether you've added hot dogs or not).

Serving suggestion: If you wish, mix ½ cup bread crumbs and 2 Tbsp. melted butter together. Sprinkle over dish just before serving. Or top instead with crushed potato chips.

Variations:

1. Use 3 cups evaporated milk, instead of 13-oz. can evaporated milk and 1½ cups milk.

2. Add more onion, up to ¼ cup total, in Step 1.

3. Add ½ tsp. pepper in Step 1.

Stacy Petersheim, Mechanicsburg, PA
Sara Wilson, Blairstown, MO

Extra Cheesy Mac and Cheese

Karen Ceneviva, Seymour, CT
Wafi Brandt, Manheim, PA

Makes 8-10 servings

Prep Time: 30 minutes
Cooking Time: 4¼ hours
Ideal slow-cooker size: 5-qt.

16-oz. pkg. elbow macaroni, uncooked
½ stick (¼ cup) butter, melted
2 eggs, beaten
12-oz. can evaporated milk
10¾-oz. can condensed cheddar cheese soup
1 cup milk
¼ tsp. onion, *or* garlic, powder
¼ tsp. pepper
1 tsp. dry mustard
4 cups (16 oz.) cheddar cheese, shredded, *divided*

1. Cook macaroni according to pkg. directions. Drain and place in slow cooker. Stir in melted butter.

2. In a bowl combine eggs, evaporated milk, soup, milk, onion or garlic powder, pepper, dry mustard, and 3 cups cheese.

3. Pour over macaroni. Stir to combine.

4. Cover. Cook on Low 4 hours.

5. Sprinkle with remaining cheese. Cook 15 minutes longer, or until cheese is melted.

Serving suggestion: Sprinkle with ⅛ tsp. paprika just before serving.

Pot-Roasted Rabbit

Donna Treloar, Gaston, IN

Makes 4 servings

Prep. Time: 5-10 minutes
Cooking Time: 10-12 hours
Ideal slow-cooker size: 5-qt.

2 onions, sliced
4-5-lb. roasting rabbit
salt to taste
pepper to taste
1 garlic clove, sliced
2 bay leaves
1 whole clove
1 cup hot water
2 Tbsp. soy sauce
2 Tbsp. flour
½ cup cold water

1. Place onion in bottom of slow cooker.

2. Rub rabbit with salt and pepper. Insert garlic in cavity. Place rabbit in slow cooker.

3. Add bay leaves, clove, hot water, and soy sauce.

4. Cover. Cook on Low 10-12 hours.

5. Remove rabbit and thicken gravy by stirring 2 Tbsp. flour blended into ½ cup water into simmering juices in cooker. Continue stirring until gravy thickens.

Serving suggestion: Cut rabbit into serving-size pieces and serve with gravy.

Baked Lamb Shanks

Irma H. Schoen, Windsor, CT

Makes 4-6 servings

Prep. Time: 10 minutes
Cooking Time: 4-10 hours
Ideal slow-cooker size: 4-qt.

1 medium onion, thinly
   sliced
2 small carrots, cut in thin
   strips
1 rib celery, chopped
3 lamb shanks, cracked
1-2 cloves garlic, split
1½ tsp. salt
¼ tsp. pepper
1 tsp. dried oregano
1 tsp. dried thyme
2 bay leaves, crumbled
½ cup dry white wine
8-oz. can tomato sauce

1. Place onions, carrots, and celery in slow cooker.
2. Rub lamb with garlic and season with salt and pepper. Add to slow cooker.
3. Mix remaining ingredients together in separate bowl and add to meat and vegetables.
4. Cover. Cook on Low 8-10 hours, or on High 4-6 hours.

Herbed Lamb Stew

Jan Mast, Lancaster, PA

Makes 6 servings

Prep Time: 20-30 minutes
Cooking Time: 8¼-10¼ hours
Ideal slow-cooker size: 6-qt.

1½-2 lbs. lamb, cut into
   1- to 2-inch cubes
1 Tbsp. oil
2 medium onions, chopped
4 cups beef broth
3-4 medium potatoes,
   peeled and thinly sliced
½-1 tsp. salt, according to
   your taste preferences
¼ tsp. pepper
¼ tsp. celery seed
¼ tsp. marjoram
¼ tsp. thyme
10-oz. pkg. frozen peas
6 Tbsp. flour
½ cup cold water

1. Brown lamb cubes in skillet in oil over medium-high heat. Do in two batches so that cubes brown and don't just steam.
2. Transfer browned meat to slow cooker.
3. Add remaining ingredients except peas, flour, and water.
4. Cover. Cook on Low 8-10 hours, or just until meat is tender.
5. Stir in peas.
6. In a small bowl, dissolve flour in water. When smooth, stir into pot.
7. Cover. Turn cooker to High and cook an additional 15 to 20 minutes, or until broth thickens.

Lamb Rice

Nanci Keatley, Salem, OR

Makes 6 servings

Prep Time: 20 minutes
Cooking Time: 6-8 hours
Ideal slow-cooker size: 4-qt.

2 lbs. lamb shoulder meat
1 Tbsp. vegetable oil
1 cup pine nuts
2 cups long-grain basmati
   rice, uncooked
4 cups chicken stock
1 tsp. crushed allspice
1 tsp. salt
1 tsp. pepper

1. Cut lamb into ½-inch pieces.
2. Brown in oil in skillet, over medium-high heat, just until browned.
3. Add pine nuts to meat.
4. Cook 3-4 minutes.
5. Put all ingredients in slow cooker. Mix well.
6. Cover. Cook 6-8 hours on Low, or until rice and meat are tender but not overcooked or dry.

Note:
I learned to love this dish as I was growing up. We always eat it with dollops of plain yogurt.

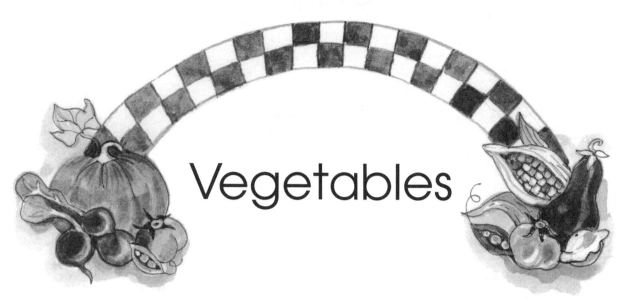

Vegetables

Very Special Spinach

Jeanette Oberholtzer, Manheim, PA

Makes 8 servings

Prep. Time: 10 minutes
Cooking Time: 5 hours
Ideal slow-cooker size: 4-qt.

3 10-oz. boxes frozen spinach, thawed and drained
2 cups cottage cheese
1½ cups grated cheddar cheese
3 eggs
¼ cup flour
1 tsp. salt
½ cup butter, *or* margarine, melted

1. Mix together all ingredients.
2. Pour into slow cooker.
3. Cook on High 1 hour.

Reduce heat to Low and cook 4 more hours.

Barbecued Green Beans

Arlene Wengerd, Millersburg, OH

Makes 4-6 servings

Prep. Time: 20 minutes
Cooking Time: 3-8 hours
Ideal slow-cooker size: 3- to 4-qt.

1 lb. bacon
¼ cup chopped onions
¾ cup ketchup
½ cup brown sugar
3 tsp. Worcestershire sauce
¾ tsp. salt
4 cups green beans

1. Brown bacon in skillet until crisp and then break into pieces. Reserve 2 Tbsp. bacon drippings.
2. Sauté onions in bacon drippings.
3. Combine ketchup, brown sugar, Worcestershire sauce, and salt. Stir into bacon and onions.
4. Pour mixture over green beans and mix lightly.
5. Pour into slow cooker and cook on High 3-4 hours, or on Low 6-8 hours.

If you're having guests, and those dinners that require last-minute attention drive you crazy, do your side-dish vegetables in your small slow cooker. They won't demand any of your attention until they're ready to be served.

Dutch Green Beans

Edwina Stoltzfus, Narvon, PA

Makes 4-6 servings

Prep. Time: 20 minutes
Cooking Time: 4½ hours
Ideal slow-cooker size: 4- to 5-qt.

½ lb. bacon, *or* ham chunks
4 medium onions, sliced
2 qts. fresh, *or* frozen, *or* canned, green beans
4 cups canned stewed tomatoes, *or* diced fresh tomatoes
½-¾ tsp. salt
¼ tsp. pepper

1. Brown bacon until crisp in skillet. Drain, reserving 2 Tbsp. drippings. Crumble bacon into small pieces.
2. Sauté onions in bacon drippings.
3. Combine all ingredients in slow cooker.
4. Cover. Cook on Low 4½ hours.

Orange Glazed Carrots

Cyndie Marrara, Port Matilda, PA

Makes 6 servings

Prep. Time: 5-10 minutes
Cooking Time: 3-4 hours
Ideal slow-cooker size: 3½-qt.

32-oz. (2 lbs.) pkg. baby carrots
½ cup packed brown sugar
½ cup orange juice
3 Tbsp. butter, *or* margarine
¾ tsp. cinnamon
¼ tsp. nutmeg
2 Tbsp. cornstarch
¼ cup water

1. Combine all ingredients except cornstarch and water in slow cooker.
2. Cover. Cook on Low 3-4 hours, until carrots are tender crisp.
3. Put carrots in serving dish and keep warm, reserving cooking juices. Put reserved juices in small saucepan. Bring to boil.
4. Mix cornstarch and water in small bowl until blended. Add to juices. Boil one minute or until thickened, stirring constantly.
5. Pour over carrots and serve.

Glazed Root Vegetable Medley

Teena Wagner, Waterloo, ON

Makes 6 servings

Prep. Time: 20 minutes
Cooking Time: 3 hours
Ideal slow-cooker size: 4-qt.

2 medium parsnips
4 medium carrots
1 turnip, about 4½ inches around
1 tsp. salt
½ cup water
½ cup sugar
3 Tbsp. butter
½ tsp. salt

1. Clean and peel vegetables. Cut in 1-inch pieces.
2. Dissolve 1 tsp. salt in water in saucepan. Add vegetables and boil for 10 minutes. Drain, reserving ½ cup liquid.
3. Place vegetables in slow cooker. Add liquid.
4. Stir in sugar, butter, and ½ tsp. salt.
5. Cover. Cook on Low 3 hours.

Caramelized Onions

Mrs. J. E. Barthold, Bethlehem, PA

Makes 6-8 servings

Prep. Time: 10 minutes
Cooking Time: 12 hours
Ideal slow-cooker size: 4-qt.

6-8 large Vidalia, *or* other sweet, onions
4 Tbsp. butter, *or* margarine
10-oz. can chicken, *or* vegetable, broth

1. Peel onions. Remove stems and root ends. Place in slow cooker.
2. Pour butter and broth over.
3. Cook on Low 12 hours.

Serving suggestion: Serve as a side dish, or use onions and liquid to flavor soups or stews, or as topping for pizza.

Acorn Squash

Valerie Hertzler, Weyers Cave, VA

Makes 2 servings

Prep. Time: 5 minutes
Cooking Time: 8-10 hours
Ideal slow-cooker size: 4- to 5-qt.

1 acorn squash
salt
cinnamon
butter

1. Place whole, rinsed squash in slow cooker.
2. Cover. Cook on Low 8-10 hours.
3. Split and remove seeds. Sprinkle each half with salt and cinnamon, dot with butter, and serve.

Zucchini Special

Louise Stackhouse, Benten, PA

Makes 4 servings

Prep. Time: 10 minutes
Cooking Time: 6-8 hours
Ideal slow-cooker size: 4-qt.

1 medium to large zucchini, peeled and sliced
1 medium onion, sliced
1 qt. stewed tomatoes with juice, *or* 2 14½-oz. cans stewed tomatoes with juice
¼ tsp. salt
1 tsp. dried basil
8 oz. mozzarella cheese, shredded

1. Layer zucchini, onion, and tomatoes in slow cooker.
2. Sprinkle with salt, basil, and cheese.
3. Cover. Cook on Low 6-8 hours.

Squash Casserole

Sharon Anders, Alburtis, PA

Makes 4-6 servings

Prep. Time: 15 minutes
Cooking Time: 7-9 hours
Ideal slow-cooker size: 4-qt.

2 lbs. yellow summer squash, *or* zucchini, thinly sliced (about 6 cups)
half a medium onion, chopped
1 cup peeled, shredded carrot
10¾-oz. can condensed cream of chicken soup
1 cup sour cream
¼ cup flour
8-oz. pkg. seasoned stuffing crumbs
½ cup butter, *or* margarine, melted

1. Combine squash, onion, carrots, and soup.
2. Mix together sour cream and flour. Stir into vegetables.
3. Toss stuffing mix with butter. Spread half in bottom of slow cooker. Add vegetable mixture. Top with remaining crumbs.
4. Cover. Cook on Low 7-9 hours.

To get maximum flavor from fresh herbs and spices, add them during the last 10 minutes of cooking time.

Doris' Broccoli and Cauliflower with Cheese

Doris G. Herr, Manheim, PA

Makes 8 servings

Prep. Time: 5 minutes
Cooking Time: 1½-3 hours
Ideal slow-cooker size: 3-qt.

1 lb. frozen cauliflower, chopped
2 10-oz. pkgs. frozen broccoli, chopped
½ cup water
2 cups shredded cheddar cheese

1. Place cauliflower and broccoli in slow cooker.
2. Add water. Top with cheese.
3. Cook on Low 1½-3 hours, depending upon how crunchy or soft you want the vegetables.

Golden Cauliflower

Carol Peachey, Lancaster, PA

Makes 4-6 servings

Prep. Time: 10 minutes
Cooking Time: 3½-5 hours
Ideal slow-cooker size: 3-qt.

2 10-oz. pkgs. frozen cauliflower, chopped, thawed
8-oz. jar cheese sauce
4 slices bacon, crisply browned and crumbled

1. Place cauliflower in slow cooker
2. Pour cheese over top. Top with bacon.
3. Cover. Cook on High 1½ hours and then reduce to Low for an additional 2 hours. Or cook only on Low 4-5 hours.

Broccoli Cheese Casserole

Janie Steele, Moore, OK

Makes 8-10 servings

Prep. Time: 10 minutes
Cooking Time: 1½ hours
Ideal slow-cooker size: 2-qt.

10-oz. pkg. frozen chopped broccoli, thawed
1 cup cooked rice

¼ cup chopped celery
10¾-oz. can cream of chicken soup
4-oz. jar cheese sauce
4-oz. can mushrooms, *optional*
⅛ tsp. garlic powder
⅛ tsp. pepper
¼-½ tsp. salt

1. Mix together all ingredients in slow cooker.
2. Cook on Low 1½ hours, or until heated through.

Sweet-Sour Cabbage

Irma H. Schoen, Windsor, CT

Makes 6 servings

Prep. Time: 20 minutes
Cooking Time: 3-5 hours
Ideal slow-cooker size: 6-qt.

1 medium-sized head red, *or* green, cabbage, shredded
2 onions, chopped
4 tart apples, pared, quartered
½ cup raisins
¼ cup lemon juice
¼ cup cider, *or* apple juice
3 Tbsp. honey
1 Tbsp. caraway seeds
⅛ tsp. allspice
½ tsp. salt

1. Combine all ingredients in slow cooker.

2. Cook on High 3-5 hours, depending upon how crunchy or soft you want the cabbage and onions.

Bavarian Cabbage

Joyce Shackelford, Green Bay, WI

Makes 4-8 servings, depending upon the size of the cabbage head

Prep. Time: 10 minutes
Cooking Time: 3-8 hours
Ideal slow-cooker size: 4-qt.

1 small head red cabbage, sliced
1 medium onion, chopped
3 tart apples, cored and quartered
2 tsp. salt
1 cup hot water
2 Tbsp. sugar
⅓ cup vinegar
3 Tbsp. bacon drippings

1. Place all ingredients in slow cooker in order listed.
2. Cover. Cook on Low 8 hours, or on High 3 hours. Stir well before serving.

Variation:
Add 6 slices bacon, browned until crisp and crumbled.
Jean M. Butzer, Batavia, NY

Vegetable Medley

Janie Steele, Moore, OK

Makes 6-8 servings
Prep Time: 25-30 minutes
Cooking Time: 1½-2 hours
Ideal slow-cooker size: 4-qt.

large raw potato, peeled and cut into small cubes
2 onions, chopped
2 carrots, sliced thin
¾ cup uncooked long-grain rice
2 Tbsp. lemon juice
⅓ cup, plus 2 Tbsp., olive oil
2 1-lb. cans diced tomatoes, *divided*
1 cup water, *divided*
large green pepper, chopped
2 zucchini squash, chopped
2 Tbsp. parsley, chopped
half a 1-lb. pkg. frozen green peas
1 Tbsp. salt
1 cup cheese, grated
hot sauce, *optional*

1. Combine potato, onions, carrots, rice, lemon juice, olive oil, 1 can of tomatoes, and ½ cup water in slow cooker.
2. Cover and cook on High 1 hour.
3. Stir in remaining ingredients—except grated cheese and hot sauce. Cover and cook 30-60 minutes, or until vegetables are tender but not mushy.

Serving suggestion: Serve in bowls, topped with grated **cheese**. *Pass* **hot sauce** *to be added individually.*

Vegetable Curry

Sheryl Shenk, Harrisonburg, VA

Makes 8-10 servings
Prep. Time: 15 minutes
Cooking Time: 3-10 hours
Ideal slow-cooker size: 4- to 5-qt.

16-oz. pkg. baby carrots
3 medium potatoes, cubed
1 lb. fresh, *or frozen*, green beans, cut in 2-inch pieces
1 green pepper, chopped
1 onion, chopped
1-2 cloves garlic, minced
15-oz. can garbanzo beans, drained
28-oz. can crushed tomatoes
3 Tbsp. minute tapioca
3 tsp. curry powder
2 tsp. salt
2 tsp. chicken bouillon granules, *or 2 chicken bouillon cubes*
1¾ cups boiling water

1. Combine carrots, potatoes, green beans, pepper, onion, garlic, garbanzo beans, and crushed tomatoes in large bowl.
2. Stir in tapioca, curry powder, and salt.
3. Dissolve bouillon in boiling water. Pour over vegetables. Mix well. Spoon into large cooker, or two medium-sized ones.
4. Cover. Cook on Low 8-10 hours, or on High 3-4 hours.

Serving suggestion: Serve with cooked **rice**.

Variation:
Substitute canned green beans for fresh beans but add toward the end of the cooking time.

293

Wild Mushrooms Italian

Connie Johnson, Loudon, NH

Makes 4-5 servings

Prep. Time: 20 minutes
Cooking Time: 6-8 hours
Ideal slow-cooker size: 5-qt.

---

2 large onions, chopped
3 large red bell peppers, chopped
3 large green bell peppers, chopped
2-3 Tbsp. oil
12-oz. pkg. oyster mushrooms, cleaned and chopped
4 garlic cloves, minced
3 fresh bay leaves
10 fresh basil leaves, chopped
1 Tbsp. salt
1½ tsp. pepper
28-oz. can Italian plum tomatoes, crushed, *or* chopped

1. Sauté onions and peppers in oil in skillet until soft. Stir in mushrooms and garlic. Sauté just until mushrooms begin to turn brown. Pour into slow cooker.
2. Add remaining ingredients. Stir well.
3. Cover. Cook on Low 6-8 hours.

*Serving suggestion: Serve as an appetizer with a spoon, or spread on **pita bread**. For a main dish, serve over **rice** or **pasta**.*

Corn on the Cob

Donna Conto, Saylorsburg, PA

Makes 3-4 servings

Prep. Time: 10 minutes
Cooking Time: 2-3 hours
Ideal slow-cooker size: 5- to 6-qt.

6-8 ears of corn (in husk)
½ cup water

1. Remove silk from corn, as much as possible, but leave husks on.
2. Cut off ends of corn so ears can stand in the cooker.
3. Add water.
4. Cover. Cook on Low 2-3 hours.

Cheesy Corn

Tina Snyder, Manheim, PA
Jeannine Janzen, Elbing, KS
Nadine Martinitz, Salina, KS

Makes 10 servings

Prep. Time: 5-7 minutes
Cooking Time: 4 hours
Ideal slow-cooker size: 4-qt.

---

3 16-oz. pkgs. frozen corn
8-oz. pkg. cream cheese, cubed
¼ cup butter, cubed
3 Tbsp. water
3 Tbsp. milk
2 Tbsp. sugar
6 slices American cheese, cut into squares

1. Combine all ingredients in slow cooker. Mix well.
2. Cover. Cook on Low 4 hours, or until heated through and the cheese is melted.

Corn Stuffing Balls

Jan Mast, Lancaster, PA

Makes 6-8 servings

Prep Time: 15 minutes
Cooking Time: 3-4 hours
Ideal slow-cooker size: 4- to 6-qt.

½ cup celery, chopped
1 Tbsp. celery leaves, chopped
1 small onion, diced
15-oz. can creamed corn
¼ cup milk
⅛ tsp. pepper
8-oz. pkg. herb stuffing cubes
2 eggs, slightly beaten
¼ cup butter, melted

1. Combine all ingredients except butter in a large bowl.
2. Shape into 6-8 balls and place in slow cooker.
3. Pour melted butter over balls.
4. Cover and cook on Low 3-4 hours.

Tip:
If you have trouble forming the stuffing into balls, add 2 Tbsp. milk, or just enough to allow the balls to hold their shape.

Slow-Cooker Rice

Dorothy Horst, Tiskilwa, IL

Makes 10 servings

Prep. Time: 5 minutes
Cooking Time: 2-3 hours
Ideal slow-cooker size: 5½-qt.

1 Tbsp. butter
4 cups converted long-grain rice, uncooked
10 cups water
4 tsp. salt

1. Pour rice, water, and salt into greased slow cooker.
2. Cover. Cook on High 2-3 hours, or until rice is tender, but not overcooked. Stir occasionally.

Wild Rice

Ruth S. Weaver, Reinholds, PA

Makes 4-5 servings

Prep. Time: 10 minutes
Cooking Time: 2½-3 hours
Ideal slow-cooker size: 3-qt.

1 cup wild rice, *or* wild rice mixture, uncooked
½ cup sliced mushrooms
½ cup diced onions
½ cup diced green, *or* red, peppers
1 Tbsp. oil
½ tsp. salt
¼ tsp. pepper
2½ cups chicken broth

1. Layer rice and vegetables in slow cooker. Pour oil, salt, and pepper over vegetables. Stir.
2. Heat chicken broth. Pour over ingredients in slow cooker.
3. Cover. Cook on High 2½-3 hours, or until rice is soft and liquid is absorbed.

Risi Bisi (Peas and Rice)

Cyndie Marrara, Port Matilda, PA

Makes 6 servings

Prep. Time: 10-15 minutes
Cooking Time: 2½-3½ hours
Ideal slow-cooker size: 4-qt.

1½ cups converted long-grain white rice, uncooked
¾ cup chopped onions
2 garlic cloves, minced
2 14½-oz. cans reduced-sodium chicken broth
⅓ cup water
¾ tsp. Italian seasoning
½ tsp. dried basil leaves
½ cup frozen baby peas, thawed
¼ cup grated Parmesan cheese

1. Combine rice, onions, and garlic in slow cooker.
2. In saucepan, mix together chicken broth and water. Bring to boil. Add Italian seasoning and basil leaves. Stir into rice mixture.
3. Cover. Cook on Low 2-3 hours, or until liquid is absorbed.
4. Stir in peas. Cover. Cook 30 minutes. Stir in cheese.

Green Rice Casserole

Ruth Hofstetter, Versailles, Missouri

Makes 6 servings

Prep. Time: 10-15 minutes
Cooking Time: 5-7 hours
Ideal slow-cooker size: 3½-qt.

1⅓ cups evaporated milk
2 Tbsp. vegetable oil
3 eggs
one-fourth of a small onion, minced
half a small carrot, minced, *optional*
2 cups minced fresh parsley, *or* 10-oz. pkg. frozen chopped spinach, thawed and drained
2 tsp. salt
¼ tsp. pepper
1 cup shredded sharp cheese
3 cups cooked long-grain rice

1. Beat together milk, oil, and eggs until well combined.
2. Stir in remaining ingredients. Mix well. Pour into greased slow cooker.
3. Cover. Cook on High 1 hour. Stir. Reduce heat to Low and cook 4-6 hours.

Butter-Rubbed Baked Potatoes

Lucille Metzler, Wellsboro, PA
Elizabeth Yutzy, Wauseon, OH
Glenda S. Weaver, Manheim, PA
Mary Jane Musser, Manheim, PA
Esther Becker, Gordonville, PA

Makes 6 servings

Prep. Time: 5 minutes
Cooking Time: 3-10 hours
Ideal slow-cooker size: 5-qt.

6 medium baking potatoes
butter, *or* **margarine**

1. Prick potatoes with fork. Rub each with either butter or margarine. Place in slow cooker.
2. Cover. Cook on High 3-5 hours, or on Low 6-10 hours.

Baked Potatoes in Foil

Valerie Hertzler, Weyers Cave, VA
Carol Peachey, Lancaster, PA
Janet L. Roggie, Lowville, NY

Prep. Time: 5 minutes
Cooking Time: 2½-10 hours
Ideal slow-cooker size: 4-qt.

potatoes

1. Prick potatoes with fork and wrap in foil.
2. Cover. Do not add water.

Cook on High 2½-4 hours, or on Low 8-10 hours.

Potluck Potatoes

Lovina Baer, Conrath, WI

Makes 6-8 servings

Prep. Time: 30 minutes
Cooking Time: 3-4 hours
Ideal slow-cooker size: 2½-qt.

4 cups potatoes, cooked, peeled, diced
10¾-oz. can cream of chicken soup
1 cup sour cream
1 cup shredded cheddar cheese
⅓ cup butter, *or* **margarine, melted**
¼ cup chopped onions
½ tsp. garlic salt
½ tsp. salt
½ tsp. pepper

1. Combine all ingredients in slow cooker. Mix well.
2. Cover. Cook on Low 3-4 hours.

Variations:
1. If you prefer soft onions, sauté in skillet in butter or margarine before combining with other ingredients.
Tracey Yohn, Harrisburg, PA

2. Add chopped ham or dried beef.

German Potato Salad

Lauren Eberhard, Seneca, IL

Makes 8 servings

Prep. Time: 30 minutes
Cooking Time: 4 hours
Ideal slow-cooker size: 3-qt.

6 slices bacon
¾ cup chopped onions
10¾-oz. can cream of chicken soup
¼ cup water
2 Tbsp. cider vinegar
½ tsp. sugar
pepper to taste
4 cups parboiled, cubed potatoes
parsley

1. Brown bacon in skillet and then crumble. Reserve 2 Tbsp. bacon drippings. Sauté onions in drippings.
2. Blend together soup, water, vinegar, sugar, and pepper. Add bacon and onions. Mix well.
3. Add potatoes and parsley. Mix well. Pour into slow cooker.
4. Cover. Cook on Low 4 hours.

Serving suggestion: Serve warm or at room temperature.

Potatoes O'Brien

Rebecca Meyerkorth, Wamego, KS

Makes 6 servings

Prep. Time: 10 minutes
Cooking Time: 4-5 hours
Ideal slow-cooker size: 4-qt.

32-oz. pkg. shredded
  potatoes
¼ cup chopped onions
¼ cup chopped green
  peppers
2 Tbsp. chopped pimento,
  optional
1 cup chopped ham, *optional*
¾ tsp. salt
¼ tsp. pepper
3 Tbsp. butter
3 Tbsp. flour
½ cup milk
10¾-oz. can cream of
  mushroom soup
1 cup shredded cheddar
  cheese, *divided*

1. Place potatoes, onions, green peppers, pimento, and ham in slow cooker. Sprinkle with salt and pepper.

2. Melt butter in saucepan. Stir in flour; then add half of milk. Stir rapidly to remove all lumps. Stir in remaining milk. Stir in mushroom soup and ½ cup cheese. Pour over potatoes.

3. Cover. Cook on Low 4-5 hours. Sprinkle remaining cheese on top about ½ hour before serving.

Slow-Cooker Scalloped Potatoes

Ruth S. Weaver, Reinholds, PA

Makes 10 servings

Prep. Time: 20 minutes
Cooking Time: 4-10 hours
Ideal slow-cooker size: 4-qt.

½ tsp. cream of tartar
1 cup water
8-10 medium potatoes,
  thinly sliced
half an onion, chopped
salt to taste
pepper to taste
1 cup grated American, *or*
  cheddar, cheese
10¾-oz. can cream of
  celery, *or* mushroom, *or*
  chicken, soup
1 tsp. paprika

1. Dissolve cream of tartar in water. Add potatoes and toss together. Drain.

2. Place half of potatoes in slow cooker. Sprinkle with onions, salt, pepper, and half of cheese.

3. Repeat with remaining potatoes and cheese.

4. Spoon soup over the top. Sprinkle with paprika.

5. Cover. Cook on Low 8-10 hours, or on High 4 hours.

Variations:

1. For thicker scalloped potatoes, sprinkle each layer of potatoes with 2 Tbsp. flour.
Ruth Hershey, Paradise, PA

2. Instead of sprinkling the layers of potatoes with grated cheese, place ¼ lb. Velveeta, or American, cheese slices over top during last 30 minutes of cooking.
Pat Bishop, Bedminster, PA
Mary Ellen Musser, Reinholds, PA
Annabelle Unternahrer, Shipshewana, IN

Saucy Scalloped Potatoes

Sue Pennington, Bridgewater, VA

Makes 4-6 servings

Prep. Time: 15 minutes
Cooking Time: 7-9 hours
Ideal slow-cooker size: 3½-qt.

4 cups peeled, thinly sliced
  potatoes
10¾-oz. can cream of celery,
  or mushroom, soup
12-oz. can evaporated milk
1 large onion, sliced
2 Tbsp. butter, *or* margarine
½ tsp. salt
¼ tsp. pepper
1½ cups chopped, fully
  cooked ham

1. Combine potatoes, soup, evaporated milk, onion, butter, salt, and pepper in slow cooker. Mix well.

2. Cover. Cook on High 1 hour. Stir in ham. Reduce to Low. Cook 6-8 hours, or until potatoes are tender.

Extra Good Mashed Potatoes

Zona Mae Bontrager, Kokomo, IN
Mary Jane Musser, Manheim, PA
Elsie Schlabach, Millersburg, OH
Carol Sommers, Millersburg, OH
Edwina Stoltzfus, Narvon, PA
Barbara Hershey, Lancaster, PA

Makes 12 servings

Prep. Time: 45 minutes
Cooking Time: 5-6 hours
Ideal slow-cooker size: 5- to 6-qt.

5 lbs. potatoes, peeled and cooked
2 cups milk, heated to scalding
2 Tbsp. butter, melted in hot milk
8-oz. pkg. fat-free cream cheese, softened
1½ cups fat-free sour cream
1 tsp. onion, *or* garlic, salt
1 tsp. salt
¼-½ tsp. pepper

1. Mash all ingredients together in a large mixing bowl until smooth.
2. Pour into slow cooker.
3. Cover. Cook on Low 4-6 hours, or until heated through.

Note:
These potatoes may be prepared 3-4 days in advance of serving and kept in the refrigerator until ready to use.

Variations:
1. Add 1½ cups shredded cheddar cheese to Step 1.
 Maricarol Magill, Freehold, NJ

2. Sprinkle with paprika before cooking.
 Pat Unternahrer, Wayland, IA

Potato Cheese Puff

Mary Sommerfeld, Lancaster, PA

Makes 10 servings

Prep. Time: 45 minutes
Cooking Time: 2½-4 hours
Ideal slow-cooker size: 4- to 5-qt.

12 medium potatoes, boiled and mashed
1 cup milk
6 Tbsp. butter
¾ tsp. salt
2¼ cups Velveeta cheese, cubed
2 eggs, beaten

1. Combine all ingredients. Pour into slow cooker.
2. Cover. Cook on High 2½ hours, or on Low 3-4 hours.

Pizza Potatoes

Margaret Wenger Johnson, Keezletown, VA

Makes 4-6 servings

Prep. Time: 15 minutes
Cooking Time: 6-10 hours
Ideal slow-cooker size: 4-qt.

6 medium potatoes, sliced
1 large onion, thinly sliced
2 Tbsp. olive oil
2 cups grated mozzarella cheese
2 oz. sliced pepperoni
1 tsp. salt
8-oz. can pizza sauce

1. Sauté potato and onion slices in oil in skillet until onions appear transparent. Drain well.
2. In slow cooker, combine potatoes, onions, cheese, pepperoni, and salt.
3. Pour pizza sauce over top.
4. Cover. Cook on Low 6-10 hours, or until potatoes are soft.

Creamy Red Potatoes

Mrs. J. E. Barthold, Bethlehem, PA

Makes 4-6 servings

Prep. Time: 10 minutes
Cooking Time: 8 hours
Ideal slow-cooker size: 4-qt.

2 lbs. small red potatoes, quartered
8-oz. pkg. cream cheese, softened
10¾-oz. can cream of potato soup
1 envelope dry Ranch salad dressing mix

1. Place potatoes in slow cooker.
2. Beat together cream cheese, soup, and salad dressing mix. Stir into potatoes.
3. Cover. Cook on Low 8 hours, or until potatoes are tender.

Creamy Hash Browns

Judy Buller, Bluffton, OH
Elaine Patton, West Middletown, PA
Melissa Raber, Millersburg, OH
Moreen Weaver, Bath, NY

Makes 14 servings

Prep. Time: 15 minutes
Cooking Time: 4-5 hours
Ideal slow-cooker size: 4- to 5-qt.

2-lb. pkg. frozen, shredded potatoes
2 cups (8 oz.) shredded sharp cheddar cheese
2 cups (1 pint) sour cream
10¾-oz. can cream of celery soup
10¾-oz. can cream of chicken soup
½-1 lb. bacon, cooked and crumbled

1 large onion, chopped
4 Tbsp. (¼ cup) butter, melted
¼ tsp. pepper

1. Place potatoes in slow cooker.
2. Combine remaining ingredients and pour over potatoes. Mix well.
3. Cover. Cook on Low 4-5 hours, or until potatoes are tender.

Cheesy Hash Brown Potatoes

Clarice Williams, Fairbank, IA

Makes 6-8 servings

Prep. Time: 10 minutes
Cooking Time: 4-4½ hours
Ideal slow-cooker size: 4-qt.

2 10¾-oz. cans cheddar cheese soup
1⅓ cups buttermilk
2 Tbsp. butter, *or* margarine, melted
½ tsp. seasoned salt
¼ tsp. garlic powder
¼ tsp. pepper
2-lb. pkg. frozen, cubed hash brown potatoes
¼ cup grated Parmesan cheese
1 tsp. paprika

1. Combine soup, buttermilk, butter, seasoned salt, garlic powder, and pepper in slow cooker. Mix well.

2. Stir in hash browns. Sprinkle with Parmesan cheese and paprika.
3. Cover. Cook on Low 4-4½ hours, or until potatoes are tender.

Slow-Cooker Cheese Potatoes

Bernice M. Wagner, Dodge City, KS,
Marilyn Yoder, Archbold, OH

Makes 6 servings

Prep. Time: 5 minutes
Cooking Time: 7 hours
Ideal slow-cooker size: 4-qt.

2-lb. pkg. frozen hash browns
10¾-oz. can cream of potato soup
10¾-oz. can cream of mushroom soup
8 oz. (2 cups) shredded cheddar cheese
1 cup grated Parmesan cheese
1 pint sour cream

1. Mix together all ingredients in slow cooker.
2. Cover. Cook on Low 7 hours.

Scalloped Taters

Sara Wilson, Blairstown, MD

Makes 6-8 servings

Prep. Time: 10 minutes
Cooking Time: 3-4 hours
Ideal slow-cooker size: 4-qt.

½ cup melted margarine
¼ cup dried onions
16-oz. pkg. frozen hash brown potatoes
10¾-oz. can cream of chicken soup
1½ cups milk
1 cup shredded cheddar cheese
⅛ tsp. black pepper
1 cup crushed cornflakes, *divided*

1. Stir together margarine, onions, potatoes, soup, milk, cheese, pepper, and ½ cup cornflakes. Pour into greased slow cooker. Top with remaining cornflakes.
2. Cover. Cook on High 3-4 hours.

Slow-Cooker Cottage Potatoes

Marjora Miller, Archbold, OH

Makes 10-12 servings

Prep. Time: 10 minutes
Cooking Time: 4 hours
Ideal slow-cooker size: 4-qt.

1 pint sour cream
10¾-oz. can cream of chicken soup
dash of pepper
2 cups Velveeta cheese, cubed
½ cup chopped onions
¾ tsp. salt
¼ tsp. pepper
2 lbs. frozen hash brown potatoes

1. Combine all ingredients except potatoes in large bowl. Then fold in potatoes. Spoon into slow cooker.
2. Cover. Cook on High 1½ hours, and then on Low 2½ hours.

Candied Sweet Potatoes

Julie Weaver, Reinholds, PA

Makes 8 servings

Prep. Time: 45 minutes
Cooking Time: 4 hours
Ideal slow-cooker size: 5-qt.

6-8 medium sweet potatoes
½ tsp. salt
¼ cup butter, *or* margarine, melted
20-oz. can crushed pineapples, undrained
¼ cup brown sugar
1 tsp. nutmeg
1 tsp. cinnamon

1. Cook sweet potatoes until soft. Peel. Slice and place in slow cooker.
2. Combine remaining ingredients. Pour over sweet potatoes.
3. Cover. Cook on High 4 hours.

It's quite convenient to use a slow cooker to cook potatoes for salads or for fried potatoes or as baked potatoes. Just fill the slow cooker with cleaned potatoes and cook all day until done. Darla Sathre, Baxter, MN

Potato Filling

Miriam Nolt, New Holland, PA

Makes 16-20 servings

Prep. Time: 40 minutes
Cooking Time: 3 hours
Ideal slow-cooker size: 10-qt.

1 cup celery, chopped fine
1 medium onion, minced
1 cup butter
2 15-oz. pkgs. bread cubes
6 eggs, beaten
1 qt. milk
1 qt. mashed potatoes
3 tsp. salt
2 pinches saffron
1 cup boiling water
1 tsp. pepper

1. Sauté celery and onion in butter in skillet for about 15 minutes.
2. Combine sautéed mixture with bread cubes. Stir in remaining ingredients. Add more milk if mixture isn't very moist.
3. Pour into large, or several medium-sized, slow cookers. Cook on High 3 hours, stirring up from bottom every hour or so to make sure the filling isn't sticking.

Slow-Cooker Stuffing with Poultry

Pat Unternahrer, Wayland, IA

Makes 18 servings

Prep. Time: 15 minutes
Cooking Time: 7-9 hours
Ideal slow-cooker size: 6- to 7-qt.

1 large loaf dried bread, cubed
1½-2 cups chopped cooked turkey, *or* chicken, meat and giblets
1 large onion, chopped
3 ribs celery with leaves, chopped
½ cup butter, melted
4 cups chicken broth
1 Tbsp. poultry seasoning
1 tsp. salt
4 eggs, beaten
½ tsp. pepper

1. Mix together all ingredients. Pour into slow cooker.
2. Cover and cook on High 1 hour, then reduce to Low 6-8 hours.

Fresh Herb Stuffing

Barbara J. Fabel, Wausau, WI

Makes 6-8 servings

Prep. Time: 25 minutes
Cooking Time: 4-5 hours
Ideal slow-cooker size: 6-qt.

2 onions, chopped
3 celery ribs, chopped
½ cup butter
½ cup chopped fresh parsley
1 Tbsp. chopped fresh rosemary
1 Tbsp. chopped fresh thyme
1 Tbsp. chopped fresh marjoram
1 Tbsp. chopped fresh sage
1 tsp. salt
½ tsp. freshly ground pepper
1 loaf stale sourdough bread, cut in 1-inch cubes
1½-2 cups chicken broth

1. Sauté onions and celery in butter in skillet for 10 minutes. Remove from heat and stir in fresh herbs and seasonings.
2. Place bread cubes in large bowl. Add onion/herb mixture. Add enough broth to moisten. Mix well. Turn into greased slow cooker.
3. Cover. Cook on High 1 hour. Reduce heat to Low and continue cooking 3-4 hours.

Moist Poultry Dressing

Virginia Bender, Dover, DE
Josie Boilman, Maumee, OH
Sharon Brubaker, Myerstown, PA
Joette Droz, Kalona, IA
Jacqueline Stefl, E. Bethany, NY

Makes 14 servings

Prep. Time: 25 minutes
Cooking Time: 5 hours
Ideal slow-cooker size: 5-qt.

2 4½-oz. cans sliced
   mushrooms, drained
4 celery ribs, chopped
   (about 2 cups)
2 medium onions, chopped
¼ cup minced fresh parsley
¼-¾ cup margarine
   (enough to flavor bread)
13 cups cubed day-old bread
1½ tsp. salt
1½ tsp. sage
1 tsp. poultry seasoning
1 tsp. dried thyme
½ tsp. pepper
2 eggs
1 *or* 2 14½-oz. cans chicken
   broth (enough to moisten
   bread)

1. In large skillet, sauté
mushrooms, celery, onions,
and parsley in margarine until
vegetables are tender.
2. Toss together bread
cubes, salt, sage, poultry
seasoning, thyme, and pepper.
Add mushroom mixture.
3. Combine eggs and broth
and add to bread mixture.
Mix well.
4. Pour into greased slow
cooker. Cook on Low 5 hours,
or until meat thermometer
reaches 160°.

Note:

This is a good way to free
up the oven when you're
making a turkey.

Variations:

1. Use 2 bags bread cubes
for stuffing. Make one mixed
bread (white and wheat) and
the other corn bread cubes.
2. Add ½ tsp. dried marjoram to Step 2.

   Arlene Miller, Hutchinson, KS

Slow-Cooker Stuffing

Dede Peterson, Rapid City, SD

Makes 10 servings

Prep. Time: 35-40 minutes
Cooking Time: 4 hours
Ideal slow-cooker size: 6-qt.

12 cups toasted bread
   crumbs, *or* dressing mix
1 lb. bulk sausage, browned
   and drained
¼-1 cup butter, *or*
   margarine (enough to
   flavor bread)
1 cup, *or* more, finely
   chopped onions
1 cup, *or* more, finely
   chopped celery
8-oz. can sliced mushrooms,
   with liquid
¼ cup chopped fresh
   parsley
2 tsp. poultry seasoning
   (omit if using dressing
   mix)
dash of pepper
½ tsp. salt
2 eggs, beaten
4 cups chicken stock

1. Combine bread crumbs
and sausage.
2. Melt butter in skillet.
Add onions and celery and
sauté until tender. Stir in
mushrooms and parsley. Add
seasonings. Pour over bread
crumbs and mix well.
3. Stir in eggs and chicken
stock.
4. Pour into slow cooker and
cook on High 1 hour, and on
Low an additional 3 hours.

Variations:

1. For a drier stuffing,
reduce the chicken stock
to 1½ cups (or 14½-oz. can
chicken broth) and eliminate
the sausage.
2. For a less spicy stuffing,
reduce the poultry seasoning
to ½ tsp.

   Dolores Metzler, Mechanicsburg, PA

3. Substitute 3½-4½ cups
cooked and diced giblets in
place of sausage. Add another
can mushrooms and 2 tsp.
sage in Step 2.

   Mrs. Don Martins, Fairbank, IA

Desserts

Bread Pudding with Vanilla Sauce

Winifred Ewy, Newton, KS
Helen King, Fairbank, IA
Elaine Patton, West Middletown, PA

Makes 6 servings

Prep. Time: 20 minutes
Cooking Time: 3-4 hours
Ideal slow-cooker size: 4-qt.

8 slices bread (raisin bread
   is especially good), cubed
4 eggs
2 cups milk
¼ cup sugar
¼ cup melted butter, *or*
   margarine
½ cup raisins (use only ¼ cup
   if using raisin bread)
½ tsp. cinnamon

Sauce:
2 Tbsp. butter, *or* margarine
2 Tbsp. flour
1 cup water
¾ cup sugar
1 tsp. vanilla

1. Place bread cubes in greased slow cooker.
2. Beat together eggs and milk. Stir in sugar, butter, raisins, and cinnamon. Pour over bread and stir.
3. Cover and cook on High 1 hour. Reduce heat to Low and cook 3-4 hours, or until thermometer reaches 160°.
4. Make sauce just before pudding is done baking. Begin by melting butter in saucepan. Stir in flour until smooth. Gradually add water, sugar, and vanilla. Bring to boil. Cook, stirring constantly for 2 minutes, or until thickened.

Serving suggestion: Serve sauce over warm bread pudding.

Variations:

1. Use dried cherries instead of raisins. Use cherry flavoring in sauce instead of vanilla.
    Char Hagnes, Montague, MI

2. Use ¼ tsp. ground cinnamon and ¼ tsp. ground nutmeg, instead of ½ tsp. ground cinnamon in pudding.

3. Use 8 cups day-old unfrosted cinnamon rolls instead of the bread.
    Beatrice Orgist, Richardson, TX

4. Use ½ tsp. vanilla and ¼ tsp. ground nutmeg instead of ½ tsp. cinnamon.
    Nanci Keatley, Salem, OR

When you use a slow cooker for side dishes and desserts it frees up your stove top and oven. I have four slow cookers and use them all.
Colleen Heatwole, Burton, MI

Old-Fashioned Rice Pudding

Ann Bender, Fort Defiance, VA
Gladys M. High, Ephrata, PA
Mrs. Don Martins, Fairbank, IA

Makes 6 servings

Prep. Time: 10 minutes
Cooking Time: 2-6 hours
Ideal slow-cooker size: 4-qt.

2½ cups cooked rice
1½ cups evaporated, *or* scalded, milk
⅔ cup brown, *or* white, sugar
1 Tbsp. soft butter
2 tsp. vanilla
½-1 tsp. nutmeg
1 egg, beaten
½-1 cup raisins

1. Mix together all ingredients. Pour into lightly greased slow cooker.

2. Cover and cook on High 2 hours, or on Low 4-6 hours. Stir after first hour.

Serving suggestion: Serve warm or cold.

Mama's Rice Pudding

Donna Barnitz, Jenks, OK
Shari Jensen, Fountain, CO

Makes 4-6 servings

Prep. Time: 5 minutes
Cooking Time: 6-7 hours
Ideal slow-cooker size: 4-qt.

½ cup white rice, uncooked
½ cup sugar
1 tsp. vanilla
1 tsp. lemon extract
1 cup plus 2 Tbsp. milk
1 tsp. butter
2 eggs, beaten
1 tsp. cinnamon
½ cup raisins
1 cup whipping cream, whipped
nutmeg

1. Combine all ingredients except whipped cream and nutmeg in slow cooker. Stir well.

2. Cover pot. Cook on Low 6-7 hours, until rice is tender and milk absorbed. Be sure to stir once every 2 hours during cooking.

3. Pour into bowl. Cover with plastic wrap and chill.

4. Before serving, fold in whipped cream and sprinkle with nutmeg.

Dolores' Rice Pudding

Dolores Metzler, Mechanicsburg, PA

Makes 8-10 servings

Prep. Time: 5-10 minutes
Cooking Time: 3½ hours
Ideal slow-cooker size: 5½-qt.

1 cup white uncooked rice
1 cup sugar
4 cups milk
3 eggs
1½ cups milk
2 tsp. vanilla
¼ tsp. salt
nutmeg, *or* cinnamon

1. In slow cooker, mix together rice, sugar, and 4 cups milk.

2. Cook on High 3 hours.

3. Beat together eggs, 1½ cups milk, vanilla, and salt. Add to slow cooker. Stir.

4. Cook on High 25-30 minutes.

5. Sprinkle with nutmeg or cinnamon.

Serving suggestion: Serve warm.

Slow-Cooker Tapioca

Nancy W. Huber, Green Park, PA

Makes 10-12 servings

Prep. Time: 5 minutes
Cooking Time: 3½ hours
Ideal slow-cooker size: 4½-qt.

2 quarts milk
1 cup small pearl tapioca
1-1½ cups sugar
4 eggs, beaten
1 tsp. vanilla

1. Combine milk, tapioca, and sugar in slow cooker. Cook on High 3 hours.
2. Mix together eggs, vanilla, and a little hot milk from slow cooker. Add to slow cooker. Cook on High 20 more minutes. Chill.

*Serving suggestion: Serve topped with **whipped cream** or **fruit** of choice.*

Tapioca Salad

Karen Ashworth, Duenweg, MO

Makes 10-12 servings

Prep. Time: 10 minutes
Cooking Time: 3 hours
Ideal slow-cooker size: 4½-qt.

10 Tbsp. large pearl tapioca
½ cup sugar to taste
dash salt
4 cups water
1 cup grapes, cut in half
1 cup crushed pineapple
1 cup whipped cream

1. Mix together tapioca, sugar, salt, and water in slow cooker.
2. Cook on High 3 hours, or until tapioca pearls are almost translucent.
3. Cool thoroughly in refrigerator.

4. Stir in remaining ingredients.

Serving suggestion: Serve cold.

Variation:
Add 1 small can mandarin oranges, drained, when adding rest of fruit.

Blushing Apple Tapioca

Julie Weaver, Reinholds, PA

Makes 8-10 servings

Prep. Time: 15-20 minutes
Cooking Time: 3-4 hours
Ideal slow-cooker size: 4-qt.

8-10 tart apples
½ cup sugar
4 Tbsp. minute tapioca
4 Tbsp. red cinnamon candy
½ cup water

1. Pare and core apples. Cut into eighths lengthwise and place in slow cooker.
2. Mix together sugar, tapioca, candy, and water. Pour over apples.
3. Cook on High 3-4 hours.

*Serving suggestion: Serve hot or cold. Top with **whipped cream**, if you wish.*

Marshmallow Applesauce Dessert

Marla Folkerts, Holland, OH

Makes 6-8 servings

Prep Time: 5 minutes
Cooking Time: 1½-4 hours
Ideal slow-cooker size: 4-qt.

4 cups applesauce
¼ tsp. allspice
½ tsp. cinnamon
2 cups mini-marshmallows

1. Spray slow cooker with nonfat cooking spray.
2. In the cooker, mix applesauce, allspice, and cinnamon together.
3. Sprinkle marshmallows on top.
4. Cook on Low 3-4 hours, or on High 1½-2 hours.

Serving suggestion: Serve warm from slow cooker.

Note:
This is delicious over ice cream and cake! We've even used it as a fondue for fruit!

Apple Topping

Donna Lantgen, Arvada, CO

Makes 6 servings

Prep Time: 10-12 minutes
Cooking Time: 6 hours
Ideal slow-cooker size: 6-qt.

6-8 cups apples, cored,
   peeled, and chopped
¼ cup brown sugar
1 cup apple cider
½ cup maple syrup

1. Put apples in slow cooker.
2. Mix brown sugar, apple cider, and maple syrup in a bowl.
3. Drizzle cider mixture over apples.
4. Cook 6 hours on Low.

Serving suggestion: This recipe is great on top of **vanilla ice cream** *or on* **waffles**.

Baked Apples with Raisins

Vera Schmucker, Goshen, IN
Connie B. Weaver, Bethlehem, PA

Makes 6-8 servings

Prep. Time: 20 minutes
Cooking Time: 2½-9 hours
Ideal slow-cooker size: 4-qt.

6-8 medium-sized baking
   apples, cored
2 Tbsp. raisins
¼ cup sugar, plus additional
   for sprinkling
1 tsp. cinnamon
1 Tbsp. butter
½ cup water

1. Remove top inch of peel from each apple.
2. Mix together raisins and sugar. Spoon into center of apples.
3. Sprinkle with additional sugar and dot with butter.
4. Place apples in slow cooker. Add water. Cover and cook on Low 7-9 hours, or on High 2½-3½ hours.

Raisin Nut-Stuffed Apples

Margaret Rich, North Newton, KS

Makes 6 servings

Prep. Time: 15 minutes
Cooking Time: 6-8 hours
Ideal slow-cooker size: 5-qt.

6 baking apples, cored
2 Tbsp. butter, *or*
   margarine, melted
¼ cup packed brown sugar
¾ cup raisins
3 Tbsp. chopped walnuts
½ cup water

1. Peel a strip around each apple about one-third of the way below the stem end to prevent splitting.
2. Mix together butter and brown sugar. Stir in raisins and walnuts. Stuff into apple cavities.
3. Place apples in slow cooker. Add water.
4. Cover and cook on Low 6-8 hours.

You can use a 2-lb. coffee can, 2 1-lb. coffee cans, 3 16-oz. vegetable cans, a 6-7 cup mold, or a 1½-2-quart baking dish for "baking" cakes in a slow cooker. Leave the cooker lid slightly open to let extra moisture escape.
Eleanor J. Ferreira, North Chelmsford, MA

Fruit/Nut Baked Apples

Cyndie Marrara, Port Matilda, PA

Makes 4 servings

Prep. Time: 25 minutes
Cooking Time: 1½-3 hours
Ideal slow-cooker size: 4-qt.

4 large firm baking apples
1 Tbsp. lemon juice
⅓ cup chopped dried apricots
⅓ cup chopped walnuts,
    or pecans
3 Tbsp. packed brown sugar
½ tsp. cinnamon
2 Tbsp. melted butter
½ cup water, *or* apple juice

1. Scoop out center of apples creating a cavity 1½ inches wide and stopping ½ inch from the bottom of each. Peel top of each apple down about 1 inch. Brush edges with lemon juice.

2. Mix together apricots, nuts, brown sugar, and cinnamon. Stir in butter. Spoon mixture evenly into apples.

3. Put ½ cup water or juice in bottom of slow cooker. Put 2 apples in bottom, and 2 apples above, but not squarely on top of other apples. Cover and cook on Low 1½-3 hours, or until tender.

Serving suggestion: Serve warm or at room temperature. Top each apple with a **pecan** *half, if desired.*

Caramel Apples

Elaine Patton, West Middletown, PA
Rhonda Lee Schmidt, Scranton, PA
Renee Shirk, Mount Joy, PA

Makes 4 servings

Prep. Time: 15 minutes
Cooking Time: 4-6 hours
Ideal slow-cooker size: 4-qt.

4 very large tart apples, cored
½ cup apple juice
8 Tbsp. brown sugar
12 hot cinnamon candies
4 Tbsp. butter, *or* margarine
8 caramel candies
¼ tsp. ground cinnamon

1. Remove ½-inch-wide strip of peel off the top of each apple and place apples in slow cooker.

2. Pour apple juice over apples.

3. Fill the center of each apple with 2 Tbsp. brown sugar, 3 hot cinnamon candies, 1 Tbsp. butter, or margarine, and 2 caramel candies. Sprinkle with cinnamon.

4. Cover and cook on Low 4-6 hours, or until tender.

Serving suggestion: Serve hot topped with **whipped cream**.

Golden Fruit Compote

Cindy Krestynick, Glen Lyon, PA,
Judi Manos, West Islip, NY

Makes 6-8 servings

Prep. Time: 5 minutes
Cooking Time: 6-8 hours
Ideal slow-cooker size: 2-qt.

29-oz. can peach, *or* pear,
    slices, undrained
½ cup dried apricots
¼ cup golden raisins
⅛ tsp. cinnamon
⅛ tsp. nutmeg
¾ cup orange juice

1. Combine undrained peach or pear slices, apricots, raisins, cinnamon, and nutmeg in slow cooker. Stir in orange juice. Completely immerse fruit in liquid.

2. Cover and cook on Low 6-8 hours.

Serving suggestion: Serve cold with **angel food**, *or* **pound, cake**, *or* **ice cream**. *Or serve warm as a side dish in the main meal.*

Variation:

If you prefer a thicker compote, mix together 2 Tbsp. cornstarch and ¼ cup cold water until smooth. Stir into hot fruit 15 minutes before end of cooking time. Stir until absorbed in juice.

Fruit Compote Dessert

Beatrice Orgish, Richardson, TX

Makes 8 servings

Prep. Time: 15 minutes
Cooking Time: 3-4 hours
Ideal slow-cooker size: 3½-qt.

2 medium tart apples, peeled
2 medium fresh peaches,
    peeled and cubed
2 cups unsweetened
    pineapple chunks
1¼ cups unsweetened
    pineapple juice
¼ cup honey
2¼-inch thick lemon slices
3½-inch cinnamon stick
1 medium firm banana,
    thinly sliced

1. Cut apples into ¼-inch slices and then in half horizontally. Place in slow cooker.
2. Add peaches, pineapple, pineapple juice, honey, lemon, and cinnamon. Cover and cook on Low 3-4 hours.
3. Stir in banana slices just before serving.

*Serving suggestion: Garnish with **whipped cream**, sliced **almonds**, and **maraschino cherries**, if you wish.*

Hot Curried Fruit Compote

Cathy Boshart, Lebanon, PA

Makes 12 servings

Prep. Time: 15 minutes
Cooking Time: 2 hours
Ideal slow-cooker size: 5-qt.

1-lb. can peach halves
1-lb. can pear halves
1-lb. can apricot halves
1-lb. can pineapple chunks
4 medium bananas, sliced
15 maraschino cherries
⅓ cup walnut halves
⅓ cup margarine
⅔ cup brown sugar
½ tsp. curry powder (or to
    taste)

1. Drain fruit. Pour canned fruit into slow cooker. Add bananas.
2. Scatter cherries and walnuts on top.
3. In skillet, melt margarine. Mix in sugar and curry powder. Pour over fruit.
4. Cook on Low 2 hours.

*Serving suggestion: Serve hot as a side dish to **beef**, **pork**, or **poultry**; serve warm as a dessert; or serve cold as a topping for **ice cream**.*

Scandinavian Fruit Soup

Willard E. Roth, Elkhart, IN

Makes 12 servings

Prep. Time: 5 minutes
Cooking Time: 8 hours
Ideal slow-cooker size: 4-qt.

1 cup dried apricots
1 cup dried sliced apples
1 cup dried pitted prunes
1 cup canned pitted red
    cherries
½ cup quick-cooking tapioca
1 cup grape juice, *or* red wine
3 cups water, *or* more
½ cup orange juice
¼ cup lemon juice
1 Tbsp. grated orange peel
½ cup brown sugar

1. Combine apricots, apples, prunes, cherries, tapioca, and grape juice in slow cooker. Cover with water.
2. Cook on Low for at least 8 hours.
3. Before serving, stir in remaining ingredients.

*Serving suggestion: Serve warm or cold, as a soup or dessert. Delicious served chilled over **vanilla ice cream** or **frozen yogurt**.*

Hot Fruit Compote

Sue Williams, Gulfport, MS

Makes 4-6 servings

Prep. Time: 5 minutes
Cooking Time: 3-8 hours
Ideal slow-cooker size: 4-qt.

1 lb. dried prunes
1⅓ cups dried apricots
13½-oz. can pineapple chunks, undrained
1-lb. can pitted dark sweet cherries, undrained
¼ cup dry white wine
2 cups water
1 cup sugar

1. Mix together all ingredients in slow cooker.
2. Cover and cook on Low 7-8 hours, or on High 3-4 hours.

Serving suggestion: Serve warm.

Fruit Medley

Angeline Lang, Greeley, CO

Makes 6-8 servings

Prep. Time: 10 minutes
Cooking Time: 2¼-3¼ hours
Ideal slow-cooker size: 2½-qt.

1½ lbs. mixed dried fruit
2½ cups water
1 cup sugar
1 Tbsp. honey
peel of half a lemon, cut into thin strips
⅛ tsp. nutmeg
1 cinnamon stick
3 Tbsp. cornstarch
¼ cup cold water
¼ cup Cointreau

1. Place dried fruit in slow cooker. Pour in water.
2. Stir in sugar, honey, lemon peel, nutmeg, and cinnamon.
3. Cover and cook on Low 2-3 hours. Turn cooker to High.
4. Mix cornstarch into water until smooth. Stir into fruit mixture. Cook on High 10 minutes, or until thickened.
5. Stir in Cointreau.

*Serving suggestion: Serve warm or chilled. Serve as a side dish with the main course, as a dessert on its own, or as a topping for **ice cream**.*

Rhubarb Sauce

Esther Porter, Minneapolis, MN

Makes 4-6 servings

Prep. Time: 10 minutes
Cooking Time: 4-5 hours
Ideal slow-cooker size: 1½-qt.

1½ lbs. rhubarb
⅛ tsp. salt
½ cup water
½-⅔ cup sugar

1. Cut rhubarb into ½-inch slices.
2. Combine all ingredients in slow cooker. Cook on Low 4-5 hours.

Serving suggestion: Serve chilled.

Variation:
Add 1 pint sliced strawberries about 30 minutes before removing from heat.

Chopping dried fruit can be difficult. Make it easier by spraying your kitchen scissors with nonstick cooking spray before chopping. Fruits won't stick to the blade.
Cyndie Marrara, Port Matilda, PA

Desserts

Strawberry Rhubarb Sauce

Tina Snyder, Manheim, PA

Makes 6-8 servings

Prep. Time: 10 minutes
Cooking Time: 6-7 hours
Ideal slow-cooker size: 3½-qt.

6 cups chopped rhubarb
1 cup sugar
1 cinnamon stick
½ cup white grape juice
2 cups sliced strawberries

1. Place rhubarb in slow cooker. Pour sugar over rhubarb. Add cinnamon stick and grape juice. Stir well.
2. Cover and cook on Low 5-6 hours, or until rhubarb is tender.
3. Stir in strawberries. Cook 1 hour longer.
4. Remove cinnamon stick. Chill.

*Serving suggestion: Serve over **cake** or **ice cream**.*

Chunky Applesauce

Joan Becker, Dodge City, KS
Rosanne Hankins, Stevensville, MD

Makes 8-10 servings

Prep. Time: 10 minutes
Cooking Time: 3-10 hours
Ideal slow-cooker size: 4-qt.

8 apples, peeled, cored, and cut into chunks *or* slices (6 cups)
1 tsp. cinnamon
½ cup water
½-1 cup sugar, *or* cinnamon red hot candies

1. Combine all ingredients in slow cooker.
2. Cook on Low 8-10 hours, or on High 3-4 hours.

Quick Yummy Peaches

Willard E. Roth, Elkhart, IN

Makes 6 servings

Prep. Time: 10 minutes
Cooking Time: 5 hours
Ideal slow-cooker size: 3½-qt.

⅓ cup buttermilk baking mix
⅔ cup dry quick oats
½ cup brown sugar
1 tsp. cinnamon

4 cups sliced peaches (canned *or* fresh)
½ cup peach juice, *or* water

1. Mix together baking mix, oats, brown sugar, and cinnamon in greased slow cooker.
2. Stir in peaches and peach juice.
3. Cook on Low for at least 5 hours. (If you like a drier cobbler, remove lid for last 15-30 minutes of cooking.)

*Serving suggestion: Serve with **frozen yogurt** or **ice cream**.*

Scalloped Pineapples

Shirley Hinh, Wayland, IA

Makes 8 servings

Prep. Time: 10 minutes
Cooking Time: 3 hours
Ideal slow-cooker size: 4-qt.

2 cups sugar
3 eggs
¾ cup butter, melted
¾ cup milk
1 large can crushed pineapple, drained
8 slices bread (crusts removed), cubed

1. Mix together all ingredients in slow cooker.
2. Cook on High 2 hours. Reduce heat to Low and cook 1 more hour.

*Serving suggestion: Delicious served as a side dish to **ham** or **poultry**, or as a dessert served warm or cold. Eat hot or chilled with **vanilla ice cream** or **frozen yogurt**.*

Black and Blue Cobbler

Renee Shirk, Mount Joy, PA

Makes 6 servings

Prep. Time: 20 minutes
Cooking Time: 2-2½ hours
Ideal slow-cooker size: 5-qt.

---

1 cup flour
¾ cup sugar
1 tsp. baking powder
¼ tsp. salt
¼ tsp. ground cinnamon
¼ tsp. ground nutmeg
2 eggs, beaten
2 Tbsp. milk
2 Tbsp. vegetable oil
2 cups fresh, *or* frozen, blueberries
2 cups fresh, *or* frozen, blackberries
¾ cup water
1 tsp. grated orange peel
¾ cup sugar

1. Combine flour, ¾ cup sugar, baking powder, salt, cinnamon, and nutmeg.
2. Combine eggs, milk, and oil. Stir into dry ingredients until moistened.
3. Spread the batter evenly over bottom of greased slow cooker.
4. In saucepan, combine berries, water, orange peel, and ¾ cup sugar. Bring to boil. Remove from heat and pour over batter. Cover.
5. Cook on High 2-2½ hours, or until toothpick inserted into batter comes out clean. Turn off cooker.
6. Uncover and let stand 30 minutes before serving.

*Serving suggestion: Spoon from cooker and serve with **whipped topping** or **ice cream** if desired.*

Cranberry Pudding

Margaret Wheeler, North Bend, OR

Makes 8-10 servings

Prep. Time: 20 minutes
Cooking Time: 3-4 hours
Ideal slow-cooker size: 4- to 5-qt.

Pudding:
1⅓ cups flour
½ tsp. salt
2 tsp. baking soda
⅓ cup boiling water
½ cup dark molasses
2 cups whole cranberries
½ cup chopped nuts
½ cup water

Butter Sauce:
1 cup confectioners sugar
½ cup heavy cream, *or* evaporated milk
½ cup butter
1 tsp. vanilla

1. Mix together flour and salt.
2. Dissolve soda in boiling water. Add to flour and salt.
3. Stir in molasses. Blend well.
4. Fold in cranberries and nuts.
5. Pour into well-greased and floured bread or cake pan that will fit in your cooker. Cover with greased tin foil.
6. Pour ½ cup water into cooker. Place foil-covered pan in cooker. Cover with cooker lid and steam on High 3-4 hours, or until pudding tests done with a wooden pick.
7. Remove pan and uncover. Let stand 5 minutes, then unmold.
8. To make butter sauce, mix together all ingredients in saucepan. Cook, stirring over medium heat until sugar dissolves.

Serving suggestion: Serve warm butter sauce over warm cranberry pudding.

Apple Caramel Pie

Sue Hamilton, Minooka, IL

Makes 8-10 servings

Prep Time: 5 minutes
Cooking Time: 3 hours
Ideal slow-cooker size: 4- to 5-qt.

2-crust refrigerated pie
  dough pkg.
2 22-oz. cans apple pie
  filling
1 tsp. cinnamon
12 caramel candies

1. Press one crust into half the bottom of a cold slow cooker, and an inch or so up half its interior side. Overlap by ¼ inch the second crust with the first crust in center of slow cooker bottom. Press remainder of second crust an inch or so up the remaining side of the cooker. Press seams flat where two crusts meet.

2. Cover. Cook on High 1½ hours.

3. In a bowl, mix together pie filling, cinnamon, and caramels.

4. Pour mixture into hot crust.

5. Cover. Cook on High an additional 1½ hours.

Slow-Cooker Pumpkin Pie Pudding

Joette Droz, Kalona, IA

Makes 4-6 servings

Prep. Time: 5-7 minutes
Cooking Time: 6-7 hours
Ideal slow-cooker size: 3-qt.

15-oz. can solid pack
  pumpkin
12-oz. can evaporated milk
¾ cup sugar
½ cup buttermilk baking mix
2 eggs, beaten
2 Tbsp. melted butter, *or*
  margarine
1 Tbsp. pumpkin pie spice
2 tsp. vanilla

1. Mix together all ingredients. Pour into greased slow cooker.

2. Cover and cook on Low 6-7 hours, or until thermometer reads 160°.

*Serving suggestion: Serve in bowls topped with **whipped cream.***

Lemon Pudding Cake

Jean Butzer, Batavia, NY

Makes 5-6 servings

Prep. Time: 15 minutes
Cooking Time: 2-3 hours
Ideal slow-cooker size: 3- to 4-qt.

3 eggs, separated
1 tsp. grated lemon peel
¼ cup lemon juice
3 Tbsp. melted butter
1½ cups milk
¾ cup sugar
¼ cup flour
⅛ tsp. salt

1. Beat egg whites until stiff peaks form. Set aside.

2. Beat egg yolks. Blend in lemon peel, lemon juice, butter, and milk.

3. In separate bowl, combine sugar, flour, and salt. Add to egg-lemon mixture, beating until smooth.

4. Fold into beaten egg whites.

5. Spoon into slow cooker.

6. Cover and cook on High 2-3 hours.

Serving suggestion: Serve with spoon from cooker.

Apple Cake

Esther Becker, Gordonville, PA
Wanda S. Curtin, Bradenton, FL

Makes 8-10 servings

Prep. Time: 15 minutes
Cooking Time: 3½-4 hours
Ideal slow-cooker size: 4- to 5-qt.

2 cups sugar
1 cup oil
2 eggs
1 tsp. vanilla
2 cups chopped apples
2 cups flour
1 tsp. salt
1 tsp. baking soda
1 tsp. nutmeg
1 cup chopped walnuts, *or* pecans

1. Beat together sugar, oil, and eggs. Add vanilla.
2. Add apples. Mix well.
3. Sift together flour, salt, baking soda, and nutmeg. Add dry ingredients and nuts to apple mixture. Stir well.
4. Pour batter into greased and floured bread or cake pan that fits into your slow cooker. Cover with pan's lid, or greased tin foil. Place pan in slow cooker. Cover cooker.
5. Bake on High 3½-4 hours. Let cake stand in pan for 5 minutes after removing from slow cooker.

Serving suggestion: Remove cake from pan, slice, and serve.

Apple Peanut Crumble

Phyllis Attig, Reynolds, IL
Joan Becker, Dodge City, KS
Pam Hochstedler, Kalona, IA

Makes 4-5 servings

Prep. Time: 10 minutes
Cooking Time: 5-6 hours
Ideal slow-cooker size: 4-qt.

4-5 cooking apples, peeled and sliced
⅔ cup packed brown sugar
½ cup flour
½ cup quick-cooking dry oats
½ tsp. cinnamon
¼-½ tsp. nutmeg
⅓ cup butter, softened
2 Tbsp. peanut butter

1. Place apple slices in slow cooker.
2. Combine brown sugar, flour, oats, cinnamon, and nutmeg.
3. Cut in butter and peanut butter. Sprinkle over apples.
4. Cover cooker and cook on Low 5-6 hours.

*Serving suggestion: Serve warm or cold, plain or with **ice cream** or **whipped cream**.*

Harvey Wallbanger Cake

Roseann Wilson, Albuquerque, NM

Makes 8 servings

Prep. Time: 10 minutes
Cooking Time: 2½-3½ hours
Ideal slow-cooker size: 4- to 5-qt.

Cake:
16-oz. pkg. pound cake mix
⅓ cup vanilla instant pudding (reserve rest of pudding from 3-oz. pkg. for glaze)
¼ cup salad oil
3 eggs
2 Tbsp. Galliano liqueur
⅔ cup orange juice

Glaze:
remaining pudding mix
⅔ cup orange juice
1 Tbsp. Galliano liqueur

1. Mix together all ingredients for cake. Beat for 3 minutes. Pour batter into greased and floured bread or cake pan that will fit into your slow cooker. Cover pan.
2. Bake in covered slow cooker on High 2½-3½ hours.
3. Invert cake onto serving platter.
4. Mix together glaze ingredients. Spoon over cake.

A slow cooker provides enough warmth to raise a dough.

Donna Barnitz, Jenks, OK

Cherry Delight

Anna Musser, Manheim, PA
Marianne J. Troyer, Millersburg, OH

Makes 10-12 servings

Prep. Time: 5 minutes
Cooking Time: 2-4 hours
Ideal slow-cooker size: 2½-qt.

21-oz. can cherry pie filling
1 pkg. yellow cake mix
½ cup butter, melted
⅓ cup walnuts, *optional*

1. Place pie filling in greased slow cooker.
2. Combine dry cake mix and butter (mixture will be crumbly). Sprinkle over filling. Sprinkle with walnuts.
3. Cover and cook on Low 4 hours, or on High 2 hours.

*Serving suggestion: Allow to cool, then serve in bowls with dips of **ice cream**.*

Note:

For a less rich, less sweet dessert, use only half the cake mix and only ¼ cup butter, melted.

Chocolate Fondue

Eleanor J. Ferreira, North Chelmsford, MA

Makes 6 servings

Prep. Time: 5 minutes
Cooking Time: 1-1½ hours
Ideal slow-cooker size: 2-qt.

1 pkg. (8 squares) semisweet chocolate
4-oz. pkg. sweet cooking chocolate
¾ cup sweetened condensed milk
¼ cup sugar
2 Tbsp. kirsch

1. Break both chocolates into pieces and place in cooker. Set cooker to High and stir chocolate constantly until it melts.
2. Turn cooker to Low and stir in milk and sugar. Stir until thoroughly blended.
3. Stir in kirsch. Cover and cook on Low until fondue comes to a very gentle simmer.

*Serving suggestion: Bring fondue to table, along with fresh **cherries** with stems and **sponge cake** squares to dip into it.*

Hot Fudge Cake

Maricarol Magill, Freehold, NJ

Makes 6-8 servings

Prep. Time: 10 minutes
Cooking Time: 2-3 hours
Ideal slow-cooker size: 3½-qt.

1 cup packed brown sugar
1 cup flour
3 Tbsp. unsweetened cocoa powder
2 tsp. baking powder
½ tsp. salt
½ cup milk
2 Tbsp. melted butter
½ tsp. vanilla
¾ cup packed brown sugar
¼ cup unsweetened cocoa powder
1¾ cups boiling water

1. Mix together 1 cup brown sugar, flour, 3 Tbsp. cocoa, baking powder, and salt.
2. Stir in milk, butter, and vanilla. Spread over the bottom of slow cooker.
3. Mix together ¾ cup brown sugar and ¼ cup cocoa. Sprinkle over mixture in slow cooker.
4. Pour in boiling water. Do not stir.
5. Cover and cook on High 2-3 hours, or until a toothpick inserted comes out clean.

*Serving suggestion: Serve warm with **vanilla ice cream**.*

Self-Frosting Fudge Cake

Mary Puterbaugh, Elwood, IN

Makes 8-10 servings

Prep. Time: 10 minutes
Cooking Time: 2-3 hours
Ideal slow-cooker size: 4- to 5-qt.

2½ cups of 18½-oz. pkg. chocolate fudge pudding cake mix
2 eggs
¾ cup water
3 Tbsp. oil
⅓ cup pecan halves
¼ cup chocolate syrup
¼ cup warm water
3 Tbsp. sugar

1. Combine cake mix, eggs, ¾ cup water, and oil in electric mixer bowl. Beat 2 minutes.
2. Pour into greased and floured bread or cake pan that will fit into your slow cooker.
3. Sprinkle nuts over mixture.
4. Blend together chocolate syrup, ¼ cup water, and sugar. Spoon over batter.
5. Cover. Bake on High 2-3 hours.

Serving suggestion: Serve warm from slow cooker.

Chocolate Pudding Cake

Lee Ann Hazlett, Freeport, IL
Della Yoder, Kalona, IA

Makes 10-12 servings

Prep. Time: 5-10 minutes
Cooking Time: 3-7 hours
Ideal slow-cooker size: 4-qt.

18½-oz. pkg. chocolate cake mix
3.9-oz. pkg. instant chocolate pudding mix
2 cups (16 oz.) sour cream
4 eggs
1 cup water
¾ cup oil
1 cup (6 oz.) semisweet chocolate chips

1. Combine cake mix, pudding mix, sour cream, eggs, water, and oil in electric mixer bowl. Beat on medium speed for 2 minutes. Stir in chocolate chips.
2. Pour into greased slow cooker. Cover and cook on Low 6-7 hours, or on High 3-4 hours, or until toothpick inserted near center comes out with moist crumbs.

*Serving suggestion: Serve with **whipped cream** or **ice cream**, if you wish.*

Peanut Butter and Hot Fudge Pudding Cake

Sara Wilson, Blairstown, MO

Makes 6 servings

Prep. Time: 10 minutes
Cooking Time: 2-3 hours
Ideal slow-cooker size: 4-qt.

½ cup flour
¼ cup sugar
¾ tsp. baking powder
⅓ cup milk
1 Tbsp. oil
½ tsp. vanilla
¼ cup peanut butter
½ cup sugar
3 Tbsp. unsweetened cocoa powder
1 cup boiling water

1. Combine flour, ¼ cup sugar, and baking powder. Add milk, oil, and vanilla. Mix until smooth. Stir in peanut butter. Pour into slow cooker.
2. Mix together ½ cup sugar and cocoa powder. Gradually stir in boiling water. Pour mixture over batter in slow cooker. Do not stir.
3. Cover and cook on High 2-3 hours, or until toothpick inserted comes out clean.

*Serving suggestion: Serve warm with **vanilla ice cream**.*

The great thing about using a slow cooker in hot weather is that it doesn't heat up your kitchen like an oven does.

Carol Peachey, Lancaster, PA

Chocolate Fudge Sauce

Nanci Keatley, Salem, OR

Makes 1½-2 cups sauce

Prep Time: 10-15 minutes
Cooking Time: 1½ hours
Ideal slow-cooker size: 4- to 5-qt.

5 squares unsweetened
  baking chocolate
1 stick (½ cup) butter, cut
  in pieces
5.3-oz. can evaporated milk
3 cups powdered sugar
1½ tsp. vanilla extract

1. Mix all ingredients in slow cooker.

2. Cover and cook on High 30 minutes. Stir.

3. Cover and cook up to another hour, or until chocolate and butter are melted and sauce is smooth.

4. Store in refrigerator.

Serving suggestion: Serve over ice cream and cake! Or use it as a fondue for fruit!

Variation:
  Add ½ cup smooth or chunky peanut butter to Step 1.

Seven Layer Bars

Mary W. Stauffer, Ephrata, PA

Makes 6-8 servings

Prep. Time: 5-10 minutes
Cooking Time: 2-3 hours
Ideal slow-cooker size: 4- to 5-qt.

¼ cup melted butter
½ cup graham cracker
  crumbs
½ cup chocolate chips
½ cup butterscotch chips
½ cup flaked coconut
½ cup chopped nuts
½ cup sweetened
  condensed milk

1. Layer ingredients in a bread or cake pan that fits in your slow cooker, in the order listed. Do not stir.

2. Cover and bake on High 2-3 hours, or until firm.
  Remove pan and uncover. Let stand 5 minutes.

3. Unmold carefully on plate and cool.

Easy Chocolate Clusters

Marcella Stalter, Flanagan, IL

Makes 3½ dozen clusters

Prep. Time: 5 minutes
Cooking Time: 2 hours
Ideal slow-cooker size: 4-qt.

2 lbs. white coating
  chocolate, broken into
  small pieces
2 cups (12 oz.) semisweet
  chocolate chips
4-oz. pkg. sweet German
  chocolate
24-oz. jar roasted peanuts

1. Combine coating chocolate, chocolate chips, and German chocolate. Cover and cook on High 1 hour. Reduce heat to Low and cook 1 hour longer, or until chocolate is melted, stirring every 15 minutes.

2. Stir in peanuts. Mix well.

3. Drop by teaspoonfuls onto waxed paper. Let stand until set. Store at room temperature.

Very Special Spinach, page 289

Black and Blue Cobbler, page 311

Seven Layer Bars,
page 316

Beverages

Apple Honey Tea

Jeanne Allen, Rye, CO

Makes 6 1-cup servings

Prep. Time: 5 minutes
Cooking Time: 1-2 hours
Ideal slow-cooker size: 1-qt.

12-oz. can frozen apple
   juice/cider concentrate
2 Tbsp. instant tea powder
1 Tbsp. honey
½ tsp. ground cinnamon

1. Reconstitute the apple juice/cider concentrate according to package directions. Pour into slow cooker.
2. Add tea powder, honey, and cinnamon. Stir to blend.
3. Heat on Low 1-2 hours.

Serving suggestion: Stir well before serving since cinnamon tends to settle on bottom.

Hot Mulled Cider

Phyllis Attig, Reynolds, IL
Jean Butzer, Batavia, NY
Doris G. Herr, Manheim, PA
Mary E. Martin, Goshen, IN
Leona Miller, Millersburg, OH
Marjora Miller, Archbold, OH
Janet L. Roggie, Lowville, NY
Shirley Sears, Tiskilwa, IL
Charlotte Shaffer, East Earl, PA
Berenice M. Wagner, Dodge City, KS
Connie B. Weaver, Bethlehem, PA
Maryann Westerberg, Rosamond, CA
Carole Whaling, New Tripoli, PA

Makes 8 1-cup servings

Prep. Time: 5 minutes
Cooking Time: 2-8 hours
Ideal slow-cooker size: 3½-qt.

¼-½ cup brown sugar
2 quarts apple cider
1 tsp. whole allspice
1½ tsp. whole cloves
2 cinnamon sticks
2 oranges sliced, with peels on

1. Combine brown sugar and cider in slow cooker.
2. Put spices in tea strainer or tie in cheesecloth. Add to slow cooker. Stir in orange slices.
3. Cover and simmer on Low 2-8 hours.

Variation:
  Add a dash of ground nutmeg and salt.
      Marsha Sabus, Fallbrook, CA

Autumn Sipper

Shari Jensen, Fountain, CO

Makes 8 1-cup servings

Prep. Time: 5-10 minutes
Cooking Time: 4 hours
Ideal slow-cooker size: 3½-qt.

1 Tbsp. whole allspice
3 3-inch cinnamon sticks
2 whole cloves
1 piece each lemon and orange peel, each about the size of a half dollar
1 piece crystallized ginger, about the size of a quarter
5 cups apple juice
3 cups apricot nectar

1. Place spices, citrus peels, and ginger in a cheesecloth or coffee filter. Tie securely. Place in bottom of slow cooker.
2. Pour in apple juice and nectar. Cover.
3. Cook on High 1 hour, then on Low 3 hours.

*Serving suggestion: Garnish filled glasses with fresh **cinnamon sticks** and **orange slices**, if you wish.*

Hot Apricot Zinger

Jan Mast, Lancaster, PA

Makes 12 servings

Prep Time: 10 minutes
Cooking Time: 2-4 hours
Ideal slow-cooker size: 4-qt.

46-oz. can apricot juice, *or* nectar
3 cups orange juice
2 Tbsp. lemon juice
½ cup brown sugar
3 cinnamon sticks
½ tsp. whole cloves

1. Stir juices and brown sugar together in slow cooker.
2. Tie cinnamon sticks and cloves in a cheesecloth bag or coffee filter.
3. Add spice pack to juices.
4. Cook on Low 2-4 hours. Serve hot.

Hot Mulled Apple Tea

Barbara Tenney, Delta, PA

Makes 16 1-cup servings

Prep. Time: 5-10 minutes
Cooking Time: 2 hours
Ideal slow-cooker size: 4½-qt.

½ gallon apple cider
½ gallon strong tea

1 sliced lemon
1 sliced orange
3 3-inch cinnamon sticks
1 Tbsp. whole cloves
1 Tbsp. allspice
brown sugar to taste

1. Combine all ingredients in slow cooker.
2. Heat on Low 2 hours.

Autumn Tea

Shelia Heil, Lancaster, PA

Makes 12 servings

Prep Time: 15 minutes
Cooking Time: 2-3 hours
Ideal slow-cooker size: 4- to 5-qt.

5 individual tea bags
5 cups boiling water
5 cups unsweetened apple juice
2 cups cranberry juice
⅓ cup lemon juice
½ cup sugar
½ tsp. pumpkin pie spice

1. Place tea bags in slow cooker. Pour in boiling water. Cover and steep for 10 minutes.
2. Remove and discard tea bags.
3. Add juices, sugar, and pumpkin pie spice.
4. Stir until sugar is dissolved.
5. Heat in slow cooker on High 2-3 hours, or until flavors have blended and tea is heated through.

Serving suggestion: Serve warm.

Mulled Holiday Wassail

Marcia S. Myer, Manheim, PA

Makes 15-18 servings

Prep Time: 5-10 minutes
Cooking Time: 3-4 hours
Ideal slow-cooker size: 5-qt.

3 qts. apple cider
½ cup brown sugar
2 6-oz. cans pineapple juice
⅓ cup orange juice
juice of 1 fresh lemon
1 heaping Tbsp. mulling
  spice, placed in cheesecloth
  or coffee filter and tied
  shut with strong string

1. Combine all ingredients in slow cooker.
2. Cook on High 3-4 hours.

Yummy Hot Cider

Char Hagner, Montague, MI

Makes 10-11 1-cup servings

Prep. Time: 5 minutes
Cooking Time: 2 hours
Ideal slow-cooker size: 3-qt.

3 3-inch sticks cinnamon
2 tsp. whole cloves
1 tsp. whole nutmeg, *or*
  ½ tsp. ground nutmeg

½ gallon apple cider
1 cup sugar
2 cups orange juice
½ cup lemon juice

1. Tie spices in cheesecloth or tea strainer and place in slow cooker.
2. Add apple cider and sugar, stirring well.
3. Cover. Simmer on Low 1 hour. Remove spices and stir in orange juice and lemon juice. Continue heating 1 more hour.

Serving suggestion: Serve cider from cooker, set on Low.

Great Mulled Cider

Charlotte Shaffer, East Earl, PA
Barbara Sparks, Glen Burnie, MD

Makes 8-10 1-cup servings

Prep. Time: 5 minutes
Cooking Time: 3 hours
Ideal slow-cooker size: 4-qt.

½ tsp. ground allspice, *or*
  1 tsp. whole allspice
1½ tsp. whole cloves
2 cinnamon sticks
2 qts. apple cider
½ cup frozen orange juice
  concentrate
½ cup brown sugar
orange slices

1. Tie all whole spices in cheesecloth bag, then combine

all ingredients in slow cooker.
2. Cover and simmer on Low 3 hours.

Hot Caramel Apple Cider

Shelia Heil, Lancaster, PA

Makes 8-10 servings

Prep Time: 5 minutes
Cooking Time: 2-3 hours
Ideal slow-cooker size: 3- to 4-qt.

½ gallon fresh apple cider
2-4 Tbsp. brown sugar,
  depending on the
  sweetness of the cider
¼ cup caramel ice cream
  topping

1. Combine cider, sugar, and caramel topping in slow cooker.
2. Cook on High 2-3 hours, stirring frequently.

*Serving suggestion: Pour into mugs and top with frozen **whipped topping**, thawed.*

Note:
This is a good fall drink for young and old, served with popcorn.

Spiced Cider

Mary Puterbaugh, Elwood, IN

Makes 12 1-cup servings

Prep. Time: 5 minutes
Cooking Time: 3-4 hours
Ideal slow-cooker size: 3-qt.

12 whole cloves
½ gallon apple cider
⅔ cup red hot candies
¼ cup dry orange drink mix
1 qt. water

1. Place cloves in cheesecloth bag or tea ball.
2. Combine all ingredients in slow cooker.
3. Cover. Cook on Low 3-4 hours.

Serving suggestion: Serve hot from cooker during fall, or on Halloween.

Hot Wassail Drink

Dale Peterson, Rapid City, SC

Makes 24-27 1-cup servings

Prep. Time: 10 minutes
Cooking Time: 1-2 hours
Ideal slow-cooker size: 2 5- or 6-qt.

12-oz. can frozen orange juice
12-oz. can frozen lemonade
2 qts. apple juice
2 cups sugar, *or less*
3 Tbsp. whole cloves
2 tbsp. ground ginger

4 tsp. ground cinnamon
10 cups hot water
6 cups strong tea

1. Mix juices, sugar, and spices in slow cooker.
2. Add hot water and tea.
3. Heat on High until hot (1-2 hours).

Serving suggestion: Set slow cooker to Low while serving.

Apricot-Pineapple Wassail

Dolores S. Kratz, Souderton, PA

Makes 8 1-cup servings

Prep. Time: 10 minutes
Cooking Time: 3-4 hours
Ideal slow-cooker size: 4-qt.

16-oz. can apricot halves, undrained
4 cups unsweetened pineapple juice
2 cups apple cider
1 cup orange juice
18 whole cloves
6 3½-inch cinnamon sticks, broken

1. In blender or food processor, blend apricots and liquid until smooth.
2. Place cloves and cinnamon sticks in cheesecloth bag.
3. Put all ingredients in slow cooker. Cook on Low 3-4 hours.

Serving suggestion: Serve hot.

Hot Cider

Ilene Bontrager, Arlington, KS

Makes 18-20 1-cup servings

Prep. Time: 5 minutes
Cooking Time: 5-6 hours
Ideal slow-cooker size: 4½-qt.

1 gallon cider
1 qt. cranberry juice
5-6 cinnamon sticks
2 tsp. whole cloves
½ tsp. ginger

1. Combine cider and cranberry juice in slow cooker.
2. Place cinnamon sticks and cloves in cheesecloth bag and add to slow cooker. Stir in ginger.
3. Heat on High 5-6 hours.

*Serving suggestion: Float **orange slices** on top before serving.*

Wassail

John D. Allen, Rye, CO
Susan Yoder Graber, Eureka, IL
Jan Pembleton, Arlington, TX

Makes 12 1-cup servings

Prep. Time: 5-10 minutes
Cooking Time: 5-9 hours
Ideal slow-cooker size: 4-qt.

2 qts. cider
1 pint cranberry juice
⅓-⅔ cup sugar
1 tsp. aromatic bitters

2 sticks cinnamon
1 tsp. whole allspice
1 small orange, studded
   with whole cloves
1 cup rum, *optional*

1. Put all ingredients into cooker. Cover and cook on High 1 hour, then on Low 4-8 hours.

Serving suggestion: Serve warm from cooker.

Note:

If the wassail turns out to be too sweet for you, add more cranberry juice until you find the flavor balance to be more pleasing.

Holiday Spice Punch

Maryland Massey, Millington, MD

Makes 10 1-cup servings

Prep. Time: 5 minutes
Cooking Time: 2 hours
Ideal slow-cooker size: 4-qt.

2 qts. apple cider
2 cups cranberry juice
2 Tbsp. mixed whole spices
   —allspice, coriander,
   cloves, and ginger

1. Pour cider and juice into slow cooker. Place mixed spices in muslin bag or tea ball. Add to juice.
2. Cover and simmer on Low 2 hours.

*Serving suggestion: Float broken **cinnamon sticks** and **lemon** or **orange** slices, studded with **whole cloves**, in individual mugs as you serve.*

Hot Cranberry-Apple Punch

Barbara Sparks, Glen Burnie, MD
Shirley Thieszen, Larkin, KS

Makes 10-11 1-cup servings

Prep. Time: 10 minutes
Cooking Time: 2 hours
Ideal slow-cooker size: 4-qt.

4½ cups cranberry juice
6 cups apple juice
¼ cup plus 1 Tbsp. brown
   sugar
¼ tsp. salt
3 cinnamon sticks
1 tsp. whole cloves

1. Pour juices into slow cooker. Mix in brown sugar and salt. Stir until sugar is dissolved.
2. Tie cinnamon sticks and cloves in cheesecloth and drop into liquid.
3. Cover. Simmer on High 2 hours. Remove spice bag. Keep warm on Low.

Josie's Hot Cranberry Punch

Josie Boilman, Maumee, OH

Makes 6 1-cup servings

Prep. Time: 5 minutes
Cooking Time: 3-4 hours
Ideal slow-cooker size: 2½-qt.

32-oz. bottle cranberry juice

2 sticks cinnamon
6-oz. can frozen lemonade
12-oz. can frozen orange
   juice

1. Mix together all ingredients in slow cooker.
2. Cook on High 3-4 hours.

Hot Cranberry Citrus Punch

Marianne Troyer, Millersburg, OH

Makes 13-14 1-cup servings

Prep. Time: 5-10 minutes
Cooking Time: 2-3 hours
Ideal slow-cooker size: 6-qt.

2 qts. hot water
1½ cups sugar
1 qt. cranberry juice
¾ cup orange juice
¼ cup lemon juice
12 whole cloves, *optional*
½ cup red hot candies

1. Combine water, sugar, and juices. Stir until sugar is dissolved.
2. Place cloves in double thickness of cheesecloth and tie with string. Add to slow cooker.
3. Add cinnamon candies.
4. Cover and Cook on Low 2-3 hours, or until heated thoroughly.
5. Remove spice bag before serving.

321

Hot Fruit Punch

Karen Stoltzfus, Alto, MI

Makes 10 1-cup servings

Prep. Time: 5-10 minutes
Cooking Time: 1 hour
Ideal slow-cooker size: 4½-qt.

1 qt. cranberry juice
3 cups water
6-oz. can frozen orange
  juice concentrate, thawed
10-oz. pkg. frozen red
  raspberries, thawed
2 oranges, sliced
6 sticks cinnamon
12 whole allspice

1. Combine all ingredients in slow cooker.
2. Heat on High 1 hour, or until hot.

Serving suggestion: Turn to Low while serving.

Hot Spicy Lemonade Punch

Mary E. Herr,
The Hermitage, Three Rivers, MI

Makes 9-10 1-cup servings

Prep. Time: 5-10 minutes
Cooking Time: 3-4 hours
Ideal slow-cooker size: 4-qt.

4 cups cranberry juice
⅓-⅔ cup sugar
12-oz. can lemonade

concentrate, thawed
4 cups water
1-2 Tbsp. honey
6 whole cloves
2 cinnamon sticks, broken
1 lemon, sliced

1. Combine juice, sugar, lemonade, water, and honey in slow cooker.
2. Tie cloves and cinnamon in small cheesecloth square. Add spice bag and lemon slices to slow cooker.
3. Cover and cook on Low 3-4 hours. Remove spice bag.

Serving suggestion: Keep hot in slow cooker until ready to serve.

Punch

Kathy Hertzler, Lancaster, PA

Makes 12 1-cup servings

Prep. Time: 5 minutes
Cooking Time: 6 hours
Ideal slow-cooker size: 5½-qt.

1 tsp. whole cloves
5 cups pineapple juice
5 cups cranberry juice
2¼ cups water
½ cup brown sugar
2 cinnamon sticks
¼ tsp. salt

1. Place cloves in small cheesecloth bag or tea ball.
2. Mix together all ingredients in slow cooker.
3. Cook on Low 6 hours. Remove cloves.

Serving suggestion: Serve hot.

Wine Cranberry Punch

C.J. Slagle, Roann, IN

Makes 8 1-cup servings

Prep. Time: 5-10 minutes
Cooking Time: 1-2 hours
Ideal slow-cooker size: 3-qt.

1 pint cranberry juice
  cocktail
1 cup water
¾ cup sugar
2 sticks cinnamon
6 whole cloves
⅘ qt. burgundy wine
1 lemon, sliced thin

1. Combine ingredients in slow cooker.
2. Heat on Low 1-2 hours. Strain and serve hot.

Serving suggestion: Keep hot and serve from slow cooker set on lowest setting.

Hot Spiced Cranberry Punch

Barbara Aston, Ashdown, AR

Makes 10 1-cup servings

Prep. Time: 10 minutes
Cooking Time: 4½-5 hours
Ideal slow-cooker size: 7½-qt.

2 16-oz. cans jellied
  cranberry sauce

2 qts. water
2 cups frozen orange juice
concentrate
1 qt. pineapple juice, *optional*
half a stick of butter
¾ cup firmly packed brown
sugar
½ tsp. ground cinnamon
½ tsp. ground allspice
¼ tsp. ground cloves
¼ tsp. ground nutmeg
¼ tsp. salt

1. Mix together all ingredients.
2. Heat on High until boiling, then reduce to Low for 4 hours.

Serving suggestion: Serve hot.

Kate's Mulled Cider / Wine

Mitzi McGlynchey, Downingtown, PA

Makes 8-10 1-cup servings

Prep. Time: 5 minutes
Cooking Time: 3-4 hours
Ideal slow-cooker size: 2½-qt.

½ tsp. whole cloves
½ tsp. whole allspice
½ gallon apple cider, *or* red
burgundy wine
2 3-inch cinnamon sticks
1 tsp. ground nutmeg

1. Place cloves and allspice in cheesecloth bag or tea ball.
2. Combine spices, apple cider or wine, 2 cinnamon sticks, and nutmeg in slow cooker.
3. Cook on High 1 hour. Reduce heat, and simmer 2-3 hours.

*Serving suggestion: Garnish individual servings with **orange slices** or fresh **cinnamon sticks**.*

Slow-Cooker Chai

Kathy Hertzler, Lancaster, PA

Makes 18 servings

Prep Time: 10 minutes
Cooking Time: 1-1½ hours
Ideal slow-cooker size: 5-qt.

1 gallon water
16 regular black tea bags
8 opened cardamom pods
9 whole cloves
3 Tbsp. ginger root, freshly
grated, *or* chopped fine
3 cinnamon sticks
8-oz. can sweetened
condensed milk
12-oz. can evaporated milk
(regular *or* fat-free are
equally good)

1. Pour one gallon water into slow cooker. Turn cooker to High and bring water to a boil.
2. Tie tea bag strings together. Remove paper tags. Place in slow cooker, submerging in boiling water.
3. Place cardamom seeds and pods, cloves, and ginger in a tea ball.
4. Place tea ball, and cinnamon sticks in boiling water in slow cooker. Reduce heat to Low and steep, along with tea bags, for 10 minutes.
5. After 10 minutes, remove tea bags. Allow spices to remain in cooker. Increase heat to High.
6. Add condensed milk and evaporated milk. Bring mixture to a boil.
7. Immediately turn back to Low. Remove spices 30 minutes later.

Serving suggestion: Serve tea from the slow cooker, but do not allow it to boil.

Note:
We love this after leaf-raking or for a fall party, especially when we serve it with muffins and fruit.

Almond Tea

Frances Schrag, Newton, KS

Makes 12 1-cup servings

Prep. Time: 5-10 minutes
Cooking Time: 1 hour
Ideal slow-cooker size: 5-qt.

10 cups boiling water
1 Tbsp. instant tea
⅔ cup lemon juice
1 cup sugar
1 tsp. vanilla
1 tsp. almond extract

1. Mix together all ingredients in slow cooker.
2. Turn to High and heat thoroughly (about 1 hour).

Serving suggestion: Turn to Low while serving.

Homestyle Tomato Juice

Jean Butzer, Batavia, NY

Makes 4-5 1-cup servings

Prep. Time: 10 minutes
Cooking Time: 4-6 hours
Ideal slow-cooker size: 5-qt.

10-12 large tomatoes
1 tsp. salt
1 tsp. seasoned salt
¼ tsp. pepper
1 Tbsp. sugar

1. Wash and drain tomatoes. Remove cores and blossom ends. Place in slow cooker.
2. Cover and cook on Low 4-6 hours, or until tomatoes are soft.
3. Press through sieve or food mill.
4. Stir in seasonings. Chill.

Spiced Coffee

Jan Mast, Lancaster, PA

Makes 10-12 servings

Prep Time: 10 minutes
Cooking Time: 2-3 hours
Ideal slow-cooker size: 4-qt.

2 quarts strong hot coffee
¼ cup chocolate syrup
⅓ cup sugar

¼-½ tsp. anise flavoring, optional
4 cinnamon sticks
1½ tsp. whole cloves

1. Combine hot coffee, chocolate syrup, sugar, and anise if you wish in slow cooker.
2. Tie cinnamon sticks and whole cloves in cheesecloth or a coffee filter and tie shut with strong string. Add to slow cooker, submerging in liquid.
3. Cook on Low 2-3 hours.

*Serving suggestion: Serve hot with a garnish of **whipped cream** and a dash of **cinnamon** if you wish on each individual serving.*

Carolers' Hot Chocolate

Pat Unternahrer, Wayland, IA

Makes 12-14 1-cup servings

Prep. Time: 10 minutes
Cooking Time: 2-2½ hours
Ideal slow-cooker size: 5-qt.

10 cups milk
¾ cup sugar
½ tsp. salt
¾ cup cocoa, *or* hot chocolate mix
2 cups hot water

1. Measure milk into slow cooker. Turn on High.
2. Mix together sugar, salt, and cocoa in heavy pan. Add hot water. Stir and boil 3 minutes, stirring often.
3. Pour into milk. Cook on High 2-2½ hours.

*Serving suggestion: Top with **marshmallows**.*

Minty Hot Chocolate

Jan Mast, Lancaster, PA

Makes 6-8 servings

Prep Time: 5 minutes
Cooking Time: 2 hours
Ideal slow-cooker size: 3- to 4-qt.

6 small peppermint patties
6 cups milk
½ cup chocolate malt mix
1 tsp. vanilla

1. Combine all ingredients in slow cooker.
2. Cook on Low 2 hours.
3. Whisk or hand-beat until thoroughly mixed and frothy.

*Serving suggestion: Serve hot, topping each individual serving with **whipped cream**.*

Equivalent Measurements

dash = little less than ⅛ tsp.

3 teaspoons = 1 Tablespoon

2 Tablespoons = 1 oz.

4 Tablespoons = ¼ cup

5 Tablespoons plus 1 tsp. = ⅓ cup

8 Tablespoons = ½ cup

12 Tablespoons = ¾ cup

16 Tablespoons = 1 cup

1 cup = 8 ozs. liquid

2 cups = 1 pint

4 cups = 1 quart

4 quarts = 1 gallon

1 stick butter = ¼ lb.

1 stick butter = ½ cup

1 stick butter = 8 Tbsp.

Beans, 1 lb. dried = 2-2½ cups (depending upon the size of the beans)

Bell peppers, 1 large = 1 cup chopped

Cheese, hard (for example, cheddar, Swiss, Monterey Jack, mozzarella), 1 lb. grated = 4 cups

Cheese, cottage, 1 lb. = 2 cups

Chocolate chips, 6-oz. pkg. = 1 scant cup

Crackers (butter, saltines, snack), 20 single crackers = 1 cup crumbs

Herbs, 1 Tbsp. fresh = 1 tsp. dried

Lemon, 1 medium-sized = 2-3 Tbsp. juice

Lemon, 1 medium-sized = 2-3 tsp. grated rind

Mustard, 1 Tbsp. prepared = 1 tsp. dry or ground mustard

Oatmeal, 1 lb. dry = about 5 cups dry

Onion, 1 medium-sized = ½ cup chopped

Pasta

Macaronis, penne, and other small or tubular shapes, 1 lb. dry = 4 cups uncooked

Noodles, 1 lb. dry = 6 cups uncooked

Spaghetti, linguine, fettucine, 1 lb. dry = 4 cups uncooked

Potatoes, white, 1 lb. = 3 medium-sized potatoes = 2 cups mashed

Potatoes, sweet, 1 lb. = 3 medium-sized potatoes = 2 cups mashed

Rice, 1 lb. dry = 2 cups uncooked

Sugar, confectioners, 1 lb. = 3½ cups sifted

Whipping cream, 1 cup unwhipped = 2 cups whipped

Whipped topping, 8-oz. container = 3 cups

Yeast, dry, 1 envelope (¼ oz.) = 1 Tbsp.

From-Scratch Replacement Recipes

When I first began making cookbooks, I was a purist. No canned cream-of-xxx soups for me, whether I was working on cookbooks or making dinner. I resolutely turned any reference to canned creamed soups into a multi-step process, which wasn't too bad if I took a magazine along to the stove or the microwave. I would do Steps 1-4 (on next page); then I'd whip out the magazine while I stirred. It made the time fly.

But when I became a mom, I began to compromise on a few things. It was a little harder to hold a wiggly child than it was to read a magazine while I stirred up a creamy soup.

Then I heard from other people who were juggling things that didn't always allow them to stand and read while stirring. So I switched and began to permit canned soups in recipes.

If you like to know exactly what you are eating, and if you have the time, I applaud your making cream soups and bases from scratch. Here is a recipe for doing this on the stove-top or in the microwave.

If you're tight time-wise, or aren't sure you want to make the extra effort to create a creamy soup or base, you'll find canned cream soups in the ingredient lists of many recipes in this cookbook. Because my first intent is to make sure you can make a meal at home and serve it to your friends and family, no matter how full or chaotic your life is.

Homemade Cream of Mushroom Soup – on the stove

Makes about 1¼ cups (10 oz.)

3 Tbsp. butter
¼ cup mushrooms, chopped
1 Tbsp. onion, chopped
3 Tbsp. flour
1 cup milk (skim, 1%, 2%, or whole)

1. In a small saucepan, melt butter.
2. Sauté mushrooms and onion in butter until tender. Stir frequently.
3. Add flour and stir until smooth. Cook over low heat for a minute or so to cook off the raw flour taste.
4. Continuing over low heat, gradually add milk, stirring the whole time.
5. Stir frequently to keep soup from sticking. When soup begins to bubble, stir continuously until it thickens to a creamy consistency.

Homemade Cream of Mushroom Soup – in the microwave

Makes about 1¼ cups (10 oz.)

3 Tbsp. butter
¼ cup mushrooms, chopped
1 Tbsp. onion, chopped
3 Tbsp. flour
1 cup milk (skim, 1%, 2%, or whole)

1. In a 1- or 2-qt. microwave-safe container, melt 3 Tbsp. butter on high for 30 seconds.
2. Stir chopped mushrooms and onions into melted butter.
3. Microwave on high for 1 minute, or just enough to make the vegetables tender.
4. Stir in flour until well blended.
5. Microwave on high for 1 minute, just enough to overcome the raw flour taste.
6. Gradually stir in milk until as well blended as possible.
7. Microwave on Power 5 for 45 seconds.
8. Stir until well blended.
9. Microwave on Power 5 for another 45 seconds. The mixture should be starting to bubble and thicken.
10. Stir again until well blended.
11. If the mixture isn't fully bubbling and thickened, microwave on high for 20 seconds.
12. Stir. If the mixture still isn't fully bubbling and thickened, microwave on high for 20 more seconds.
13. Repeat Step 12 if needed.

Note:

If your microwave is fairly new and powerful, you will probably have a creamy soup by the end of Step 8 or 10 below. If you're working with an older, less powerful, microwave, you will likely need to go through Step 12, and maybe Step 13.

Homemade Cornbread Mix

Makes the equivalent of an 8½-oz. box of Jiffy Cornbread Mix

⅔ cup flour
½ cup cornmeal
3 Tbsp. sugar
1 Tbsp. baking powder
¼ tsp. salt
2 Tbsp. oil

Variation:

To make muffins from this mix, add:

1 egg
⅓ cup milk

1. Stir just until combined.
2. Fill muffin cups half-full.
3. Bake at 400° for 15-20 minutes, or until toothpick inserted in center of muffins comes out clean.

Homemade Frozen Hash Browns

1. Bake potatoes until tender.
2. Cool.
3. Grate coarsely.
4. Freeze.

Substitute Ingredients
for when you're in a pinch

For one cup **buttermilk**—use 1 cup plain yogurt; or pour 1⅓ Tbsp. lemon juice or vinegar into a 1-cup measure. Fill the cup with milk. Stir and let stand for 5 minutes. Stir again before using.

For 1 oz. **unsweetened baking chocolate**—stir together 3 Tbsp. unsweetened cocoa powder and 1 Tbsp. butter, softened.

For 1 Tbsp. **cornstarch**—use 2 Tbsp. all-purpose flour; or 4 tsp. minute tapioca.

For 1 **garlic clove**—use ¼ tsp. garlic salt (reduce salt in recipe by ⅛ tsp.); or ⅛ tsp. garlic powder.

For 1 Tbsp. **fresh herbs**—use 1 tsp. dried herbs.

For ½ lb. **fresh mushrooms**—use 1 6-oz. can mushrooms, drained.

For 1 Tbsp. **prepared mustard**—use 1 tsp. dry or ground mustard.

For 1 **medium-sized fresh onion**— use 2 Tbsp. minced dried onion; or 2 tsp. onion salt (reduce salt in recipe by 1 tsp.); or 1 tsp. onion powder. Note: These substitutions will work for meat balls and meat loaf, but not for sautéing.

For 1 cup **sour milk**—use 1 cup plain yogurt; or pour 1 Tbsp. lemon juice or vinegar into a 1-cup measure. Fill with milk. Stir and then let stand for 5 minutes. Stir again before using.

For 2 Tbsp. **tapioca**—use 3 Tbsp. all-purpose flour.

For 1 cup canned **tomatoes**—use 1⅓ cups diced fresh tomatoes, cooked gently for 10 minutes.

For 1 Tbsp. **tomato paste**—use 1 Tbsp. ketchup.

For 1 Tbsp. **vinegar**—use 1 Tbsp. lemon juice.

For 1 cup **heavy cream**—add ⅓ cup melted butter to ¾ cup milk. *Note: This will work for baking and cooking, but not for whipping.*

For 1 cup **whipping cream**—chill thoroughly ⅔ cup evaporated milk, plus the bowl and beaters, then whip; or use 2 cups bought whipped topping.

For ½ cup **wine**—pour 2 Tbsp. wine vinegar into a ½-cup measure. Fill with broth (chicken, beef, or vegetable). Stir and then let stand for 5 minutes. Stir again before using.

Index

A

10-Layer Slow-Cooker Dish, 177
"Absent Cook" Stew, 94
Acorn Squash, 291
African Chicken Treat, 255
A Hearty Western Casserole, 176
All-American Snack, 84
All-Day Roast, 151
Allen's Beans, 275
Almond Tea, 323
Almonds
   Curried Almonds, 83
Ann's Boston Baked Beans, 282
Ann's Chicken Cacciatore, 246
Anona's Beef Vegetable Soup, 94
Another Chicken in a Pot, 235
Apple Bean Bake, 281
Apple-Bean Pot, 281
Apple Cake, 313
Apple Caramel Pie, 312
Apple Honey Tea, 317
Apple Oatmeal, 90
Apple Peanut Crumble, 313
Apple Topping, 306
Apples
   Ann's Boston Baked Beans, 282
   Apple Bean Bake, 281
   Apple-Bean Pot, 281
   Apple Cake, 313
   Apple Oatmeal, 90
   Apple Peanut Crumble, 313
   Apple Topping, 306
   Autumn Brisket, 154
   Baked Apples with Raisins, 306
   Bavarian Cabbage, 293
   Blushing Apple Tapioca, 305
   Caramel Apples, 307
   Charlotte's Apple Butter, 85
   Chunky Applesauce, 310
   Cider and Pork Stew, 129
   Fruit Compote Dessert, 308
   Fruit/Nut Baked Apples, 307
   Old World Sauerkraut Supper, 218
   Polish Kraut 'n' Apples, 218
   Pork and Cabbage Dinner, 209
   Pork and Kraut, 220
   Pork and Sauerkraut, 220
   Pork Spareribs with
     Sauerkraut, 221
   Raisin Nut-Stuffed Apples, 306
   Rhonda's Apple Butter, 85
   Sauerkraut and Pork, 222
   Scandinavian Fruit Soup, 308
   Shirley's Apple Butter, 85
   Sweet-Sour Cabbage, 292
Applesauce
   Dolores' Apple Butter, 86
   Lilli's Apple Butter, 86
   Marshmallow Applesauce
     Dessert, 305
Apricot-Pineapple Wassail, 320
Apricots
   Apricot-Pineapple Wassail, 320
   Barbecue Beef, 196
   Barbecued Hot Dogs, 226
   Fruit/Nut Baked Apples, 307
   Golden Fruit Compote, 307
   Hot Curried Fruit Compote, 308
   Hot Fruit Compote, 309
   Peach or Apricot Butter, 86
   Pork and Apricots with Mashed
     Sweet Potatoes, 202
   Scandinavian Fruit Soup, 308
Artichokes, 83
Artichokes
   Artichokes, 83
   Chicken on a Whim, 259
   Roasted Pepper and Artichoke
     Spread, 82
Asian-Style Country Ribs, 213
Aunt Lavina's Sauerkraut, 219
Autumn Brisket, 154
Autumn Chicken and Veggies, 253
Autumn Pork Chops, 205
Autumn Sipper, 318
Autumn Tea, 318
Awesome Chicken Marinade, 56
Awfully Easy Barbecued Ribs, 213

B

Bacon *See Pork, Bacon*
Baked Apples with Raisins, 306
Baked Bean Soup, 127
Baked Brie with Cranberry
   Chutney, 82
Baked Chicken Breasts, 236
Baked Lamb Shanks, 288
Baked Oatmeal, 90
Baked Potatoes in Foil, 296
Baked Steak, 157
Bananas
   Chocolate Chip Banana Bread,
     48
   Fruit Compote Dessert, 308
   Hot Curried Fruit Compote,
     308
Barbara's Calico Beans, 279
Barbara's Creole Chicken, 255
Barbara's Scalloped Potatoes with
   Ham, 210
Barbecue Beef, 196
Barbecue Beef Sandwiches, 197
Barbecue Brisket, 170
Barbecue Chicken for Buns, 263
Barbecued Beans, 269
Barbecued Green Beans, 289
Barbecued Ham Sandwiches,
   227
Barbecued Hot Dogs, 226
Barbecued Lentils, 286
Barbecued Lima Beans, 266
Barbecued Meatballs, 186
Barbecued Mini-Franks, 226
Barbecued Pork, 215
Barbecued Pork and Beef
   Sandwiches, 215
Barbecued Pork in the Slow
   Cooker, 215
Barbecued Pork Steaks, 203
Barbecued Ribs, 214
Barbecued Roast Beef, 169
Barbecued Sausage Pieces, 225
Barbecued Spareribs, 212
Barbecued Spoonburgers, 197
Barbecue Hamburger Steaks, 174
Barley
   Chicken Barley Chili, 113
   Hamburger Soup with Barley,
     101
   Vegetarian Minestrone Soup,
     134
Barley, Pearl
   Beef Roast with Mushroom
     Barley, 153
Basil
   Wild Mushrooms Italian, 294
Bavarian Cabbage, 293
BBQ Meatballs, 184
Bean Soup, 133
Bean Tater Tot Casserole, 181
Beans and Tomato Chili, 131
Beans with Rice, 272
Beans, Baked
   Ann's Boston Baked Beans, 282
   Apple-Bean Pot, 281
   Baked Bean Soup, 127
   Crock-O-Beans, 275
   Doris' Sweet-Sour Bean Trio,
     279
   Four-Bean Medley, 276
   Fruity Baked Bean Casserole,
     281
   Linda's Baked Beans, 282
   Lizzie's California Beans, 277
   Lotsa-Beans Chili, 109
   Lotsa Beans Vegetarian Chili,
     132
   Main Dish Baked Beans, 280
   Marcia's California Beans, 277
   Mary Ellen's Three-Bean Dish,
     271
   Mixed Slow-Cooker Beans, 277
   Nan's Barbecued Beans, 273
   Pork Chops in Bean Sauce, 204
   Sausage Bean Quickie, 272
Beans, Barbecue
   Marcia's California Beans, 277

Index

Index

Index

Index

Index

Index

Index

Index

Index

About the Author

Phyllis Pellman Good is a *New York Times* bestselling author whose books have sold more than 10 million copies.

Good is the author of the nationally acclaimed *Fix-It and Forget-It* slow-cooker cookbooks, several of which have appeared on *The New York Times* bestseller list, as well as the bestseller lists of *USA Today*, *Publishers Weekly*, and *Book Sense*.

In addition to this book, the series includes:

- **Fix-It and Forget-It Cookbook (Revised and Updated)**
  700 Great Slow-Cooker Recipes

- **Fix-It and Forget-It Lightly (Revised and Updated)**
  600 Healthy, Low-Fat Recipes for Your Slow Cooker

- **Fix-It and Forget-It Christmas Cookbook**
  600 Slow-Cooker Holiday Recipes

- **Fix-It and Forget-It 5-Ingredient Favorites**
  Comforting Slow-Cooker Recipes

- **Fix-It and Forget-It Diabetic Cookbook**
  Slow-Cooker Favorites to Include Everyone
  (with the American Diabetes Association)

- **Fix-It and Forget-It Vegetarian Cookbook**
  565 Delicious Slow-Cooker, Stove-Top, Oven, and Salad Recipes, plus 50 Suggested Menus

- **Fix-It and Forget-It Kids' Cookbook**
  50 Favorite Recipes to Make in a Slow Cooker

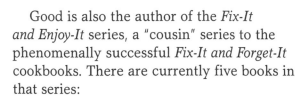

Good is also the author of the *Fix-It and Enjoy-It* series, a "cousin" series to the phenomenally successful *Fix-It and Forget-It* cookbooks. There are currently five books in that series:

- **Fix-It and Enjoy-It Cookbook**
  All-Purpose, Welcome-Home Recipes

- **Fix-It and Enjoy-It Potluck Heaven**
  543 Stove-Top and Oven Recipes That Everyone Loves

- **Fix-It and Enjoy-It 5-Ingredient Recipes**
  Quick and Easy—for Stove-Top and Oven!

- **Fix-It and Enjoy-It Diabetic Cookbook**
  Stove-Top and Oven Recipes—for Everyone!
  (with the American Diabetes Association)

- **Fix-It and Enjoy-It Healthy Cookbook**
  400 Great Stove-Top and Oven Recipes
  (with nutritional expertise from Mayo Clinic)

Phyllis Pellman Good is Executive Editor at Good Books. (Good Books has published hundreds of titles by more than 135 authors.) She received her B.A. and M.A. in English from New York University. She and her husband, Merle, live in Lancaster, Pennsylvania. They are the parents of two young-adult daughters.

For a complete listing of books by Phyllis Pellman Good, as well as excerpts and reviews, visit www.Fix-ItandForget-It.com or www.GoodBooks.com.

Good and her family are also proprietors of **The Good Cooking Store** in the small Lancaster County village of Intercourse. Located near the Good Books offices, the Store is the home of *Fix-It and Forget-It* cookbooks, as well as offering gadgets and wares for your kitchen, and cooking classes. Visit **www.GoodCookingStore.com** for more information.

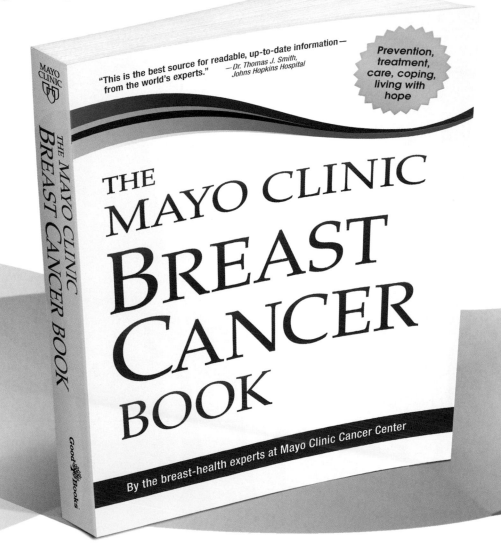

National Bestsellers!

Phyllis' cookbooks have already sold more than **11 million** copies!

Phyllis Pellman Good

  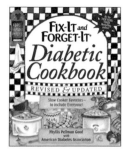  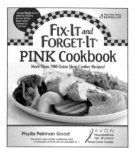